2016

by
Jack Gillis

and
Amy Curran
Richard Eckman

with
Dr. Carl Nash
Peter Kitchen

Foreword by
Clarence Ditlow
Center for Auto Safety

A Center for Auto Safety Publication

ACKNOWLEDGMENTS

Taking over as co-author, Richard "Ricky" Eckman did an extraordinary job of managing and organizing this 36th edition of *The Car Book*. It is a monumental effort as literally thousands of data points go into compiling the book and all of its ratings. As a 25 year veteran of *The Car Book*, Amy Curran prepared all of the graphics necessary to clearly present the data as well as managed the logistics necessary to get a printed book in the hands of the public. Last year's co-author, Peter Kitchen, returned providing key research. In addition, important new safety advice and content was provided by noted auto safety expert and former National Highway Traffic Safety Administration official, Dr. Carl Nash. Thanks to Amy, Ricky, and the team, consumers have the information they need to make a smart, sensible new car choice.

As has been the case for 35 years, this year's edition would not have been possible without the essential contributions from Clarence Ditlow and the staff of the Center for Auto Safety, including Michael Brooks and Jon Robinson.

As always, the most important factor in being able to bring this information to the American car buyer for 36 years is the encouragement, support, and love from my brilliant and beautiful wife, Marilyn Mohrman-Gillis. For her and our four terrific children–Katie, John, Brian and Brennan–I am eternally grateful.

—J.G.

As Always,
for Marilyn &
Katie, John, Brian, and Brennan

CLARENCE DITLOW

Until the fall of 1966, no federal regulatory law or agency–not one–protected Americans from death and injury on the nation's highways. In 1966, 50,894 people were killed and 1.9 million injured. From the advent of the automobile to 1966, motor vehicle accidents killed more than 1.6 million people in the United States. Then Congress passed two landmark pieces of legislation–the National Traffic and Motor Vehicle Safety Act and the Highway Safety Act.

If the 1966 fatality rate of 5.50 deaths per hundred million vehicle miles traveled (VMT) had continued, 167,956 people would have been killed in vehicle crashes in 2014. Instead, the death rate was 1.07–a decline of 80% over 50 years–with 32,675 killed. The 1966 federal laws, federal agency and general measures they created—have averted 3.5 million auto deaths over the past 50 years.

In 1965, Ralph Nader's "Unsafe at Any Speed" exposed the deplorable safety records of auto companies. The book—and subsequent investigation of Nader by General Motors, which put private detectives on his trail—led to Congressional hearings overseen by Senators Warren Magnuson and Abraham Ribicoff. At the Senate hearing, GM President James Roche apologized to Mr. Nader for his company's probes.

Within months, Congress unanimously passed the Vehicle and Highway Safety Acts, which President Lyndon B. Johnson signed on September 16th. The President stated: "In this century, more than one and a half million of our fellow citizens have died on our streets and highways; nearly three times as many Americans as we have lost in all our wars. . . . I'm proud at this moment to sign these bills–which promise, in the years to come, to cure the highway disease: to end the years of horror and give us years of hope."

When Congress passed the Vehicle Safety Act in 1966, the auto industry fought one provision more than any–criminal penalties for violating the Act. Why? Because putting their executives behind bars like common criminals was simply too much to bear. Drunk drivers that kill innocent consumers are put in jail. Why not jail auto executives who approve unsafe designs to save a buck when those designs kill consumers just like drunk drivers do?

Under the influence of corporate lobbyists, Congress imposed civil penalties–but no criminal penalties–on auto companies breaking the law. Penalties amount to, at most, a few dollars per car. Rather than restraining auto companies from breaking the law, the penalties encourage auto companies to violate it by shaving manufacturing costs. The result: Profits go up, and so do the number of unsafe vehicles on the road. If caught, the worst that can happen is a recall and slap-on-the-wrist civil penalty. It's cheaper to stonewall than recall.

Even worse, civil penalties encourage manufacturers to hire lobbyists to build bigger loopholes into safety regulations rather than hire engineers to build safer vehicles. Weak roofs on rollover-prone vehicles saved the auto industry hundreds of millions of dollars every year while thousands of consumers died because weak roofs on vehicles collapsed in rollovers. Auto lobbyists watered down the original roof-crush standard in 1971, while auto engineers lamented seat belts would restrain occupants in place only to by killed or injured by crushing roofs.

What other safety hazards would never have occurred if auto executives knew they could be held criminally responsible for their designs? To name a few: Exploding Pinto and Jeep gas tanks; collapsing seat backs that kill children; Takata airbag inflators that explode; GM ignition switches that shut off airbags in crashes; Firestone tires that fail catastrophically and Toyotas that suddenly accelerate.

Until Congress adds criminal penalties to the Safety Act, the 2016 *Car Book* is your answer to finding a new car that has the fewest defects and the most advanced safety features, among them lane-departure correction, radar braking and adaptive cruise control, active pre-crash safety, and automatic crash notification. Use *The Car Book*'s new comprehensive crash safety rating to buy a car to protect you in a crash. Use the Safety Chapter to find the optional safety features you want when you buy a new vehicle. Your buying decision can save your life and send a message to automakers not to withhold vital safety features.

By using *The Car Book* to buy a safer car, you have taken an important first step toward your personal vehicle safety and helping CAS reach our Vision of Zero Traffic Deaths by 2050. The next step is to support CAS which works every day on your behalf to ensure that all Americans ride in safe and reliable vehicles. Go to www.autosafety.org and find out how you can support the Center and have us be your safety and lemon insurance.

JACK GILLIS

The auto industry is back! Last year, car-makers sold more than ever before—17.5 million vehicles—a far cry from the 10.4 million vehicles purchased in 2009. In fact, sales were so bad then that the U.S. government had to bail out some of the manufacturers. With today's improved economy and lower gas prices, folks are flocking back into new car showrooms. In spite of the record number of recalls plaguing previously sold vehicles, there are plenty of good choices among the 2016 models—if you know what to look for!

Amazingly, this is the 36th year we've been bringing consumers the information they need to make a smart and safe choice among the new vehicles. While the driverless car is still a few years down the road, many of today's new cars have a variety of highly technical crash avoidance systems. From automatic braking to backup cameras and self-parking, the many new and life-saving features once only on high priced cars are becoming available on vehicles the rest of us can afford.

One of the most exciting developments is the growing number of electric vehicles. This year we include a special section at the end of the book to guide you through the 20 EVs being offered for sale this year. Amazingly, based on family size and driving needs of the typical family, EVs would work for nearly half of Americans! EVs work like your cell phone—imagine plugging them in each night and then gliding silently and smoothly throughout your driving day.

Not only are vehicles getting better, so is the buying experience. More dealers are abandoning the difficult negotiation process in favor of a straightforward posted price. So with lots of new electronics, improved safety features, and some improvements in the showroom, *The Car Book* is ready to guide you to a great new 2016 vehicle!

Working closely with the Center for Auto Safety's Clarence Ditlow and his staff, as we have for 35 years, my goal is to sift through the myriad of government and industry data on cars and present the information so you can actually use it. Thirty-six years ago, *The Car Book* was the first publication to give you the ability to make an informed choice on one of the most important and complex items that you will ever purchase. In setting out to change the way people buy their cars, *The Car Book* was able to change the way car companies made them.

The Center's Clarence Ditlow has been the primary advocate who has brought media, consumer and Congressional attention to the many serious auto defects that have been in the news. His efforts have saved lives and brought about important changes in auto company practices and government regulations. This year, renowned auto safety expert and former NHTSA official, Dr. Carl Nash, provided invaluable updates to the safety information you are about to read.

In keeping with *The Car Book*'s philosophy of making it as easy as possible to identify the truly good performers in the government crash tests, we provide a unique *Car Book* Combined Crash Test Rating which combines all of the complex government test-

ing into a simple, straightforward number. In addition, we take the step of comparing the vehicles on a relative basis to each other so you can easily tell the best performers from the worst.

Before *The Car Book*, consumers had no idea which warranties were better, what you could expect to pay for typical repairs, which cars cost the most and least to insure, or how they stacked up in government complaints. Now you have this information all in one place.

Our exclusive car-by-car ratings at the end of the book provide an overview of all the criteria you need to make a good choice. Here, you'll be able to quickly assess key features and see how the car you're interested in stacks up against its competition so you can make sure your selection is the best car for you.

While the choices get better each year, it's still a challenge to separate the lemons from the peaches. There are differences in how cars protect you in a crash, how much they cost to maintain, and the benefits of their warranties. Nevertheless, by using *The Car Book*, there's no reason why your next car shouldn't last at least 150,000 miles. Finally, our "Showroom Strategies" section will give you the keys to getting the best deal.

The information in *The Car Book* is based on data collected and developed by our staff, the U.S. Department of Transportation, and the Center for Auto Safety. With all of this information in hand, you'll find some great choices for 2016.

—*Jack*

USING THE BUYING GUIDE

T he "Buying Guide" provides a quick comparison of the 2016 cars in terms of their safety, warranty, fuel economy, complaint rating, and price range—arranged by size class. To fully understand the information in the charts, it is important to read the related section in the book.

Overall Rating: This shows how well this car stacks up on a scale of 1 to 10 when compared to all others on the market. Because safety is the most important component of our ratings, cars with no crash test results at printing are not given an overall rating.

Combined Crash Test Rating: This indicates how well the car performed in the government's frontal and side crash test programs compared to this year's vehicles tested to date. See page 18 for details.

Warranty Rating: This is an overall comparative assessment of the car's warranty.

Fuel Economy: This is the EPA city/highway mpg for, what is expected to be, the most popular version of each model.

Complaint Rating: This is based on complaints received by the U.S. Department of Transportation. If not rated, the vehicle is too new to have a complaint rating.

Price Range: This will give you a general idea of the "sticker," or suggested retail price.

 Indicates a *Car Book* Best Bet. See page 13.

ABOUT THE CAR BOOK BEST BETS

TIP It is important to consult the specific chapters to learn more about how *The Car Book* ratings are developed and to look on the car pages, beginning on page 81, for more details on these vehicles. In order to be considered as a "Best Bet" the vehicle must have a crash test rating as safety is a critical factor in gaining that recognition. Vehicles with "Poor" (3 or 4) or "Very Poor" (1 or 2) in Combined Crash Tests, or Front or Side Crash Test Ratings, or an additional injury warning were not considered a "Best Bet." Because most people are considering vehicles in the same size category, the "Best Bets" are by size—indicating how these vehicles compared against others in the same size class.

Vehicle	Page #	Overall Rating	Combined Crash Test Rating	Warranty Rating	Fuel Economy	Complaint Rating	Price Range
Subcompact							
BMW i3	98			Good	137/111		$42-$46,000
Chevrolet Sonic	119	10	Good	Average	25/35	Average	$14-$21,000
Chevrolet Spark	120			Average	31/41		$12-$25,000
Fiat 500	133	4	Very Poor	Poor	27/34	Very Poor	$16-$22,000
Ford Fiesta	141	1	Poor	Poor	27/37	Very Poor	$14-$18,000
Honda Fit	155	7	Very Good	Very Poor	33/41	Very Poor	$15-$21,000
Hyundai Accent	159	6	Very Poor	Very Good	26/37	Very Good	$14-$17,000
Hyundai Veloster	167	6	Poor	Very Good	28/36		$18-$23,000
Kia Rio	182	6	Very Poor	Very Good	27/37	Very Good	$14-$20,000
Kia Soul	185	7	Very Good	Very Good	23/31	Poor	$31-$35,000
Mazda MX-5 Miata	206			Very Poor	27/36		$24-$31,000
Mini Cooper	215			Very Good	27/32		$20-$30,000
Mini Countryman	216			Very Good	27/34	Very Good	$22-$35,000
Mitsubishi Mirage	218	4	Very Poor	Very Good	37/44	Poor	$12-$15,000
Nissan 370Z	221			Very Poor	19/26	Poor	$29-$49,000
Nissan Versa	234	3	Very Poor	Very Poor	31/40	Average	$11-$17,000
Smart ForTwo	239			Poor	34/39		$13-$25,000
Toyota Yaris	259	6	Poor	Very Poor	30/36	Very Good	$14-$17,000
Volkswagen Beetle	260	3	Poor	Average	25/33	Average	$19-$36,000
Compact							
Acura ILX	81	9	Average	Average	24/35	Very Good	$27-$32,000
Audi A3	85	5	Average	Good	24/33	Poor	$30-$48,000
Audi A4	86	8	Average	Good	22/31	Very Good	$33-$43,000
BMW 2 Series	92			Good	23/35		$32-$46,000
BMW 3 Series	93	8	Good	Good	23/36	Average	$33-$45,000
BMW 4 Series	94			Good	23/35	Good	$41-$58,000
Buick Verano	106	10	Very Good	Good	21/32		$23-$28,000
Cadillac ATS	107	8	Good	Very Good	21/33	Poor	$33-$49,000
Chevrolet Cruze	114			Average	26/38		$17-$24,000
Chevrolet Volt	125			Average	43/42		$33-$37,000
Dodge Dart	131	6	Good	Poor	24/34		$16-$23,000
Fiat 500L	134			Poor	22/30	Very Poor	$19-$24,000
Ford C-MAX	135	5	Poor	Poor	42/37	Very Poor	$24-$31,000
Ford Focus	143	6	Good	Poor	27/40	Very Poor	$17-$29,000

Vehicle	Page #	Overall Rating	Combined Crash Test Rating	Warranty Rating	Fuel Economy	Complaint Rating	Price Range
Compact (cont.)							
Honda Civic	149			Very Poor	31/41		$18-$24,000
Hyundai Elantra	161	7	Poor	Very Good	28/38	Good	$17-$21,000
Kia Forte	180	5	Poor	Very Good	25/36	Poor	$15-$21,000
Lexus CT	190			Average	43/40	Average	$31-$31,000
Lexus IS	194	7	Average	Average	21/30	Very Good	$36-$43,000
Lexus RC	196			Average	22/32		$42-$62,000
Mazda Mazda3	204	8	Average	Very Poor	30/41	Good	$17-$25,000
Mercedes-Benz C-Class	207	4	Poor	Very Poor	22/31	Poor	$39-$63,000
Mercedes-Benz CLA-Class	208			Very Poor	26/38	Very Poor	$31-$48,000
Nissan Leaf	226	3	Very Poor	Very Poor	126/101	Very Poor	$29-$35,000
Nissan Sentra	232	6	Poor	Very Poor	30/39	Good	$16-$20,000
Scion FR-S	237	3	Poor	Very Poor	25/34	Good	$25-$26,000
Scion tC	238	5	Average	Very Poor	23/31	Very Good	$19-$20,000
Subaru Impreza	241	5	Poor	Very Poor	28/37	Good	$18-$23,000
Toyota Corolla	249	9	Very Good	Very Poor	27/36	Very Good	$17-$23,000
Toyota Prius	251			Very Poor	54/50		$23-$34,000
Toyota Prius C	252	6	Very Poor	Very Poor	53/46	Good	$19-$24,000
Volkswagen Golf	262	3	Poor	Average	26/36	Very Poor	$18-$29,000
Volkswagen Jetta	263	7	Good	Average	28/39		$18-$25,000
Intermediate							
Acura TLX	84	10	Very Good	Average	20/31	Very Poor	$31-$41,000
Audi A5	87			Good	22/32	Very Good	$40-$50,000
Audi A6	88	9	Good	Good	20/30	Very Good	$46-$63,000
BMW 5 Series	95	8	Average	Good	23/34	Average	$50-$62,000
BMW 6 Series	96			Good	17/25	Very Good	$76-$98,000
Buick Regal	105	5	Average	Good	19/31	Good	$28-$36,000
Cadillac CTS	108	8	Good	Very Good	18/29	Average	$45-$64,000
Chevrolet Camaro	111			Average	19/28		$25-$41,000
Chevrolet Corvette	113			Average	16/29	Good	$55-$64,000
Chevrolet Malibu	117	9	Average	Average	27/37	Good	$23-$30,000
Chrysler 200	126	10	Good	Poor	23/36	Very Poor	$21-$31,000
Ford Fusion	144	7	Average	Poor	22/34	Poor	$22-$32,000
Ford Fusion Energi	145	8	Good	Poor	40/36		$33-$35,000
Ford Mustang	146			Poor	19/28	Very Poor	$23-$47,000
Honda Accord	152	10	Very Good	Very Poor	27/36	Average	$22-$34,000
Hyundai Azera	160			Very Good	20/29	Poor	$34-$38,000
Hyundai Sonata	165	10	Very Good	Very Good	25/37	Poor	$21-$26,000
Infiniti Q50	168	5	Poor	Good	20/29	Very Good	$37-$46,000

Vehicle	Page #	Overall Rating	Combined Crash Test Rating	Warranty Rating	Fuel Economy	Complaint Rating	Price Range
Intermediate (cont.)							
Infiniti Q70	169			Good	18/24	Poor	$49-$67,000
Kia Cadenza	179			Very Good	19/28	Very Poor	$34-$43,000
Kia Optima	181	8	Average	Very Good	23/34	Good	$21-$35,000
Lexus GS	192			Average	19/29	Very Good	$48-$61,000
Lincoln MKZ	200	6	Average	Good	18/27	Good	$35-$47,000
Mazda Mazda6	205	8	Good	Very Poor	26/38	Poor	$21-$30,000
Mitsubishi Lancer	217	4	Very Poor	Very Good	26/34	Average	$16-$40,000
Nissan Altima	222	7	Average	Very Poor	27/38	Average	$22-$31,000
Nissan Maxima	227	5	Good	Very Poor	22/30		$32-$39,000
Subaru Legacy	242	7	Very Good	Very Poor	26/36	Very Poor	$21-$29,000
Toyota Camry	248	7	Average	Very Poor	25/35	Very Good	$23-$31,000
Toyota Prius V	253	9	Average	Very Poor	44/40	Very Good	$26-$30,000
Volkswagen CC	261			Average	22/31	Average	$32-$43,000
Volkswagen Passat	264	7	Good	Average	25/38		$21-$35,000
Volvo S60	267	10	Very Good	Good	25/37	Very Good	$33-$47,000
Volvo V60	268			Good	25/37		$35-$49,000
Large							
BMW 7 Series	97			Good	21/29		$81-$97,000
Buick LaCrosse	104	8	Good	Good	18/28	Good	$33-$40,000
Cadillac XTS	110	9	Very Good	Very Good	18/28	Good	$45-$72,000
Chevrolet Impala	116	6	Good	Average	18/28	Average	$27-$40,000
Chrysler 300	127	4	Poor	Poor	19/31	Poor	$35-$45,000
Dodge Challenger	129	5	Good	Poor	19/30	Poor	$26-$62,000
Dodge Charger	130	5	Average	Poor	19/31	Very Poor	$27-$65,000
Ford Taurus	147	4	Good	Poor	19/29	Good	$26-$40,000
Hyundai Genesis	162	7	Very Good	Very Good	18/29	Very Poor	$26-$51,000
Lexus ES	191	8	Average	Average	21/31	Very Good	$38-$40,000
Lincoln MKS	199	5	Good	Good	19/28	Good	$38-$45,000
Mercedes-Benz E-Class	209	5	Poor	Very Poor	20/29	Very Good	$52-$101,000
Mercedes-Benz S-Class	214			Very Poor	17/26	Poor	$94-$222,000
Tesla Model S	245	10	Very Good	Very Good	88/90		$69-$105,000
Toyota Avalon	247	8	Good	Very Poor	21/31	Average	$32-$41,000
Minivan							
Chrysler Town and Country	129	3	Very Poor	Poor	17/25	Very Poor	$29-$37,000
Honda Odyssey	157	8	Good	Very Poor	19/28	Average	$29-$44,000
Kia Sedona	183	7	Good	Very Good	18/24	Average	$26-$39,000
Nissan Quest	230			Very Poor	20/27	Average	$26-$43,000
Toyota Sienna	256	3	Average	Very Poor	18/25	Average	$28-$46,000

Vehicle	Page #	Overall Rating	Combined Crash Test Rating	Warranty Rating	Fuel Economy	Complaint Rating	Price Range
Small SUV							
Acura RDX	83	10	Very Good	Average	19/27	Very Good	$35-$40,000
Audi Q3	89			Good	20/28	Very Good	$33-$40,000
Audi Q5	90	5	Very Poor	Good	20/28	Very Good	$40-$55,000
BMW X1	99			Good	22/32		$31-$39,000
BMW X3	100	7	Average	Good	21/28	Good	$38-$46,000
Buick Encore	103	10	Good	Good	23/30	Good	$24-$31,000
Cadillac SRX	109	6	Average	Very Good	17/24	Good	$37-$51,000
Chevrolet Trax	124	9	Good	Average	24/31	Very Good	$20-$26,000
Ford Escape	137	5	Average	Poor	22/31	Average	$23-$31,000
Honda CR-V	154	7	Good	Very Poor	26/33	Poor	$23-$32,000
Honda HR-V	156	5	Poor	Very Poor	28/35		$19-$25,000
Hyundai Tucson	166	7	Very Poor	Very Good	24/28	Very Good	$22-$31,000
Jeep Cherokee	173	7	Average	Good	21/28	Very Poor	$23-$30,000
Jeep Compass	174	4	Very Poor	Good	20/23	Average	$19-$25,000
Jeep Patriot	176	3	Very Poor	Good	20/23	Poor	$17-$25,000
Jeep Renegade	177	2	Poor	Good	21/29	Very Poor	$17-$26,000
Jeep Wrangler	178			Good	17/21	Very Poor	$23-$36,000
Kia Sportage	186	5	Average	Very Good	21/28	Very Good	$22-$31,000
Land Rover Range Rvr Evoque	188			Poor	21/30	Average	$41-$56,000
Lexus NX	195	5	Good	Average	22/28	Average	$34-$41,000
Lincoln MKC	198	4	Poor	Good	19/26	Poor	$33-$48,000
Mazda CX-5	202	3	Poor	Very Poor	26/32	Poor	$21-$29,000
Mercedes-Benz GLA-Class	210			Very Poor	24/32	Poor	$31-$48,000
Nissan Juke	225	2	Very Poor	Very Poor	26/31	Good	$20-$30,000
Porsche Macan	235			Average	17/23		$49-$72,000
Subaru Forester	240	4	Good	Very Poor	24/32	Poor	$22-$33,000
Subaru XV Crosstrek	244	5	Poor	Very Poor	26/34	Very Good	$21-$29,000
Toyota RAV4	254	5	Average	Very Poor	22/29	Very Good	$23-$29,000
Volkswagen Tiguan	265	1	Very Poor	Average	21/26	Poor	$24-$34,000
Mid-Size SUV							
Acura MDX	82	6	Good	Average	18/27	Very Poor	$42-$57,000
Audi Q7	91			Good			$48-$65,000
BMW X5	101	6	Good	Good	18/27	Very Good	$53-$70,000
Chevrolet Equinox	115	2	Very Poor	Average	22/32	Average	$25-$31,000
Dodge Journey	132	1	Very Poor	Poor	17/25	Very Poor	$20-$33,000
Ford Edge	136	9	Very Good	Poor	20/30	Good	$28-$40,000
Ford Explorer	139	3	Good	Poor	17/23	Poor	$30-$52,000
GMC Terrain	151	3	Very Poor	Average	22/32	Good	$26-$35,000

Vehicle	Page #	Overall Rating	Combined Crash Test Rating	Warranty Rating	Fuel Economy	Complaint Rating	Price Range
Mid-Size SUV (cont.)							
Honda Pilot	158	9	Good	Very Poor	19/27		$29-$46,000
Hyundai Santa Fe	163			Very Good	18/25	Poor	$30-$36,000
Hyundai Santa Fe Sport	164	5	Good	Very Good	20/27		$24-$33,000
Infiniti QX60	170	3	Average	Good	19/26	Very Poor	$42-$46,000
Infiniti QX70	171			Good	16/22	Very Good	$45-$47,000
Jeep Grand Cherokee	175	5	Average	Good	14/20	Very Poor	$29-$64,000
Kia Sorento	184	5	Average	Very Good	21/29		$26-$43,000
Land Rover Range Rover Sport	189			Poor	14/19	Average	$63-$92,000
Lexus RX	197			Average	20/28		$40-$48,000
Mazda CX-9	203	2	Very Poor	Very Poor	16/22	Average	$29-$36,000
Mercedes-Benz GLC	211			Very Poor	18/25		$38-$40,000
Mercedes-Benz GLE	213			Very Poor	18/24		$51-$99,000
Mitsubishi Outlander	219	4	Average	Very Good	24/29	Very Poor	$22-$30,000
Mitsubishi Outlander Sport	220	3	Poor	Very Good	25/32	Average	$19-$24,000
Nissan Murano	228	5	Poor	Very Poor	21/28	Poor	$29-$40,000
Nissan Pathfinder	229	1	Average	Very Poor	19/26	Very Poor	$29-$43,000
Nissan Rogue	231	2	Very Poor	Very Poor	25/32	Good	$23-$29,000
Subaru Outback	243	7	Very Good	Very Poor	25/33	Very Poor	$24-$33,000
Volkswagen Touareg	266			Average	17/23	Average	$42-$63,000
Volvo XC60	269	10	Very Good	Good	17/24	Good	$36-$51,000
Volvo XC70	270			Good	23/31		$37-$47,000
Large SUV							
Buick Enclave	102	5	Good	Good	17/24	Average	$39-$49,000
Cadillac Escalade	122			Very Good	14/21	Average	$72-$84,000
Cadillac Escalade ESV	121			Very Good	14/20	Average	$75-$87,000
Chevrolet Suburban	122	3	Average	Average	15/22	Very Poor	$49-$67,000
Chevrolet Tahoe	123	4	Good	Average	16/22	Very Poor	$47-$64,000
Chevrolet Traverse	123	4	Good	Average	17/24	Average	$31-$44,000
Ford Expedition	138	7	Very Good	Poor	15/20	Good	$40-$63,000
Ford Flex	142			Poor	18/25	Poor	$29-$42,000
GMC Acadia	148	4	Good	Average	17/24	Poor	$34-$49,000
GMC Yukon	122	5	Good	Average	14/21	Good	$48-$68,000
GMC Yukon XL	121	3	Average	Average	14/20	Very Good	$50-$70,000
Infiniti QX80	172			Good	14/20	Average	$63-$66,000
Land Rover Range Rover	187			Poor	14/19	Poor	$83-$137,000
Lexus GX	193			Average	15/20	Very Good	$50-$61,000
Lincoln Navigator	201	9	Very Good	Good	15/20	Very Good	$63-$74,000
Mercedes-Benz GL-Class	212			Very Poor	19/26		$63-$119,000

Vehicle	Page #	Overall Rating	Combined Crash Test Rating	Warranty Rating	Fuel Economy	Complaint Rating	Price Range
Large SUV (cont.)							
Nissan Armada	223			Very Poor	13/19	Poor	$38-$53,000
Toyota 4Runner	246	3	Very Poor	Very Poor	17/21	Very Good	$33-$43,000
Toyota Highlander	250	7	Good	Very Poor	18/24	Good	$29-$50,000
Toyota Sequoia	255			Very Poor	13/17	Very Good	$44-$64,000
Compact Pickup							
Chevrolet Colorado	112	3	Poor	Average	20/27	Poor	$20-$34,000
GMC Canyon	149	1	Poor	Average	17/24	Very Poor	$20-$37,000
Nissan Frontier	224			Very Poor	15/21	Average	$17-$34,000
Toyota Tacoma	257			Very Poor	19/23		$23-$33,000
Standard Pickup							
Chevrolet Silverado	118	5	Very Good	Average	16/22	Good	$26-$51,000
Ford F-150	140	9	Very Good	Poor	17/23	Very Good	$25-$54,000
GMC Sierra	150	5	Very Good	Average	16/22	Poor	$26-$52,000
Nissan Titan	233			Very Poor			$29-$43,000
Ram 1500	236	4	Poor	Poor	13/19	Poor	$25-$50,000
Toyota Tundra	258			Very Poor	13/17	Very Good	$29-$49,000

BEST BETS

The following is our list of the highest rated vehicles in each size category. The ratings are based on expected performance in nine important categories–Combined Crash Rating, Safety Features, Rollover, Preventive Maintenance, Repair Costs, Warranty, Fuel Economy, Complaints, and Insurance Costs–with the heaviest emphasis placed on safety. (See box on page 6.)

CHEVROLET SONIC — SUBCOMPACT

BEST The CAR Book BET

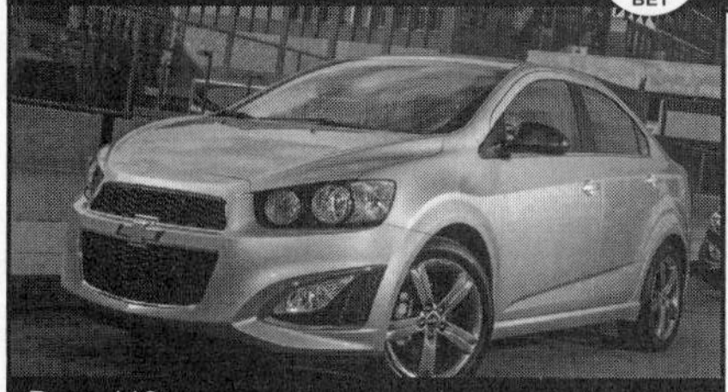

Page 119

Combo Crash Tests	8	Warranty	6
Safety Features	8	Fuel Economy	7
Rollover	7	Complaints	6
PM	9	Insurance	1
Repair Costs	10	**OVERALL RATING**	**10**

HONDA FIT — SUBCOMPACT

BEST The CAR Book BET

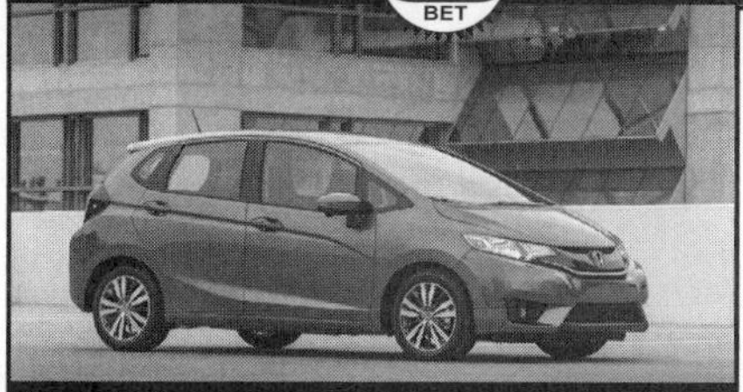

Page 155

Combo Crash Tests	9	Warranty	1
Safety Features	3	Fuel Economy	9
Rollover	5	Complaints	2
PM	10	Insurance	5
Repair Costs	8	**OVERALL RATING**	**7**

KIA SOUL — SUBCOMPACT

BEST The CAR Book BET

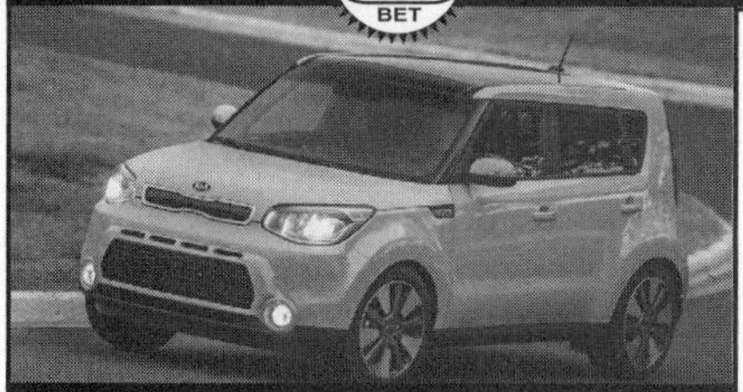

Page 185

Combo Crash Tests	9	Warranty	9
Safety Features	2	Fuel Economy	5
Rollover	5	Complaints	3
PM	5	Insurance	1
Repair Costs	9	**OVERALL RATING**	**7**

BMW 3 SERIES — COMPACT

BEST The CAR Book BET

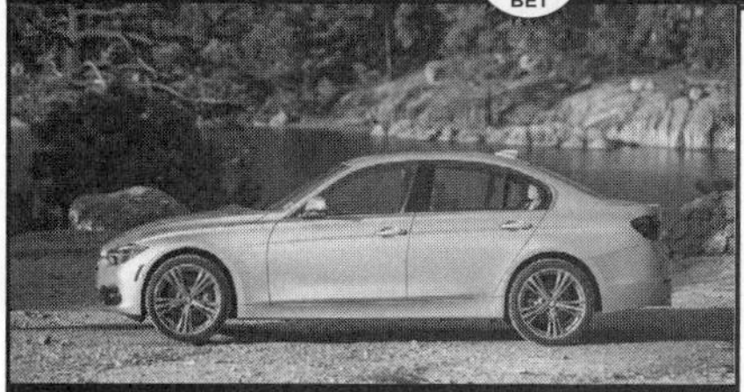

Page 93

Combo Crash Tests	7	Warranty	8
Safety Features	6	Fuel Economy	6
Rollover	10	Complaints	6
PM	5	Insurance	5
Repair Costs	3	**OVERALL RATING**	**8**

BUICK VERANO — COMPACT

BEST The CAR Book BET

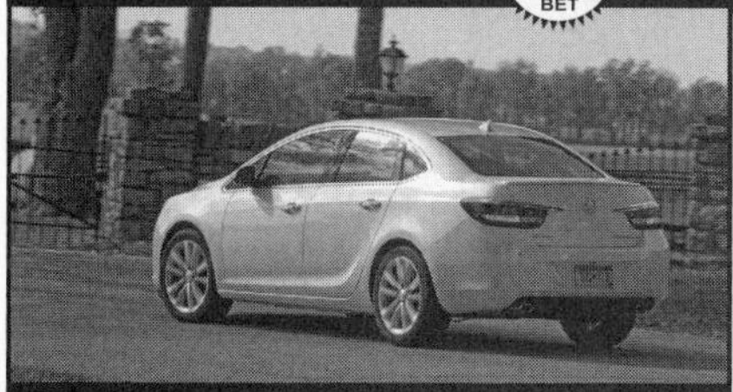

Page 106

Combo Crash Tests	10	Warranty	7
Safety Features	8	Fuel Economy	5
Rollover	8	Complaints	—
PM	7	Insurance	3
Repair Costs	7	**OVERALL RATING**	**10**

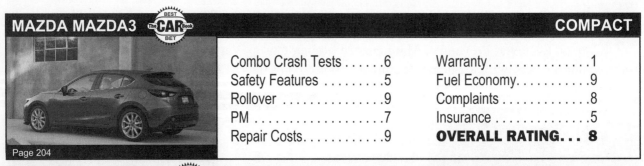

MAZDA MAZDA3 COMPACT

Page 204

Combo Crash Tests	6	Warranty	1
Safety Features	5	Fuel Economy	9
Rollover	9	Complaints	8
PM	7	Insurance	5
Repair Costs	9	**OVERALL RATING... 8**	

TOYOTA COROLLA COMPACT

Page 249

Combo Crash Tests	9	Warranty	2
Safety Features	2	Fuel Economy	8
Rollover	7	Complaints	9
PM	9	Insurance	3
Repair Costs	9	**OVERALL RATING... 9**	

VOLKSWAGEN JETTA COMPACT

Page 263

Combo Crash Tests	7	Warranty	5
Safety Features	4	Fuel Economy	9
Rollover	8	Complaints	6
PM	5	Insurance	1
Repair Costs	5	**OVERALL RATING... 7**	

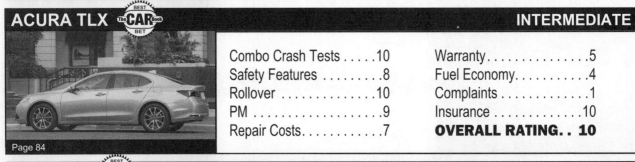

ACURA TLX INTERMEDIATE

Page 84

Combo Crash Tests	10	Warranty	5
Safety Features	8	Fuel Economy	4
Rollover	10	Complaints	1
PM	9	Insurance	10
Repair Costs	7	**OVERALL RATING.. 10**	

AUDI A6 INTERMEDIATE

Page 88

Combo Crash Tests	8	Warranty	7
Safety Features	8	Fuel Economy	4
Rollover	10	Complaints	9
PM	4	Insurance	5
Repair Costs	1	**OVERALL RATING... 8**	

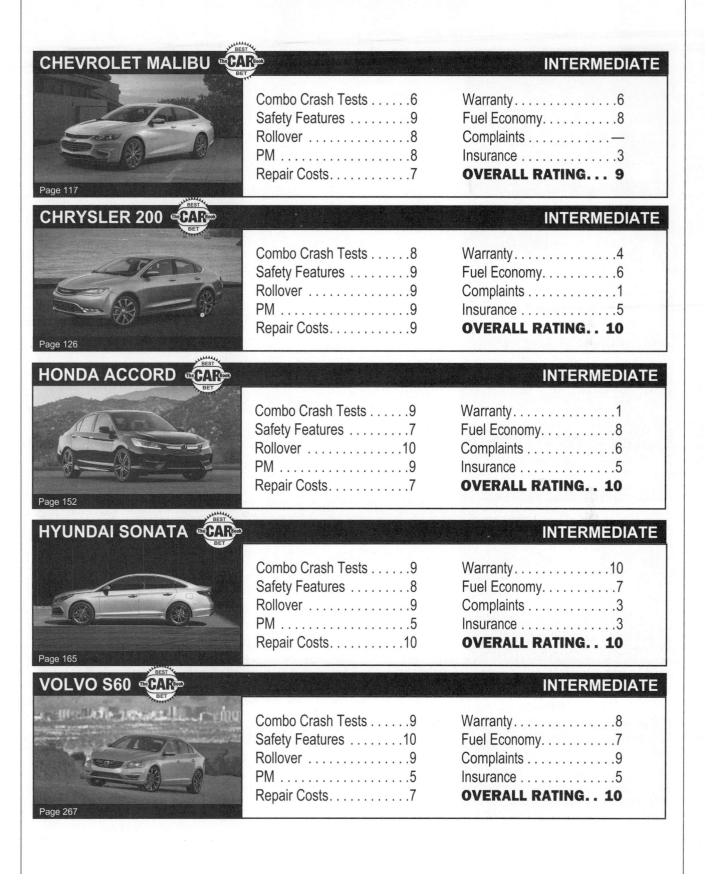

CHEVROLET MALIBU — INTERMEDIATE

Combo Crash Tests 6
Safety Features 9
Rollover 8
PM 8
Repair Costs 7
Warranty 6
Fuel Economy 8
Complaints . . . . —
Insurance 3
OVERALL RATING . . . 9

Page 117

CHRYSLER 200 — INTERMEDIATE

Combo Crash Tests 8
Safety Features 9
Rollover 9
PM 9
Repair Costs 9
Warranty 4
Fuel Economy 6
Complaints 1
Insurance 5
OVERALL RATING . . 10

Page 126

HONDA ACCORD — INTERMEDIATE

Combo Crash Tests 9
Safety Features 7
Rollover 10
PM 9
Repair Costs 7
Warranty 1
Fuel Economy 8
Complaints 6
Insurance 5
OVERALL RATING . . 10

Page 152

HYUNDAI SONATA — INTERMEDIATE

Combo Crash Tests 9
Safety Features 8
Rollover 9
PM 5
Repair Costs 10
Warranty 10
Fuel Economy 7
Complaints 3
Insurance 3
OVERALL RATING . . 10

Page 165

VOLVO S60 — INTERMEDIATE

Combo Crash Tests 9
Safety Features 10
Rollover 9
PM 5
Repair Costs 7
Warranty 8
Fuel Economy 7
Complaints 9
Insurance 5
OVERALL RATING . . 10

Page 267

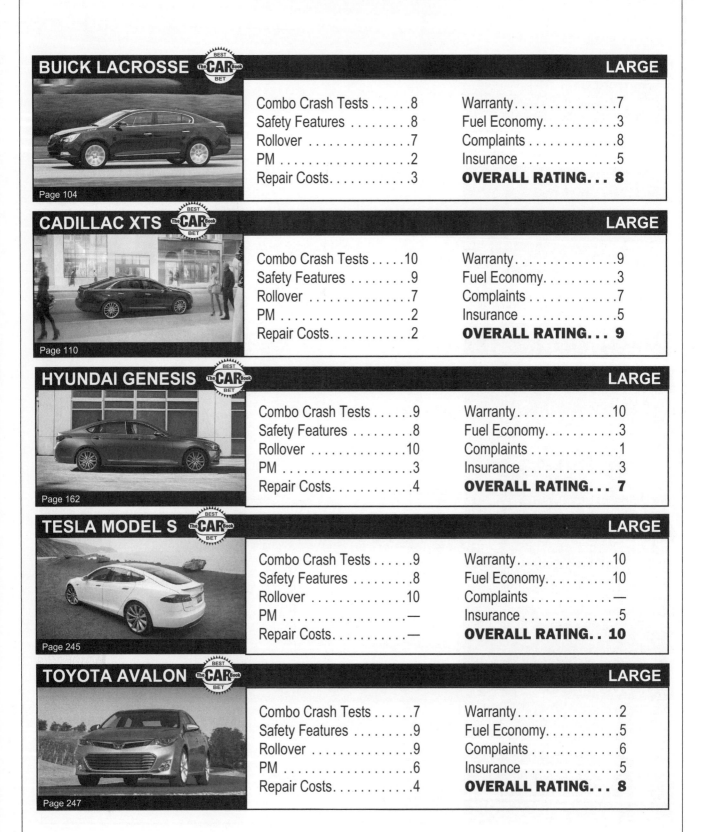

BUICK LACROSSE   LARGE

Page 104

Combo Crash Tests 8   Warranty 7
Safety Features 8   Fuel Economy 3
Rollover 7   Complaints 8
PM 2   Insurance 5
Repair Costs 3   **OVERALL RATING. . . 8**

CADILLAC XTS   LARGE

Page 110

Combo Crash Tests 10   Warranty 9
Safety Features 9   Fuel Economy 3
Rollover 7   Complaints 7
PM 2   Insurance 5
Repair Costs 2   **OVERALL RATING. . . 9**

HYUNDAI GENESIS   LARGE

Page 162

Combo Crash Tests 9   Warranty 10
Safety Features 8   Fuel Economy 3
Rollover 10   Complaints 1
PM 3   Insurance 3
Repair Costs 4   **OVERALL RATING. . . 7**

TESLA MODEL S   LARGE

Page 245

Combo Crash Tests 9   Warranty 10
Safety Features 8   Fuel Economy 10
Rollover 10   Complaints . . . .—
PM . . . .—   Insurance 5
Repair Costs . . . .—   **OVERALL RATING. . 10**

TOYOTA AVALON   LARGE

Page 247

Combo Crash Tests 7   Warranty 2
Safety Features 9   Fuel Economy 5
Rollover 9   Complaints 6
PM 6   Insurance 5
Repair Costs 4   **OVERALL RATING. . . 8**

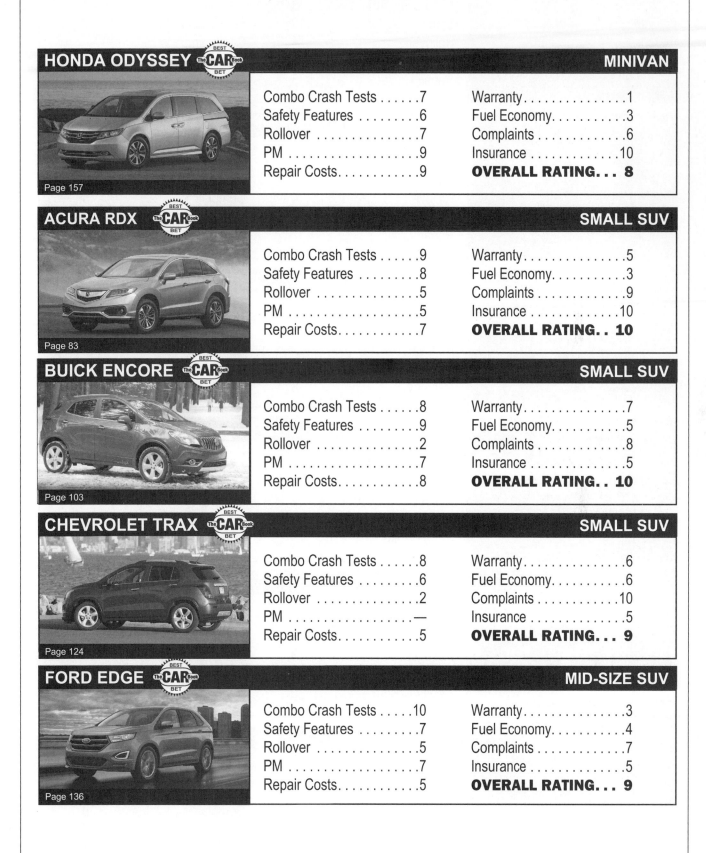

HONDA ODYSSEY — MINIVAN

Page 157

Combo Crash Tests 7	Warranty 1
Safety Features 6	Fuel Economy 3
Rollover 7	Complaints 6
PM 9	Insurance 10
Repair Costs 9	**OVERALL RATING. . . 8**

ACURA RDX — SMALL SUV

Page 83

Combo Crash Tests 9	Warranty 5
Safety Features 8	Fuel Economy 3
Rollover 5	Complaints 9
PM 5	Insurance 10
Repair Costs 7	**OVERALL RATING. . 10**

BUICK ENCORE — SMALL SUV

Page 103

Combo Crash Tests 8	Warranty 7
Safety Features 9	Fuel Economy 5
Rollover 2	Complaints 8
PM 7	Insurance 5
Repair Costs 8	**OVERALL RATING. . 10**

CHEVROLET TRAX — SMALL SUV

Page 124

Combo Crash Tests 8	Warranty 6
Safety Features 6	Fuel Economy 6
Rollover 2	Complaints 10
PM . . . .—	Insurance 5
Repair Costs 5	**OVERALL RATING. . . 9**

FORD EDGE — MID-SIZE SUV

Page 136

Combo Crash Tests 10	Warranty 3
Safety Features 7	Fuel Economy 4
Rollover 5	Complaints 7
PM 7	Insurance 5
Repair Costs 5	**OVERALL RATING. . . 9**

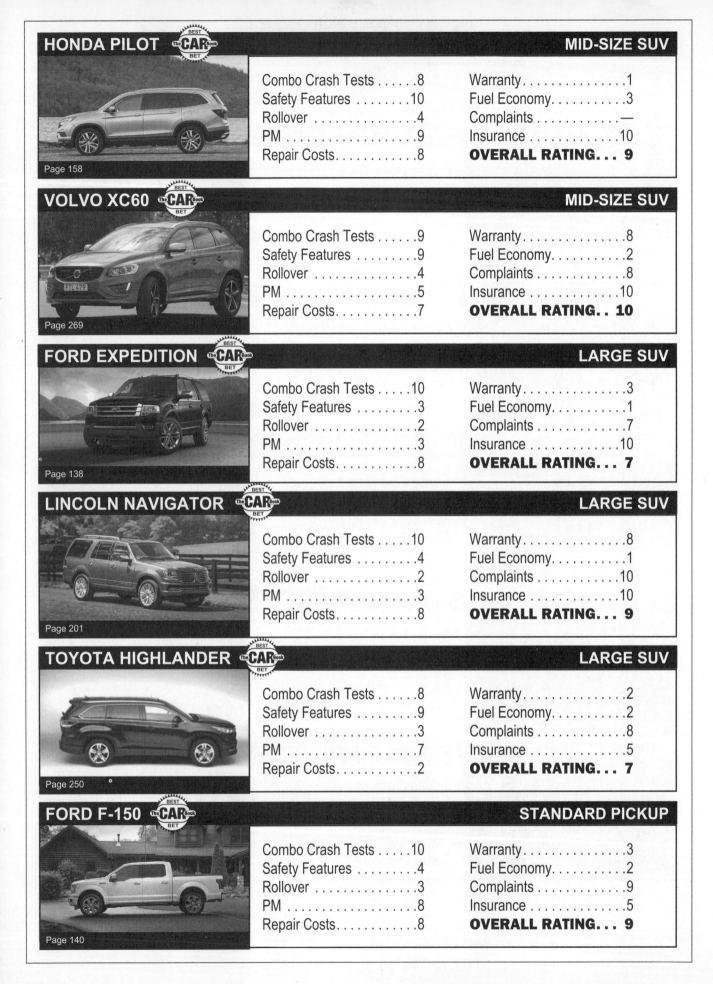

HONDA PILOT — MID-SIZE SUV

Page 158

Combo Crash Tests	8	Warranty	1
Safety Features	10	Fuel Economy	3
Rollover	4	Complaints	—
PM	9	Insurance	10
Repair Costs	8	**OVERALL RATING**	**9**

VOLVO XC60 — MID-SIZE SUV

Page 269

Combo Crash Tests	9	Warranty	8
Safety Features	9	Fuel Economy	2
Rollover	4	Complaints	8
PM	5	Insurance	10
Repair Costs	7	**OVERALL RATING**	**10**

FORD EXPEDITION — LARGE SUV

Page 138

Combo Crash Tests	10	Warranty	3
Safety Features	3	Fuel Economy	1
Rollover	2	Complaints	7
PM	3	Insurance	10
Repair Costs	8	**OVERALL RATING**	**7**

LINCOLN NAVIGATOR — LARGE SUV

Page 201

Combo Crash Tests	10	Warranty	8
Safety Features	4	Fuel Economy	1
Rollover	2	Complaints	10
PM	3	Insurance	10
Repair Costs	8	**OVERALL RATING**	**9**

TOYOTA HIGHLANDER — LARGE SUV

Page 250

Combo Crash Tests	8	Warranty	2
Safety Features	9	Fuel Economy	2
Rollover	3	Complaints	8
PM	7	Insurance	5
Repair Costs	2	**OVERALL RATING**	**7**

FORD F-150 — STANDARD PICKUP

Page 140

Combo Crash Tests	10	Warranty	3
Safety Features	4	Fuel Economy	2
Rollover	3	Complaints	9
PM	8	Insurance	5
Repair Costs	8	**OVERALL RATING**	**9**

CRASH TESTS

Safety is likely the most important factor that most of us consider when choosing a new car. In the past, evaluating safety was difficult. Now, thanks to the information in *The Car Book*, it's much easier to pick a safe vehicle. The bottom line: For the greatest protection, you'll want the maximum number of safety features (See Safety Checklist, pages 78-80) and good crash test results (the following tables).

A key factor in occupant protection is how well the car protects you in a crash. This depends on its ability to absorb the force of the impact rather than transfer it to the occupant.

In the frontal test, the vehicle impacts a solid barrier at 35 mph. In the side test, a moving barrier is crashed into the side of the vehicle at 38.5 mph. A second side test simulates hitting a tree or roadside pole by smashing a vertical pole into the driver side door at 20 mph. The only occupant in this side pole test is a small female dummy in the driver seat.

The dummies measure the impact on the head, chest, neck and thighs.

Not all 2016 vehicles have undergone a crash test. The good news is that by carrying forward previous tests from cars that haven't changed, we have results for 139 2016 models. The bad news is that there are 60 models for which we don't have crash test results.

How the Cars are Rated: The combined crash test ratings are based on the relative performance of the vehicles tested to date using the new test. *This is a big difference from the government's "star" program.* Rather than large groups of undifferentiated vehicles in the government's star ratings, *The Car Book* rates them from best to worst. This means that those manufacturers really working

on safety, each year, will rise to the top.

The first column provides *The Car Book's* Combined Crash Test Rating. The cars are rated from 10 Best to 1 Worst. The front is weighted 60%, the side 36%, and the pole test 4% with results compared among all new 2016 crash tests to date.

Next are the individual front and side tests. Again, relative to all other 2016 vehicles tested, we indicate if the vehicle was Very Good, Good, Average, Poor or Very Poor. For side tests, the cars are rated separately from the

trucks. Because of their construction the dynamics of a side test are different in cars and trucks.

The next five columns indicate the likelihood of the occupant sustaining a life-threatening injury. The percent likelihood is listed for the driver and front passenger in the front test, the driver and rear passenger in the side test, and the driver in the side pole test. Lower percentages mean a lower likelihood of being seriously injured. This information is taken directly from the government's analysis of the crash test results.

USING CRASH TEST DATA

One of the most important results of our being the first to publish crash test data, and later develop our relative comparative ratings, is that it has put enormous pressure on the manufacturers to improve. Whereas years ago, when competition was based on style and horsepower, thanks to *The Car Book*, today's manufacturers are feverously competing on safety features. While the most important factors in evaluating the safety of today's vehicles are crash test performance and advanced safety features, size and weight do play a role. It is important to compare vehicles in the size classes that follow. For example, in a frontal collision between a subcompact and SUV rated 'Very Good,' you'll be better off in the SUV. Nevertheless, selecting the best performers in whatever size class you are buying, is fundamental to protecting yourself. And remember, these tests are conducted with fully belted dummies, if you are not wearing your safety belt, then test results do not really apply.

CRASH TESTS

Crash Test Performance (10=Best, 1=Worst)	Combined Car Book Crash Test Rating	Test Type	Car Book Crash Test Rating-Index (Lower numbers are better)	Likelihood of Life Threatening Injury				
				Front Fixed Barrier		Side Moving Barrier		Side Pole
				Front Driver	Front Pass.	Side Driver	Side Pass.	Pole Driver
Subcompact								
Chevrolet Sonic	8	Front	Very Good-166	8.7%	8.7%			
		Side	Average-113			7.0%	4.6%	7.1%
Fiat 500	2	Front	Very Poor-256	11.4%	16.0%			
		Side	Poor-148			5.3%	8.0%	15.8%
Ford Fiesta	3	Front	Average-199	8.2%	12.8%			
		Side	Very Poor-381			11.3%	31.5%	3.6%
Honda Fit	8	Front	Good-175	9.2%	9.1%			
		Side	Very Good-85			6.8%	2.5%	3.5%
Hyundai Accent	2	Front	Poor-209	9.2%	12.8%			
		Side	Very Poor-234			8.6%	17.0%	4.3%
Hyundai Veloster	4	Front	Poor-205	12.4%	9.2%			
		Side	Average-131			6.9%	7.8%	1.5%
Kia Rio	2	Front	Very Poor-230	10.8%	13.7%			
		Side	Very Poor-177			13.5%	7.0%	3.5%
Kia Soul	8	Front	Good-180	7.6%	11.2%			
		Side	Very Good-81			4.7%	4.0%	2.6%
Mitsubishi Mirage	3	Front	Poor-218	12.6%	10.5%			
		Side	Very Poor-169			7.4%	9.8%	9.6%
Nissan Versa	1	Front	Very Poor-295	12.2%	19.7%			
		Side	Very Poor-256			16.4%	13.5%	4.7%
Toyota Yaris	3	Front	Poor-217	9.9%	13.1%			
		Side	Poor-159			7.3%	8.7%	10.1%
Volkswagen Beetle	4	Front	Poor-216	9.6%	13.2%			
		Side	Average-125			7.3%	6.0%	5.3%
Compact								
Acura ILX	5	Front	Poor-209	9.5%	12.5%			
		Side	Good-105			5.6%	4.4%	9.5%
Audi A3	5	Front	Average-197	11.2%	9.6%			
		Side	Average-113			7.0%	5.1%	4.2%
Audi A4	6	Front	Good-178	9.5%	9.1%			
		Side	Poor-152			12.8%	4.8%	3.8%
BMW 3 Series	6	Front	Average-194	11.6%	8.9%			
		Side	Good-108			7.9%	4.3%	2.3%
Buick Verano	10	Front	Very Good-155	7.5%	8.7%			
		Side	Very Good-75			6.1%	1.9%	4.3%
Cadillac ATS	8	Front	Very Good-162	8.2%	8.7%			
		Side	Poor-138			7.5%	7.4%	4.8%

CRASH TESTS

Crash Test Performance (10=Best, 1=Worst)	Combined Car Book Crash Test Rating	Test Type	Car Book Crash Test Rating-Index (Lower numbers are better)	Likelihood of Life Threatening Injury				
				Front Fixed Barrier		Side Moving Barrier		Side Pole
				Front Driver	Front Pass.	Side Driver	Side Pass.	Pole Driver
Compact (cont.)								
Dodge Dart	8	Front	Average-188	9.2%	10.6%			
		Side	Very Good-78			4.1%	4.1%	2.4%
Ford C-MAX	3	Front	Very Poor-224	10.9%	12.9%			
		Side	Average-119			6.2%	5.7%	8.1%
Ford Focus	6	Front	Average-192	8.1%	12.1%			
		Side	Good-97			6.7%	3.9%	3.4%
Hyundai Elantra	5	Front	Average-199	9.7%	11.3%			
		Side	Poor-146			12.0%	3.9%	7.8%
Kia Forte	4	Front	Poor-208	10.1%	11.9%			
		Side	Poor-156			9.0%	8.4%	2.7%
Lexus IS	5	Front	Very Poor-226	10.8%	13.2%			
		Side	Very Good-85			5.4%	3.2%	5.9%
Mazda Mazda3	6	Front	Good-185	8.5%	10.9%			
		Side	Average-119			11.5%	2.4%	2.8%
Mercedes-Benz C-Class	3	Front	Poor-203	7.8%	13.6%			
		Side	Very Poor-170			5.7%	12.2%	4.8%
Nissan Leaf	2	Front	Very Poor-229	9.2%	15.1%			
		Side	Very Poor-215			5.6%	17.0%	5.0%
Nissan Sentra	3	Front	Very Poor-242	11.8%	14.0%			
		Side	Average-118			6.6%	6.5%	1.7%
Scion FR-S	4	Front	Average-195	10.1%	10.5%			
		Side	Very Poor-166			15.6%	4.0%	3.3%
Scion tC	6	Front	Poor-201	9.1%	12.1%			
		Side	Good-89			2.7%	6.1%	4.0%
Subaru Impreza	4	Front	Very Poor-240	12.1%	13.6%			
		Side	Good-96			6.0%	2.4%	12.8%
Toyota Corolla	8	Front	Good-176	8.6%	9.8%			
		Side	Very Good-87			3.0%	5.1%	6.6%
Toyota Prius C	2	Front	Poor-215	12.2%	10.5%			
		Side	Very Poor-239			14.8%	12.0%	8.1%
Volkswagen Golf	4	Front	Poor-203	12.4%	9.0%			
		Side	Average-128			5.0%	8.1%	6.0%
Volkswagen Jetta	7	Front	Average-200	10.0%	11.1%			
		Side	Very Good-78			4.2%	3.9%	3.8%

CRASH TESTS

Crash Test Performance (10=Best, 1=Worst)	Combined Car Book Crash Test Rating	Test Type	Car Book Crash Test Rating-Index (Lower numbers are better)	Likelihood of Life Threatening Injury				
				Front Fixed Barrier		Side Moving Barrier		Side Pole
				Front Driver	Front Pass.	Side Driver	Side Pass.	Pole Driver
Intermediate								
Acura TLX	10	Front	Very Good-156	7.3%	8.9%			
		Side	Very Good-58			4.4%	1.7%	3.4%
Audi A6	8	Front	Very Good-163	9.3%	7.7%			
		Side	Average-115			8.1%	3.9%	7.0%
BMW 5 Series	5	Front	Very Poor-233	13.1%	11.7%			
		Side	Very Good-85			8.4%	0.8%	5.5%
Buick Regal	5	Front	Average-199	9.9%	11.1%			
		Side	Average-116			4.1%	7.8%	4.3%
Cadillac CTS	7	Front	Good-184	8.1%	11.2%			
		Side	Good-102			6.9%	3.3%	7.9%
Chevrolet Malibu	6	Front	Average-198	10.1%	10.7%			
		Side	Good-111			5.6%	6.1%	4.1%
Chrysler 200	7	Front	Good-173	8.3%	9.9%			
		Side	Average-116			4.7%	7.0%	5.9%
Ford Fusion	6	Front	Good-176	7.5%	10.9%			
		Side	Very Poor-195			18.4%	5.0%	2.8%
Ford Fusion Energi	7	Front	Very Good-154	7.3%	8.7%			
		Side	Poor-158			14.6%	3.6%	4.7%
Honda Accord	8	Front	Very Good-169	8.7%	8.9%			
		Side	Good-104			2.9%	7.7%	3.0%
Hyundai Sonata	8	Front	Very Good-147	7.5%	7.8%			
		Side	Average-114			5.8%	6.2%	4.6%
Infiniti Q50	5	Front	Very Poor-246	10.7%	15.6%			
		Side	Very Good-68			6.5%	1.2%	2.6%
Kia Optima	6	Front	Good-174	8.6%	9.6%			
		Side	Very Poor-167			16.8%	2.0%	7.9%
Lincoln MKZ	6	Front	Good-176	7.5%	10.9%			
		Side	Very Poor-195			18.4%	5.0%	2.8%
Mazda Mazda6	7	Front	Good-185	7.6%	11.7%			
		Side	Good-96			8.2%	2.5%	3.5%
Mitsubishi Lancer	2	Front	Poor-214	9.4%	13.3%			
		Side	Very Poor-199			4.0%	16.4%	5.6%
Nissan Altima	6	Front	Very Good-165	7.2%	10.0%			
		Side	Very Poor-189			17.7%	4.4%	4.9%
Nissan Maxima	7	Front	Good-185	8.7%	10.8%			
		Side	Good-111			6.0%	4.3%	11.4%
Subaru Legacy	10	Front	Very Good-161	8.9%	7.9%			
		Side	Very Good-80			3.3%	4.7%	4.0%

CRASH TESTS

Crash Test Performance (10=Best, 1=Worst)	Combined Car Book Crash Test Rating	Test Type	Car Book Crash Test Rating-Index (Lower numbers are better)	Likelihood of Life Threatening Injury				
				Front Fixed Barrier		Side Moving Barrier		Side Pole
				Front Driver	Front Pass.	Side Driver	Side Pass.	Pole Driver
Intermediate (cont.)								
Toyota Camry	6	Front	Average-195	11.2%	9.4%			
		Side	Good-107			6.1%	3.8%	11.3%
Toyota Prius V	6	Front	Poor-211	10.3%	12.0%			
		Side	Very Good-70			4.3%	1.5%	10.5%
Volkswagen Passat	8	Front	Very Good-155	7.7%	8.5%			
		Side	Poor-137			13.1%	2.7%	3.9%
Volvo S60	8	Front	Very Good-158	8.3%	8.2%			
		Side	Average-119			9.8%	3.7%	3.2%
Large								
Buick LaCrosse	8	Front	Very Good-169	7.9%	9.8%			
		Side	Average-112			5.7%	4.9%	10.5%
Cadillac XTS	9	Front	Very Good-160	7.6%	9.1%			
		Side	Good-88			4.2%	4.3%	6.7%
Chevrolet Impala	6	Front	Good-173	7.5%	10.6%			
		Side	Poor-142			10.1%	6.1%	2.9%
Chrysler 300	4	Front	Poor-221	12.7%	12.5%			
		Side	Average-120			12.9%	0.8%	5.1%
Dodge Challenger	6	Front	Poor-204	11.7%	9.8%			
		Side	Very Good-56			4.7%	1.4%	2.6%
Dodge Charger	6	Front	Average-190	9.7%	10.3%			
		Side	Average-128			13.5%	0.7%	7.0%
Ford Taurus	7	Front	Very Good-164	8.4%	8.7%			
		Side	Poor-154			8.3%	8.3%	5.8%
Hyundai Genesis	9	Front	Very Good-153	7.7%	8.3%			
		Side	Good-108			10.9%	0.9%	6.5%
Lexus ES	6	Front	Good-187	9.7%	9.9%			
		Side	Poor-134			11.7%	2.9%	6.9%
Lincoln MKS	7	Front	Very Good-164	8.4%	8.7%			
		Side	Poor-154			8.3%	8.3%	5.8%
Mercedes-Benz E-Class	3	Front	Very Poor-265	13.7%	14.8%			
		Side	Average-116			2.2%	6.7%	17.8%
Tesla Model S	8	Front	Good-180	9.4%	9.5%			
		Side	Very Good-58			3.5%	1.5%	7.9%
Toyota Avalon	7	Front	Average-194	10.1%	10.4%			
		Side	Good-92			6.2%	2.3%	10.2%
Minivan								
Chrysler Town and Country	3	Front	Poor-207	11.2%	10.7%			
		Side	Very Poor-152			7.4%	8.8%	5.5%

CRASH TESTS

Crash Test Performance (10=Best, 1=Worst)	Combined Car Book Crash Test Rating	Test Type	Car Book Crash Test Rating-Index (Lower numbers are better)	Likelihood of Life Threatening Injury				
				Front Fixed Barrier		Side Moving Barrier		Side Pole
				Front Driver	Front Pass.	Side Driver	Side Pass.	Pole Driver
Minivan (cont.)								
Honda Odyssey	7	Front	Average-187	9.9%	9.8%			
		Side	Good-57			2.9%	2.3%	5.6%
Kia Sedona	7	Front	Very Good-153	7.7%	8.3%			
		Side	Very Poor-108			10.9%	0.9%	6.5%
Toyota Sienna	5	Front	Average-197	8.6%	12.1%			
		Side	Average-71			2.9%	4.0%	4.5%
Small SUV								
Acura RDX	8	Front	Very Good-149	7.0%	8.5%			
		Side	Average-62			2.2%	2.9%	7.9%
Audi Q5	3	Front	Very Poor-230	14.6%	9.9%			
		Side	Poor-74			2.7%	4.4%	4.9%
BMW X3	6	Front	Average-188	8.8%	11.0%			
		Side	Poor-75			4.9%	3.5%	0.9%
Buick Encore	8	Front	Very Good-165	8.3%	9.0%			
		Side	Average-66			3.3%	3.0%	5.4%
Cadillac SRX	6	Front	Average-191	8.6%	11.4%			
		Side	Average-67			2.7%	1.7%	14.8%
Chevrolet Trax	8	Front	Very Good-165	8.3%	9.0%			
		Side	Average-66			3.3%	3.0%	5.4%
Ford Escape	5	Front	Poor-202	10.2%	11.2%			
		Side	Good-60			2.0%	3.5%	5.0%
Honda CR-V	6	Front	Good-178	8.8%	9.9%			
		Side	Poor-73			3.1%	3.9%	5.7%
Honda HR-V	4	Front	Poor-214	11.9%	10.8%			
		Side	Average-70			4.4%	2.6%	5.1%
Hyundai Tucson	4	Front	Poor-210	11.2%	11.1%			
		Side	Average-72			3.7%	1.7%	12.8%
Jeep Cherokee	5	Front	Very Poor-228	11.2%	13.1%			
		Side	Very Good-45			3.2%	1.7%	1.6%
Jeep Compass	1	Front	Very Poor-314	17.4%	17.0%			
		Side	Very Poor-106			9.3%	2.4%	4.8%
Jeep Patriot	1	Front	Very Poor-296	18.6%	13.5%			
		Side	Very Poor-108			6.4%	4.5%	7.3%
Jeep Renegade	3	Front	Poor-207	10.4%	11.6%			
		Side	Very Poor-187			3.8%	15.7%	2.4%
Kia Sportage	6	Front	Good-185	8.9%	10.5%			
		Side	Very Poor-101			7.7%	3.5%	3.3%
Lexus NX	7	Front	Very Good-147	7.5%	7.8%			
		Side	Very Poor-114			5.8%	6.2%	4.6%

CRASH TESTS

Crash Test Performance (10=Best, 1=Worst)	Combined Car Book Crash Test Rating	Test Type	Car Book Crash Test Rating-Index (Lower numbers are better)	Likelihood of Life Threatening Injury				
				Front Fixed Barrier		Side Moving Barrier		Side Pole
				Front Driver	Front Pass.	Side Driver	Side Pass.	Pole Driver
Small SUV (cont.)								
Lincoln MKC	3	Front	Poor-213	8.9%	13.7%			
		Side	Poor-84			2.5%	5.8%	3.4%
Mazda CX-5	4	Front	Very Poor-227	7.3%	16.7%			
		Side	Average-64			2.2%	3.4%	7.0%
Nissan Juke	1	Front	Very Poor-289	12.5%	18.7%			
		Side	Very Poor-185			11.7%	9.1%	4.8%
Subaru Forester	7	Front	Poor-205	9.0%	12.7%			
		Side	Good-56			3.1%	2.6%	2.9%
Subaru XV Crosstrek	4	Front	Average-200	10.4%	10.7%			
		Side	Poor-82			3.8%	2.8%	12.8%
Toyota RAV4	6	Front	Poor-204	10.6%	10.9%			
		Side	Very Good-49			3.2%	1.1%	6.5%
Volkswagen Tiguan	2	Front	Very Poor-287	13.2%	17.9%			
		Side	Poor-86			3.3%	4.2%	10.0%
Mid-Size SUV								
Acura MDX	7	Front	Very Good-168	8.3%	9.2%			
		Side	Average-68			2.5%	4.2%	3.6%
BMW X5	7	Front	Good-177	8.9%	9.7%			
		Side	Average-62			2.4%	3.1%	6.7%
Chevrolet Equinox	2	Front	Poor-216	9.5%	13.4%			
		Side	Very Poor-120			11.7%	2.0%	4.5%
Dodge Journey	2	Front	Very Poor-222	9.6%	13.9%			
		Side	Very Poor-168			3.7%	11.8%	13.5%
Ford Edge	9	Front	Very Good-161	8.3%	8.5%			
		Side	Good-53			2.6%	2.7%	2.9%
Ford Explorer	7	Front	Good-183	10.4%	8.8%			
		Side	Average-63			4.2%	1.6%	7.1%
GMC Terrain	2	Front	Poor-216	9.5%	13.4%			
		Side	Very Poor-120			11.7%	2.0%	4.5%
Honda Pilot	7	Front	Average-189	9.9%	10.0%			
		Side	Very Good-46			2.5%	1.0%	8.1%
Hyundai Santa Fe Sport	7	Front	Good-184	9.2%	10.1%			
		Side	Average-71			3.6%	3.2%	6.3%
Infiniti QX60	5	Front	Average-196	11.2%	9.5%			
		Side	Average-64			4.9%	1.8%	4.2%
Jeep Grand Cherokee	6	Front	Good-178	9.4%	9.3%			
		Side	Poor-93			8.3%	2.3%	2.4%
Kia Sorento	6	Front	Good-177	8.8%	9.7%			
		Side	Poor-84			3.2%	5.3%	3.7%

CRASH TESTS

Crash Test Performance (10=Best, 1=Worst)	Combined Car Book Crash Test Rating	Test Type	Car Book Crash Test Rating-Index (Lower numbers are better)	Likelihood of Life Threatening Injury				
				Front Fixed Barrier		Side Moving Barrier		Side Pole
				Front Driver	Front Pass.	Side Driver	Side Pass.	Pole Driver
Mid-Size SUV (cont.)								
Mazda CX-9	2	Front	Very Poor-302	16.6%	16.2%			
		Side	Poor-100			4.0%	5.7%	6.8%
Mitsubishi Outlander	5	Front	Average-195	12.4%	8.0%			
		Side	Poor-91			3.8%	4.7%	7.8%
Mitsubishi Outlander Sport	4	Front	Poor-203	10.0%	11.3%			
		Side	Poor-97			2.8%	6.3%	6.8%
Nissan Murano	3	Front	Very Poor-261	9.9%	18.0%			
		Side	Average-66			6.1%	0.9%	4.3%
Nissan Pathfinder	5	Front	Average-196	11.2%	9.5%			
		Side	Average-64			4.9%	1.8%	4.2%
Nissan Rogue	2	Front	Very Poor-240	10.5%	15.0%			
		Side	Very Poor-116			6.5%	4.6%	10.4%
Subaru Outback	9	Front	Very Good-161	8.9%	7.9%			
		Side	Good-50			2.9%	1.9%	4.0%
Volvo XC60	8	Front	Very Good-165	8.2%	9.0%			
		Side	Good-60			4.0%	2.1%	4.0%
Large SUV								
Buick Enclave	7	Front	Good-181	9.6%	9.3%			
		Side	Good-57			2.1%	3.4%	3.8%
Cadillac Escalade		Front	No Index					
		Side	Very Good-45			3.0%	0.4%	8.6%
Cadillac Escalade ESV		Front	No Index					
		Side	Average-69			4.5%	1.0%	12.2%
Chevrolet Suburban	5	Front	Average-195	10.4%	10.2%			
		Side	Average-69			4.5%	1.0%	12.2%
Chevrolet Tahoe	8	Front	Good-185	9.7%	9.7%			
		Side	Very Good-45			3.0%	0.4%	8.6%
Chevrolet Traverse	7	Front	Good-181	9.6%	9.3%			
		Side	Good-57			2.1%	3.4%	3.8%
Ford Expedition	9	Front	Very Good-167	9.1%	8.4%			
		Side	Very Good-37			2.5%	0.5%	6.5%
GMC Acadia	7	Front	Good-181	9.6%	9.3%			
		Side	Good-57			2.1%	3.4%	3.8%
GMC Yukon	8	Front	Good-185	9.7%	9.7%			
		Side	Very Good-45			3.0%	0.4%	8.6%
GMC Yukon XL	5	Front	Average-195	10.4%	10.2%			
		Side	Average-69			4.5%	1.0%	12.2%
Lincoln Navigator	9	Front	Very Good-167	9.1%	8.4%			
		Side	Very Good-37			2.5%	0.5%	6.5%

CRASH TESTS

Crash Test Performance (10=Best, 1=Worst)	Combined Car Book Crash Test Rating	Test Type	Car Book Crash Test Rating-Index (Lower numbers are better)	Likelihood of Life Threatening Injury				
				Front Fixed Barrier		Side Moving Barrier		Side Pole
				Front Driver	Front Pass.	Side Driver	Side Pass.	Pole Driver
Large SUV (cont.)								
Toyota 4Runner	2	Front	Very Poor-255	11.9%	15.5%			
		Side	Poor-88			7.1%	0.9%	11.7%
Toyota Highlander	8	Front	Average-192	11.2%	9.0%			
		Side	Very Good-45			2.4%	1.1%	7.3%
Compact Pickup								
Chevrolet Colorado	4	Front	Poor-208	10.4%	11.1%			
		Side	Poor-73			6.0%	1.2%	6.4%
GMC Canyon	4	Front	Poor-208	10.4%	11.1%			
		Side	Poor-73			6.0%	1.2%	6.4%
Standard Pickup								
Chevrolet Silverado	9	Front	Very Good-156	8.1%	8.1%			
		Side	Poor-80			2.7%	3.7%	11.7%
Ford F-150	9	Front	Very Good-167	8.1%	9.4%			
		Side	Very Good-43			3.6%	0.7%	3.9%
GMC Sierra	9	Front	Very Good-156	8.1%	8.1%			
		Side	Poor-80			2.7%	3.7%	11.7%
Ram 1500	5	Front	Poor-214	10.8%	11.9%			
		Side	Good-59			5.2%	0.3%	7.3%
Toyota Tundra		Front	Very Poor-236	12.0%	13.2%			
		Side	No Index			2.7%		7.5%

CHILD SAFETY

Incorrect Child Safety Seat Installation: Surveys show up to 85 percent of parents do not install their child seats properly. Incorrect installation of a child safety seat can deny the child lifesaving protection and may even contribute to further injuring the child. Read the installation instructions carefully. If you have any questions about the correct installation in your particular car, go to www.safercar.gov/parents. There you will find a list of inspection stations near you where you can go for a free check up and advice by trained experts.

Child Safety Seat Recalls: Manufacturers are required to put address cards in child seat packages. Mail the registration card as soon as you open the box! You can also register your own seat at www.safercars.gov/parents for notification about recalls on your particular seat(s).These are the only ways you will receive notification of a seat recall. Keep a copy of the manufacturer's address and contact the manufacturer if you move. To find out if the seat you are using has ever been recalled go to www-odi.nhtsa.dot.gov/owners/SearchSafety Issues. You can also contact the Auto Safety Hotline at 800-424-9393.

Seat Belts for Kids: How long should children use car seats? For children, a car seat is twice as effective in preventing injury as an adult lap and shoulder harness so use it for as long as possible. Most children can start using seat belts at 4'9" or tall enough for the shoulder belt to cross the chest, not the neck. The lap section of the belt should be snug and as low on the hips as possible. If the shoulder belt does cross the face or neck, use a booster seat.

AUTOMATIC SAFETY PROTECTION

The concept of automatic safety protection is not new. Automatic fire sprinklers in public buildings, oxygen masks in airplanes, purification of drinking water, and pasteurization of milk are all commonly accepted forms of automatic safety protection. Airbags provide automatic crash protection in cars.

Automatic crash protection protects people from what is called the "second collision," when the occupant collides with the interior of the vehicle. Because the "second collision" occurs within milliseconds, providing automatic rather than manual protection dramatically improves the chances of escaping injury.

Automatic crash protection comes in two basic forms, airbags and automatic control of safety features.

Since airbags were introduced over 30 years ago, they have been so successful in saving lives that car makers now include a variety of types which deploy from as many as 10 different points.

The automatic control of safety features was first introduced with anti-lock brakes. Today, Electronic Stability Control (ESC) and other automatic functions such as Collision Avoidance Braking and Lane Departure Warnings are improving the safety of new cars.

Electronic Stability Control (ESC) takes advantage of anti-lock brake technology and helps minimize the loss of control. Each car maker will have its own name for this feature, but they all work in a similar fashion.

For ESC, anti-lock brakes work by using speed sensors on each wheel to determine if one or more of the wheels is locking up or skidding. ESC then uses these speed sensors and a unit that determines the steering angle to monitor what's happening with the vehicle. A special control device measures the steering and rotation of the tires in order to detect when a vehicle is about to go in a direction different from the one indicated by the steering wheel–or out of control! This will typically occur during a hard turn or on slippery surfaces. The control unit will sense whether the car is over-steering (turning sharper than you intended resulting in the back wheels slipping sideways) or under-steering (continuing to move forward despite your intended turn). When either of these events occur, the control unit will automatically apply the brakes to the appropriate wheels to correct the situation and, in some cases, automatically slow down the engine.

ESC will not keep the vehicle under control in severely out of control situations nor does it work as well on curvey roads as on straight roads. Nevertheless, according to the IIHS, ESC can reduce the chance of a single vehicle crash by over 50%. Its benefit is that it will prevent more typical losses of control from escalating into a crash. For more details on key automatic safety features, see pages 78-80.

TELEMATICS

Telematic systems are subscription-based services ($100-$300 per year) that use a combination of cellular technology and global positioning systems to provide a variety of safety and convenience features. The main safety feature is automatic crash notification (ACN) which connects the vehicle's occupants to a private call center that directs emergency medical teams to the car. This system can be activated by pressing a button on the dash or rear view mirror or it is automatically activated if the airbag deploys. Once the system is activated, the call center receives the exact location of your vehicle and notifies the local emergency response team. This can potentially reduce the time it takes for an emergency team to reach your vehicle. Other safety features can include roadside assistance, remote door unlocking, stolen vehicle tracking, and driving directions.

Caution! Some manufacturers are adding cell phone capability to the ACN system which increases the risk of a crash 4-fold when talking on the ACN cell phone. This is about the same effect as drinking and driving. Don't drink and drive or phone and drive!

WHAT'S COMING IN THE FUTURE

Crashworthiness and Occupant Protection

Among the great successes in auto safety are the improved occupant protection from air bags and better designed safety belts. Recently, new regulations and technologies have resulted in a dramatic reduction in rollover casualties. Rollovers, especially SUVs and pickups, had been responsible for one third of all road fatalities. Unfortunately, many people bought SUVs because they thought they were safe when they were not. Poor handling qualities and weak roofs meant that despite their greater bulk and weight, SUVs had higher fatality rates than many smaller cars.

Today, all new light vehicles have electronic stability control systems to keep them under better control, much stronger roofs, and side curtain air bags with improved designs to control ejection even when one is not wearing a safety belt. As a consequence, rollover fatalities in recent models have dropped by about 25%.

Rear End Collisions

Although the crashworthiness of new vehicles is dramatically better than in cars of the past, there is still a problem in rear impacts. The front seats and head restraints of some vehicles are still so weak that they will collapse and cause even belted occupants to slide into the rear seat or even out the back window when a vehicle is hit from behind. Children in the rear seat – which is where they should be – are, tragically, right in the path of a collapsing front seat.

Research and testing has shown how to design seating systems that can protect both the people in these seats, and the kids sitting behind them. The Insurance Institute for Highway Safety (iihs.org) has ratings for rear impact safety that are useful in differentiating relatively safe from unsafe vehicles in rear impacts. Unfortunately, not all makes and models are rated.

What's Next?

Two major changes are occurring in motor vehicle design. First, the fuel economy standards are becoming dramatically more rigorous. Cars ten years from now will have to go twice as far on a gallon of gas as they did only a few years ago; advances in electronics, sensors and computing power are being used to both improve safety and take over more of the driving; and, the electric vehicle is breaking into showrooms.

While the dramatic safety improvements have been in protecting people when crashes occur, future technology will be devoted to reducing the potential that a crash will even occur. Advanced sensors, electronics and computers will act as a co-pilot to either warn a driver of a potential collision or actually take over control of the vehicle to avoid a crash.

Unquestionably, the self-driving car is coming, but today's vehicles are already "computers on wheels". Computers control emissions, transmissions, crash sensing, braking and many other critical actions. Manufacturers now offer systems that not only *warn* about vehicles in your blind spot, inadvertent lane changing or upcoming crashes, but actually *take action* to avoid potential collisions.

Lane Keeping Assist monitors the position of the vehicle within a lane and makes an automatic correction if the vehicle drifts out of the center. It also warns if a driver attempts to change lanes when it is not safe to do so.

Smart cruise control, which can vary travel speeds automatically to accommodate traffic conditions, is becoming common.

Automatic braking, which will stop a car when a potential rear end collision or pedestrian is sensed, is also being installed in some cars.

Because of the popularity of these life-saving devices, manufacturers are rushing them to market with varying degrees of effectiveness and reliability. Both NHTSA and IIHS are developing tests and ratings for the performance of such systems. For some of these features, back up cameras, lane changing and forward crash warnings, NHTSA has voluntary standards which define good performance. For the first time *The Car Book's* car pages at the back of the book, indicates which of these features do and do not meet the government requirements.

The good news is that more and more of this technology is becoming available in the cars most of us buy. With all of the information in *The Car Book*, safety features have always been our top priority. Whether buying for yourself or your new teenage driver, focusing on the safety features of today's new vehicles can be your most important buying decision.

ROLLOVER

The bad news is that until recently 10,000 people died in rollovers annually. The good news is that most rollover casualties today are in older cars or in very severe or complex crashes.

The risk that a vehicle will rollover is a significant safety challenge, especially with sport utility vehicles pickups and vans. Because of their relatively high center of gravity, they are less stable than most passenger cars. As a result, they are more likely to roll over on a sharp turn or if they go out of control. A typical rollover occurs when a driver is not paying attention and drifts off the road, and then responds with a major steering correction. Until about five years ago, many cars and light trucks were not only more vulnerable to rolling over, they did a poor job of protecting occupants when they did. Drivers and passengers too often received critical head or neck injuries from collapsing roofs.

New vehicle buyers are in luck in that the Federal government has finally addressed the problems of rollover with several recent requirements:

Electronic Stability Control: ESC judiciously applies braking to wheels selectively when a vehicle is on the verge of going out of control. This can keep the vehicle from sliding and rotating so that it is travelling sideways, making it vulnerable to rolling over. This feature has substantially reduced the likelihood of a rollovers.

Ejection Control: Since half of all rollover fatalities are thrown out of the vehicle, this feature is designed to keep passengers in the car even if they are not wearing their safety belts. This feature includes improved side window glass that continues to block the window even when the glass breaks and window curtain air bags that cover the side windows in a rollover. These curtains cushion the occupant and further reduce the potential that they will be ejected.

Roof Strength: Until recently, the requirements for roof strength were very weak, and few manufacturers bothered to

Center for Auto Safety Roof Crush Test Results

A few years ago, to identify vehicles which have strong roofs, the Center for Auto Safety had the Center for Injury Research conduct dynamic rollover roof crush tests using the Jordan Rollover System. Funded by the Santos Family Foundation, the testing played a major role in NHTSA going to two-sided testing in its new standard.

The table below shows the results of the testing. The cumulative crush is how much the roof will crush inward after two full rolls. More than 5 inches of roof crush is unacceptable because an occupant's head is likely to be hit. The Strength to Weight Ratio (SWR) is how much weight the roof on one side will support before crushing inward 5 inches when tested in a static fashion as the government does.

Vehicle*	Cumulative Crush (in.)	Dynamic SWR	Static SWR	Rating
Kia Soul 2010-12	1.6	5.2	4.3	Very Good
Volvo XC90 2005-09	1.8	5.2	4.6	Very Good
Toyota Highlander Hybrid 2008-12	2.3	4.9	4.7	Very Good
VW Tiguan 2009-11	2.4	4.9	4.4	Very Good
VW Jetta 2007-09	3.4	4.4	5.1	Good
Honda CR-V 2007-10	3.6	4.3	2.6	Good
Toyota Camry Hybrid 2007-10	4.3	4.2	3.9	Good
Toyota Prius 2010	3.8	4.2	4.2	Good
Toyota Camry 2007-09	4.3	4	4.3	Good
Nissan Versa 2009-10	4.4	4	3.7	Good
Subaru Forester 2003-08	4.6	3.9	4.3	Moderate
Hyundai Sonata 2006-09	4.6	3.9	3.2	Moderate
Chevrolet Mailbu 2009-10	5	3.7	4.4	Moderate
Pontiac G6 2006-09	7	2.8	2.3	Poor
Ford F-150 Supercab 2010-12	7.2	2.7	4.7	Poor
Chrysler 300 2006-09	7.4	2.6	2.5	Poor
Jeep Gr. Cherokee 2007-10	9.1	1.8	2.2	Very Poor
Scion xB 2008-10	10.4	1.2	6.8	Very Poor
Chevy Tahoe 2007-09	10.9	1	2.1	Very Poor
Honda Ridgeline 2006-09	10.9	1	2.4	Very Poor

*Year tested is first model year listed with later models having similar roof strength and design.

This work was funded by the Santos Family Foundation on sixteen vehicles donated by the State Farm Insurance Company.

ROLLOVER

design roofs that could withstand the forces when a vehicle rolled. Prodded by the dynamic rollover roof crush tests sponsored by the Cetner for Auto Safety, NHTSA has substantially increased the roof strength requirement and IIHS has begun rating roof strength, requiring even greater strength to get a "good" rating. The result is that most new vehicle roofs can withstand a force of more than four times the weight of the vehicle without significant distortion. The table on the previous page shows some of the difference in roof strength that led to the new standards.

Padding in the Roof: This standard ensures that if your head strikes the roof in a rollover, the impact will be lessened by the padding, reducing the likelihood of a concussion or other head injury.

Static Stability Index: In addition to these factors, the Static Stability Index, a measure of a vehicle's roll stability. The SSI is a ratio of the height of the car's center of gravity to half of its track width (the distance between two wheels). In the past, some SUVs had SSIs that were little more than "1" making them exceptionally unstable and vulnerable to rolling over. Traditionally, many SUVs were built on pickup chassis and had poor a SSI (typically 1.1 to 1.15) along with very crude suspension systems. Combined with their very weak roofs, this was a major reason for the high rollover casualty rates in SUVs. Today, many SUVs are built on passenger car platforms and have much higher SSIs: typically 1.2 to 1.3. Most passenger cars have SSIs greater than 1.35. The higher the SSI, the more stable the vehicle.

In buying a new car, minivan, or normal-sized pickup you can be reasonably confident – thanks to NHTSA's standards – that the vehicle will have a reasonable level of rollover resistance and will provide good protection in most simple rollovers.

Rollover and Your Next Vehicle Purchase: If you have a car or light truck that is more than five or ten years old, you might consider whether to replace it because of its poor rollover safety. For example, the danger of rollover with sport utilities was so severe that manufacturers were actually required to place a rollover warning sticker where it could be seen by the driver.

Rollover Ratings for 2016 Vehicles: Following are rollover ratings for many 2016 vehicles. We published these ratings for years before the National Highway Traffic Safety Administration adopted this rating system.

The rollover rating is based on the Static Stability Index (SSI) and consists of a formula that uses the track width of the vehicle (tire to tire) and height to determine which vehicles are more or less likely to roll over when compared to each other. You can't use this information to exactly predict rollovers. However, all things being equal, if two vehicles are in the same situation where a rollover could occur, the one with a high SSI is less likely to roll over than one with a lower SSI. Because this formula doesn't consider such things as driver behavior, the weight of the vehicle, and the effectiveness of the vehicle's electronic stability control, some experts do not believe it tells the whole story. We agree, and urged the government to provide an even better rollover rating system.

In the meantime, knowing a vehicle's SSI can be a key consideration in your evaluation of the vehicle. Again, the lower the SSI, the more stable the vehicle.

STATIC STABILITY INDEX

Vehicle	SSI (High=Better)/ Chance of Rollover		Vehicle	SSI (High=Better)/ Chance of Rollover		Vehicle	SSI (High=Better)/ Chance of Rollover	
Acura ILX	1.42	Low	Ford Taurus	1.39	Moderate	Mercedes-Benz GLA-Class	1.33*	Moderate
Acura MDX	1.26	High	GMC Acadia	1.23	High	Mercedes-Benz GLC-Class	1.21*	High
Acura RDX	1.26	High	GMC Canyon	1.16	Very High	Mercedes-Benz GL-Class	1.19*	Very High
Acura TLX	1.46	Low	GMC Sierra	1.21	High	Mercedes-Benz GLE-Class	1.20*	High
Audi A3	1.41	Low	GMC Terrain	1.19	Very High	Mercedes-Benz S-Class	1.46*	Low
Audi A4	1.46	Low	GMC Yukon	1.14	Very High	Mini Cooper	1.41*	Low
Audi A5	1.53*	Very Low	GMC Yukon XL	1.16	Very High	Mini Countryman	1.32*	Moderate
Audi A6	1.51	Very Low	Honda Accord	1.46	Low	Mitsubishi Lancer	1.36	Moderate
Audi Q3	1.32*	Moderate	Honda Civic	1.35*	Moderate	Mitsubishi Mirage	1.24	High
Audi Q5	1.27	High	Honda CR-V	1.22	High	Mitsubishi Mirage	1.24	High
Audi Q7	1.29*	High	Honda Fit	1.28	High	Mitsubishi Mirage	1.24	High
BMW 2 Series	1.45*	Low	Honda HR-V	1.26	High	Mitsubishi Mirage	1.24	High
BMW 3 Series	1.48	Low	Honda Odyssey	1.34	Moderate	Mitsubishi Outlander	1.24	High
BMW 4 Series	1.52*	Very Low	Honda Pilot	1.22	High	Mitsubishi Outlander Sport	1.23	High
BMW 5 Series	1.49	Low	Hyundai Accent	1.35	Moderate	Nissan 370Z	1.59*	Very Low
BMW 6 Series	1.59*	Very Low	Hyundai Azera	1.46*	Low	Nissan Altima	1.44	Low
BMW 7 Series	1.47*	Low	Hyundai Elantra	1.41	Low	Nissan Armada	1.14*	Very High
BMW i3	1.33*	Moderate	Hyundai Genesis	1.48	Low	Nissan Frontier	1.15*	Very High
BMW X1	1.31*	Moderate	Hyundai Santa Fe	1.29*	High	Nissan Juke	1.27	High
BMW X3	1.24	High	Hyundai Santa Fe Sport	1.27	High	Nissan Leaf	1.41	Low
BMW X5	1.21	High	Hyundai Sonata	1.43	Low	Nissan Maxima	1.48	Low
Buick Enclave	1.23	High	Hyundai Tucson	1.21	High	Nissan Murano	1.25	High
Buick Encore	1.18	Very High	Hyundai Veloster	1.43	Low	Nissan Pathfinder	1.22	High
Buick LaCrosse	1.37	Moderate	Infiniti Q50	1.47	Low	Nissan Quest	1.24*	High
Buick Regal	1.41	Low	Infiniti Q70	1.33*	Moderate	Nissan Rogue	1.24	High
Buick Verano	1.39	Moderate	Infiniti QX60	1.22	High	Nissan Sentra	1.37	Moderate
Cadillac ATS	1.45	Low	Infiniti QX70	1.29*	High	Nissan Sentra	1.37	Moderate
Cadillac CTS	1.45	Low	Infiniti QX80	1.16*	Very High	Nissan Sentra	1.37	Moderate
Cadillac Escalade	1.14	Very High	Jeep Cherokee	1.22	High	Nissan Sentra	1.37	Moderate
Cadillac Escalade ESV	1.16	Very High	Jeep Compass	1.20	High	Nissan Titan		
Cadillac SRX	1.21	High	Jeep Grand Cherokee	1.17	Very High	Nissan Versa	1.29	High
Cadillac XTS	1.37	Moderate	Jeep Patriot	1.15	Very High	Porsche Macan	1.33*	Moderate
Chevrolet Camaro	1.58*	Very Low	Jeep Renegade	1.18*	Very High	Ram 1500	1.18	Very High
Chevrolet Colorado	1.15	Very High	Jeep Wrangler	1.13*	Very High	Scion FR-S	1.66	Very Low
Chevrolet Corvette	1.71*	Very Low	Kia Cadenza	1.45*	Low	Scion tC	1.41	Low
Chevrolet Cruze	1.40*	Low	Kia Forte	1.44	Low	Smart ForTwo	1.24*	High
Chevrolet Equinox	1.19	Very High	Kia Optima	1.48	Low	Subaru Forester	1.23	High
Chevrolet Impala	1.36	Moderate	Kia Rio	1.38	Moderate	Subaru Impreza	1.46	Low
Chevrolet Malibu	1.40	Low	Kia Rio	1.38	Moderate	Subaru Legacy	1.45	Low
Chevrolet Silverado	1.21	High	Kia Rio	1.38	Moderate	Subaru Outback	1.22	High
Chevrolet Sonic	1.34	Moderate	Kia Rio	1.38	Moderate	Subaru XV Crosstrek	1.27	High
Chevrolet Spark	1.24*	High	Kia Sedona	1.33	Moderate	Tesla Model S	1.83	Very Low
Chevrolet Suburban	1.16	Very High	Kia Sorento	1.25	High	Toyota 4Runner	1.12	Very High
Chevrolet Tahoe	1.14	Very High	Kia Soul	1.28	High	Toyota Avalon	1.42	Low
Chevrolet Traverse	1.23	High	Kia Sportage	1.22	High	Toyota Camry	1.40	Low
Chevrolet Trax	1.18	Very High	Land Rover Range Rover	1.19*	Very High	Toyota Corolla	1.37	Moderate
Chevrolet Volt	1.45*	Low	Land Rover Rng Rvr Evoque	1.29*	High	Toyota Highlander	1.20	High
Chrysler 200	1.42	Low	Land Rover Rng Rver Sport	1.23*	High	Toyota Prius	1.39*	Moderate
Chrysler 300	1.39	Moderate	Lexus CT	1.39*	Moderate	Toyota Prius C	1.37	Moderate
Chrysler Town and Country	1.24	High	Lexus ES	1.40	Low	Toyota Prius V	1.31	Moderate
Dodge Challenger	1.40	Low	Lexus GS	1.45*	Low	Toyota RAV4	1.23	High
Dodge Charger	1.45	Low	Lexus GX	1.09*	Very High	Toyota Sequoia	1.19*	Very High
Dodge Dart	1.42	Low	Lexus IS	1.48	Low	Toyota Sienna	1.30	Moderate
Dodge Journey	1.20	High	Lexus NX	1.25	High	Toyota Tacoma	1.16*	Very High
Fiat 500	1.29	High	Lexus RC	1.51*	Very Low	Toyota Tundra	1.15	Very High
Fiat 500L	1.20*	High	Lexus RX	1.23*	High	Toyota Yaris	1.31	Moderate
Ford C-MAX	1.29	High	Lincoln MKC	1.24	High	Volkswagen Beetle	1.43	Low
Ford Edge	1.26	High	Lincoln MKS	1.39	Moderate	Volkswagen CC	1.46*	Low
Ford Escape	1.19	Very High	Lincoln MKZ	1.41	Low	Volkswagen Golf	1.40	Low
Ford Expedition	1.16	Very High	Lincoln Navigator	1.16	Very High	Volkswagen Jetta	1.40	Low
Ford Explorer	1.24	High	Mazda CX-5	1.22	High	Volkswagen Passat	1.42	Low
Ford F-150	1.19	Very High	Mazda CX-9	1.27	High	Volkswagen Tiguan	1.20	High
Ford Fiesta	1.29	High	Mazda Mazda3	1.43	Low	Volkswagen Touareg	1.25*	High
Ford Flex	1.23*	High	Mazda Mazda6	1.44	Low	Volvo S60	1.45	Low
Ford Focus	1.38	Moderate	Mazda MX-5 Miata	1.62*	Very Low	Volvo V60	1.41*	Low
Ford Fusion	1.41	Low	Mercedes-Benz C-Class	1.40	Low	Volvo XC60	1.22	High
Ford Fusion Energi	1.41*	Low	Mercedes-Benz CLA-Class	1.43*	Low	Volvo XC70	1.29*	High
Ford Mustang	1.56*	Very Low	Mercedes-Benz E-Class	1.46	Low			

*Calculated

As gas prices bounce up and down, regular driving still takes a big bite out of our pocketbooks. The good news is that higher fuel efficiency standards are forcing car companies to provide more fuel efficient vehicles. Buying right and practicing more fuel efficient driving will make a huge difference in your vehicle's operating costs. With the current low gas prices, many consumers are buying fuel inefficient vehicles. Beware, when gas prices go back up, and they will, you'll be stuck with a budget-busting gas guzzler.

Using the EPA ratings is the best way to incorporate fuel efficiency in selecting a new car. By comparing these ratings, even among cars of the same size, you'll find that fuel efficiency varies greatly. One compact car might get 36 miles per gallon (mpg) while another compact gets only 22 mpg. If you drive 15,000 miles a year and you pay $2.10 per gallon for fuel, the 36 mpg car will save you $570 *a year* over the "gas guzzler." Imagine what's going to happen when gas prices go back up!

In 2008, the EPA changed the way it estimates miles per gallon to better represent today's driving conditions. Their new method adjusts for aggressive driving (high speeds and faster acceleration), air conditioning use, and cold temperature operation.

Octane Ratings: Once you've purchased your car, you'll be faced with choosing the right gasoline. Oil companies spend millions of dollars trying to get you to buy so-called higher performance or high octane fuels. Using high octane fuel can add considerably to your gas bill, and the vast majority of vehicles do not need it. Check your owner's manual and only use what's recommended, which is usually 87. Very few vehicles require "premium" gasoline.

The octane rating of a gasoline is not a measure of power or quality. It is simply a measure of the gas' resistance to engine knock, which is the pinging sound you hear when the air and fuel mixture in your engine ignites prematurely during acceleration.

Your engine may knock when accelerating a heavily loaded car uphill or when the humidity is low. This is normal and does not call for a higher-octane gasoline.

FIVE FACTORS AFFECTING FUEL ECONOMY

1. Engine Size: The smaller the engine the better your fuel efficiency. A 10% increase in the size of your engine can increase your fuel consumption rate by 6%. Smaller engines can be cheaper to maintain as well.

2. Transmission: If used properly, manual transmissions are generally more fuel-efficient than automatics. In fact, a 5-speed manual can add up to 6.5 mpg over a 4-speed automatic transmission. Getting an automatic with an overdrive gear can improve your fuel economy by up to 9 percent.

3. Cruise Control: Using cruise control can save fuel because driving at a constant speed uses less fuel than changing speeds frequently.

4. Hybrids: Most manufacturers offer hybrid vehicles that have both gasoline and electric engines. Hybrids can offer 30% better fuel economy and lower emissions.

5. Electrics: All electric vehicles can keep you out of the gas station altogether. See our new section on page 271.

TWELVE WAYS TO SAVE MONEY AT THE PUMP

Here are a few simple things you can do that will save you a lot of money. Note: Savings are based on gas at $2.60.

1. Make Sure Your Tires are Inflated Properly: 27% of vehicles have tires that are under-inflated. Properly inflated tires can improve mileage by 3%, which is like getting 8 cents off a gallon of gas. Check the label on your door or glove box to find out what the pressure range should be for your tires. Don't use the "max pressure" written on your tire. Electronic gauges are fast, easy to use and accurate. Don't rely on the numbers on the air pump.

2. Check Your Air Filter: A dirty air filter by itself can rob a car by as much as 10% percent of its mileage. If an engine doesn't get enough air, it will burn too much gasoline. Replacing a dirty filter can knock 26 cents off a gallon of gas.

3. Check Your Alignment: Not only does poor alignment cause your tires to wear out faster and cause poor handling, but it can cause your engine to work harder and reduce your fuel efficiency by 10%.

4. Don't Use High Octane Gas: Check your owner's manual. Very, very few cars actually need high-octane gas. Using 87-octane gas will save you over 10 cents per gallon over mid-grade and 20 cents over premium.

5. Get a Tune Up: A properly tuned engine is a fuel saver. Have a trusted mechanic tune your engine to exact factory specifications and you could save up to 10 cents a gallon.

6. Check Your Gas Cap: It is estimated that nearly 15 % of the cars on the road have broken or missing gasoline caps. This hurts your mileage and can harm the environment by allowing your gasoline to evaporate. Many Ford products have a capless gas filler, which is a great convenience.

7. Don't Speed: A car moving at 55 mph gets better fuel economy than the same car at 65 mph. For every 5 mph you reduce your highway speed, you can reduce fuel consumption by 7%, which is like getting 18 cents off a gallon of gas.

8. Avoid Excess Idling: An idling car gets 0 mpg. Cars with larger engines typically waste more gas at idle than cars with smaller engines.

9. Drive Smoother: The smoother your accelerations and decelerations, the better your mileage. A smooth foot can save 43 cents a gallon.

10. Combine Trips: Short trips can be expensive because they usually involve a "cold" vehicle. For the first mile or two before the engine gets warmed up, a cold vehicle only gets 30 to 40% of the mileage it gets at full efficiency.

11. Empty your Roof Rack and Trunk: 50% of engine power, traveling at highway speed, is used in overcoming aerodynamic drag or wind resistance. Any protrusion on a vehicle's roof can reduce gas mileage, typical roof racks reduce fuel economy by about 6 mpg. 100 lbs. of extra weight will reduce your mileage by .5 mpg.

12. Choose Your Gas Miser: If you own more than one vehicle, choosing to drive the one with better gas mileage will save you money. If you drive 15,000 miles per year, half in a vehicle with 20 mpg and half with a 30 mpg vehicle and switch to driving 75% of your trips in the 30 mpg vehicle, you will save $162.50 annually with gas at $2.63.

FUEL ECONOMY

Get up-to-date information about fuel economy at www.fueleconomy.gov, a joint website created by the U.S. Department of Energy and the EPA. There you'll find the EPA's Fuel Economy Guide, allowing you to compare fuel economy estimates for 2016 models back to 1985 models. You'll also find out about the latest technological advances pertaining to fuel efficiency. The site is extremely useful and easy to navigate. We've added fuel economy ratings and a Fuel Factor section to the At-a-glance box on our car rating pages.

FUEL ECONOMY MISERS AND GUZZLERS

Because the success of the EPA program depends on consumers' ability to compare the fuel economy ratings easily, we have included key mileage figures on our ratings pages. Listed below are the best and worst of this year's ratings according to annual fuel cost. The complete EPA fuel economy guide is available at www. fueleconomy.gov.

FUEL ECONOMY MISERS AND GUZZLERS

Vehicle	Specifications	MPG (city/hwy)	Annual Fuel Cost
THE BEST			
Plug In Hybrid Electric Vehicles (PHEVs)*			
Chevrolet Volt	1.4L, 4 cyl., Continuously Variable, FWD	35/40	$900
Toyota Prius Plug-in Hybrid	1.8L, 4 cyl., Continuously Variable, FWD	51/49	$950
Honda Accord Plug-in Hybrid	2L, 4 cyl., Continuously Variable, FWD	47/46	$950
Ford Fusion Energi Plug-in Hybrid	2L, 4 cyl., Continuously Variable, FWD	44/41	$950
Gas			
Toyota Prius	1.8L, 4 cyl., Continuously Variable, FWD	51/48	$1,036
Honda Accord	2L, 4 cyl., Continuously Variable, FWD	50/45	$1,077
Ford Fusion Hybrid FWD	2L, 4 cyl., Continuously Variable, FWD	47/47	$1,095
Lincoln MKZ Hybrid FWD	2L, 4 cyl., Continuously Variable, FWD	45/45	$1,143
Honda Insight	1.3L, 4 cyl., Continuously Variable, FWD	41/44	$1,215
Toyota Prius v	1.8L, 4 cyl., Continuously Variable, FWD	44/40	$1,219
Lexus CT 200h	1.8L, 4 cyl., Continuously Variable, FWD	43/40	$1,235
Toyota Camry Hybrid LE	2.5L, 4 cyl., Continuously Variable, FWD	43/39	$1,249
Volkswagen Jetta Hybrid	1.4L, 4 cyl., 7-sp. Automated Manual, FWD	42/48	$1,252
Mitsubishi Mirage	1.2L, 3 cyl., Continuously Variable, FWD	37/44	$1,281
Lexus ES 300h	2.5L, 4 cyl., Selectable Continuously Variable, FWD	40/39	$1,301
Toyota Avalon Hybrid	2.5L, 4 cyl., Selectable Continuously Variable, FWD	40/39	$1,301
Toyota Camry Hybrid XLE/SE	2.5L, 4 cyl., Continuously Variable, FWD	40/38	$1,335
Ford Fiesta SFE FWD	1L, 3 cyl., 5 sp. Manual, FWD	32/45	$1,359
Mitsubishi Mirage	1.2L, 3 cyl., 5 sp. Manual, FWD	34/42	$1,368
Honda CR-Z	1.5L, 4 cyl., Selectable Continuously Variable, FWD	36/39	$1,378
Scion iQ	1.3L, 4 cyl., Continuously Variable, FWD	36/37	$1,412
BMW 328d xDrive	2L, 4 cyl., 8 sp. Automatic, AWD	31/43	$1,413
Acura ILX	1.5L, 4 cyl., Selectable Continuously Variable, FWD	39/38	$1,431
Toyota Corolla LE ECO	1.8L, 4 cyl., Continuously Variable, FWD	30/42	$1,453
Nissan Versa	1.6L, 4 cyl., Continuously Variable, FWD	31/40	$1,468
BMW 328d	2L, 4 cyl., 8 sp. Automatic, RWD	32/45	$1,478
Chevrolet Spark	1.2L, 4 cyl., Continuously Variable, FWD	30/39	$1,511
Volkswagen Passat	2L, 4 cyl., 6 sp. Manual, FWD	31/43	$1,537
Mercedes-Benz Smart fortwo (COUPE)	1L, 3 cyl., 5 sp. Automated Manual, RWD	34/38	$1,563
THE WORST**			
Ford F150 Raptor Pickup 4WD	6.2L, 8 cyl., 6 sp. Semi-Automatic, 4WD	11/16	$4,223
Ford F150 Pickup 4WD	6.2L, 8 cyl., 6 sp. Semi-Automatic, 4WD	12/16	$4,054
Mercedes-Benz G 63 AMG	5.5L, 8 cyl., 7 sp. Automatic, 4WD	12/14	$3,988
Mercedes-Benz G 550	5.5L, 8 cyl., 7 sp. Automatic, RWD	12/15	$3,854
Audi R8 Spyder	5.2L, 10 cyl., 6 sp. Manual, AWD	12/18	$3,806
Chevrolet/GMC Camaro	6.2L, 8 cyl., 6 sp. Semi-Automatic, RWD	12/18	$3,806
Cadillac CTS/CTS V/CTS Wagon	6.2L, 8 cyl., 6 sp. Semi-Automatic, RWD	12/18	$3,806
Mercedes-Benz CL 65 AMG	6L, 12 cyl., 5 sp. Automatic, RWD	12/18	$3,806
Toyota Sequoia 4WD	5.7L, 6 cly., 8 sp. Semi-Automatic, 4WD	13/17	$3,780
BMW X6 M	4.4L, 6 sp. Semi-Automatic, AWD	13/17	$3,780
Audi R8	4.2L, 8 cyl., 6 sp. Manual, AWD	11/20	$3,718
Audi R8	5.2L, 10 cyl., 6 sp. Manual, AWD	12/19	$3,693
NissanTitan 4WD	5.6L, 8 cyl., 5 sp. Automatic, 4WD	12/17	$3,611
Audi R8 Spyder	4.2L, 8 cyl., 6 sp. Manual, AWD	11/20	$3,587
Mercedes-Benz CL 600	5.5L, 12 cyl., 5 sp. Automatic, RWD	12/18	$3,500
Nissan Armada 4WD	5.6L, 8 cyl., 5 sp. Automatic, 4WD	12/18	$3,500
BMW 760Li	6L, 12 cyl., 8 sp. Semi-Automatic, RWD	13/20	$3,464
Cadillac Escalade AWD	6.2L, 8 cyl., 6 sp. Automatic, AWD	13/18	$3,374
Ford Expedition 4WD FFV	5.4, 8 cyl., 6 sp. Automatic, 4WD	13/18	$3,374
Ford F150 Pickup 2WD	6.2L, 8 cyl., 6 sp. Semi-Automatic, RWD	13/18	$3,374
Chevrolet/GMC G1500 Savana 2WD Cargo	5.3L, 8 cyl., 4 sp. Automatic, RWD	13/18	$3,374
GMC K10 Yukon Denali AWD	6.2L, 8 cyl., 6 sp. Automatic, AWD	13/18	$3,374
Jeep Grand Cherokee SRT8	6.4L, 8 cyl., 8 sp. Automatic, 4WD	13/19	$3,277
Land Rover Range Rover	5.0L, 8 cyl., 8 sp. Semi-Automatic, 4WD	13/19	$3,277

Note: 2016 annual fuel cost based on driving 15,000 miles and a projected regular gas price of $2.64; #=Premium Required; *=Fuel Economy rating based on hybrid function only; annual cost based on epa estimate for gas and electric use; **=Low volume exotic vehicles (over $120,000) and cargo vans were excluded.

COMPARING WARRANTIES

After buying your car, maintenance will be a significant portion of your operating costs. The strength of your warranty and the cost of repairs after the warranty expires will determine these costs. Comparing warranties and repair costs, before you buy, can save you thousands of dollars down the road.

Along with your new car comes a warranty which is a promise from the manufacturer that the car will perform as it should. Most of us never read the warranty until it is too late. In fact, because warranties are often difficult to read and understand, most of us don't really know what our warranty covers.

To keep your warranty in effect, you must operate and maintain your car according to the instructions in your owner's manual. It is important to keep a record of all maintenance performed on your car.

Do not confuse a warranty with a service contract. A service contract must be purchased separately while a warranty is yours at no extra cost when you buy the car.

Warranties are difficult to compare because they contain fine print and confusing language. The following table will help you compare this year's warranties. Because the table does not contain all the details about each warranty, review the actual warranty to understand its fine points. You have the right to inspect a warranty before you buy—it's the law.

The table provides information on five critical items in a warranty:

The **Basic Warranty** covers most parts against manufacturer's defects. Tires, batteries, and items you add to the car are covered under separate warranties. The table describes coverage in terms of months and miles. For example, 48/50 means the warranty is good for 48 months or 50,000 miles, whichever comes first. This is the most important part of your warranty because it covers the items most likely to fail. We give the basic warranty the most weight.

The **Power Train Warranty** often lasts longer than the basic warranty. Because each manufacturer's definition of the power train is different, it is important to find out exactly what your warranty will cover. Power train coverage should include the engine, transmission, and drive train. Some luxury cars will cover additional systems such as steering, suspension, and electrical systems. We give the powertrain warranty less weight than the basic because it doesn't cover as much as the basic warranty. Even with less weight in our rating, it can have a lot of influence in the overall index if it is very long.

The **Corrosion Warranty** usually applies only to actual holes due to rust. Read this section carefully because many corrosion warranties do not apply to what the manufacturer may describe as cosmetic rust or bad paint.

The **Roadside Assistance** column indicates whether or not the manufacturer offers a program for helping with breakdowns, lockouts, jump starts, flat tires, running out of gas, and towing. Some have special limitations or added features. Because each one is different, check yours carefully.

The **Scheduled Maint. (Free)** column indicates whether or not free scheduled maintenance is included and for how long. These programs cover parts scheduled to be replaced such as filters. If there is an asterisk next to the coverage, that means the manufacturer also covers the cost of <u>any</u> parts that need to be replaced because of wear. Covering the cost of "wear" parts is a terrific feature and offered by very few manufacturers.

The last column, the **Warranty Rating Index**, provides an overall assessment of this year's warranties. **The higher the Index number, the better the warranty.** We give the most weight to the basic and power train components of the warranties. Roadside assistance was weighted somewhat less, and the corrosion warranty received the least weight.

Finally, we also considered special features such as extra coverage on batteries or wheel alignment. These benefits added to the overall ratings, whereas certain limitations (shortened transferability) took away from the rating.

The best ratings are in *BOLD*.

WARRANTY COMPARISON

Manufacturer	Basic Warranty	Power Train Warranty	Corrosion Warranty	Roadside Assistance	Scheduled Maint. (Free)	Index	Warranty Rating
Acura[1]	48/50	72/70	60/75	48/50		1106	Average
Audi	48/50	48/50	144/180	48/Unlimited	12/5	1203	Good
BMW	48/50	48/50	144/180	48/Unlimited	48/50[1]	1288	Good
Buick	48/50	72/70	72/90	72/70	24/24	1229	Good
Cadillac[2]	**48/50**	**72/70**	**72/90[3]**	**72/70**	**48/50**	**1320**	**Very Good**
Chevrolet	36/36	60/60	72/90[4]	60/100	24/24	1122	Average
Chrysler[5]	36/36	60/60	60/75[6]	60/100		1070	Poor
Dodge[7]	36/36	60/60	60/75[8]	60/100		1070	Poor
Fiat[9]	48/50	48/50	60/75[10]	48/Unlimited		1048	Poor
Ford[11]	36/36	60/60	60/75	60/60		974	Poor
GMC	36/36	60/60	72/90	60/100	24/24	1086	Average
Honda[12]	36/36	60/60	60/75	36/36		897	Very Poor
Hyundai[13]	**60/60**	**120/100[14]**	**84/Unlimited**	**60/Unlimited**		**1448**	**Very Good**
Infiniti[15]	48/60	72/70	84/105	48/Unlimited		1233	Good
Jeep[16]	36/36	60/100	60/75[17]	60/100		1190	Good
Kia[18]	**60/60**	**120/100[19]**	**60/75**	**60/60**		**1341**	**Very Good**
Land Rover	48/50	48/50	72/90	48/50	12/15	1015	Poor
Lexus[20]	48/50	72/70	72/90	48/Unlimited	12/10	1182	Average
Lincoln[21]	48/50	72/70	60/75	72/70[22]	24/24	1256	Good
Mazda	36/36	60/60	60/75	36/36		891	Very Poor
Mercedes-Benz[23]	48/50	48/50	48/50	48/50		931	Very Poor
Mini	**48/50**	**48/50**	**144/Unlimited**	**48/Unlimited**	**36/36[23]**	**1334**	**Very Good**
Mitsubishi	**60/60**	**120/100**	**84/100[24]**	**60/Unlimited**		**1429**	**Very Good**
Nissan[25]	36/36	60/60	60/75			789	Very Poor
Porsche	48/50	48/50	144/180	48/50		1157	Average
Ram	36/36	60/60	60/75[26]	60/100		1064	Poor
Scion[27]	36/36	60/60	60/75	24/Unlimited		879	Very Poor
Smart[28]	48/50	48/50	48/50	48/50		937	Poor
Subaru[29]	36/36	60/60	60/75	36/36		918	Very Poor
Tesla	**48/50**	**96/Unlimited**	**48/50**	**48/50**		**1357**	**Very Good**
Toyota[30]	36/36	60/60	60/75	24/Unlimited	24/25	916	Very Poor
Volkswagen	36/36	60/60	144/180	36/36	12/10	1096	Average
Volvo	48/50	48/50	144/180	48/Unlimited	36/36	1244	Good

[1] Wheel Alignment and Balancing 12/12
[2] Wheel Alignment and Balancing 12/7.5
[3] All Corrosion 48/50
[4] All Corrosion 36/36
[5] Wheel Alignment and Balancing 12/12
[6] All Corrosion 36/Unlimited
[7] Wheel Alignment and Balancing 12/12
[8] All Corrosion 36/Unlimited
[9] Wheel Alignment and Balancing 12/12
[10] All Corrosion 36/Unlimited
[11] Wheel Alignment and Balancing 12/12; Brake Pads 12/18
[12] Wheel Alignment and Balancing 12/12
[13] Wheel Alignment and Balancing 12/12; Wear Items 12/12
[14] Only transferable up to 60/60
[15] Wheel Alignment and Balancing 12/12
[16] Wheel Alignment and Balancing 12/12
[17] All Corrosion 36/Unlimited
[18] Wheel Alignment and Balancing 12/12
[19] Transferable only to 60/60
[20] Wheel Alignment and Balancing 12/12
[21] Wheel Alignment and Balancing 12/12; Brake Pads 12/18
[22] Lifetime for original owner
[23] Wheel Alignment and Balancing 12/12
[24] Transferable only up to 60/60
[25] Wheel Alignment and Balancing 12/12
[26] All Corrosion 36/Unlimited
[27] Wheel Alignment and Balancing 12/12
[28] Wheel Alignment and Balancing 12/12
[29] Wear Items 36/36
[30] Wheel Alignment and Balancing 12/12

SECRET WARRANTIES

If dealers report a number of complaints about a certain part and the manufacturer determines that the problem is due to faulty design or assembly, the manufacturer may permit dealers to repair the problem at no charge to the customer even though the warranty is expired. In the past, this practice was often reserved for customers who made a big fuss. The availability of the free repair was never publicized, which is why we call these "secret warranties."

Manufacturers deny the existence of secret warranties. They call these free repairs "policy adjustments" or "goodwill service." Whatever they are called, most consumers never hear about them.

Many secret warranties are disclosed in service bulletins that the manufacturers send to dealers. These bulletins outline free repair or reimbursement programs, as well as other problems and their possible causes and solutions.

Service bulletins from many manufacturers may be on file at the National Highway Traffic Safety Administration. You can visit www.nhtsa.gov to access NHTSA's Service Bulletin database.

If you find that a secret warranty is in effect and repairs are being made at no charge after the warranty has expired, contact the Center for Auto Safety, 1825 Connecticut Ave. NW, #330, Washington, DC 20009, www.autosafety.org. They will publish the information so others can benefit.

Disclosure Laws: Spurred by the proliferation of secret warranties and the failure of the FTC to take action, California, Connecticut, Virginia, Wisconsin, and Maryland have passed legislation that requires consumers to be notified of secret warranties on their cars. Several other states have introduced similar warranty bills.

Typically, the laws require the following: direct notice to consumers within a specified time after the adoption of a warranty adjustment policy; notice of the disclosure law to new car buyers; reimbursement within a number of years after payment to owners who paid for covered repairs before they learned of the extended warranty service; and dealers must inform consumers who complain about a covered defect that it is eligible for repair under warranty.

If you live in a state with a secret warranty law already in effect, write your state attorney general's office (in care of your state capital) for information. To encourage passage of such a bill, contact your state representative (in care of your state capital).

Some state lemon laws require dealers and manufacturers to give you copies of Technical Service Bulletins on problems affecting your vehicle. These bulletins may alert you to a secret warranty on your vehicle or help you make the case for a free repair if there isn't a secret warranty. See page 59 for an overview of your state's lemon law. If you would like to see the complete law, go to www.autosafety.org to view your state's lemon laws.

LITTLE SECRETS OF THE AUTO INDUSTRY

Every auto company makes mistakes building cars. When they do, they often issue technical service bulletins telling dealers how to fix the problem. Rarely do they publicize these fixes, many of which are offered for free, called secret warranties. The Center for Auto Safety has published a book called *Little Secrets of the Auto Industry*, a consumer guide to secret warranties. This book explains how to find out about secret warranties, offers tips for going to small claims court and getting federal and state assistance, and lists information on state secret warranty laws. To order a copy, send $17.50 to: Center for Auto Safety, Pub. Dept. CB, 1825 Connecticut Ave. NW, Suite 330, Washington, DC 20009.

KEEPING IT GOING

Comparing maintenance costs before you buy can help decide which car to purchase. These costs include preventive maintenance servicing—such as changing the oil and filters—as well as the cost of repairs after your warranty expires. The following tables enable you to compare the costs of preventive maintenance and nine likely repairs for the 2016 models.

Preventive Maintenance: The first column in the table is the periodic servicing, specified by the manufacturer, that keeps your car running properly. For example, regularly changing the oil and oil filter. Every owner's manual specifies a schedule of recommended servicing for at least the first 60,000 miles and many now go to 100,000 miles. The tables on the following pages estimate the labor cost of following this preventive maintenance schedule for 60,000 miles, the length of a typical warranty. Service parts are not included in this total.

Repairs Costs: The tables also list the costs for nine repairs that typically occur during the first 100,000 miles. There is no precise way to predict exactly when a repair will be needed. But if you keep a car for 75,000 to 100,000 miles, it is likely that you will experience most of these repairs at least once. The last column provides a relative indication of how expensive these nine repairs are for many cars. Repair cost is rated as Very Good if the total for nine repairs is in the lowest fifth of all the cars rated, and Very Poor if the total is in the highest fifth.

Most repair shops use "flat-rate manuals" to estimate repair costs. These manuals list the approximate time required for repairing many items. Each automobile manufacturer publishes its own manual and there are several independent manuals as well. For many repairs, the time varies from one manual to another. Some repair shops even use different manuals for different repairs. To determine a repair bill, a shop multiplies the time listed in its manual by its hourly labor rate and then adds the cost of parts.

Some dealers and repair shops create their own maintenance schedules which call for more frequent (and thus more expensive) servicing than the manufacturer's recommendations. If the service recommended by your dealer or repair shop doesn't match what the manufacturer recommends, make sure you understand and agree to the extra items. Our cost estimates are based on published repair times multiplied by a nationwide average labor rate of $90 per hour and include the cost of replaced parts and related adjustments.

Prices in the following tables may not predict the exact costs of these repairs. For example, labor rates for your area may be more or less than the national average. However, the prices will provide you with a relative comparison of costs for various automobiles.

! SAVE YOUR RECEIPTS !

Keeping it going means taking advantage of your warranty and, if you've purchased a service agreement, getting what's coming to you. Because warranties and service agreements are protected against consumer abuse, sometimes the repair shop may try to blame the mechanical problem on your failure to properly maintain the vehicle. Unscrupulous service providers do this in order to keep from having to reimburse you for the repair. According to the Center for Auto Safety, a common claim is to blame the problem on your failure to regularly change the oil. To insure that you get the warranty coverage you have a right to, or the service contract coverage you paid for, religiously keep your receipts. That's the best way to prove that you're not the one at fault.

	PM Costs to 60,000 Miles	Front Brake Pads	Starter	Fuel Injector	Fuel Pump	Struts/ Shocks	Timing Belt/Chain	Water Pump	Muffler	Headlamps	Relative Repair Cost*
Subcompact											
BMW i3		154				232		855		1,505	?????
Chevrolet Sonic	504	198	375	81	386	168	277	328	622	789	Vry. Gd.
Chevrolet Spark	540	198	313	138	443	160	458	299	432	898	Vry. Gd.
Fiat 500	630	170	308	394	558	89	365	453	284	760	Vry. Gd.
Ford Fiesta	1,065	130	454	104	514	160	380	321	476	643	Vry. Gd.
Honda Fit	477	146	631	217	495	380	579	290	246	881	Good
Hyundai Accent	864	122	430	173	464	175	390	316	359	284	Vry. Gd.
Hyundai Veloster	882	163	351	138	431	320	538	350	402	702	Vry. Gd.
Kia Rio	774	129	421	203	360	224	378	309	75	642	Vry. Gd.
Kia Soul	954	129	425	212	313	266	355	309	435	1,026	Vry. Gd.
Mazda MX-5 Miata	864	191	341	219	480	362	474	261	624	1,572	Good
Mini Cooper	1,701	206	550	198	628	358	1,032	448	503	1,502	Poor
Mini Countryman	1,701	221	462	198	425	365	1,032	423	632	851	Average
Mitsubishi Mirage	612	200	848	21,699	132	343	621	576	431	1,347	Vry. Pr.
Nissan 370Z	594	175	502	358	525	566	763	677	604	1,971	Poor
Nissan Versa	594	191	401	275	522	189	437	209	323	673	Vry. Gd.
Smart ForTwo	1,127	98	463	198	438	510	1,436	470	971	766	Poor
Toyota Yaris	486	139	393	223	460	286	504	240	249	686	Vry. Gd.
Volkswagen Beetle	918	185	552	298	430	327	986	477	900	1,107	Poor
Compact											
Acura ILX	576	142	591	155	506	446	551	390	173	1,095	Good
Audi A3		190	407	249	440	676	740	638	641	856	Average
Audi A4	972	231	784	509	700	710	530	793	641	982	Poor
BMW 2 Series	999	242	585	419	473	349	1,336	750	673	1,173	Poor
BMW 3 Series	945	106	585	419	474	349	1,292	732	684	1,200	Poor
BMW 4 Series	945	243	655	216	500	389	1,066	771	870	1,354	Poor
Buick Verano	720	293	351	424	514	212	589	624	273	1,016	Good
Cadillac ATS	1,179	201	578	412	406	450	493	420	1,143	1,071	Average
Chevrolet Cruze	963	198	259	230	524	173	777	432	623	602	Good
Chevrolet Volt	1,080	174	0	119	380	139	1,254	451	572	1,005	Good
Dodge Dart	630	177	228	391	573	235	607	316	507	1,516	Average
Fiat 500L	630	170	308	394	558	91	367	453	284	760	Vry. Gd.
Ford C-MAX	594	181	288	136	342	249	630	179	263	641	Vry. Gd.
Ford Focus	882	148	420	288	479	122	695	242	313	668	Vry. Gd.
Honda Civic	423	142	555	218	443	209	641	257	204	747	Vry. Gd.
Hyundai Elantra	981	149	358	173	285	208	421	262	368	768	Vry. Gd.
Kia Forte	585	165	236	194	332	210	544	291	331	535	Vry. Gd.
Lexus CT	558	143	0	445	455	244	1,707	702	598	2,262	Vry. Pr.
Lexus IS	756	156	940	634	414	490	2,026	535	865	1,346	Vry. Pr.
Mazda Mazda3	792	177	333	305	580	204	452	297	428	712	Vry. Gd.
Mercedes-Benz C-Class	1,287	183	719	328	1,061	487	409	731	931	1,144	Poor
Mercedes-Benz CLA-Class	1,269	192	1,025	375	579	669	1,200	689	973	1,212	Vry. Pr.
Nissan Leaf	666	151	0	0	0	224	0	714	0	0	Vry. Gd.
Nissan Sentra	702	155	344	356	562	175	592	238	407	649	Vry. Gd.
Scion FR-S	972	185	637	575	692	355	648	389	618	984	Average
Scion tC	513	169	661	373	452	320	1,379	308	270	682	Average
Subaru BRZ	918	181	585	456	438	311	585	361	559	545	Good
Subaru Impreza	1,008	154	504	230	453	620	393	455	404	824	Good
Toyota Corolla	549	152	467	309	427	333	640	259	387	533	Vry. Gd.
Toyota Prius	558	138	0	445	429	351	1,666	693	285	861	Average
AVERAGE OF ALL VEHICLES	**$891**	**$199**	**$459**	**$502**	**$532**	**$363**	**$1006**	**$507**	**$1358**	**$1085**	

	PM Costs to 60,000 Miles	REPAIR COSTS									
		Front Brake Pads	Starter	Fuel Injector	Fuel Pump	Struts/ Shocks	Timing Belt/Chain	Water Pump	Muffler	Headlamps	Relative Repair Cost*
Compact (cont.)											
Toyota Prius C	558	138	0	263	467	212	503	626	275	863	Vry. Gd.
Volkswagen Golf	1,089	180	684	206	365	415	551	457	458	606	Good
Volkswagen Jetta	918	161	670	413	535	420	600	665	721	770	Average
Intermediate											
Acura TLX	576	142	603	137	441	299	452	221	711	1,521	Good
Audi A5	972	208	779	420	476	482	525	775	1,496	1,941	Vry. Pr.
Audi A6	972	231	931	531	685	548	672	501	750	1,127	Poor
BMW 5 Series	567	259	646	837	663	702	1,699	731	974	1,650	Vry. Pr.
BMW 6 Series	1,251	241	732	572	492	651	1,156	731	756	4,176	Vry. Pr.
Buick Regal	1,251	282	351	337	359	744	544	624	1,065	1,058	Poor
Cadillac CTS	1,179	271	333	239	911	422	745	417	1,270	1,021	Poor
Chevrolet Camaro	1,251	474	288	373	632	351	662	435	634	509	Good
Chevrolet Corvette	1,062	548	585	348	3,010	203	875	455	847	2,356	Vry. Pr.
Chevrolet Malibu	711	282	351	463	529	388	616	633	479	513	Good
Chrysler 200	585	126	244	109	422	203	540	223	589	1,080	Vry. Gd.
Ford Fusion	684	163	192	125	301	123	596	206	402	1,020	Vry. Gd.
Ford Fusion Energi	846	163	0	0	0	123	0	0	0	1,020	Vry. Gd.
Ford Mustang	603	152	175	191	399	155	890	273	255	748	Vry. Gd.
Honda Accord	504	150	506	466	476	262	494	227	457	1,079	Good
Hyundai Azera	972	113	420	161	457	175	345	318	368	284	Vry. Gd.
Hyundai Sonata	891	149	285	187	327	280	189	376	645	749	Vry. Gd.
Infiniti Q50	1,440	168	456	408	494	556	1,346	686	631	2,035	Vry. Pr.
Infiniti Q70	702	248	442	367	458	846	1,346	686	694	2,611	Vry. Pr.
Kia Cadenza	972	106	252	197	112	218	553	291	836	534	Vry. Gd.
Kia Optima	864	170	236	194	332	210	526	291	331	535	Vry. Gd.
Lexus GS	657	165	715	544	468	415	2,686	373	835	2,283	Vry. Pr.
Lincoln MKZ	684	167	435	173	338	788	1,448	1,331	436	3,688	Vry. Pr.
Mazda Mazda6	799	184	240	224	535	232	542	226	360	699	Vry. Gd.
Mitsubishi Lancer	504	187	870	353	628	334	616	569	422	1,300	Poor
Nissan Altima	954	148	372	335	449	311	652	280	408	695	Good
Nissan Maxima	828	151	407	412	472	238	984	410	664	881	Average
Subaru Legacy	1,323	163	557	203	417	537	318	420	384	889	Good
Toyota Camry	864	138	489	328	434	560	2,117	313	405	901	Poor
Toyota Prius V	558	166	0	443	467	351	1,696	456	271	864	Average
Volkswagen CC	1,098	181	635	324	492	328	713	847	520	855	Average
Volkswagen Passat	918	171	706	251	480	382	1,714	469	706	680	Poor
Volvo S60	909	196	449	311	801	263	569	452	678	502	Good
Volvo V60	1,116	196	449	320	792	263	434	452	669	502	Good
BMW 7 Series	585	145	646	536	528	2,395	1,274	731	741	3,276	Vry. Pr.
Large											
Cadillac XTS	1,242	302	415	390	548	279	781	426	838	2,490	Vry. Pr.
Chevrolet Impala	1,251	263	410	309	711	195	544	624	613	613	Good
Chrysler 300	630	222	227	179	365	140	737	359	971	1,802	Average
Dodge Challenger	630	222	219	179	242	135	735	168	977	682	Vry. Gd.
Dodge Charger	630	231	219	179	244	137	726	253	1,084	674	Good
Ford Taurus	909	157	399	213	342	171	1,092	981	688	1,358	Poor
Hyundai Genesis	1,044	233	451	215	431	341	1,735	372	575	1,050	Poor
Lexus ES	864	134	489	427	434	865	1,842	453	460	3,345	Vry. Pr.
Lincoln MKS	900	169	408	164	482	179	1,029	1,092	634	2,311	Vry. Pr.
AVERAGE OF ALL VEHICLES	**$891**	**$199**	**$459**	**$502**	**$532**	**$363**	**$1006**	**$507**	**$1358**	**$1085**	

	PM Costs to 60,000 Miles	REPAIR COSTS									Relative Repair Cost*
		Front Brake Pads	Starter	Fuel Injector	Fuel Pump	Struts/ Shocks	Timing Belt/ Chain	Water Pump	Muffler	Headlamps	
Large (cont.)											
Mercedes-Benz E-Class	1,017	187	800	583	489	493	1,127	765	1,139	1,304	Vry. Pr.
Mercedes-Benz S-Class	1,017	298	740	442	518	2,959	375	952	1,475	1,933	Vry. Pr.
Toyota Avalon	864	138	476	355	466	533	1,837	370	377	901	Poor
Minivan											
Chrysler Town and Country	504	516	409	388	543	156	901	271	568	536	Good
Honda Odyssey	540	158	490	101	415	191	379	423	657	717	Vry. Gd.
Kia Sedona	990	161	248	344	372	335	1,278	374	539	329	Good
Nissan Quest	702	155	510	301	521	375	1,018	279	608	774	Average
Toyota Sienna	1,116	149	503	402	1,051	296	1,780	353	409	1,033	Poor
Small SUV											
Acura RDX	909	168	512	236	480	292	289	443	358	1,733	Good
Audi Q3		213	757	321	639	482	18,904	775	652	1,185	Vry. Pr.
Audi Q5	972	213	757	321	684	482	561	775	652	1,187	Poor
BMW X1	783	238	585	437	581	520	1,343	714	743	1,115	Vry. Pr.
BMW X3	1,242	242	585	270	617	576	895	651	956	350	Average
Buick Encore	720	311	268	111	433	198	723	360	607	664	Good
Cadillac SRX	1,251	202	379	417	434	188	754	399	935	1,163	Average
Chevrolet Trax		299	388	313	544	219	1,195	498	621	1,041	Average
Ford Escape	855	148	224	49	369	172	713	215	310	959	Vry. Gd.
Honda CR-V	504	142	591	165	341	405	560	221	398	760	Vry. Gd.
Honda HR-V	747	150	578	176	362	427	578	145	395	796	Vry. Gd.
Hyundai Tucson	972	131	367	143	336	216	457	430	578	580	Vry. Gd.
Jeep Cherokee	270	225	336	254	726	192	855	244	844	791	Good
Jeep Compass	450	155	395	110	351	233	554	259	568	1,006	Good
Jeep Patriot	450	117	284	110	342	176	472	259	572	435	Vry. Gd.
Jeep Renegade	1,224	131	288	88	348	240	540	243	572	445	Vry. Gd.
Jeep Wrangler	369	212	248	260	530	114	855	369	357	374	Vry. Gd.
Kia Sportage	927	156	236	223	349	268	558	403	633	2,119	Average
Land Rover Range Rover Evoque	441	280	575	511	688	704	533	298	715	532	Average
Lexus NX	2,466	144	745	383	474	243	1,759	1,191	118,781	1,159	Vry. Pr.
Lincoln MKC	855	172	417	165	499	188	984	1,083	90	2,282	Poor
Mazda CX-5	792	165	383	350	331	224	396	240	463	627	Vry. Gd.
Mercedes-Benz GLA-Class	486	320	770	551	546	620	324	882	830	1,390	Vry. Pr.
Mercedes-Benz GLC-Class	0	333	750	573	546	590	318	837	830	1,390	Poor
Nissan Juke	945	151	515	343	501	287	1,432	311	362	612	Good
Porsche Macan		380	597	424	579	1,405	1,309	501	1,755	1,016	Vry. Pr.
Subaru Forester	1,026	154	549	239	417	537	666	457	357	840	Good
Subaru XV Crosstrek	1,008	163	549	266	468	490	738	429	404	824	Good
Toyota RAV4	963	178	467	319	693	246	1,838	254	896	690	Poor
Volkswagen Tiguan	1,053	180	670	459	414	414	910	799	431	934	Average
Mid-Size SUV											
Acura MDX	1,242	161	544	184	442	257	397	470	656	1,823	Average
Audi Q7	1,080	270	754	593	829	1,732	1,955	392	1,067	2,367	Vry. Pr.
BMW X5	1,053	298	619	683	518	561	935	798	1,480	3,683	Vry. Pr.
Chevrolet Equinox	1,278	295	369	283	870	195	544	624	634	927	Average
Dodge Journey	423	216	413	188	702	344	1,045	271	1,420	656	Poor
Ford Edge	756	184	408	192	456	243	1,124	1,065	612	924	Average
Ford Explorer	909	157	399	307	686	292	1,052	1,026	903	1,365	Vry. Pr.
GMC Terrain	1,278	295	369	283	870	194	544	624	634	927	Average
Honda Pilot	504	158	513	209	495	209	379	513	655	830	Good
Hyundai Santa Fe	972	174	258	138	410	260	511	329	572	1,100	Good
AVERAGE OF ALL VEHICLES	$891	$199	$459	$502	$532	$363	$1006	$507	$1358	$1085	

	PM Costs to 60,000 Miles	REPAIR COSTS									Relative Repair Cost*
		Front Brake Pads	Starter	Fuel Injector	Fuel Pump	Struts/ Shocks	Timing Belt/ Chain	Water Pump	Muffler	Headlamps	
Mid-Size SUV (cont.)											
Hyundai Santa Fe Sport	972	174	258	138	455	260	512	1,749	572	1,108	Average
Infiniti QX60	1,440	155	419	390	458	673	1,661	686	678	3,638	Vry. Pr.
Infiniti QX70	702	176	419	390	458	258	1,661	686	678	3,588	Vry. Pr.
Jeep Grand Cherokee	630	225	336	254	726	192	855	244	844	791	Good
Kia Sorento	936	146	253	312	473	269	1,854	462	674	919	Poor
Land Rover Range Rover Sport	1,458	242	660	642	631	791	2,262	381	476	295	Vry. Pr.
Lexus RX	900	151	753	378	476	190	1,860	1,191	1,207	1,171	Vry. Pr.
Mazda CX-9	774	190	308	227	568	308	1,101	1,096	602	870	Poor
Mercedes-Benz GLE-Class	1,610	328	770	572	556	608	370	900	848	1,399	Vry. Pr.
Mitsubishi Outlander	981	187	317	266	759	233	623	524	413	783	Good
Mitsubishi Outlander Sport	792	277	906	360	780	483	623	529	459	1,477	Poor
Nissan Murano	702	194	455	385	526	264	1,099	458	513	836	Average
Nissan Pathfinder	1,440	173	458	408	508	189	1,097	487	612	968	Average
Nissan Rogue	1,053	155	376	363	747	198	1,123	338	623	1,610	Poor
Subaru Outback	1,323	163	557	203	417	537	288	420	294	289	Vry. Gd.
Volkswagen Touareg	1,080	231	724	873	462	869	1,410	751	912	1,328	Vry. Pr.
Volvo XC60	909	270	441	244	731	234	630	397	593	542	Good
Volvo XC70	738	280	415	246	734	241	648	402	611	570	Good
Large SUV											
Buick Enclave	1,206	284	379	322	647	176	1,393	462	634	1,748	Poor
Cadillac Escalade	1,278	283	318	292	924	223	866	542	1,125	2,025	Vry. Pr.
Cadillac Escalade ESV	1,278	283	524	301	679	193	866	524	1,099	2,025	Vry. Pr.
Chevrolet Suburban	1,278	283	318	283	697	193	866	528	239	630	Good
Chevrolet Tahoe	1,278	283	318	292	920	223	866	524	1,125	630	Average
Chevrolet Traverse	1,206	284	379	322	559	222	1,393	462	621	731	Average
Ford Expedition	1,098	176	300	172	578	259	925	275	627	607	Good
Ford Flex	801	148	399	191	430	199	1,097	1,047	734	1,458	Poor
GMC Acadia	1,206	284	379	322	559	176	1,303	462	621	1,748	Poor
GMC Yukon	1,278	283	318	291	920	223	866	524	1,125	630	Average
GMC Yukon XL	1,278	283	318	16,700	679	193	866	524	239	560	Vry. Pr.
Infiniti QX80	1,080	173	523	300	523	513	1,427	291	378	1,639	Poor
Land Rover Range Rover	837	242	660	642	631	791	2,262	381	476	295	Vry. Pr.
Lexus GX	819	155	889	445	623	154	1,288	593	534	1,054	Poor
Lincoln Navigator	1,125	176	300	172	579	256	925	275	627	607	Good
Mercedes-Benz GL-Class	1,062	320	755	619	551	599	369	869	830	1,390	Vry. Pr.
Nissan Armada	1,080	164	496	300	530	374	1,716	296	626	917	Poor
Toyota 4Runner	558	151	537	350	632	239	1,869	447	513	842	Poor
Toyota Highlander	720	144	499	398	986	643	1,894	559	1,180	682	Vry. Pr.
Toyota Land Cruiser	1,899	180	504	338	668	270	1,757	265	907	674	Poor
Toyota Sequoia	819	303	864	373	757	390	1,230	517	508	835	Poor
Compact Pickup											
Chevrolet Colorado	1,278	283	381	292	650	209	866	497	900	705	Average
GMC Canyon	1,278	283	381	292	650	209	866	497	900	705	Average
Nissan Frontier	1,080	164	439	363	558	200	856	308	407	725	Good
Toyota Tacoma	558	148	522	345	816	171	1,432	249	466	767	Average
Standard Pickup											
Chevrolet Silverado	1,278	283	381	292	651	209	866	497	900	706	Average
Ford F-150	612	184	459	518	621	126	811	269	473	586	Good
GMC Sierra	1,278	283	381	292	650	209	816	497	220	706	Good
Nissan Titan	1,620	164	577	300	563	199	1,815	307	124	753	Average
Ram 1500	576	152	294	140	406	162	520	399	400	455	Vry. Gd.
Toyota Tundra	819	168	826	317	859	220	1,017	447	508	835	Poor
AVERAGE OF ALL VEHICLES	**$891**	**$199**	**$459**	**$502**	**$532**	**$363**	**$1006**	**$507**	**$1358**	**$1085**	

SERVICE CONTRACTS

Service contracts are one of the most expensive options you can buy. In fact, service contracts are a major profit source for many dealers.

A service contract is not a warranty. It is more like an insurance plan that, in theory, covers repairs that are not covered by your warranty or that occur after the warranty runs out. They are often inaccurately referred to as "extended warranties."

Service contracts are generally a poor value. The companies who sell contracts are very sure that, on average, your repairs will cost considerably less than what you pay for the contract—if not, they wouldn't be in business.

Here are some important questions to ask before buying a service contract:

How reputable is the company responsible for the contract? If the company offering the contract goes out of business, you will be out of luck. The company may be required to be insured, but find out if they actually are and by whom. Check with your Better Business Bureau or office of consumer affairs if you are not sure of a company's reputation. Service contracts from car and insurance companies are more likely to remain in effect than those from independent companies.

Exactly what does the contract cover and for how long? Service contracts vary considerably—different items are covered and different time limits are offered. This is true even among service contracts offered by the same company. For example, one company has plans that range from 4 years/36,000 miles maximum coverage to 6 years/100,000 miles maximum coverage, with other options for only power train coverage. Make sure you know what components are covered because if a breakdown occurs on a part that is not covered, you are responsible for the repairs.

If you plan to resell your car in a few years, you won't want to purchase a long-running service contract. Some service contracts automatically cancel when you resell the car, while others require a hefty transfer fee before extending privileges to the new owner.

Some automakers offer a "menu" format, which lets you pick the items you want covered in your service contract. Find out if the contract pays for preventive maintenance, towing, and rental car expenses. If not written into the contract, assume they are not covered.

Make sure the contract clearly specifies how you can reach the company. Knowing this before you purchase a service contract can save you time and aggravation in the future.

How will the repair bills be paid? It is best to have the service contractor pay bills directly. Some contracts require you to pay the repair bill, and reimburse you later.

Where can the car be serviced? Can you take the car to any mechanic if you have trouble on the road? What if you move?

What other costs can be expected? Most service contracts will have a deductible expense. Compare deductibles on various plans. Also, some companies charge the deductible for each individual repair while other companies pay per visit, regardless of the number of repairs being made.

What are your responsibilities? Make sure you know what you have to do to uphold the contract. For example if you have to follow the manufacturer's recommended maintenance, keep detailed records or the contract could be voided. You will find your specific responsibilities in the contact. Be sure to have the seller point them out.

SERVICE CONTRACTS VS. SAVINGS ACCOUNT

One alternative to buying a service contract is to deposit the cost of the contract into a savings account. If the car needs a major repair not covered by your warranty, the money in your account will cover the cost. Most likely, you'll be building up a down payment for your next car!

TIPS FOR DEALING WITH A MECHANIC

Call around. Don't choose a shop simply because it's nearby. Calling a few shops may turn up estimates cheaper by half.

Don't necessarily go for the lowest price. A good rule is to eliminate the highest and lowest estimates; the mechanic with the highest estimate is probably charging too much, and the lowest may be cutting too many corners.

Check the shop's reputation. Call your local consumer affairs agency and the Better Business Bureau. They don't have records on every shop, but unfavorable reports on a shop should disqualify it.

Look for certification. Mechanics can be certified by the National Institute for Automotive Service Excellence, an industry-wide yardstick for competence. Certification is offered in eight areas of repair and shops with certified mechanics are allowed to advertise this fact. However, make sure the mechanic working on your car is certified for the repair you need.

Take a look around. A well-kept shop reflects pride in workmanship. A skilled and efficient mechanic would probably not work in a messy shop.

Don't sign a blank check. The service order you sign should have specific instructions or describe your vehicle's symptoms. Avoid signing a vague work order. Be sure you are called for final approval before the shop does extra work. Many states require a written estimate signed by you and require that the shop get your permission for repairs that exceed the estimate by 10%.

Show interest. Ask about the repair. But don't act like an expert if you don't really understand what's wrong. Express your satisfaction. If you're happy with the work, compliment the mechanic and ask for him or her the next time you come in. You will get to know each other and the mechanic will get to know your vehicle.

Take a test-drive. Before you pay for a major repair, you should take the car for a test-drive. The few extra minutes you spend checking out the repair could save you a trip back to the mechanic. If you find that the problem still exists, there will be no question that the repair wasn't properly completed.

REPAIR PROTECTION BY CREDIT CARD

Paying your auto repair bills by credit card can provide a much needed recourse if you are having problems with an auto mechanic. According to federal law, you have the right to withhold payment for sloppy or incorrect repairs. Of course, you may withhold no more than the amount of the repair in dispute.

In order to use this right, you must first try to work out the problem with the mechanic. Also, unless the credit card company owns the repair shop (this might be the case with gasoline credit cards used at gas stations), two other conditions must be met. First, the repair shop must be in your home state (or within 100 miles of your current address), and second, the cost of repairs must be over $50. Until the problem is settled or resolved in court, the credit card company cannot charge you interest or penalties on the amount in dispute.

If you decide to take action, send a letter to the credit card company and a copy to the repair shop, explaining the details of the problem and what you want as settlement. Send the letter by certified mail with a return receipt requested.

Sometimes the credit card company or repair shop will attempt to put a "bad mark" on your credit record if you use this tactic. Legally, you can't be reported as delinquent if you've given the credit card company notice of your dispute, but a creditor can report that you are disputing your bill, which goes in your record. However, you have the right to challenge any incorrect information and add your side of the story to your file.

For more information, write to the Federal Trade Commission, Credit Practices Division, 601 Pennsylvania Avenue, NW, Washington, DC 20580.

TIRE RATINGS

Buying tires has become an infrequent task because today's radial tires last much longer than the tires of the past. Surprisingly, a tire has to perform more functions simultaneously than any other part of the car (steering, bearing the load, cushioning the ride, and stopping).

Because comparing tires is difficult, many consumers mistakenly use price and brand name to determine quality. Because there are hundreds of tire lines to choose from, and only a few tire manufacturers, the difference in many tires may only be the brand name.

But there is help. The U.S. government requires tires to be rated according to their safety and expected mileage.

Treadwear, traction, and heat resistance grades are printed on the sidewall and are attached to the tire on a paper label. Ask the dealer for the grades of the tires they sell. Using this rating system, a sampling of top rated tires follows on page 48.

Treadwear: The treadwear grade gives you an idea of the mileage you can expect from a tire. It is shown in numbers–720, 700, 680, 660, and so forth. Higher numbers mean longer tire life. A tire with a grade of 600 should give you twice as much mileage as one rated 300. Use the treadwear grade as a relative basis of comparison.

Traction: Traction grades of AA, A, B, and C describe the tire's ability to stop on wet surfaces. Tires graded AA will stop on a wet road in a shorter distance than tires graded B or C. Tires rated C have poor traction.

Heat Resistance: Heat resistance is graded A, B, and C. An A rating means the tire will run cooler than one rated B or C and be less likely to fail if driven over long distances at highway speeds. Tires that run cooler tend to be more fuel-efficient. Hot-running tires can result in blow-outs or tread separation.

TIRE CARE

Pump 'em Up: An estimated one-third of us are driving on underinflated tires. Because even good tires lose air, it is important to check your tire pressure monthly. Underinflated tires can be dangerous, use more fuel and cause premature tire failure. When checking your tires, be sure to use an accurate gauge and inflate to the pressure indicated in your owner's manual, not the maximum pressure printed on your tire.

When to Replace: If any part of Lincoln's head is visible when you insert the top of a penny into a tread groove, it's time to replace the tire. While this old rule of thumb is still valid, today's tires also have a built-in wear indicator. A series of horizontal bars appear across the surface when the tread depth reaches the danger zone.

GETTING THE BEST PRICE

The price of the same tire can vary depending on where you shop so shopping around is vital to finding a good buy. Most tire ads appear in the sports section of your Wednesday and Saturday daily newspaper. You are most likely to find the best prices at independent tire dealers who carry a variety of tire brands.

The price of a tire is based on its size, and tires come in as many as nine sizes. For example, the list price of the same tire can range from $74.20 to $134.35, depending on its size.

To get the best buy:

1. Check to see which manufacturer makes the least expensive "off brand." Only a few manufacturers produce the over 1,800 types of tires sold in the U.S.

2. Don't forget to compare balancing and mounting costs. These extra charges can add up to more than $25 or be offered at no cost.

3. Never pay list price for a tire. A good rule of thumb is to pay at least 30-40 percent off the suggested list price.

4. Use the treadwear grade the same way you would the "unit price" in a supermarket. The tire with the lowest cost per grade point is the best value. For example, if tire A costs $100 and has a treadwear grade of 600, and tire B costs $80 and has a treadwear grade of 300, tire A is the better buy, even though its initial cost is more.

Tire A: $100÷600=$0.17 per point
Tire B: $80÷300=$0.27 per point

Where you live is a key factor in how long your tires will last. In addition to construction and design, tire wear is affected by the level of abrasive material in the road surface. Generally, the road surfaces of the West Coast, Great Lakes region, and northern New England are easiest on tires. The Appalachian and Rocky Mountain areas are usually hardest on tires.

HOW TO READ A TIRE

Labels on tire diagram:
- 1. Tire Type
- 2. Width
- 3. Height
- 4. Construction
- 5. Wheel Diameter
- 6. Load Index
- 7. Speed Rating
- 9. U.S. DOT Tire Identification Number
- 10. Tire ply composition and material
- 11. Treadwear, traction, and temperature grades
- 12. Max. Load
- 13. Max. Pressure

P215/65R15 95H

Tire Type and Size: The most important information on a tire are the letters and the numbers indicating its type and size.

1. Tire Type: The P at the beginning of the tire size indicates that the tire is a passenger vehicle tire. LT indicates light truck tire, and T indicates a temporary or spare tire.

2. Tire Width is the first part of the number and is measured in millimeters, from sidewall to sidewall.

3. Tire Height is the next number and tells you the height of the tire from the bead to the tread. This is described as a percentage of the tire width. In our example, the tire's height is 65 percent of its width. The smaller the aspect ratio, the wider the tire in relation to its height.

4. Tire Construction designates how the tire was made. R indicates radial construction which is the most common type. Older tires were made using diagonal bias D or bias belted B construction, but these tire types are no longer used on passenger vehicles.

5. Wheel Diameter identifies the wheel rim diameter (in inches-15) needed for this tire.

6. Load Index: The load rating indicates the maximum load for that tire. A higher number indicates a higher load capacity. The rating 95, for example, corresponds to a load capacity of 1521 pounds. Larger vehicles, SUVs and pickups need tires with a higher load capacity.

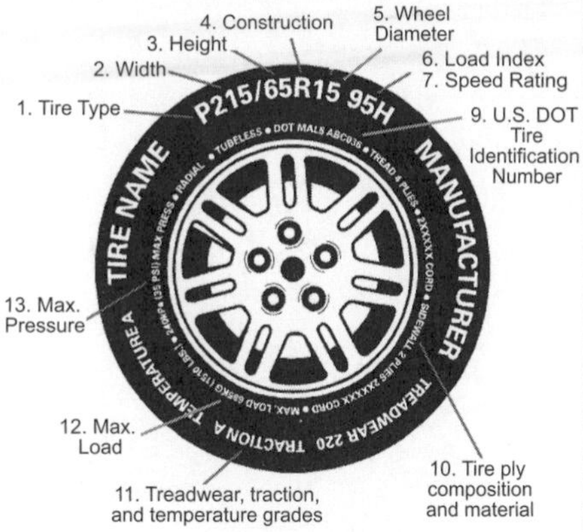

7. Speed Rating indicates the maximum speed that the tire can sustain a ten minute endurance test without being in danger. All passenger car tires are rated at least S and pass the test at speeds up to 112 mph. Other ratings are as follows: T up to 118 mph, H up to 130 mph, V up to 149 mph and Z 150 mph or higher. Other types of tires, temporary spares and snow tires are lower on the rating scale.

8. Severe Conditions: M+S indicates the tire meets the Rubber Manu. Association's definition of a mud and snow tire. There are no performance tests for this standard. If the tire has an M+S and a "mountain and snowflake" symbol then the traction is at least 10% better than the regular version of the tire. These symbols are not in the above example.

9. Tire Identification Number
Example: DOT NJ HR 2AF 5212
The letters DOT certify compliance with all applicable safety standards established by the U.S. Department of Transportation. The next four characters is a code where the first two characters indicate the manufacturer and the second two characters indicate the plant where the tire was made.

Next you may see an optional string of three to four characters. Most manufacturers use these to record company specific information they use to identify their products or that can be used to identify tires in the market for recall purposes.

The last four digits determine the week and year the tire was made. The digits 5212 would signify that the tire was made during the 52nd week of 2012. Don't buy tires more than two years old. Tires naturally degrade with age, so you want the newest possible tires for the longest life (and safe operation.)

10. Tire Ply Composition and Material indicates the type of cord (polyester or steel) and number of plies in the tire, 4-ply, 6-ply, 8-ply, for both the tread and the sidewall.

11. Treadwear, Traction and Temperature Grades are three performance grades assigned to the tire and are the best way to truly evaluate the tires expected performance in these three critical areas. See page 46 for more information.

12. Max Load Limit tells you the cold inflation load limit in lbs. (pounds) and in kg (kilograms). The number corresponds to the load index.

13. Max Pressure is the maximum recommended pressure in psi (pounds per square inch) and in kPa (kilopascals). However, this is not the tire pressure for your car. You must check your owner's manual for the proper tire pressure for the tires on your car.

A Sampling of Top Rated Tires

Brand Name	Model	Description	Traction	Heat	Treadwear
Michelin	DEFENDER	All Sizes	A	B	820
Bridgestone	DUELER H/L ALENZA PLUS "H" & "V" Spd Rtd	All Sizes	A	A	800
Toyo	TOYO ULTRA Z900 (H-rated)	All sizes	A	A	800
Bridgestone	DUELER H/L ALENZA PLUS "T" Spd Rtd	All Sizes	A	B	800
Mastercraft	Avenger Touring LSR (TR)	15"-18"	A	A	780
Cooper	CS5 Grand Touring	All sizes	A	B	780
Big O	EURO TOUR (T RATED)	All sizes	A	A	740
Bridgestone	TURANZA SERENITY "H" Spd Rtd	All sizes	A	A	740
Cooper	Discoverer SRX (H)	All sizes	A	A	740
Goodyear	ASSURANCE COMFORTRED TOURING (T&H)	All sizes	A	B	740
Hankook	Optimo H725 (OE)	P235/60R17	A	B	740
Maxxis	MA-T1 Escapade	All sizes	A	A	720
Michelin	LTX M/S2	All Sizes	A	A	720
Big O	LEGACY TOUR PLUS (S & T RATED)	All sizes	A	B	720
Falken	SN211	All sizes	A	B	720
Michelin	LATITUDE TOUR	All Sizes except	A	B	720
Michelin	X RADIAL LT2	All Sizes	A	B	720
Vogue	CUSTOM BUILT IX (S)	P225/60R16	A	B	720
Vogue	WIDE TRAC TOURING II (S)	All sizes	A	B	720
Nokian	Nokian eNTYRE	All sizes	A	A	700
Big O	LEGACY TOUR PLUS	P205,215,225 & 235/70R15 T	A	B	700
Bridgestone	DUELER H/L ALENZA "T" Spd Rtd	All sizes	A	B	700
Bridgestone	TURANZA LS-T	All sizes	A	B	700
Co-op	GOLDENMARK LUXURY TOURING (T)	All sizes	A	B	700
Cooper	Discoverer CTS (T-rated)	All sizes	A	B	700
Cordovan	CENTURY	All sizes	A	B	700
Cordovan	GRAND SPIRIT TOURING LS	All sizes	A	B	700
Delta	ESTEEM XLE	P235/75R15	A	B	700
Goodyear	ASSURANCE COMFORTRED	All sizes	A	B	700
Hankook	DynaPro HT	All sizes	A	B	700
Hankook	Optimo H725	All sizes	A	B	700
Hankook	ROADHANDLER	All sizes	A	B	700
Hankook	Route Master UH70	All sizes	A	B	700
Laramie	GRANDEUR TOURING GT 60/65/70 ser.	14 -16	A	B	700
Mentor	VANTAGE TOURING LE	All sizes	A	B	700
Monarch	ULTRA TOUR LS	All sizes	A	B	700
Multi-Mile	EXCEL	All sizes	A	B	700
National	OVATION	P235/75R15	A	B	700
Spartan	AVISTA	P205/65R16 94T	A	B	700
Spartan	AVISTA (S & T)	ALL EXCEPT	A	B	700
Sumitomo	Enhance L/X (T-Rated)	All sizes	A	B	700
Sumitomo	TOURING LST	All sizes	A	B	700
Toyo	VERSADO LX	T	A	B	700
Toyo	TOUREVO LS	T	A	B	700
Toyo	800 ULTRA	ALL	A	B	700
Yokohama	AVID TRZ	P195/70R14 90T	A	B	700
Hankook	DynaPro HT (OE)	265/60R18, 265/60R18	B	A	700
Hankook	veNtus S1 noble2 (OE)	235/55R17, 235/55ZR17	B	A	700
Bridgestone	DUELER H/L ALENZA "S" Spd Rtd	All sizes	B	B	700
Cordovan	TOUR PLUS LST (T rated)	All sizes	A	A	680
Eldorado	LEGEND TOUR (T rated)	All sizes	A	A	680
Hercules	ROADTOUR XUV	235/60R17T, 235/65R18T, P255/65R18T	A	A	680
Jetzon	GENESIS LST (T rated)	All sizes	A	A	680
Multi-Mile	GRAND TOUR LS (T rated)	All sizes	A	A	680
Sigma	REGENT TOURING LS (T rated)	All sizes	A	A	680
Telstar	ECHELON ULTRA LST (T rated)	All sizes	A	A	680
Vanderbilt	TOURING LSE (T rated)	All sizes	A	A	680

For a complete listing of all the tires on the market, you can call the Auto Safety Hot Line toll free, at 888-327-4236 or 800-424-9153 (TTY). Or, go to www.safercar.gov

WARNING

As tires age, they naturally dry out and can become potentially dangerous. Some experts recommend getting rid of a six-year-old tire no matter what condition it is in. Recently, a national news organization went undercover and found 12 year old tires for sale, so be sure to check your tire date before purchasing. Ask for tires that are less than one year old.

Insurance is a big part of ownership expenses, yet it's often forgotten in the showroom. As you shop, remember that the car's design and accident history may affect your insurance rates. Some cars cost less to insure because experience has shown that they are damaged less, less expensive to fix after a collision, or stolen less.

Auto insurance covers different aspects of damage and injury. The term "first party" means you and "third party" means someone else who was involved in a crash with your vehicle. The critical parts of your insurance are:

Liability (third party): This pays for damage or injury you or your vehicle may inflict on others. It is generally limited (in some cases to only $10,000 but may be several hundred thousand dollars) so that if you severely or fatally injure someone, the liability insurance will not be adequate to pay the costs. For minor or moderate damage or injury, insurance companies generally negotiate payments, but for major ones, there may be lawsuits.

Collision Damage (first party): This pays for crash damage to your own car when no other party is found to be at fault for the accident. If you lease your vehicle or have an outstanding loan on it, you will be required to have collision damage insurance.

Uninsured or Under-insured drivers: This pays your expenses when someone else is at fault, but lacks sufficient insurance or personal resources to pay for the damage or injury. The amount typically covers property damage, but may not cover serious injuries.

Comprehensive (first party): This covers the cost of some types of damage not related to crashes including theft.

Additional forms of insurance that may apply when auto insurance doesn't cover loss are health insurance, which may pay the cost of more serious injuries, life insurance which pays if you are killed in a crash, and umbrella policy insurance which may pay liability costs beyond what is covered by your auto policy. An umbrella policy may be important if you want to protect assets such as savings, your house a business, or other major assets.

Shop Around: You can save hundreds of dollars by shopping around for insurance.

There are a number of factors that determine what coverage will cost you. A car's design can affect both the chances and severity of an accident. For example, a well-designed bumper may escape damage in a low-speed crash. Some cars are easier to repair than others or may have less expensive parts. Cars with four doors tend to be damaged less than cars with two doors.

Other factors that affect your insurance costs include:

Your Annual Mileage: The more you drive, the more your vehicle will be "exposed" to a potential accident. Driving less than 5,000 to 7,500 miles per year often gets a discount. Ask your insurer if they offer this option.

Where You Drive and Park: If you regularly drive and park in the city, you will most likely pay more than if you drive in rural areas. You may get a discount if you garage your car.

Youthful Drivers: Usually the highest premiums are paid by male drivers under the age of 25. Whether or not the under-25-year-old male is married also affects insurance rates. (Married males pay less.) As the driver gets older, and if he or she has good driving record, rates are lowered.

Insurance discounts and surcharges depend upon the way a vehicle is traditionally driven. Sports cars, for example, are usually surcharged due, in part, to the typical driving habits of their owners. Four-door sedans and station wagons generally merit discounts. Not all companies offer discounts or surcharges, and many cars receive neither. Some companies offer a discount or impose a sur-

REDUCING INSURANCE COSTS

charge on collision premiums only. Others apply discounts and surcharges on both collision and comprehensive coverage. Discounts and surcharges usually range from 10 to30 percent. Remember that one company may offer a discount on a particular car while another may not.

Major crashes are rare events for individuals, but more than 30,000 people are killed and double that number suffer serious injuries in crashes each year. In a very severe crash with major injury or death, the limits on first and third party auto insurance will be inadequate to cover the costs. NHTSA estimates that the economic cost of a fatality may range from several million to more than ten million dollars, and injuries such as quadriplegia and serious brain damage could easily have a lifetime cost of ten million dollars for each individual. If a crash is not deemed to be the fault of another motorist (such as with a single vehicle crash), your health insurance may cover the cost of your injuries, but is unlikely to cover such things as long-term rehabilitation and loss of income.

Get Your Discounts: After you have shopped around and found the best deal by comparing the costs of different coverages, be sure you get all the discounts you are entitled to.

Most insurance companies offer discounts of 5 to 30 percent on various parts of your insurance bill. Ask your insurance company for a complete list of the discounts that it offers.

These can vary by company and from state to state.

Here are some of the most common insurance discounts:

Driver Education/Defensive Driving Courses: Discounts for completing a state-approved driver education course can mean a $40 reduction in the cost of coverage. Discounts of 5 to 15 percent are available in some states to those who complete a defensive driving course.

Good Student Discounts of up to 25 percent for full-time high school or college students who are in the upper 20 percent of their class, on the dean's list, or have a B or better grade point average.

Good Driver Discounts are available to drivers with an accident and violation-free record, (or no incidents in the past 3 years).

Mature Driver Credit: Drivers ages 50 and older may qualify for up to a 10 percent discount or a lower price bracket.

Sole Female Driver: Some companies offer discounts of 10 percent for females, ages 30 to 64, who are the only driver in a household.

Non-Drinkers and Non-Smokers: A limited number of companies offer incentives ranging from 10–25 percent to those who abstain.

Farmer Discounts: Many companies offer farmers either a discount of 10 to 30 percent or a lower price bracket.

! DON'T SPEED !

Besides endangering the lives of your passengers and other drivers, speeding tickets will increase your insurance premium. It only takes one speeding ticket to lose your "preferred" or "good driver" discount, which requires a clean driving record. Two or more speeding tickets or accidents can increase your premium by 40% to 200%. Some insurers may simply drop your coverage. According to the Insurance Institute for Highway Safety (IIHS), you are 17% more likely to be in an accident if you have just one speeding ticket. Insurance companies know this and will charge you for it.

Car Pooling: Commuters sharing driving may qualify for discounts of 5 to 25 percent or a lower price bracket.

Children away at school don't drive the family car very often, so if they're on your policy and they're at school, let your company know. If you insure them separately, discounts of 10–40 percent or a lower price bracket are available.

Desirable Cars: Premiums are usually much higher for cars with high collision rates or that are the favorite target of thieves.

Anti-Theft Device Credits: Discounts of 5-15 percent are offered in some states for cars equipped with a hood lock and an alarm or a disabling device (active or passive) that prevents the car from being started.

Multi-policy and Multicar Policy Discount: Some companies offer discounts of up to 10–20 percent for insuring your home and auto with the same company, or more than one car.

First Accident Allowance: Some insurers offer a "first accident allowance," which guarantees that if a customer achieves five accident-free years, his or her rates won't go up after the first at-fault accident.

Deductibles: Opting for the largest reasonable deductible is the obvious first step in reducing premiums. Increasing your deductible to $500 from $200 could cut your collision premium about 20 percent. Raising the deductible to $1,000 from $200 could lower your premium about 45 percent. The discounts may vary by company.

Collision Coverage: The older the car, the less the need for collision insurance. Consider dropping collision insurance entirely on an older car. Regardless of how much coverage you carry, the insurance company will only pay up to the car's "book value." For example, if your car requires $1,000 in repairs, but its "book value" is only $500, the insurance company is required to pay only $500.

Organizations: If you are a member of AARP, AAA, the military, a union, a professional group, an alumni association, or similar organization, you may be able to get a discount. Often insurance companies will enter joint ventures with organizations.

YOUNG DRIVERS

TIP

Each year, teenagers account for about 15 percent of highway deaths. According to the Insurance Institute for Highway Safety (IIHS), the highest driver death rate per 100,000 people is among 18-year-olds. Parents need to make sure their children are fully prepared to be competent, safe drivers before letting them out on the road. All states issue learner's permits. However, only 35 states and the District of Columbia require permits before getting a driver's license. It isn't difficult for teenagers to get a license and only 14 states prohibit teenagers from driving during night and early morning. Call your state's MVA for young driver laws.

LOW-SPEED COLLISION DAMAGE

The main purpose of a bumper is to protect your car in low-speed collisions. Unfortunately, the bumpers on today's cars and light trucks mostly fail to prevent or minimize such damage. That leaves many of us victims of a $500 to $5,000 repair bill after a minor impact, and the possibility of an increased insurance bill.

More than 30 years ago, the federal government required that new cars have bumpers capable of withstanding impacts at up to 5 with no damage. Some manufacturers were able to meet this requirement at minimal cost with attractive bumpers. Under the anti-regulatory fervor of the early 1980s, the government rolled back this along with some safety requirements. (The requirement for air bags was initially a victim of deregulation, but a Supreme Court ruling followed by a creative rulemaking gave us both air bags and safety belt use laws.)

Today, the federal law only requires that bumpers protect the safety features of cars in 2.5 mph collisions: less than a walking pace. This standard also requires that passenger car bumpers match each other in height to reduce the likelihood of under-ride in a collision.

Even this minimal requirement does not apply to SUVs, pickups, and vans. With such a high percentage of these vehicles on the road, bumper mismatches in crashes are quite common which results in excessive damage and costly repairs. The roll-back of the bumper standard enabled car companies to sell lots of expensive parts, and has cost consumers millions of dollars in increased insurance premiums and repair costs.

California requires that companies disclose which bumpers meet the old 5 mph standard; but few, if any manufacturers disclose this information.

In order to see how well bumpers actually protect our vehicles, the Insurance Institute for Highway Safety used to conduct low-speed collision damage tests. It was shocking how poorly the bumpers of recent models protected them. IIHS found that repairs after a 10 mph rear end collisions between a car and an SUV from the same manufacturer, repairs would cost as much as $6,000 per vehicle, with the average being around $3,000 (see below). Despite the fact that IIHS is funded by the insurance industry, there seems to have been no interest in continuing this test program.

Consumers Union, which also used to conduct bumper tests and report on the results in Consumer Reports has also discontinued these tests. The result is that consumers are left with neither an effective bumper standard nor consumer information on low speed crash protection.

Bumpers on most contemporary vehicles are mostly minor structures covered by plastic facings that hide their function. Styling is a more important criterion for bumper design than protection. Consumers and insurance companies have lost interest in whether bumpers provide any collision protection. Until we demand that all cars and light trucks provide better low speed collision protection, car owners will be stuck with the consequent repair bills and high insurance costs.

DAMAGE REPAIR COSTS IN 10 MPH FRONT-INTO-REAR CRASH TESTS

Source: Insurance Institute for Highway Safety

SUV INTO CAR	SUV Damage	Car Damage	Total Damage
Honda CR-V into Honda Civic	$1,721	$1,274	$2,995
Toyota RAV4 into Toyota Corolla	$1,434	$2,327	$3,761
Hyundai Tucson into Kia Forte	$850	$3,223	$4,073
Volkswagen Tiguan into Volkswagen Golf	$2,329	$2,058	$4,387
Jeep Patriot into Dodge Caliber	$1,415	$3,095	$4,510
Ford Escape into Ford Focus	$1,470	$3,386	$4,856
Nissan Rogue into Nissan Sentra	$2,884	$4,560	$7,444

CAR INTO SUV	Car Damage	SUV Damage	Total Damage
Kia Forte into Hyundai Tucson	$1,510	$2,091	$3,601
Dodge Caliber into Jeep Patriot	$2,559	$1,338	$3,897
Honda Civic into Honda CR-V	$4,921	$1,053	$5,974
Volkswagen Golf into Volkswagen Tiguan	$4,555	$1,872	$6,427
Nissan Sentra into Nissan Rogue	$5,114	$1,428	$6,542
Ford Focus into Ford Escape	$5,203	$2,208	$7,411
Corolla into Toyota RAV4	$3,852	$6,015	$9,867

See www.IIHS.org

COMPLAINTS

Americans spend billions of dollars on vehicle repairs every year. While many of those repairs are satisfactory, there are times when getting your vehicle fixed can be a very difficult process. In fact, vehicle defects and repairs are the number one cause of consumer complaints, according to the Federal Trade Commission. This chapter is designed to help you resolve your complaint, whether it's for a new vehicle still under warranty or for one you've had for years. In addition, we offer a guide to arbitration, the names and addresses of consumer groups, federal agencies, and the manufacturers themselves. Finally, we tell you how to take the important step of registering your complaint with the U.S. Department of Transportation.

No matter what your complaint, keep accurate records. Copies of the following items are indispensable in helping to resolve your problems:

☑ your service invoices

☑ bills you have paid

☑ letters you have written to the manufacturer or the repair facility owner

☑ written repair estimates from your independent mechanic.

☑ notes on discussion with company representatives including names and dates.

RESOLVING COMPLAINTS

Here are some basic steps to help you resolve your problem:

1 First, return your vehicle to the repair facility that did the work. Bring a written list of the problems and make sure that you keep a copy of the list. Give the repair facility a reasonable opportunity to examine your vehicle and attempt to fix it. Speak directly to the service manager (not to the service writer who wrote up your repair order), and ask him or her to test drive the vehicle with you so that you can point out the problem.

2 If that doesn't resolve the problem, take the vehicle to a diagnostic center for an independent examination. This may cost $45 to $60. Get a written statement defining the problem and outlining how it may be fixed. Give your repair shop a copy. If your vehicle is under warranty, do not allow any warranty repair by an independent mechanic; you may not be reimbursed by the manufacturer.

3 If your repair shop does not respond to the independent assessment, present your problem to an arbitration panel. These panels hear both sides of the story and try to come to a resolution.

If the problem is with a new vehicle dealer, or if you feel that the manufacturer is responsible, you may be able to use one of the manufacturer's arbitration programs.

If the problem is solely with an independent dealer, a local Better Business Bureau (BBB) may be able to mediate your complaint. It may also offer an arbitration hearing. In any case, the BBB should enter your complaint into its files on that establishment.

When contacting any arbitration program, determine how long the process takes, who makes the final decision, whether you are bound by that decision, and whether the program handles all problems or only warranty complaints.

Beware of "binding arbitration" because you give up your right to pursue legal action.

4 If there are no arbitration programs in your area, contact private consumer groups, local government agencies, or your local "action line" newspaper columnist, newspaper editor, or radio/TV broadcaster. A phone call or letter from them may persuade a repair facility to take action. Send a copy of your letter to the repair shop.

5 One of your last resorts is to bring a lawsuit against the dealer, manufacturer, or repair facility in small claims court. The fee for filing such an action is usually small, and you generally act as your own attorney, saving attorney's fees. There is a monetary limit on the amount you can claim, which varies from state to state. Your local consumer affairs office, state attorney general's office, or the clerk of the court can tell you how to file such a suit.

6 Finally, talk with an attorney. It's best to select an attorney who is familiar with handling automotive problems. Lawyer referral services can provide names of attorneys who deal with automobile problems. If you can't afford an attorney, contact the Legal Aid Society.

WARRANTY COMPLAINTS

If your vehicle is under warranty or you are having problems with a factory-authorized dealership, here are some special guidelines:

1 Have the warranty available to show the dealer. Make sure you call the problem to the dealer's attention before the end of the warranty period.

2 If you are still dissatisfied after giving the dealer a reasonable opportunity to fix your vehicle, contact the manufacturer's representative (also called the zone representative) in your area. This person can authorize the dealer to make repairs or take other steps to resolve the dispute. Your dealer will have your zone representative's name and telephone number. Explain the problem and ask for a meeting and a personal inspection of your vehicle.

3 If you can't get satisfaction from the zone representative, call or write the manufacturer's owner relations department. Your owner's manual contains this phone number and address. In each case, as you move up the chain, indicate the steps you have already taken and keep careful records of your efforts.

4 Your next option is to present your problem to a complaint handling arbitration program. Beware of "binding arbitration" because you give up your right to pursue legal action.

If you complain of a problem during the warranty period, you have a right to have the problem fixed even after the warranty runs out. If your warranty has not been honored, you may be able to "revoke acceptance," which means that you return the vehicle to the dealer. If you are successful, you may be entitled to a replacement vehicle or to a full refund of the purchase price and reimbursement of legal fees under the Magnuson-Moss Warranty Act. Or, if you are covered by one of the state lemon laws, you may be able to return the vehicle and receive a refund or replacement from the manufacturer.

NEED HELP?

If you need legal assistance with your repair problem, the Center for Auto Safety has a list of lawyers who specialize in helping consumers with auto repair problems. For the names of attorneys in your area, send a stamped, self-addressed envelope to: Center for Auto Safety, 1825 Connecticut Ave. NW, Suite 330, Washington, DC 20009. Check their website at www.autosafety.org for a shorter list of lemon law attorneys. The Center has also published *The Lemon Book*, a detailed guide to resolving automobile complaints, available for $17.50 directly from the Center.

Attorneys Take Note: For information on litigation assistance provided by the Center for Auto Safety, including *The Lemon Law Litigation Manual*, please contact the Center for Auto Safety at the above address.

VEHICLE SAFETY HOT LINE: 800-424-9393
TTY FOR HEARING IMPAIRED: 800-424-9153
WWW.SAFERCAR.GOV

The toll-free Auto Safety Hot Line can provide information on recalls, record information about safety problems, and refer you to the appropriate government experts on other vehicle related problems. You can even have recall information mailed to you within 24 hours of your call at no charge. Most importantly, you can call the hot line to report safety problems which will become part of the National Highway Traffic Safety Administration's complaint database. If you have access to the internet, www.safercar.gov is a more efficient way to register complaints and obtain recall and safety information.

COMPLAINT INDEX

Thanks to the efforts of the Center for Auto Safety, we are able to provide you with the vehicle complaints on file with the National Highway Traffic Safety Administration (NHTSA). Each year, thousands of Americans file online or call the government in order to register complaints about their vehicles.

The complaint index is the result of our analysis of these complaints. It is based on a ratio of the number of complaints for each vehicle to the sales of that vehicle. In order to predict the expected complaint performance of the 2016 models, we have examined the complaint history of that car's series. The term series refers to the fact that when a manufacturer introduces a new model, that vehicle remains essentially unchanged, on average, for four to six years. For example, the Ford Explorer was redesigned in 2011 and remains essentially the same car for 2016. As such, we have compiled the complaint experience for that series in order to give you some information to use in deciding which car to buy. For vehicles introduced or significantly changed in 2016, we do not yet have enough data to develop a complaint index.

The following table presents the projected best and worst complaint ratings for the 2016 models for which we can develop ratings. Higher index numbers mean the vehicle generated a greater number of complaints. Lower numbers indicate fewer complaints.

2016 PROJECTED COMPLAINT INDEX

THE BEST	INDEX*
Chevrolet Trax	745
Scion tC	907
Mini Countryman	1041
Lincoln Navigator	1064
Audi Q3	1066
Lexus GS	1138
Acura ILX	1169
Toyota Yaris	1178
Toyota Prius V	1209
Toyota Tundra	1245
Audi Q5	1302
Toyota 4Runner	1310
Lexus IS	1344
Lexus GX	1402
Audi A4	1446
Mercedes-Benz E-Class	1485
Kia Sportage	1557
Toyota Corolla	1616
BMW 6 Series	1630
Lexus ES	1652
Audi A6	1675

THE WORST	INDEX*
Chrysler 200	>20,000
Acura TLX	>20,000
Jeep Cherokee	>20,000
Subaru Outback	17,784
Volkswagen Golf	17,111
Subaru Legacy	16,906
GMC Canyon	14,598
Chevrolet Suburban	13,952
Jeep Grand Cherokee	13,729
Jeep Renegade	13,318
Fiat 500L	12,690
Dodge Journey	12,430
Hyundai Genesis	12,396
Ford Focus	12,081
Ford Fiesta	11,878
Mercedes-Benz CLA-Class	10,738
Nissan Pathfinder	10,293
Chrysler Town and Country	10,196
Jeep Wrangler	10,188
Fiat 500	9,122

*IMPORTANT NOTE: The numbers represent relative index scores, not the number of complaints received. The complaint index score considers sales volume and years on the road. Lower index numbers are better. We capped the complaint index at 20,000 for excessively high complaint indices.

CENTER FOR AUTO SAFETY

Every year automobile manufacturers spend millions of dollars making their voices heard in government decision making. For example, General Motors and Ford have large staffs in Detroit and Washington that work solely to influence government activity. But who looks out for the consumer?

For over 40 years, the nonprofit Center for Auto Safety (CAS) has told the consumer's story to government agencies, to Congress, and to the courts. Along with countless recalls, CAS got airbags in every car and lemon laws in every state.

CAS was established in 1970 by Ralph Nader and Consumers Union. As consumer concerns about auto safety issues expanded, so did the work of CAS. CAS' activities include:

Initiating Safety Recalls: CAS analyzes over 20,000 consumer complaints each year. CAS requests government investigations and recalls of defective vehicles. CAS was responsible for the Ford Pinto faulty gas tank recall, the Firestone 500 steel-belted radial tire recall, the record recall of over three million Evenflo One Step child seats, and Jeep Grand Cherokees with Pinto like fuel systems. Other CAS influenced recalls include Fords with transmissions that jump out of park, Toyota unintended acceleration, exploding Honda airbags, Ford cruise control switch fires and many others.

Representing the Consumer in Washington: CAS follows the activities of federal agencies and Congress to ensure that they carry out their responsibilities to the American taxpayer. CAS brings a consumer's point of view to vehicle safety policies and rule-making. Since 1970, CAS has submitted more than 500 petitions and comments on federal safety standards.

One major effort on safety standards has been the successful fight to get airbags in every car. After opposing airbags for decades, the auto industry now can't get enough lifesaving airbags in cars with some models having ten airbags. With airbags to protect consumers in front and side crashes, CAS worked to strengthen weak roofs that crush in rollovers. Beginning in 2013, vehicles will have roofs more than twice as strong as before. Between stronger roofs and Electronic Stability Control deaths and serious injuries in rollovers have already decreased by more than 30% from 27,000 in 2005.

In the 1990's, CAS uncovered a fire defect that dwarfed the highly publicized flammability of the Ford Pinto. Side saddle gas tanks on full size 1973–87 GM pickups and 1988–90 crew cabs can explode on impact. Over 2,000 people have been killed in fire crashes involving these trucks. After mounting a national campaign to warn consumers to steer clear of these GM fire hazards, the Department of Transportation granted CAS' petition and conducted one of its biggest defect investigations in history. The result—GM was asked to recall its pickups. GM, sadly, denied this request and was left off with a $50 million slap on the wrist.

Exposing Secret Warranties: CAS played a prominent role in the disclosure of secret warranties, "policy adjustments," as they are called by manufacturers. These occur when an automaker agrees to pay for repair of certain defects beyond the warranty period but refuses to notify consumers. Thanks to years of CAS prodding, DOT will soon be publishing every auto company Service Bulletin on its website with a index to guide consumes to secret warranties.

Lemon Laws: CAS' work on Lemon Laws aided in the enactment of state laws which make it easier to return a defective new automobile and get money back.

Tire Ratings: Consumers have reliable treadwear ratings to help them get the most miles for their dollar thanks to a CAS' lawsuit overturning DOT's revocation of this valuable tire information program.

Legal Action: When CAS has exhausted other means of obtaining relief for consumer problems, it initiates legal action. For example, in 1978 when the Department of Energy attempted to raise the price of unleaded gasoline four cents per gallon without notice or comment, CAS succeeded in stopping this illegal move through a lawsuit, thus

CENTER FOR AUTO SAFETY ONLINE

The Center for Auto Safety has a website at www.autosafety.org to provide information to consumers and to organize consumer campaigns against auto companies on safety defects. Detailed information and advice on defects in specific makes and models are on CAS' website. Consumers with lemons can file online complaints with CAS and get referred to lemon lawyers.

www.autosafety.org

saving consumers $2 billion over 3-years.

A 1985 Center for Auto Safety lawsuit against the Environmental Protection Agency (EPA) forced the EPA to recall polluting cars, rather than let companies promise to make cleaner cars in the future. As part of the settlement, GM (which was responsible for the polluting cars) funded a $7 million methanol bus demonstration program in New York City.

In 2003, a CAS lawsuit forced the Department of Transportation to require auto companies to use more accurate tire pressure monitors on the vehicle dash that identified which tire had low pressure versus an indirect system that only told consumers they had low tire pressure on some tire.

CAS also challenges class actions settlements that don't deliver for consumers. We have knocked off coupon settlement after coupon settlement in which consumers got useless coupons to buy a new car while trial lawyers got cold cash. In 2010 we challenged a Honda Civic Hybrid gas mileage settlement that gave consumers a DVD on how to drive better. In 2009, we challenged a Ford Explorer rollover settlement that gave consumers a restricted $300-500 coupon toward a new $30,000 Ford that only 148 out of 1,000,000 class members redeemed while attorneys got $25 million in fees and costs.

CAS is your safety and lemon insurance. CAS depends on public support to do all its good work. Annual membership is $25. All contributions are tax-deductible. To contribute by credit card, go to the CAS website at: www.auto-safety.org/make-donation-cas.

To contribute by mail, send a check to: Center for Auto Safety, 1825 Connecticut Ave., NW #330, Washington, DC 20009-5708.

Consumer Groups and Government

Below are the names of additional consumer groups you may find helpful:

Advocates for Highway and Auto Safety
750 First St., NE, Suite 1130
Washington, DC 20002
(202) 408-1711/408-1699 fax
www.saferoads.org
An alliance of consumer, health and safety groups and insurance companies.

Consumer Action
1170 Market St., Suite 500
San Francisco, CA 94102
(415) 777-9635
www.consumer-action.org
Complaint handling and advocacy related to consumer rights.

Consumers for Auto Reliability and Safety
1303 J St., Suite 270
Sacramento, CA 95814
(530) 759-9440
www.carconsumers.org
Auto safety, airbags, and lemon laws.

KIDS AND CARS
(816) 216-7085
www.kidsandcars.org
email@kidsandcars.org
Safety and advocacy related to protecting children in and around motor vehicles.

SafetyBelt Safe, U.S.A.
P.O. Box 553
Altadena, CA 91003
(800) 745-SAFE
www.carseat.org
stombrella@carseat.org
Excellent information and training on child safety seats and safety belt usage.

Several federal agencies conduct automobile-related programs. Following is each agency with a description of the type of work it performs and how to contact them.

National Highway Traffic Safety Administration
1200 New Jersey Ave., SE, West Bldg.
Washington, DC 20590
(888) 327-4236/www.nhtsa.gov
www.safercar.gov

NHTSA issues safety and fuel economy standards for new motor vehicles; investigates safety defects and enforces recall of defective vehicles and equipment; conducts research and demonstration programs on vehicle safety, fuel economy, driver safety, and automobile inspection and repair; provides grants for state highway safety programs in areas such as police traffic services, driver education and licensing, emergency medical services, pedestrian safety, and alcohol abuse.

Environmental Protection Agency
1200 Pennsylvania Ave., NW
Washington, DC 20460
(202) 272-0167/www.epa.gov
www.fueleconomy.gov
EPA's responsibilities include setting and enforcing air and noise emission standards for motor vehicles and measuring fuel economy in new vehicles (EPA Fuel Economy Guide).

Federal Trade Commission
600 Pennsylvania Ave., NW
Washington, DC 20580
(202) 326-2222/www.ftc.gov
The FTC regulates advertising, credit practices, marketing abuses, and professional services and ensures that products are properly labeled (as in fuel economy ratings). The commission covers unfair or deceptive trade practices in motor vehicle sales and repairs, as well as non-safety defects.

U.S. Department of Justice
Civil Division
950 Pennsylvania Ave., NW
Washington, DC 20530
(202) 307-0066
www.justice.gov/civil
feedback@doj.gov
The DOJ enforces federal law that requires manufacturers to label new automobiles and forbids removal or alteration of labels before delivery to consumers. Labels must contain make, model, vehicle identification number, dealer's name, suggested base price, manufacturer option costs, and manufacturer's suggested retail price.

AUTOMOBILE MANUFACTURERS

Acura (Division of Honda)
John Ikeda, Vice President-General
Manager
See Honda for address
Customer Relations: 800-382-2238

Audi (Division of Volkswagen)
Scott Keogh, President
See Volkswagen for address
Customer Relations: 800-822-2834

BMW
Ludwig Willisch, President and CEO
300 Chestnut Ridge Road
Woodcliff Lake, NJ 07677-7731
Customer Relations: 800-831-1117

Buick (Division of General Motors)
P.O. Box 33136
Detroit, MI 48232-5136
Customer Relations: 800-521-7300

Cadillac (Division of General Motors)
P.O. Box 33169
Detroit, MI 48232-5169
Customer Relations: 800-458-8006

Chevrolet (Division of General Motors)
P.O. Box 33136
Detroit, MI 48323-5136
Customer Relations: 800-222-1020

Chrysler (Chrysler, Dodge, Jeep, Ram, Fiat)
Sergio Marchionne, CEO
1000 Chrysler Drive
Auburn Hills, MI 48326
Customer Relations: 800-247-9753

Dodge (Division of Chrysler)
P.O. Box 21-8004
Auburn Hills, MI 48321-8004
Customer Relations: 800-423-6343

Fiat (Division of Chrysler)
P.O. Box 21-8004
Auburn Hills, MI 48321-8004
Customer Relations: 888-242-6342

Ford (Ford, Lincoln)
Mark Fields, President and CEO
P.O. Box 6248
Dearborn, MI 48126
Customer Relations 800-392-3673

General Motors (Buick, Cadillac, Chevrolet, GMC)
Mary Barra, CEO
300 Renaisance Center
Detorit, MI 48265

GMC (Division of General Motors)
P.O. Box 33172
Detroit, MI 48232
Customer Relations: 800-462-8782

Honda (Honda, Acura)
Takuji Yamada, President and CEO
1919 Torrance Blvd.
Torrance, CA 90501
Customer Relations: 800-999-1009

Hyundai
David Zuchowski, President and CEO
P.O. Box 20850
Fountain Valley, CA 92728-0850
Customer Relations: 800-633-5151
Email: consumeraffairs@hmausa.com

Infiniti (Division of Nissan)
Roland Krueger, President
See Nissan for address
Customer Relations: 800-662-6200

Jaguar, Land Rover
Joachim Eberhardt, President
555 MacArthur Blvd.
Mahwah, NJ 07430
Jaguar Customer Relations: 800-452-4827
Land Rover Cust. Relations: 800-637-6837

Jeep (Division of Chrysler)
P.O. Box 21-8004
Auburn Hills, MI 48321-8004
Customer Relations: 877-426-5337

Kia
Jung Won Sohn, CEO
P.O. Box 52410
Irvine, CA 92619-2410
Customer Relations: 800-333-4542

Lexus (Division of Toyota)
Jeff Bracken, Vice President and General
Manager
P.O. Box 2991-Mail Drop L201
Torrance, CA 90509-2991
Customer Relations: 800-255-3987

Lincoln (Division of Ford)
Kumar Galhotra, President
See Ford for address
Customer Relations: 800-521-4140

Mazda
Jim O' Sullivan, President and CEO
P.O. Box 19734
Irvine, CA 92623-9734
Customer Relations: 800-222-5500

Mercedes-Benz
Dietmar Exler, President and CEO
1 Mercedes Drive
Montvale, NJ 07645
Customer Relations 800-367-6372

Mini (Division of BMW)
David Duncan, Vice President
See BMW for address
Customer Relations: 866-275-6464

Mitsubishi
Ryujiro Kobashi, President and CEO
P.O. Box 6400
Cypress, CA 90630-9998
Customer Reloations: 800-648-7820

Nissan
Carlos Ghosn, President and CEO
P.O. Box 685003
Franklin, TN 37068-5003
Customer Relations: 800-647-7261

Porsche
Klaus Zellmer, President and CEO
980 Hammond Dr., Suite 1000
Atlanta, GA 30328
Customer Relations: 800-767-7243

Ram (Division of Chrysler)
P.O. Box 21-8007
Auburn Hills, MI 48321-8004
Customer Relations: 866-726-4636

Scion (Division of Toyota)
Andrew Gilleland, Vice President
D102 P.O. Box 2742
Torrance, CA 90509-2742
Customer Relations: 800-707-2466

Smart (Division of Mercedes-Benz)
Mike Nolte, General Manager
1 Mercedes Drive
Montvale, NJ 07645
Customer Relations 800-762-2466

Subaru
Tomomi Nakamura, Chairman and CEO
P.O. Box 6000
Cherry Hill, NJ 08034-6000
Customer Relations: 800-782-2783

Telsa
Elon Musk, Chairman and CEO
3500 Deer Creek
Palo Alto, CA 94304
Customer Relations: 877-798-3752

Toyota (Toyota, Lexus, Scion)
Jim Lentz, President and CEO
19001 South Western Ave. Dept. WC11
Torrance, CA 90501
Customer Relations: 800-331-4331

Volkswagen
Michael Horn, President and CEO
2200 Ferdinand Porsche Dr.
Herndon, VA 20171
Customer Relations: 800-822-8987

Volvo
Tony Nicolosi, President and CEO
One Volvo Drive
P.O. Box 914
Rockleigh, NJ 07647
Customer Relations: 800-458-1552

LEMON LAWS

Sometimes, despite our best efforts, we buy a vehicle that just doesn't work right. There may be little problem after little problem, or perhaps one big problem that never seems to be fixed. Because of the "sour" taste that such vehicles leave in the mouths of consumers who buy them, these vehicles are known as "lemons."

In the past, it's been difficult to obtain a refund or replacement if a vehicle was a lemon. The burden of proof was left to the consumer. Because it is hard to define exactly what constitutes a lemon, many lemon owners were unable to win a case against a manufacturer. And when they won, consumers had to pay for their attorneys giving them less than if they had traded in their lemon.

Thanks to "Lemon Laws" passed by all states, lemon-aide is available when consumers get stuck with a lemon. Although there are some important state-to-state variations, all of the laws have similarities: They establish a period of coverage, usually two years from delivery or the written warranty period, whichever is shorter; they may require some form of noncourt arbitration; and most importantly they define a lemon. In most states a new car, truck, or van is "presumed" to be a lemon when it has been taken back to the shop 3 to 4 times for the same problem or is out of service for a total of 30 days during the covered period. This time does not mean consecutive days and can be for different problems. 15 states have safety lemon provisions which presume a vehicle is a lemon after only 1 to 2 repairs of a defect likely to cause death or serious injury. Be sure to keep careful records of your repairs since some states now require only one of the repairs to be within the specified time period. Thirty-three states provide for the award of attorney fees with the other 17 relying on the Federal lemon law for fees.

A vehicle may be covered by the lemon law even though it doesn't meet the "presumption."

Specific information about your state's law can be obtained from your state attorney general's office or at the Center for Auto Safety's website. The following table offers a general description of the Lemon Law in your state and what you need to do to set it in motion (Notification/Trigger). We indicate where state-run arbitration programs are available. State-run programs are the best type of arbitration. Be aware, a few state lemon laws are so bad consumers should only rely on the Federal lemon law and state contract law. We have marked these bad laws with a ⊠ while the best laws have a ☑.

☑ **The Best Lemon Laws**
⊠ **The Worst Lemon Laws**

Alabama	Qualification: 3 unsuccessful repairs or 30 calendar days within shorter of 24 months or 24,000 miles, provided 1 repair attempt or 1 day out of service is within shorter of 1 year or 12,000 miles. Notice/Trigger: Certified mail to manufacturer + opportunity for final repair attempt within 14 calendar days.
Alaska	Qualification: 3 unsuccessful repairs or 30 business days out of service within shorter of 1 year or warranty. Notice/Trigger: Certified mail to manufacturer + dealer (or repair agent) that problem has not been corrected in reasonable number of attempts + refund or replacement demanded within 60 days. Manufacturer has 30 calendar days for final repair attempt.
Arizona	Qualification: 4 unsuccessful repairs or 30 calendar days out of service within warranty period or shorter of 2 years or 24,000 miles. Notice/Trigger: Written notice + opportunity to repair to manufacturer.
Arkansas ☑ BEST	Qualification: 3 unsuccessful repairs, 5 total repairs of any nonconformity, or 1 unsuccessful repair of problem likely to cause death or serious bodily injury within longer of 24 months or 24,000 miles. Notice/Trigger: Certified or registered mail to manufacturer who has 10 days to notify consumer of repair facility. Facility has 10 days to repair.

L—Law specifically applies to leased vehicles; S-C—State has certified guidelines for arbitration; S-R—State-run arbitration mechanism available

California ✓ BEST	Qualification: 4 repair attempts or 30 calendar days out of service or 2 repair attempts for defect likely to cause death or serious bodily injury within shorter of 18 months or 18,000 miles, or "reasonable" number of attempts during entire express warranty period. Notice/Trigger: Direct written notice to manufacturer at address clearly specified in owner's manual. Covers small businesses with up to 5 vehicles under 10,000 pounds GVWR.
Colorado ✗ WORST	Qualification: 4 unsuccessful repairs or 30 business days out of service within shorter of 1 year or warranty. Notice/Trigger: Prior certified mail notice + opportunity to repair for manufacturer.
Connecticut	Qualification: 4 unsuccessful repairs or 30 calendar days out of service within shorter of 2 years or 24,000 miles, or 2 unsuccessful repairs of problem likely to cause death or serious bodily injury within warranty period or 1 year. Notice/Trigger: Report to manufacturer, agent, or dealer. Written notice to manufacturer only if required in owner's manual or warranty. S-R
Delaware	Qualification: 4 unsuccessful repairs or 30 calendar days out of service within shorter of 1 year or warranty. Notice/Trigger: Written notice + opportunity to repair to manufacturer.
D.C.	Qualification: 4 unsuccessful repairs or 30 calendar days out of service or 1 unsuccessful repair of safety-related defect, within shorter of 2 years or 18,000 miles. Notice/Trigger: Report to manufacturer, agent, or dealer.
Florida	Qualification: 3 unsuccessful repairs or 15 calendar days within 24 months from delivery. Notice/Trigger: Certified or express mail notice to manufacturer who has 10 days to notify consumer of repair facility plus 10 more calendar days for final repair attempt after delivery to designated dealer. S-R
Georgia	Qualification: 1 unsuccessful repair of serious safety defect or 3 unsuccessful repair attempts or 30 calendar days out of service within shorter of 24,000 miles or 24 months. Notification/Trigger: Overnight or certified mail notice return receipt requested. Manufacturer has 7 days to notify consumer of repair facility & consumer has 14 days from manufacturer receipt of original notice to deliver vehicle to repair facility. Facility has 28 calendar days from manufacturer receipt of original notice to repair. State-run arbitration mechanism available. Law specifically applies to leased vehicles.
Hawaii	Qualification: 3 unsuccessful repair attempts, or 1 unsuccessful repair attempt of defect likely to cause death or serious bodily injury, or out of service for total of 30 days within shorter of 2 years or 24,000 miles. Notice/Trigger: Written notice + opportunity to repair to manufacturer. S-R
Idaho	Qualification: 4 repair attempts or 30 business days out of service within shorter of 2 years or 24,000 miles, or 1 repair of complete failure of braking or steering likely to cause death or serious bodily injury. Notice/Trigger: Written notice to manufacturer or dealer + one opportunity to repair to manufacturer. S-R.
Illinois	Qualification: 4 unsuccessful repairs or 30 business days out of service within shorter of 1 year or 12,000 miles. Notice/Trigger: Written notice + opportunity to repair to manufacturer.
Indiana ✗ WORST	Qualification: 4 unsuccessful repairs or 30 business days out of service within shorter of 18 months or 18,000 miles. Notice/Trigger: Written notice to manufacturer only if required in the warranty.

L—Law specifically applies to leased vehicles; S-C—State has certified guidelines for arbitration; S-R—State-run arbitration mechanism available

Iowa	Qualification: 3 unsuccessful repairs, or 1 unsuccessful repair of nonconformity likely to cause death or serious bodily injury, or 30 calendar days out of service within shorter of 2 years or 24,000 miles. Notice/Trigger: Certified registered mail + final opportunity to repair within 10 calendar days of receipt of notice to manufacturer.
Kansas	Qualification: 4 unsuccessful repairs or 30 calendar days out of service or 10 total repairs within shorter of 1 year or warranty. Notice/Trigger: Actual notice to manufacturer.
Kentucky	Qualification: 4 unsuccessful repairs or 30 calendar days out of service within shorter of 1 year or 12,000 miles. Notice/Trigger: Written notice to manufacturer.
Louisiana	Qualification: 4 unsuccessful repairs or 90 calendar days out of service within shorter of 1 year or warranty. Notice/Trigger: Report to manufacturer or dealer.
Maine	Qualification: 3 unsuccessful repairs (or 1 unsuccessful repair of serious failure of brakes or steering) or 15 business days out of service within shorter of warranty or 3 years or 18,000 miles. Applies to vehicles within first 18,000 miles or 3 years regardless of whether claimant is original owner. Notice/Trigger: Written notice to manufacturer or dealer. Manufacturer has 7 business days after receipt for final repair attempt. S-R
Maryland	Qualification: 4 unsuccessful repairs, 30 calendar days out of service or 1 unsuccessful repair of braking or steering system within shorter of 15 months or 15,000 miles. Notice/Trigger: Certified mail return receipt requested + opportunity to repair within 30 calendar days of receipt of notice to manufacturer or factory branch.
Massachusetts	Qualification: 3 unsuccessful repairs or 10 business days out of service within shorter of 1 year or 15,000 miles. Notice/Trigger: Notice to manufacturer or dealer who has 7 business days to attempt final repair. S-R
Michigan	Qualification: 4 unsuccessful repairs within 2 years from date of first unsuccessful repair or 30 calendar days within shorter of 1 year or warranty. Notice/Trigger: Certified mail return receipt requested to manufacturer who has 5 business days to repair after delivery. Consumer may notify manufacturer after third repair attempt.
Minnesota	Qualification: 4 unsuccessful repairs or 30 business days or 1 unsuccessful repair of total braking or steering loss likely to cause death or serious bodily injury within shorter of 2 years or warranty. Notice/Trigger: Written notice + opportunity to repair to manufacturer, agent, or dealer.
Mississippi	Qualification: 3 unsuccessful repairs or 15 business days out of service within shorter of 1 year or warranty. Notice/Trigger: Written notice to manufacturer who has 10 business days to repair after delivery to designated dealer.
Missouri	Qualification: 4 unsuccessful repairs or 30 business days out of service within shorter of 1 year or warranty. Notice/Trigger: Written notice to manufacturer who has 10 calendar days to repair after delivery to designated dealer.
Montana	Qualification: 4 unsuccessful repairs or 30 business days out of service after notice within shorter of 2 years or 18,000 miles. Notice/Trigger: Written notice + opportunity to repair to manufacturer. S-R
Nebraska	Qualification: 4 unsuccessful repairs or 40 calendar days out of service within shorter of 1 year or warranty. Notice/Trigger: Certified mail + opportunity to repair to manufacturer.

L—Law specifically applies to leased vehicles; S-C—State has certified guidelines for arbitration; S-R—State-run arbitration mechanism available

Nevada	Qualification: 4 unsuccessful repairs or 30 calendar days out of service within shorter of 1 year or warranty. Notice/Trigger: Written notice to manufacturer.
New Hampshire	Qualification: 3 unsuccessful repairs by same dealer or 30 business days out of service within warranty. Notice/Trigger: Report to manufacturer, distributor, agent, or dealer (on forms provided by manufacturer) + final opportunity to repair before arbitration. S-R
New Jersey ☑ BEST	Qualification: 3 Unsuccessful repairs or 20 calendar days out of service within shorter of 2 years or 24,000 miles; or 1 unsuccessful repair of a serious safety defect likely to cause death or serious bodily injury. Notice/Trigger: Certified mail notice, return receipt requested to manufacturer who has 10 days to repair. Consumer may notify manufacturer at any time after the second repair attempt, or after the first repair attempt in the case of a serious safety defect.
New Mexico ☒ WORST	Qualification: 4 unsuccessful repairs or 30 business days out of service within shorter of 1 year or warranty. Notice/Trigger: Written notice + opportunity to repair to manufacturer, agent, or dealer.
New York	Qualification: 4 unsuccessful repairs or 30 calendar days out of service within shorter of 2 years or 18,000 miles. Notice/Trigger: Notice to manufacturer, agent, or dealer.
North Carolina	Qualification: 4 unsuccessful repairs within shorter of 24 months, 24,000 miles or warranty or 20 business days out of service during any 12 month period of warranty. Notice/Trigger: Written notice to manufacturer + opportunity to repair within 15 calendar days of receipt only if required in warranty or owner's manual.
North Dakota ☒ WORST	Qualification: 3 unsuccessful repairs or 30 business days out of service within shorter of 1 year or warranty. Notice/Trigger: Direct written notice + opportunity to repair to manufacturer. (Manufacturer's informal arbitration process serves as prerequisite to consumer refund or replacement.)
Ohio ☑ BEST	Qualification: 3 unsuccessful repairs of same nonconformity, 30 calendar days out of service, 8 total repairs of any nonconformity, or 1 unsuccessful repair of problem likely to cause death or serious bodily injury within shorter of 1 year or 18,000 miles. Notice/Trigger: Report to manufacturer, its agent, or dealer.
Oklahoma	Qualification: 4 unsuccessful repairs or 30 calendar days out of service within shorter of 1 year or warranty. Notice/Trigger: Written notice + opportunity to repair to manufacturer.
Oregon	Qualification: 4 unsuccessful repairs or 30 business days within shorter of 1 year or 12,000 miles. Notice/Trigger: Direct written notice + opportunity to repair to manufacturer.
Pennsylvania	Qualification: 3 unsuccessful repairs or 30 calendar days within shorter of 1 year, 12,000 miles, or warranty. Notice/Trigger: Delivery to authorized service + repair facility. If delivery impossible, written notice to manufacturer or its repair facility obligates them to pay for delivery.
Rhode Island	Qualification: 4 unsuccessful repairs or 30 calendar days out of service within shorter of 1 year or 15,000 miles. Notice/Trigger: Report to dealer or manufacturer who has 7 days for final repair opportunity.

L—Law specifically applies to leased vehicles; S-C—State has certified guidelines for arbitration; S-R—State-run arbitration mechanism available

South Carolina	Qualification: 3 unsuccessful repairs or 30 calendar days out of service within shorter of 1 year or 12,000 miles. Notice/Trigger: Certified mail + opportunity to repair (not more than 10 business days) to manufacturer only if manufacturer informed consumer of such at time of sale.
South Dakota	Qualification: 4 unsuccessful repairs, 1 of which occurred during shorter of 1 year or 12,000 miles, or 30 calendar days out of service during shorter of 24 months or 24,000 miles. Notice/Trigger: Certified mail to manufacturer + final opportunity to repair + 7 calendar days to notify consumer of repair facility.
Tennessee	Qualification: 4 unsuccessful repairs or 30 calendar days out of service within shorter of 1 year or warranty. Notice/Trigger: Certified mail notice to manufacturer + final opportunity to repair within 10 calendar days.
Texas	Qualification: 4 unsuccessful repairs when 2 occurred within shorter of 1 year or 12,000 miles, + other 2 occur within shorter of 1 year or 12,000 miles immediately following second repair attempt; or 2 unsuccessful repairs of serious safety defect when 1 occurred within shorter of 1 year or 12,000 miles + other occurred within shorter of 1 year or 12,000 miles immediately following first repair; or 30 calendar days out of service within shorter of 2 years or 24,000 miles + at least 2 attempts were made within shorter of 1 year or 12,000 miles. Notice/Trigger: Written notice to manufacturer. S-R
Utah	Qualification: 4 unsuccessful repairs or 30 business days out of service within shorter of 1 year or warranty. Notice/Trigger: Report to manufacturer, agent, or dealer. S-R
Vermont	Qualification: 3 unsuccessful repairs when at least first repair was within warranty, or 30 calendar days out of service within warranty. Notice/Trigger: Written notice to manufacturer (on provided forms) after third repair attempt, or 30 days. Arbitration must be held within 45 days after notice, during which time manufacturer has 1 final repair. S-R Note: Repairs must been done by same authorized agent or dealer, unless consumer shows good cause for taking vehicle to different agent or dealer.
Virginia	Qualification: 3 unsuccessful repairs, or 1 repair attempt of serious safety defect, or 30 calendar days out of service within 18 months. Notice/Trigger: Written notice to manufacturer. If 3 unsuccessful repairs or 30 days already exhausted before notice, manufacturer has 1 more repair attempt not to exceed 15 days.
Washington	Qualification: 4 unsuccessful repairs, 30 calendar days out of service (15 during warranty period), or 2 repairs of serious safety defect, first reported within shorter of warranty or 24 months or 24,000 miles. One repair attempt + 15 of 30 days must fall within manufacturer's express warranty of at least 1 year of 12,000 miles. Notice/Trigger: Written notice to manufacturer. S-R Note: Consumer should receive replacement or refund within 40 calendar days of request.
West Virginia ☑ BEST	Qualification: 3 unsuccessful repairs or 30 calendar days out of service or 1 unsuccessful repair of problem likely to cause death or serious bodily injury within shorter of 1 year or warranty. Notice/Trigger: Written notice + opportunity to repair to manufacturer.
Wisconsin	Qualification: 4 unsuccessful repairs or 30 calendar days out of service within shorter of 1 year or warranty. Notice/Trigger: Report to manufacturer or dealer. Note: Consumer should receive replacement or refund within 30 calendar days after offer to return title.
Wyoming	Qualification: 3 unsuccessful repairs or 30 business days out of service within 1 year. Notice/Trigger: Direct written notice + opportunity to repair to manufacturer. S-R

L—Law specifically applies to leased vehicles; S-C—State has certified guidelines for arbitration; S-R—State-run arbitration mechanism available

5 BASIC STEPS TO CAR BUYING

Buying a car means matching wits with a seasoned professional. But if you know what to expect, you'll have a much better chance of getting a really good deal!

There's no question that buying a car can be an intimidating experience. But it doesn't have to be. First of all, you have in your hands all of the information you need to make an informed choice. Secondly, if you approach the purchase logically, you'll always maintain control of the decision. Start with the following basic steps:

1 Narrow your choice down to a particular class of car—sports, station wagon, mini-van, sedan, large luxury, SUV, truck, or economy car. These are general classifications and some cars may fit into more than one category. In most cases, *The Car Book* presents the vehicles by size class.

2 Determine what features are really important to you. Most buyers consider safety on the top of their list, which is why the "Safety Chapter" is right up front in *The Car Book*. Airbags, power options, the general size, number of passengers, as well as "hidden" elements such as maintenance and insurance costs, should be considered at this stage in your selection process.

3 Find three or four cars that meet the needs you outlined above and your pocketbook. It's important not to narrow your choice down to one car because then you lose all your bargaining power in the showroom. (Why? Because you might lose the psychological ability to walk away from a bad deal!) In fact, because cars today are more similar than dissimilar, it's not hard to keep three or four choices in mind. In the "Car Rating Pages" in the back of the book, we suggest some competitive choices for your consideration. For example, if you are interested in the Honda Accord, you should also consider the Toyota Camry, Ford Fusion, and Hyundai Sonata.

4 Make sure you take a good, long test drive. The biggest car buying mistake most of us make is to overlook those nagging problems that seem to surface only after we've brought the car home. Spend at least an hour driving the car and preferably without a salesperson. If a dealership won't allow you to test drive a car without a salesperson, go somewhere else. The test drive should include time on the highway, parking, taking the car in and out of your driveway or garage, sitting in the back seat, and using the trunk or storage area.

TIP: Whatever you do, don't talk price until you're ready to buy!

5 This is the stage most of us dread—negotiating the price. While price negotiation is a car buying tradition, a few dealers are trying to break tradition by offering so-called "no-haggle" or "posted" pricing. Since they're still in the minority and because it's very hard for an individual to establish true competition between dealers, we recommend avoiding negotiating altogether by using the non-profit CarBargains pricing service described on page 68.

THE 180-DEGREE TURN

When buying a car, remember that you have the most important weapon in the bargaining process: the 180-degree turn. Be prepared to walk away from a deal, even at the risk of losing the "very best deal" your salesperson has ever offered, and you will be in the best position to get a real "best deal." Remember: Dealerships need you, the buyer, to survive.

IN THE SHOWROOM

Being prepared is the best way to turn a potentially intimidating showroom experience into a profitable one. Here's some advice on handling what you'll find in the showroom.

Beware of silence. Silence is often used to intimidate, so be prepared for long periods of time when the salesperson is "talking with the manager." This tactic is designed to make you want to "just get the negotiation over with." Instead of becoming a victim, do something that indicates you are serious about looking elsewhere. Bring the classified section of the newspaper and begin circling other cars or review brochures from other manufacturers. By sending the message that you have other options, you increase your bargaining power and speed up the process.

Don't fall in love with a car. Never look too interested in any particular car. Advise family members who go with you against being too enthusiastic about any one car. Tip: Beat the dealers at their own game—bring along a friend who tells you that the price is "too much compared to the other deal," or "I really liked that other car much better," or "wasn't that other car much cheaper?"

Keep your wallet in your pocket. Don't leave a deposit, even if it's refundable. You'll feel pressure to rush your shopping, and you'll have to return and face the salesperson again before you are ready.

Shop at the end of the month. Salespeople anxious to meet sales goals are more willing to negotiate a lower price at this time.

Buy last year's model. The majority of new cars are the same as the previous year, with minor cosmetic changes. You can save considerably by buying in early fall when dealers are clearing space for "new" models. The important trade-off you make using this technique is that the carmaker may have added a new safety feature to an otherwise unchanged vehicle.

Buying from stock. You can often get a better deal on a car that the dealer has on the lot. However, these cars often have expensive options you may not want or need. Do not hesitate to ask the dealer to remove an option (and its accompanying charge) or sell you the car without charging for the option. The longer the car sits there, the more interest the dealer pays on the car, which increases the dealer's incentive to sell.

Ordering a car. Cars can be ordered from the manufacturer with exactly the options you want. Simply offering a fixed amount over invoice may be attractive because it's a sure sale and the dealership has not invested in the car. All the salesperson has to do is take your order.

If you do order a car, make sure when it arrives that it includes only the options you requested. Don't fall for the trick where the dealer offers you unordered options at a "special price," because it was their mistake. If you didn't order an option, don't pay for it.

BEWARE OF MANDATORY ARBITRATION AGREEMENTS

More and more dealers are adding mandatory binding arbitration agreements, which they often call "dispute resolution mechanisms," to your purchase contract. What this means is that you waive the right to sue or appeal any problem you have with the vehicle. Before you start negotiating the price, ask if the dealer requires Mandatory Binding Arbitration. If so, and they won't remove that requirement, you should buy elsewhere. Many dealers do not have this requirement.

GETTING THE BEST PRICE

One of the most difficult aspects of buying a new car is getting the best price. Most of us are at a disadvantage negotiating because we don't know how much the car actually cost the dealer. The difference between what the dealer paid and the sticker price represents the negotiable amount.

Beware, now that most savvy consumers know to check the so-called "dealer invoice," the industry has camouflaged this number. Special incentives, rebates, and kickbacks can account for $500 to $2,000 worth of extra profit to a dealer selling a car at "dealer invoice." The non-profit Center for the Study of Services recently discovered that in 37 percent of cases when dealers are forced to bid against each other, they offered the buyer a price below the "dealer invoice"—an unlikely event if the dealer was actually losing money. The bottom line is that "dealer invoice" doesn't really mean dealer cost.

You can't really negotiate with only one dealer, you need to get two or three bidding against each other. Introducing competition is the best way to get the lowest price on a new car. To do this you have to convince two or three dealers that you are, in fact, prepared to buy a car; that you have decided on the make, model, and features; and that your decision now rests solely on which dealer will give you the best price. You can try to do this by phone, but often dealers will not give you the best price, or will quote you a price over the phone that they will not honor later. Instead, you should try to do this in person. As anyone knows who has ventured into an auto showroom simply to get the best price, the process can be lengthy and terribly arduous. Nevertheless, if you can convince the dealer that you are serious and are willing to take the time to go to a number of dealers, it will pay off. Be sure the dealer knows that you simply want the best price for the particular make, model and options. Otherwise, we suggest you use the CarBargains service described on page 68.

Here are some other showroom strategies:

Shop away from home. If you find a big savings at a dealership far from your home or on the Internet, call a local dealer with the price. They may match it. If not, pick up the car from the distant dealer, knowing your trip has saved you hundreds of dollars. You can still bring it to your local dealer for warranty work and repairs.

Beware of misleading advertising. New car ads are meant to get you into the showroom. They usually promise low prices, big rebates, high trade-in, and spotless integrity—don't be deceived. Advertised prices are rarely the true selling price. They usually exclude transportation charges, service fees, or document fees. And always look out for the asterisk, both in advertisements and on invoices. It can be a signal that the advertiser has something to hide.

Don't talk price until you're ready to buy. On your first few trips to the showroom, simply look over the cars, decide what options you want, and do your test-driving.

Shop the corporate twins. Page 75 contains a list of corporate twins—nearly identical cars that carry different name plates. Check the price and options of the twins of the car you like. A higher-priced twin may have more options, so it may be a better deal than the lower-priced car without the options you want.

Watch out for dealer preparation overcharges. Before paying the dealer to clean your car, make sure that preparation is not included in the basic price. The price sticker will state: "Manufacturer's suggested retail price of this model includes dealer preparation."

If you must negotiate . . . negotiate up from the "invoice" price rather than down from the sticker price. Simply make an offer close to or at the "invoice" price. If the salesperson says that your offer is too low to make a profit, ask to see the factory invoice.

Don't trade in. Although it is more work, you can usually do better by selling your old car yourself than by trading it in. To determine what you'll gain by selling the car yourself, check the NADA Official Used Car Guide at your credit union or library. On the web, the Kelly Blue Book website at kbb.com is a good source for invoice pricing. The difference between the trade-in price (what the dealer will give you) and the retail price (what you typically can sell it for) is your extra payment for selling the car yourself. Another option is to get a bid for your car from one of the national used car chains, such as CarMax. They do buy used cars with no obligation for you to buy from them.

If you do decide to trade your car in at the dealership, keep the buying and selling separate. First, negotiate the best price for your new car, then find out how much the dealer will give you for your old car. Keeping the two deals separate ensures that you know what you're paying for your new car and simplifies the entire transaction.

Question everything the dealer writes down. Nothing is etched in stone. Because things are written down, we tend not to question them. This is wrong—always assume that anything written down is negotiable.

BUYING FOR SAFETY

So how do you buy for safety? Many consumers mistakenly believe that handling and performance are the key elements in the safety of a car. While an extremely unresponsive car could cause an accident, most new cars meet basic handling requirements. In fact, many people actually feel uncomfortable driving high performance cars because the highly responsive steering, acceleration, and suspension systems can be difficult to get used to. But the main reason handling is overrated as a safety measure is that automobile collisions are, by nature, accidents. Once they've begun, they are beyond human capacity to prevent, no matter how well your car handles. So the key to protecting yourself is to purchase a car that offers a high degree of crash protection and automatic crash avoidance features.

When it comes to crash protection there are amazing new features to look for which we describe in the Safety Chapter and in the Guide to the Ratings on pages 79-80.

Here's a general list of what you should look for:

Dynamic Head Restraints: They adjust properly in an accident.

Safety Belt Air Bags: Just being introduced.

Lane Keeping Assist: Keeps you within the white lines.

Automatic Crash Braking: Applies the brakes faster than you can.

Blind Spot Detection: Keeps you from hitting another vehicle.

Rear View Cameras: Keeps children safe and helps with parking.

Adaptive Cruise Control: Keeps you in check with surrounding highway traffic.

Roll Sensing Airbags: Offer extra protection in a rollover.

CARBARGAINS' BEST PRICE SERVICE

Even with the information that we provide you in this chapter of *The Car Book*, many of us still will not be comfortable negotiating for a fair price. In fact, as we indicated on the previous page, we believe it's really very difficult to negotiate the best price with a single dealer. The key to getting the best price is to get dealers to compete with each other.

CarBargains is a service of the non-profit Consumers' CHECK-BOOK, a consumer group that provides comparative price and quality information for many products and services.

CarBargains will "shop" the dealerships in your area and obtain at least five price quotes for the make and model of the car that you want to buy. The dealers who submit quotes know that they are competing with other area dealerships and have agreed to honor the prices that they submit. It is important to note that CarBargains is not an auto broker or "car buying" service; they have no affiliation with dealers.

Here's how the service works:

1. You provide CarBargains with the specific make, model, and style of car you wish to buy (Toyota Camry XLE, for example) by phone or mail.

2. Within two weeks, CarBargains will send you dealer quote sheets from at least five local dealers who have bid against one another to sell you that car. Each dealer's offer is actually a commitment to a dollar amount above (or below) "factory invoice cost" for that model. You get the name and phone number of the manager responsible for handling the quote.

You will also receive a print-out that enables you to figure the exact cost for each available option you might want on the vehicle.

3. Determine which dealer offers the best price using the dealer quote sheets. Add up the cost including the specific options you want. Contact the sales manager of that dealership and arrange to purchase the car.

If a car with the options you want is not available on the dealer's lot, you can, in many cases, have the dealer order the car from the factory or from another dealer at the agreed price.

When you receive your quotes, you will also get some suggestions on low-cost sources of financing and a valuation of your used car (trade-in).

The price for this service ($250) may seem expensive, but when you consider the savings that will result by having dealers bid against each other, as well as the time and effort of trying to get these bids yourself, we believe it's a great value. The dealers know they have a bona fide buyer (you've paid for the service); they know they are bidding against five to seven of their competitors; and, you have CarBargains' experts on your side.

To obtain CarBargains' competitive price quotes, call them at 800-475-7283 or visit their website at www.carbargains.org. Or, you can send a check for $250 to CarBargains, 1625 K St., NW, 8th Floor, Washington, DC 20006. Be sure to include your complete mailing address, phone number, and e-mail address (in case of questions), and the exact make, model, style, and year of the car you want to buy. You should receive your report within two weeks.

! AUTO BROKERS !

While CarBargains is a non-profit organization created to help you find the best price for the car you want to purchase, auto brokers are typically in the business to make money. As such, the price you end up paying for the car will include additional profit for the broker. There have been cases where the auto broker makes certain promises, takes your money, and you never hear from him again. While many brokers are legitimately trying to get their customers the best price, others have developed special relationships with certain dealers and may not do much shopping for you. As a consumer, it is difficult to tell which are which. This is why we recommend CarBargains. If CarBargains is not for you, then we suggest you consider using a buying service associated with your credit union or auto club. They can arrange for the purchase of a car at some fixed price over "dealer invoice."

FINANCING

You've done your test-drive, researched prices, studied crash tests, determined the options you want, and haggled to get the best price. Now you have to decide how to pay for the car.

If you have the cash, pay for the car right away. You avoid finance charges, you won't have a large debt haunting you, and the full value of the car is yours. You can then make the monthly payments to yourself to save up for your next car.

However, most of us cannot afford to pay cash for a car, which leaves two options: financing or leasing. While leasing may seem more affordable, financing will actually cost you less. When you finance a car, you own it after you finish your payments. At the end of a lease, you have nothing. We don't recommend leasing, but if you want more information, see page 71.

Shop around for interest rates. Most banks and credit unions will knock off at least a quarter of a percent for their customers. Have these quotes handy when you talk financing with the dealer.

The higher your down payment, the less you'll have to finance. This will not only reduce your overall interest charges, but often qualifies you for a lower interest rate.

Avoid long car loans. The monthly payments are lower, but you'll pay far more in overall interest charges. For example, a two-year, $25,000 loan at 4 percent will cost you $1,055 in interest; the same amount at five years will cost you $2,625— well over twice as much!

Beware of manufacturer promotional rates—the 0 to 1 percent rates you see advertised. These low rates are usually only valid on two or three-year loans and only for the most credit-worthy customers.

Read everything you are asked to sign and ask questions about anything you don't fully understand.

Make sure that an extended warranty has not been added to the purchase price. Dealers will sometimes do this without telling you. Extended warranties are generally a bad value. See the "Warranties" chapter for more information.

Credit Unions vs. Banks: Credit unions generally charge fewer and lower fees and offer better rates than banks. In addition, credit unions offer counseling services where consumers can find pricing information on cars or compare monthly payments for financing. You can join a credit union either through your employer, an organization or club, or if you have a relative who is part of a credit union.

DON'T BE TONGUE-TIED

Beware of high-pressure phrases like "I've talked to the manager and this is really the best we can do. As it is, we're losing money on this deal." Rarely is this true. Dealers are in the business to make money and most do very well. Don't tolerate a take-it-or-leave-it attitude. Simply repeat that you will only buy when you see the deal you want and that you don't appreciate the dealer pressuring you. Threaten to leave if the dealer continues to pressure you to buy today.

Don't let the dealer answer your questions with a question. If you ask, "Can I get this same car with leather seats?" and the salesperson answers, "If I get you leather seats in this car, will you buy today?" this response tries to force you to decide to buy before you are ready. Ask the dealer to just answer your question and say that you'll buy when you're ready. It's the dealer's job to answer questions, not yours.

If you are having a difficult time getting what you want, ask the dealer: "Why won't you let me buy a car today?" Most salespeople will be thrown off by this phrase as they are often too busy trying to use it on you. If they respond in frustration, "OK, what do you want?" then you can make straightforward answers to simple questions.

Get a price; don't settle for: "If you're shopping price, go to the other dealers first and then come back." This technique ensures that they don't have to truly negotiate. Your best response is: "I only plan to come back if your price is the lowest, so that's what I need today, your lowest price."

TYPICAL OPERATING COSTS

Here are the annual operating costs for some popular vehicles. These costs include operating expenses (fuel, oil, maintenance, and tires) and ownership expenses (insurance, financing, taxes, depreciation, and licensing) and are based on keeping the vehicle for 3 years and driving 20,000 miles per year. This information is from Runzheimer International. Runzheimer evaluated thirty 2016 model cars, vans, SUVs, and light trucks and determined the most and least expensive to operate among those vehicles. (Source: Runzheimer International, www.runzheimer.com)

Projected Ownership and Operating Costs for Selected 2016 Cars for 3 Years Based on Driving 20,000 miles per Year

Most Expensive	
Hyundai Equus Signature 8-cyl. 5.0L	$23,262
Mercedes-Benz E350 6-cyl. 3.5L	$20,753
Cadillac CTS Luxury 6-cyl. 3.6L	$20,409
Buick Lacrosse Leather 6-cyl. 3.6L	$16,347
Ford Taurus Limited AWD 6-cyl. 3.5L	$15,529
Least Expensive	
Nissan Altima S 4-cyl. 2.5L	$10,838
Mazda Mazda3 I Grand Touring 4-cyl. 2.0L	$10,429
Mazda Mazda3 I Touring 4-cyl. 2.0L	$9,798
Chevrolet Sonic LT 4-cyl. 1.8L	$9,323
Toyota Corolla LE 4-cyl. 1.8L	$9,197

Projected Ownership and Operating Costs for Selected 2016 Light Trucks, Vans, and SUVs

Most Expensive	
Chevrolet Tahoe LS 4WD 8-cyl. 5.3L	$17,550
Ford F250 XL 2WD 8FT 8-cyl. 6.2L	$16,032
Dodge Grand Caravan R/T 6-cyl. 3.6L	$14,299
Jeep Grand Cherokee Laredo 6-cyl. 3.6L	$13,622
Chevrolet Silverado 1500 LS 6-cyl. 4.3L	$13,316
Least Expensive	
Chev. Silverado 1500 Work 2WD 8FT 6-cyl. 4.3L	$12,895
Chev. Silverado 1500 Work 2WD 6FT 6-cyl. 4.3L	$12,619
Dodge Grand Caravan AVP 6-cyl. 3.6L	$11,926
Ford Escape SE 4-cyl. 2L	$11,841
Toyota Tacoma SR5 4-cyl. 2.7L	$10,227

Runzheimer International is providing the attached information for reference only. Any direct reproduction or publication of this data in its entirety without prior consent from Runzheimer International is strictly forbidden. Runzheimer International is an international management consulting firm that provides workforce mobility solutions relating to business vehicles, relocation, travel management, corporate aircraft, and mobile device management programs.

LEASING VS. BUYING

About 25% of new car sales are actually leases. Unfortunately, most leasees don't realize that, in spite of the low monthly payments, leasing costs more than buying.

When you pay cash or finance a car, you own an asset; leasing leaves you with nothing except all the headaches and responsibilities of ownership with none of the benefits. When you lease you pay a monthly fee for a pre-determined time in exchange for the use of a car. However, you also pay for maintenance, insurance, and repairs as if you owned the car. Finally, when it comes time to turn in the car, it has to be in top shape—otherwise, you'll have to pay for repairs, clean up, or body work.

If you are considering a lease, here are some leasing terms you need to know and some tips to get you through the process:

Capitalized Cost is the price of the car on which the lease is based. Negotiate this as if you were buying the car. Capitalized Cost Reduction is your down payment.

Know the make and model of the vehicle you want. Tell the agent exactly how you want the car equipped. You don't have to pay for options you don't request. Decide in advance how long you will keep the car.

Find out the price of the options on which the lease is based. Typically, they will be full retail price. Their cost can be negotiated (albeit with some difficulty) before you settle on the monthly payment.

Make sure options like a sunroof or stereo are added to the Capitalized Cost. When you purchase dealer-added options,

be sure they add the full cost of the option to the Capitalized Cost so that you only pay for the depreciated value of the option, not the full cost.

Find out how much you are required to pay at delivery. Most leases require at least the first month's payment. Others have a security deposit, registration fees, or other "hidden costs." When shopping around, make sure price quotes include security deposit and taxes—sales tax, monthly use tax, or gross receipt tax. Ask how the length of the lease affects your monthly cost.

Find out how the lease price was determined. Lease prices are generally based on the manufacturer's suggested retail price, less the predetermined residual value. The best values are cars with a high expected residual value. To protect themselves, leasers tend to underestimate residual value, but you can do little about this estimate.

Find out the annual mileage limit. Don't accept a contract with a lower limit than you need. Most standard contracts

allow 15,000 to 18,000 miles per year. If you go under the allowance one year, you can go over it the next. Watch out for Excess Mileage fees. If you go over, you'll get charged per mile.

Avoid "capitalized cost reduction" or "equity leases." Here the leaser offers to lower the monthly payment by asking you for more money up front—in other words, a down payment.

Ask about early termination. Between 30 and 40 percent of two-year leases are terminated early and 40–60 percent of four-year leases terminate early—this means expensive early termination fees. If you terminate the lease before it is up, what are the financial penalties? Typically, they are very high so watch out. Ask the dealer exactly what you would owe at the end of each year if you wanted out of the lease. Remember, if your car is stolen, the lease will typically be terminated. While your insurance should cover the value of the car, you still may owe addi-

---

TIP

LEASEWISE

If you must lease, why haggle when you can let someone else do it for you? LeaseWise, a service from the non-profit Center for the Study of Services, makes dealers bid for your lease. First, they get leasing bids from dealers on the vehicles you're interested in. Next, you'll receive a detailed report with all the bids, the dealer and invoice cost of the vehicle, and a complete explanation of the various bids. Then, you can lease from the lowest bidder or use the report as leverage with another dealer. The service costs $350. For more information, call 800-475-7283, or visit www.checkbook.org/auto/leasew.cfm

tional amounts per your lease contract.

Avoid maintenance contracts. Getting work done privately is cheaper in the long run. And don't forget, this is a new car with a standard warranty.

Arrange for your own insurance. By shopping around, you can generally find less expensive insurance than what's offered by the lessor.

Ask how quickly you can expect delivery. If your agent can't deliver in a reasonable time, maybe he or she can't meet the price quoted.

Retain your option to buy the car at the end of the lease at a predetermined price. The price should equal the residual value; if it is more then the leaser is trying to make an additional profit. Regardless of how the end-of-lease value is determined, if you want the car, make an offer based on the current "Blue Book" value of the car at the end of the lease.

Residual Value is the value of your car at the end of the lease.

Here's what Automotive Lease Guide estimates the residual value after five years will be for a few 2016 vehicles:

Acura MDX	44%
Subaru Impreza	40%
Hyundai Elantra	40%
Ford Edge	36%
Nissan Titan	34%

LEASING VS. BUYING

The following table compares the costs of leasing vs. buying the same car over three and six years. Your actual costs may vary, but you can use this format to compare the cars you are considering. Our example assumes the residual value to be 68 percent after three years and 43 percent after six years.

3 Years	36 month Lease	5 Yr Loan–2.7% Sell in 3 Yrs
MSRP	$33,500	$33,500
Lease Value/Purchase Price[1]	$30,150	$30,150
Initial Payment/Down Payment[2]	$3,110	$3,015
Loan Amount		$27,135
Monthly Payments[3]	$320	$484
Total Payments (first 3 years of loan)[4]	$11,520	$17,424
Excess miles and disposition fees[5]	$480	
Total Cost[6]	$15,110	$20,439
Amount Left on Loan		$11,295
Less Value of Vehicle .55 residual[7]		$18,425
Overall Cost, first 3 years	$15,110	$13,309
Savings over Leasing 3 Years		$1,801

6 Years[8]	2nd 3 Yr Lease	5 Yr Loan–2.7% Keep Car 6 yrs.
MSRP - 2nd Car 5% increase in cost	$35,175	$33,500
Lease Value/Purchase Cost of Car	$31,650	$30,150
Initial Payment/Down Payment[2]	$3,260	$3,015
Loan Amount		$27,135
Monthly Payment[3]	$320	$484
Total Payments[4]	$11,520	$29,040
Excess miles and disposition fees[5]	$480	
Total Cost of 2nd Lease[9]	$15,260	
Total Cost[6]	$27,110	$32,055
Amount Left on Loan		$–
Less Value of Vehicle .40 residual 6 yrs[10]		$13,400
Overall Cost, 6 years[11]	$27,110	$18,655
Savings Over Leasing 6 Years		$8,455

[1] Purchase price reflects that most buyer's pay about 90% of the MSRP
[2] Initial lease payment based on typical lease deals for January 2016 as reported by US News and World Report; Purchase down payment is based on typical 10% down.
[3] Monthly lease payments based on typical lease deals for January 2016 as reported by US News and World Report. Monthly finance payments are based on a 5 year loan with a 2.7% interest rate.
[4] Total amounts (lease and finance) paid for 3 years.
[5] Total average excess mileage fee of $480 based on a 12000 mile limit and averages 3 typical situations: 25% of leasers going over the 1500 mile limit at $0.15/mile; 50% of leasers pre-paying for expected mile overages of 1500 miles at $0.10/mile, and 25% of leasers not exceeding the mileage limit–plus a typical disposition fee based on average of $350.
[6] Total amount paid during period; includes down payment, monthly payments, and excess mile and disposition fees for leasing.
[7] Three-year residual value of 55 percent based on average actual 36-month residual value for the top 10 selling vehicles for model year 2016.
[8] Second 3-year lease costs assume a 5% increase for a similar vehicle. Five-year loan with 2.7 percent annual percentage rate, no monthly payments in the sixth year.
[9] Total amount paid during 2nd lease period; includes initial payment, monthly payments, and excess mile and disposition fees for leasing.
[10] Six-year residual value of 40 percent based on average actual 72-month residual value for the top 10 selling vehicles for model year 2016.
[11] Six-year overall cost for lease is total of first 3-year lease and second 3-year lease.

USING THE INTERNET

The Internet is changing the way car buyers research and shop for cars. But the Internet should be used with caution. Anyone can publish a website with no guarantee concerning the accuracy of the information on it. We advise that you only visit websites that have a familiar non-web counterpart. A good example is the Center for Auto Safety's website at www. autosafety.org where you can find information on auto safety, including publications and newsletters which are typically mailed out to subscribers.

Use the Internet as an information resource. Unfortunately, most automaker websites are nothing more than sophisticated ads with little comparative information. However, many do include a "build your own" feature which you can use to get the MSRP for the cars you are considering. While you never want to pay MSRP, it's a good way to get a general sense of the cost.

There are also several online car shopping services that have launched. We view most of them with skepticism. Many online car shopping services are tied to a limited, often non-competitive, group of dealers. They may claim the lowest price, but you'll most likely have a dealer calling you with a price that is not much better than what you'd get if you went into a dealership.

Auto insurance and financing sites are sometimes no better. Don't rely solely on these online services; getting quotes from other sources is the only way to make sure you truly have the best deal.

Finally, clicking a mouse is no substitute for going out and test-driving a car. If you are shopping for a used car, you must check out the actual car before signing on the dotted line. Do not rely on online photos. In fact, online classifieds for cars are no more reliable than looking in a newspaper.

If you do use an online car shopping service, be sure to shop around on your own. Visit dealerships, get quotes from several car shopping services, and research the value of your used car (see www.nadaguides.com). Beware that if you give anyone online your phone number, or email address, you are opening yourself up to unwanted email, junk mail, and even sales calls.

ON THE WEB

autosafety.org
The Center for Auto Safety (CAS) provides consumers with a voice for auto safety and quality in Washington and to help lemon owners fight back across the country.

carfax.com
Carfax collects information from numerous sources to provide a vehicle history on a specific vehicle, based on the Vehicle Identification Number (VIN). Carfax can help uncover costly and potentially dangerous hidden problems. Beware, however, a "clean" history may be because serious problems were never reported.

checkbook.org
The Center for the Study of Services (CSS) is an independent, nonprofit consumer organization and the creator of Consumers' CHECKBOOK. One of the few car buying services worth using, CHECKBOOK's CarBargains service pits dealers against each other, keeping you from haggling, and using the power of competitive bidding to get you a great price.

safercar.gov
The National Highway Traffic Safety Administration (NHTSA) website contains useful information on safety standards, crash tests, recalls, technical service bulletins, child seats, and safety advisories.

fueleconomy.gov
This joint effort by the Department of Energy and the Environmental Protection Agency contains EPA fuel economy ratings for passenger cars and trucks from 1985 to the present, gas saving tips, greenhouse gas and air pollution ratings, energy impact scores, a downloadable Fuel Economy Guide, and a variety of other useful information in a very user-friendly format.

DEPRECIATION

Over the past 20 years, new vehicle depreciation costs have steadily increased. A study con-ducted by Runzheimer International shows that depreciation and interest now account for just over 50 percent of the costs of owning and operating a vehicle. Recently, however, the increasing cost of depreciation has slowed down. This is due to the relatively stable prices of new vehicles and to the stabilization in finance rates.

While there is no foolproof method for predicting retained vehicle value, your best bet is to purchase a popular vehicle model. Chances are, though not always, it will also be a popular used vehicle, meaning that it will retain more of its value when you go to sell it.

Most new cars are traded in within four years and are then available on the used car market. The priciest used cars may not be the highest quality. Supply and demand, as well as appearance, are important factors in determining used car prices.

The following table indicates which of the top-selling 2012 cars held their value the best and which did not.

2012 VEHICLES WITH THE BEST AND WORST RESALE VALUE

THE BEST				THE WORST			
Model	2012 Price	2015 Price	Retain. Value	Model	2012 Price	2015 Price	Retain. Value
Toyota Tacoma	$27,835	$27,225	97.8%	Chevrolet Impala	$25,645	$11,950	46.6%
Jeep Wrangler	$29,995	$27,550	91.8%	Hyundai Elantra	$21,600	$11,150	51.6%
Toyota 4Runner	$31,090	$27,200	87.5%	Ford Focus	$16,500	$8,950	54.2%
Toyota Tundra	$30,335	$26,225	86.5%	Chrysler T&C	$30,360	$16,650	54.8%
Subaru Forester	$20,595	$17,375	84.4%	Dodge Avenger	$18,995	$10,425	54.9%
Subaru Outback	$23,295	$18,500	79.4%	Chrysler 200	$18,995	$10,525	55.4%
Nissan Versa	$10,990	$8,450	76.9%	Volkswagen Passat	$25,995	$14,450	55.6%
Jeep Grand Cherokee	$26,995	$20,750	76.9%	Mazda 3	$19,225	$10,850	56.4%
Chevrolet Silverado	$29,530	$22,325	75.6%	Chevrolet Malibu	$21,995	$12,425	56.5%
Chevrolet Camaro	$23,200	$17,500	75.4%	Ford Edge	$27,640	$15,825	57.3%
Toyota Highlander	$28,090	$21,050	74.9%	Ford Fusion	$19,850	$11,400	57.4%
Jeep Patriot	$17,745	$13,225	74.5%	Dodge Grand Caravan	$22,995	$13,275	57.7%
Chevrolet Cruze	$16,720	$12,375	74.0%	Honda Odyssey	$28,225	$16,300	57.8%
Chevrolet Equinox	$23,450	$17,100	72.9%	Scion iQ	$15,265	$8,950	58.6%
Toyota Corolla	$16,130	$11,700	72.5%	Ford Escape	$21,240	$12,600	59.3%
BMW 3 Series	$38,500	$27,750	72.1%	Hyundai Sonata	$23,095	$13,775	59.6%
Ram Pickup	$29,225	$20,950	71.7%	GMC Terrain	$26,880	$16,350	60.8%
Chevrolet Traverse	$29,430	$20,725	70.4%	Volkswagen Jetta	$16,495	$10,050	60.9%
Kia Soul	$13,900	$9,750	70.1%	Honda Civic	$20,505	$12,575	61.3%
Lexus RX	$39,075	$27,300	69.9%	GMC Sierra	$30,320	$19,000	62.7%
Honda CR-V	$25,445	$17,775	69.9%	Honda Accord	$21,380	$13,400	62.7%
Honda Pilot	$31,320	$21,750	69.4%	Toyota Camry	$21,955	$13,900	63.3%
Ford Explorer	$28,170	$19,550	69.4%	Dodge Charger	$25,495	$16,150	63.3%
Toyota RAV4	$22,650	$15,500	68.4%	Nissan Sentra	$16,060	$10,325	64.3%
Nissan Altima	$20,410	$13,925	68.2%	Toyota Sienna	$29,700	$19,100	64.3%

CORPORATE TWINS

"Corporate twins" refers to vehicles that have different names but share the same mechanics, drivetrain, and chassis. In many cases the vehicles are identical. Sometimes the difference is in body style, price, or options as with the Chevrolet Tahoe and the Cadillac Escalade.

While corporate twins share the same basic structure and running gear, some will drive and feel different because of the tuning of the suspension, the standard equipment and options available, and the the comfort and convenience features. One twin may stress a soft ride and

luxury while another a tighter, sportier feel.

Historically, corporate twins have been limited mainly to domestic car companies. Today, several Asian and European car companies have started the practice.

CORPORATE TWINS

Chrysler Corp.
Chrysler 300
Dodge Charger

Ford Motor Co.
Ford Escape
Lincoln MKC

Ford Expedition
Lincoln Navigator

Ford Fusion
Lincoln MKZ

General Motors
Buick Encore
Chevrolet Trax

Buick LaCrosse
Cadillac XTS
Chevrolet Impala

Buick Verano
Chevrolet Cruze

Cadillac Escalade
Chevrolet Tahoe
GMC Yukon

General Motors (cont.)
Cadillac Escalade ESV
Chevrolet Suburban
GMC Yukon XL

Chevrolet Colorado
GMC Canyon

Chevrolet Equinox
GMC Terrain

Chevrolet Silverado
GMC Sierra

Chevrolet Traverse
GMC Acadia

Honda
Acura TLX
Honda Accord

Hyundai–Kia
Hyundai Accent
Kia Rio

Hyundai Azera
Kia Cadenza

Hyundai–Kia (cont.)
Hyundai Elantra
Kia Forte

Nissan
Nissan Pathfinder
Infiniti QX60

Toyota
Lexus ES
Toyota Avalon

Lexus NX
Toyota RAV4

Lexus GX
Toyota 4Runner

Volkswagen-Audi
Audi A3
Volkswagen Golf

Audi Q3
Volkswagen Tiguan

Cadillac Escalade

Chevrolet Tahoe

GMC Yukon

This section provides an overview of the most important features of this year's new models. Nearly all the information you'll need to make a smart choice is concisely presented on one page. (The data are collected for the model expected to be the most popular.) Here's what you'll find and how to interpret the data we've provided:

The Ratings

These are the ratings in nine important categories, as well as an overall comparative rating. We have adopted the Olympic rating system with "10" being the best.

Overall Crash Test: This rating represents a combination of the front and side crash test ratings and provides a relative comparison of how this year's models did against each other. We give the best performers a 10 and the worst a 1. Remember to compare crash test results relative to other cars in the same size class. For details, see page 19.

Safety Features: This is an evaluation of how much extra safety is built into the car. We give credit for torso and pelvis side airbags, roll-sensing side airbags, knee bolster bag, crash imminent braking, daytime running lamps, adjustable upper seat belt anchorages, lane keeping assist, pedestrian crash avoidance, automatic crash notification, lane departure warning, dynamic brake support, and frontal collision warning. We also include dynamic head restraint, backup cameras and blind spot detection among other important safety features. See the "Safety Checklist" descriptions on the following pages.

Rollover: Many consumers are aware that vehicles with higher centers of gravity could be more likely to roll over. Comparing the tendency of a vehicle to roll over is very difficult, as there is no agreed upon comparative rating system. The U.S. government adopted the rating system that we have been using called the static stability formula (SSF). The government provides the SSF rating for some vehicles. For those vehicles not on the government list, we use the SSF formula to provide a rating. (See page 32.)

Preventive Maintenance: Each manufacturer suggests a preventive maintenance schedule designed to keep the car in good shape and to protect your rights under the warranty. Those with the lowest estimated PM costs get a 10 and the highest a 1. See pages 39-43 for the estimated costs and more information.

Repair Costs: It is virtually impossible to predict exactly what any new car will cost you in repairs. As such, we take nine typical repairs that you are likely to experience after your warranty expires and compare those costs among this year's models. Those with the lowest cost get a 10 and the highest a 1. See pages 39-43 for specific part repair cost and more information.

Warranty: This is an overall assessment of the manufacturer's basic, powertrain, corrosion, and roadside assistance warranties compared to all other manufacturer warranties. We also give credit for perks like free scheduled maintenance. We give the highest-rated warranties a 10 and the lowest a 1. For details, see page 36.

Fuel Economy: Here we compare the EPA mileage ratings of each car. The misers get a 10 and the guzzlers get a 1. For the purposes of the overall rating we pick the fuel economy rating of what is expected to be the most popular engine and drive train configuration. See page 33 for more information.

Complaints: This is where you'll find how each vehicle stacks up against hundreds of others on the road, based on the U.S. government complaint data for that vehicle. If the car has not been around long enough to have developed a complaint history, it is given a 5 (average). The least complained about cars get a 10 and the most problematic a 1. See page 55 for details.

Insurance Costs: Insurance companies rate vehicles to determine how much they plan to charge for insurance. While each insurer may have slightly different methods of rating, vehicles typically get a discount (max and min), a surcharge (max and min) or neither (average or typical). We looked at data from the insurance rating program of the largest insurer in America. This rating can predict the cost of insuring that vehicle, however, your location, age, driving record, and other factors also play a significant role in your cost of insurance. (See The Insurance Section page 49.) Vehicles with a low rating (1 or 3) are more expensive to insure than other vehicles in that class or category. On the other hand, vehicles with a high rating (8 or 10) would be less expensive to insure in that particular class of vehicles. Because insurance companies may rate vehicles differently, it's important to compare prices between companies before you buy the car.

Overall Rating: This is the "bottom line." Using a combination of all of the key ratings, this tells how this vehicle stacks up against the others on a scale of 1 to 10. Due to the importance of safety, the combined crash test rating is 20 percent of the overall rating while the other eight ratings are 10 percent each. Vehicles with no front or side crash test results, as of our publication date, cannot be given an overall rating. In other categories, if information is unavailable, an "average" is included in order to develop an overall rating.

At-a-Glance

Status: Here we tell you if a vehicle is all-new, unchanged, or has received appearance change. All-new vehicles (the minority) are brand new from the ground up. Unchanged vehicles are essentially the same, but could have some different color or feature options. Vehicles with an appearance change are those whose internal workings stayed essentially the same, but have updated body panels.

Year Series Started: Each year the model is made, the production usually improves and as a result there are fewer defects. Therefore, the longer a car has been made, the less likely you are to be plagued with manufacturing and design defects. On the other hand, the newer a car is, the more likely it is to have the latest in features and safety.

Twins: These are cars with different make and model names but share the same mechanics, drive train, and chassis. In some cases the vehicles are identical, in other cases the body style, pricing or options are different.

Body Styles: This is a listing of the various body styles available such as coupe, sedan, wagon, etc. SUVs and minivans are only offered in one body style. Data on the page are for the first style listed.

Seating: This is the number of seating positions in the most popular model. When more than one number is listed (for example, 5/6) it means that different seat configurations are available.

Anti-theft Device: This lists the anti-theft devices standard for the vehicle. An immobilizer is an electronic device fitted to an automobile which prevents the engine from running unless the correct key (or other token) is present. This prevents the car from being "hot-wired" and driven away. A car alarm is an electronic device that emits high-volume sound and can sometimes flash the vehicles headlights in an attempt to discourage theft of the vehicle itself, its contents, or both. Passive devices automati-

cally enter an armed state after the ignition is turned off and doors are closed. Active devices require the user to perform some action like pressing a button to arm and disarm the system.

Parking Index Rating: Using the car's length, wheelbase, and turning circle, we have calculated how easy it will be to maneuver this car in tight spots. This rating of "very easy" to "very hard" is an indicator of how much difficulty you may have parking.

Where Made: Here we tell you where the car was assembled. You'll find that traditional domestic companies often build their vehicles in other countries. Also, many foreign companies build their cars in the U.S.

Fuel Factor

MPG Rating (city/hwy): This is the EPA-rated fuel economy for city and highway driving measured in miles per gallon. Most models have a variety of fuel economy ratings because of different engine and transmission options. We've selected the combination expected to be most popular.

Driving Range: Given the car's expected fuel economy and gas tank size, this value gives you an idea of the number of miles you can expect to go on a tank of gas.

Fuel: The type of fuel specified by the manufacturer: regular, premium, E85.

Annual Fuel Cost: This is an estimate based on driving 15,000 miles per year at $2.10/gallon for regular and $2.35/gallon for premium. If the vehicle takes E85 (85% ethanol and 15% gasoline) or gasoline we calculated the annual cost using gasoline.

Gas Guzzler Tax: Auto companies are required to pay a gas guzzler tax on the sale of cars with exceptionally low fuel economy. This tax does not apply to light trucks.

Greenhouse Gas Emissions: This shows the amount (in tons) of greenhouse gases (carbon dioxide, nitrous oxide, and methane) that a vehicle emits per year along with the CO_2 emitted in producing and distributing the fuel.

Barrels of Oil Used Per Year: This is the number of barrels of petroleum the vehicle will likely use each year. One barrel, once refined, makes about 19.5 gallons of gas.

Competition

Here we tell you how the car stacks up with some of its key competitors. Use this information to broaden your choice of new car possibilities. This list is only a guideline, not an all-inclusive list of every possible alternative.

Price Range

This box contains information on the MSRP. When available, we offer a variety of prices between the base and the most luxurious version of the car. The difference is often substantial. Usually the more expensive versions have fancy trim, larger engines, and lots of automatic equipment. The least expensive versions usually have manual transmissions and few extra features. In addition to the price range, we provide the estimated dealer markup. Remember, prices and dealer costs can

change during the year. Use these figures for general reference and comparisons, not as a precise indication of exactly how much the car you are interested in will cost. See page 68 for a buying service designed to ensure that you get the very best price.

Safety Checklist

Crash Tests

Frontal and Side Crash Test Ratings: Here's where we tell you if the front or side crash test index was very good,

good, average, poor or very poor when compared to 2016 cars tested to date. To provide this rating we use the crash test for the vehicles with the best available safety equipment among the models when multiple models were tested. Unfortunately, not all of the 2016 models have been crash tested. If the car has been previously tested and the 2016 model is unchanged, we can carry those results forward. For details about the crash test programs, see page 19.

Airbags

All vehicles have dual front airbags and nearly all have head

TYPES OF AIRBAGS

Airbags were introduced over 30 years ago and have been so successful in saving lives that car makers now include a variety of types. Here's a rundown of the basic types of airbags available. Manufacturers have varying marketing names for these airbags.

Front: These deploy toward the front occupants and are now standard in all vehicles.
Side: These deploy from the side of the seat or door and protect both the front and rear passengers in a side impact. Bags mounted in seats offer protection in a wider range of seating positions.
Head: These deploy from above the doors and are often called curtain airbags. They can reduce head injuries, shield from spraying glass, and provide protection in rollovers.
Rollover Protection: These head curtain airbags remain inflated for five seconds to protect in a sustained rollover.
Knee Bolster: These fill space between the front occupant's knees and instrument panel protecting the knees and legs.

airbags. We've identified four additional types of airbags that the vehicle may have. The first two we list, Torso and Pelvis, have historically been seperate bag systems. Recently, most manufacturers have been combining torso and pelvis protection into one bag. When the two are combined, we list *Front Pelvis/Torso from Seat* after each airbag type. Otherwise we identify specific bag type (or not) that comes with the vehicle.

Torso Side Airbag: This airbag protects the chest from serious injury in a side impact crash.

Pelvis Side Airbag: Provides extra protection around the pelvis and hip area, the portion of the body is usually closest to the vehicles exterior.

Rollover Sensing Airbags: This is a special side airbag system which keeps the side airbags inflated longer in the event of a rollover.

Knee Bolster Airbag: This airbag fills the space between the front passenger's knees and the dashboard.

Crash Avoidance

Collision Avoidance: Great new technology is available that can react faster than you in the event of a frontal collision. There are three basic systems available: Crash Imminent Braking (CIB), Dynamic Brake Support (DBS), and Frontal Collision Warning (FCW). All of these systems use radar or laser sensors to either alert the driver (FCW) or actively intervene to apply the brakes prior to a crash. CIB will actually apply the brakes if you are about to experience a frontal crash. DBS

will increase your braking force if the sensors determine that you are not applying enough force to stop in time. FCW will merely sound an alarm in the event of an imminent frontal collision. Whenever a vehicle has CIB or DBS, it will also have a Frontal Crash Warning. We believe that Crash Imminent Braking and Dynamic Brake Support are more useful than just a Frontal Collision Warning (and thus rated higher), however FCW is still a useful safety feature. The government has set standards for FCW and we've used a ^ to indicate which systems DON'T meet the FCW requirements.

Blind Spot Detection: This is a blind spot monitor that uses radar or other technologies to detect objects in the driver's blind spot. When switching lanes a visible, audible, or vibrating alert warns if a vehicle has entered your blind spot.

Lane Keeping Assist: Going one step beyond a Lane Departure Warning, cars with Lane Keeping Assist will actually apply pressure to the brakes or adjust the steering when it senses that a car is drifting out of its lane. Lane Departure Warning (LDW) will simply alert the driver. If the vehicle has Land Keeping Assist, it will also have LDW. We have combined the two since the technology for Lane Departure Warning is required for Lane Keeping Assist, which we believe to be a better technology. The government has set standards for LDW and we've used an ^ to indicate which systems DON'T meet the low requirements.

Backup Camera: This camera allows the driver to see what is behind them on a dashboard screen. This is a critically important safety feature if you have children or drive near or around

THE BEST SAFETY FEATURES

TIP

The good news: automatic crash avoidance features are becoming more available. The bad news: it is hard to determine which ones work the best. For the first year we are indicating which of the features meet the National Highway Traffic Safety Administration standards for three important safety features: Back up cameras, Lane Depature Warning, and Frontal Collision Warning. Compliance to these standards is voluntary. In the tradition of *The Car Book*, exposing differences to stimulate market changes, we are publishing for the first time which of these three safety features meets the government standards. However, it is important to note that having one of these features that doesn't meet government standards is better than not having it at all.

children. It's also a great parking assist. For a backup camera system to meet NHTSA's voluntary standards it must meet requirements regarding image size, linger time, response time, durability and deactivation. On the safety check list we've indicated which back up cameras DON'T meet federal standards with an asterisk (*).

Pedestrian Crash Avoidance: These systems utilize a variety of technologies (infrared, camera, radar) to detect pedestrians and adjust the car's course to avoid a collision.

General

Automatic Crash Notification: Using cellular technology and global positioning systems, some vehicles have the ability to send a call for help in the event of airbag deployment or accident. Often free initially, you'll have to pay extra for this feature. There are several different types of ACN systems. Some simply dial 911 in the event of a crash while others connect your car to a call center which can determine the severity of the crash and dispatch emergency services. Some systems even send information about the crash to the call center.

Daytime Running Lights: Some cars offer daytime running lights that can reduce your chances of being in a crash by up to 40 percent by increasing the visibility of your vehicle. We indicate whether daytime running lights are standard, optional, or not available.

Safety Belts/Restraints

Dynamic Head Restraints: Many people position their seat and head restraint according to their own body and comfort requirements. This may not be the best position to protect you in a crash. These adjustors, sensing a crash, will automatically move the seat and headrest to the optimal position to help reduce injury during a rear-end crash.

Adjustable Belts: Proper positioning of the safety belt across your chest is critical to obtaining the benefits of buckling up. Some systems allow you to adjust the height of the belt so it crosses your chest properly.

Specifications

Drive: This indicates the type of drive the manufacturer offers. This could be two wheel drive in the front (FWD) or rear (RWD) or all or four wheel drive (AWD/4WD).

Engine: This is the engine size (liters) and type that is expected to be the most popular. The engine types specify V6 or V8 for six or eight cylinders and I4 for four in-line. For electric vehicles, we indicate the type of auxiliary power offered.

Transmission: This is the type of transmission expected to be the most popular. Most drivers today prefer automatic transmissions. The number listed with the transmission (5-sp.) is the number of gears or speeds. Then we list whether it's automatic or manual and if the transmission is a continuously variable transmission (CVT). CVT changes smoothly and efficiently between gears and can provide better fuel economy.

Tow Rating: Ratings of very low, low, average, high, and very high indicate the vehicle's relative ability to tow trailers or other loads. Some manufacturers do not provide a tow rating.

Head/Leg Room: This tells how roomy the front seat is. The values are given in inches and rated in comparison to all other vehicles.

Interior Space: This tells how roomy the car's passenger area should feel. This value is given in cubic feet and rated in comparison to all other vehicles. Many SUVs do not provide interior space specifications.

Cargo Space: This gives you the cubic feet available for cargo. For minivans, the volume is behind the last row of seats. In cars, it's the trunk space. We rate the roominess of the cargo space compared to all trucks, SUVs, and cars.

Wheelbase/Length: The wheelbase is the distance between the centers of the front and rear wheels and the length is the distance from front bumper to rear bumper. Wheelbase can affect the ride and length affects how big the car "feels."

Ratings—10 Best, 1 Worst

Combo Crash Tests	5
Safety Features	1
Rollover	9
Preventive Maintenance	9
Repair Costs	8
Warranty	5
Fuel Economy	6
Complaints	10
Insurance Costs	10
OVERALL RATING	**9**

Acura ILX

Safety Checklist

Crash Tests:
Frontal............................Poor
Side.............................Good

Airbags:
Torso ....Front Torso from Seat
Pelvis ....None
Roll Sensing.........................No
Knee Bolster ....None

Crash Avoidance:
Collision Avoidance ...... Optional CIB & DBS
Blind Spot Detection ....None
Lane Keeping Assist ....None
Backup Camera .... Standard
Pedestrian Crash Avoidance ....None

General:
Auto. Crash Notification... Operator Assist.-Fee
Day Running Lamps .... Standard

Safety Belt/Restraint:
Dynamic Head Restraints ....None
Adjustable Belt...............Standard Front

^Warning feature does not meet government standards.
*Backup camera does not meet government standards.

Acura ILX

At-a-Glance

Status/Year Series Started........	Unchanged/2013
Twins	–
Body Styles	Sedan
Seating	5
Anti-Theft Device	Std. Pass. Immobil. & Alarm
Parking Index Rating	Easy
Where Made...................	Greensburg, IN

Fuel Factor:
MPG Rating (city/hwy)........... Average-24/35
Driving Range (mi.) .... Very Short-369.0
Fuel Type....................... Premium
Annual Fuel Cost .... Average-$1,261
Gas Guzzler Tax .... No
Greenhouse Gas Emissions (tons/yr.).. Average-6.4
Barrels of Oil Used per year Average-11.8

How the Competition Rates

Competitors	Rating	Pg.
Audi A4	8	86
Cadillac ATS	8	107
Mercedes-Benz CLA-Class	–	208

Price Range	Retail	Markup
Base 2.0L	$27,900	8
Base 2.0L w/ Prem. Package	$29,900	8
Base 2.4L w/Prem. Package	$31,890	8
Base 2.0L w/Tech. Package	$32,900	8

Acura ILX

Specifications

Drive..................................	FWD
Engine	2.0-liter I4
Transmission	5-sp. Automatic
Tow Rating (lbs.)	–
Head/Leg Room (in.)	Cramped-38/42.3
Interior Space (cu. ft.).........	Very Cramped-89.3
Cargo Space (cu. ft.)	Very Cramped-12.3
Wheelbase/Length (in.)	105.1/179.1

Ratings—10 Best, 1 Worst

Combo Crash Tests	8
Safety Features	7
Rollover	5
Preventive Maintenance	2
Repair Costs	5
Warranty	5
Fuel Economy	3
Complaints	2
Insurance Costs	10
OVERALL RATING	**6**

Acura MDX

At-a-Glance

Status/Year Series Started. Unchanged/2014
Twins . . . . –
Body Styles . . . . SUV
Seating 7
Anti-Theft Device . . . . . . Std. Pass. Immobil. & Alarm
Parking Index Rating . . . . Hard
Where Made. . . . . Lincoln, AL
Fuel Factor:
  MPG Rating (city/hwy) Poor-18/27
  Driving Range (mi.) Average-412.9
  Fuel Type . . . . Premium
  Annual Fuel Cost . . . . Very High-$1,665
  Gas Guzzler Tax . . . . No
  Greenhouse Gas Emissions (tons/yr.) High-8.6
  Barrels of Oil Used per year High-15.7

How the Competition Rates

Competitors	Rating	Pg.
BMW X5	6	101
Infiniti QX70	–	171
Volvo XC60	10	269

Price Range

Price Range	Retail	Markup
Base	$42,865	8
SH-AWD w/Tech. Package	$47,290	8
Advance w/RES	$49,290	8
SH-AWD Advance w/RES	$57,080	8

Acura MDX

Safety Checklist

Crash Tests:
  Frontal. . . . . Very Good
  Side. . . . . Average
Airbags:
  Torso . . . . Front Pelvis/Torso from Seat
  Pelvis . . . . Front Pelvis/Torso from Seat
  Roll Sensing. . . . . Yes
  Knee Bolster . . . . Standard Driver
Crash Avoidance:
  Collision Avoidance . . . . . . Optional CIB & DBS
  Blind Spot Detection . . . . Optional
  Lane Keeping Assist . . . . Optional
  Backup Camera . . . . Standard
  Pedestrian Crash Avoidance . . . . Optional
General:
  Auto. Crash Notification . . . Operator Assist.-Fee
  Day Running Lamps . . . . Standard
Safety Belt/Restraint:
  Dynamic Head Restraints . . . . . . Standard Front
  Adjustable Belt . . . . Standard Front

^Warning feature does not meet government standards.
*Backup camera does not meet government standards.

Acura MDX

Specifications

Drive. . . . . AWD
Engine 3.5-liter V6
Transmission . . . . 6-sp. Automatic
Tow Rating (lbs.) Low-3500
Head/Leg Room (in.) . . . . . Very Cramped-38.1/41.4
Interior Space (cu. ft.). Roomy-132.3
Cargo Space (cu. ft.) Cramped-14.8
Wheelbase/Length (in.) 111/193.6

Ratings—10 Best, 1 Worst

Combo Crash Tests	9
Safety Features	8
Rollover	5
Preventive Maintenance	5
Repair Costs	7
Warranty	5
Fuel Economy	3
Complaints	9
Insurance Costs	10
OVERALL RATING	**10**

Acura RDX

Acura RDX

At-a-Glance

Status/Year Series Started	Unchanged/2013
Twins	–
Body Styles	SUV
Seating	5
Anti-Theft Device	Std. Pass. Immobil. & Alarm
Parking Index Rating	Hard
Where Made	East Liberty, OH

Fuel Factor:

MPG Rating (city/hwy)	Poor-19/27
Driving Range (mi.)	Very Short-350.8
Fuel Type	Premium
Annual Fuel Cost	Very High-$1,607
Gas Guzzler Tax	No
Greenhouse Gas Emissions (tons/yr.)	High-8.2
Barrels of Oil Used per year	High-15.0

How the Competition Rates

Competitors	Rating	Pg.
BMW X3	7	100
Buick Encore	10	103
Lexus RX	–	197

Price Range

Price Range	Retail	Markup
FWD	$35,270	8
AWD	$36,770	8
FWD w/Tech. Package	$38,970	8
AWD w/Tech. Package	$40,470	8

Safety Checklist

Crash Tests:

Frontal	Very Good
Side	Average

Airbags:

Torso	Front Pelvis/Torso from Seat
Pelvis	Front Pelvis/Torso from Seat
Roll Sensing	Yes
Knee Bolster	None

Crash Avoidance:

Collision Avoidance	Optional CIB & DBS
Blind Spot Detection	Optional
Lane Keeping Assist	Optional
Backup Camera	Standard
Pedestrian Crash Avoidance	Optional

General:

Auto. Crash Notification	Operator Assist.-Fee
Day Running Lamps	Standard

Safety Belt/Restraint:

Dynamic Head Restraints	None
Adjustable Belt	Standard Front

^Warning feature does not meet government standards.
*Backup camera does not meet government standards.

Acura RDX

Specifications

Drive	AWD
Engine	3.5-liter V6
Transmission	6-sp. Automatic
Tow Rating (lbs.)	Very Low-1500
Head/Leg Room (in.)	Cramped-38.7/42
Interior Space (cu. ft.)	Average-103.5
Cargo Space (cu. ft.)	Roomy-26.1
Wheelbase/Length (in.)	105.7/183.5

Ratings—10 Best, 1 Worst

Combo Crash Tests	10
Safety Features	8
Rollover	10
Preventive Maintenance	9
Repair Costs	7
Warranty	5
Fuel Economy	4
Complaints	1
Insurance Costs	10
OVERALL RATING	**10**

The CAR Book BEST BET

Acura TLX

Acura TLX

At-a-Glance

Status/Year Series Started	Unchanged/2015
Twins	Honda Accord
Body Styles	Sedan
Seating	5
Anti-Theft Device	Std. Pass. Immobil. & Alarm
Parking Index Rating	Hard
Where Made	Marysville, OH

Fuel Factor:

MPG Rating (city/hwy)	Poor-20/31
Driving Range (mi.)	Average-409.4
Fuel Type	Premium
Annual Fuel Cost	High-$1,481
Gas Guzzler Tax	No
Greenhouse Gas Emissions (tons/yr.)	Average-6.4
Barrels of Oil Used per year	Average-11.8

How the Competition Rates

Competitors	Rating	Pg.
Cadillac CTS	8	108
Infiniti Q70	–	169
Lexus ES	8	191

Price Range	Retail	Markup
Base 2.4L	$31,445	6%
Base 3.5L	$35,320	6%
3.5L w/Tech. Package	$39,375	7%
SH-AWD w/Advance Package	$41,575	7%

Safety Checklist

Crash Tests:

Frontal	Very Good
Side	Very Good

Airbags:

Torso	Front Pelvis/Torso from Seat
Pelvis	Front Pelvis/Torso from Seat
Roll Sensing	Yes
Knee Bolster	None

Crash Avoidance:

Collision Avoidance	Optional CIB & DBS
Blind Spot Detection	Optional
Lane Keeping Assist	Optional
Backup Camera	Standard
Pedestrian Crash Avoidance	Optional

General:

Auto. Crash Notification	Operator Assist.-Fee
Day Running Lamps	Standard

Safety Belt/Restraint:

Dynamic Head Restraints	None
Adjustable Belt	Standard Front

^Warning feature does not meet government standards.
*Backup camera does not meet government standards.

Acura TLX

Specifications

Drive	FWD
Engine	2.0-liter I4
Transmission	8-sp. Automatic
Tow Rating (lbs.)	–
Head/Leg Room (in.)	Cramped-37.2/42.6
Interior Space (cu. ft.)	Cramped-93.3
Cargo Space (cu. ft.)	Very Cramped-13.2
Wheelbase/Length (in.)	109.3/190.3

Ratings—10 Best, 1 Worst

Combo Crash Tests	5
Safety Features	8
Rollover	8
Preventive Maintenance	5
Repair Costs	6
Warranty	7
Fuel Economy	6
Complaints	3
Insurance Costs	5
OVERALL RATING	**5**

Audi A3

Audi A3

Safety Checklist

Crash Tests:
Frontal . . . . Average
Side . . . . Average

Airbags:
Torso Std. Fr. & Opt. Rr. Pelvis/Torso from Seat
Pelvis Std. Fr. & Opt. Rr. Pelvis/Torso from Seat
Roll Sensing . . . . Yes
Knee Bolster . . . . Standard Front

Crash Avoidance:
Collision Avoidance . . . . . . Optional CIB & DBS
Blind Spot Detection . . . . Optional
Lane Keeping Assist . . . . Optional
Backup Camera . . . . Standard*
Pedestrian Crash Avoidance . . . . None

General:
Auto. Crash Notification . . . . None
Day Running Lamps . . . . Standard

Safety Belt/Restraint:
Dynamic Head Restraints . . . . None
Adjustable Belt . . . . Standard Front

^Warning feature does not meet government standards.
*Backup camera does not meet government standards.

At-a-Glance

Status/Year Series Started Unchanged/2015
Twins . . . . Volkswagen Golf
Body Styles . . . . Sedan, Wagon
Seating 5
Anti-Theft Device . . . . . . Std. Pass. Immobil. & Alarm
Parking Index Rating . . . . Easy
Where Made . . . . Gyor, Hungary
Fuel Factor:
MPG Rating (city/hwy) Average-24/33
Driving Range (mi.) Short-396.7
Fuel Type . . . . Premium
Annual Fuel Cost . . . . Average-$1,288
Gas Guzzler Tax . . . . No
Greenhouse Gas Emissions (tons/yr.) . . Average-6.6
Barrels of Oil Used per year Average-12.2

Audi A3

How the Competition Rates

Competitors	Rating	Pg.
Acura ILX	9	81
Buick Verano	10	106
Mercedes-Benz CLA-Class	–	208

Specifications

Drive . . . . AWD
Engine 2.0-liter I4
Transmission . . . . 6-sp. Automatic
Tow Rating (lbs.) . . . . –
Head/Leg Room (in.) . . . . . Very Cramped-36.5/41.2
Interior Space (cu. ft.) . . . . Very Cramped-86
Cargo Space (cu. ft.) . . . . Very Cramped-10.03
Wheelbase/Length (in.) 103.8/175.4

Price Range

	Retail	Markup
1.8T Premium Sedan	$30,900	8%
2.0 TDI Premium Sedan	$33,200	8%
2.0T Premium Plus Sedan Quattro	$35,900	8%
2.0T Prestige Cabriolet Quattro	$48,450	8%

Audi A4 Compact

Ratings—10 Best, 1 Worst

Combo Crash Tests	6
Safety Features	4
Rollover	10
Preventive Maintenance	4
Repair Costs	3
Warranty	7
Fuel Economy	5
Complaints	10
Insurance Costs	5
OVERALL RATING	**8**

Audi A4

Audi A4

At-a-Glance

Status/Year Series Started........ Unchanged/2009
Twins ....–
Body Styles ....Sedan
Seating 5
Anti-Theft Device ...... Std. Pass. Immobil. & Alarm
Parking Index Rating .... Average
Where Made..................Ingolstadt, Germany

Fuel Factor:
MPG Rating (city/hwy) Average-22/31
Driving Range (mi.) Average-407.4
Fuel Type...........................Premium
Annual Fuel Cost .... High-$1,392
Gas Guzzler Tax ....No
Greenhouse Gas Emissions (tons/yr.).. Average-7.2
Barrels of Oil Used per year High-13.2

How the Competition Rates

Competitors	Rating	Pg.
BMW 3 Series	8	93
Cadillac ATS	8	107
Mercedes-Benz C-Class	3	207

Price Range

Price Range	Retail	Markup
2.0T Premium Sedan	$33,200	8%
2.0T Premium Sedan Quattro	$34,200	8%
2.0T Premium Plus Sedan Quattro	$36,900	8%
2.0T Prestige Sedan Quattro	$43,050	8%

Safety Checklist

Crash Tests:
Frontal............................ Good
Side.............................. Poor
Airbags:
Torso Std. Fr. & Opt. Rr. Pelvis/Torso from Seat
Pelvis Std. Fr. & Opt. Rr. Pelvis/Torso from Seat
Roll Sensing......................... No
Knee Bolster .... None
Crash Avoidance:
Collision Avoidance ...... Optional CIB & DBS
Blind Spot Detection .... Optional
Lane Keeping Assist ...Warning Only Optional^
Backup Camera.................. Optional*
Pedestrian Crash Avoidance .... None
General:
Auto. Crash Notification .... None
Day Running Lamps .... Standard
Safety Belt/Restraint:
Dynamic Head Restraints .... None
Adjustable Belt...............Standard Front

^Warning feature does not meet government standards.
*Backup camera does not meet government standards.

Audi A4

Specifications

Drive................................... AWD
Engine 2.0-liter I4
Transmission ....8-sp. Automatic
Tow Rating (lbs.) .... –
Head/Leg Room (in.) .....Very Cramped-36.9/41.3
Interior Space (cu. ft.).............. Cramped-91
Cargo Space (cu. ft.) ....Very Cramped-12.4
Wheelbase/Length (in.) 110.6/185.1

Ratings—10 Best, 1 Worst	
Combo Crash Tests	—
Safety Features	6
Rollover	—
Preventive Maintenance	4
Repair Costs	2
Warranty	7
Fuel Economy	5
Complaints	9
Insurance Costs	3

OVERALL RATING   —

Audi A5

Audi A5

At-a-Glance

Status/Year Series Started Appearance Change/2008
Twins .... —
Body Styles .... Coupe
Seating 5
Anti-Theft Device ...... Std. Pass. Immobil. & Alarm
Parking Index Rating .... Average
Where Made................. Ingolstadt, Germany

Fuel Factor:
  MPG Rating (city/hwy) Average-22/32
  Driving Range (mi.) Average-412.2
  Fuel Type......................... Premium
  Annual Fuel Cost .... High-$1,376
  Gas Guzzler Tax .... No
  Greenhouse Gas Emissions (tons/yr.) Low-5.7
  Barrels of Oil Used per year Average-12.7

How the Competition Rates

Competitors	Rating	Pg.
Acura ILX	9	81
BMW 4 Series	—	94
Lexus IS	7	194

Price Range	Retail	Markup
2.0T Premium Coupe Quattro	$40,500	8%
2.0T Premium Plus Coupe Quattro AT	$42,800	8%
2.0T Premium Plus Quattro AT	$43,800	8%
2.0T Prestige Cabrio Tip Quattro	$50,200	8%

Safety Checklist

Crash Tests:
  Frontal.................................. −
  Side.................................... −
Airbags:
  Torso .... Front Pelvis/Torso from Seat
  Pelvis .... Front Pelvis/Torso from Seat
  Roll Sensing........................... No
  Knee Bolster .... Standard Front
Crash Avoidance:
  Collision Avoidance ...... Optional CIB & DBS
  Blind Spot Detection .... Optional
  Lane Keeping Assist ...Warning Only Optional^
  Backup Camera .... Optional*
  Pedestrian Crash Avoidance .... None
General:
  Auto. Crash Notification.............. None
  Day Running Lamps .... Standard
Safety Belt/Restraint:
  Dynamic Head Restraints .... None
  Adjustable Belt.................... None

^Warning feature does not meet government standards.
*Backup camera does not meet government standards.

Audi A5

Specifications

Drive................................... AWD
Engine 2.0-liter I4
Transmission .... 8-sp. Automatic
Tow Rating (lbs.) .... —
Head/Leg Room (in.) .....Very Cramped-37.5/41.3
Interior Space (cu. ft.)................. —
Cargo Space (cu. ft.) ....Very Cramped-12.2
Wheelbase/Length (in.) 108.3/182.1

Audi A6

Intermediate

Audi A6

Ratings—10 Best, 1 Worst	
Combo Crash Tests	8
Safety Features	8
Rollover	10
Preventive Maintenance	4
Repair Costs	1
Warranty	7
Fuel Economy	4
Complaints	9
Insurance Costs	5
OVERALL RATING	**8**

Audi A6

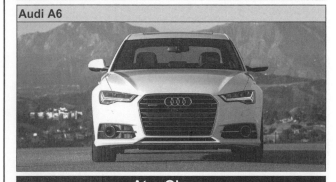

At-a-Glance

Status/Year Series Started Appearance Change/2012
Twins . . . .–
Body Styles . . . . .Sedan
Seating 5
Anti-Theft Device . . . . . . Std. Pass. Immobil. & Alarm
Parking Index Rating . . . . Hard
Where Made. . . . . Neckarsulm, Germany
Fuel Factor:
  MPG Rating (city/hwy). Poor-20/30
  Driving Range (mi.) . . . . .Very Long-465.9
  Fuel Type . . . . .Premium
  Annual Fuel Cost . . . . High-$1,498
  Gas Guzzler Tax . . . . .No
  Greenhouse Gas Emissions (tons/yr.). Low-5.1
  Barrels of Oil Used per year Average-11.8

How the Competition Rates

Competitors	Rating	Pg.
BMW 5 Series	8	95
Mercedes-Benz E-Class	5	209
Volvo S60	10	267

Price Range	Retail	Markup
2.0T Premium	$46,200	8%
2.0T Premium Plus Quattro	$52,100	8%
3.0 Prestige Quattro	$61,600	8%
3.0 Prestige TDI	$63,700	8%

Safety Checklist

Crash Tests:
  Frontal. . . . . Very Good
  Side. . . . . Average
Airbags:
  Torso Std. Fr. & Opt. Rr. Pelvis/Torso from Seat
  Pelvis Std. Fr. & Opt. Rr. Pelvis/Torso from Seat
  Roll Sensing. . . . . .Yes
  Knee Bolster . . . . .Standard Front
Crash Avoidance:
  Collision Avoidance . . . . . . Optional CIB & DBS
  Blind Spot Detection . . . . Optional
  Lane Keeping Assist . . . . Optional^
  Backup Camera . . . . Optional*
  Pedestrian Crash Avoidance . . . . None
General:
  Auto. Crash Notification . . . . None
  Day Running Lamps . . . . Standard
Safety Belt/Restraint:
  Dynamic Head Restraints . . . . None
  Adjustable Belt. . . . . .Standard Front

^Warning feature does not meet government standards.
*Backup camera does not meet government standards.

Audi A6

Specifications

Drive. . . . . AWD
Engine 3.0-liter V6
Transmission . . . . .8-sp. Automatic
Tow Rating (lbs.) . . . . –
Head/Leg Room (in.) . . . . .Very Cramped-37.2/41.3
Interior Space (cu. ft.). Average-98
Cargo Space (cu. ft.) Cramped-14.1
Wheelbase/Length (in.) 114.7/194.2

Audi Q3

Ratings—10 Best, 1 Worst

Combo Crash Tests	—
Safety Features	3
Rollover	—
Preventive Maintenance	—
Repair Costs	4
Warranty	7
Fuel Economy	4
Complaints	10
Insurance Costs	5
OVERALL RATING	**—**

Audi Q3

Audi Q3

At-a-Glance

Status/Year Series Started	Appearance Change/2015
Twins	Volkswagen Tiguan
Body Styles	SUV
Seating	5
Anti-Theft Device	Std. Pass. Immobil & Alarm
Parking Index Rating	Average
Where Made	Martorell, Spain

Fuel Factor:

MPG Rating (city/hwy)	Poor-20/28
Driving Range (mi.)	Short-387.9
Fuel Type	Premium
Annual Fuel Cost	High-$1,536
Gas Guzzler Tax	No
Greenhouse Gas Emissions (tons/yr.)	High-7.8
Barrels of Oil Used per year	High-14.3

How the Competition Rates

Competitors	Rating	Pg.
BMW X1	—	99
Lexus NX	5	195
Mercedes-Benz GLA-Class	—	210

Price Range

	Retail	Markup
2.0T Premium Plus	$33,700	8%
2.0T Premium Plus Quattro	$35,800	8%
2.0T Prestige	$38,600	8%
2.0T Prestige Quattro	$40,700	8%

Safety Checklist

Crash Tests:

Frontal	—
Side	—

Airbags:

Torso	Front Pelvis/Torso from Seat
Pelvis	Front Pelvis/Torso from Seat
Roll Sensing	Yes
Knee Bolster	None

Crash Avoidance:

Collision Avoidance	None
Blind Spot Detection	Optional
Lane Keeping Assist	None
Backup Camera	Standard*
Pedestrian Crash Avoidance	None

General:

Auto. Crash Notification	None
Day Running Lamps	Standard

Safety Belt/Restraint:

Dynamic Head Restraints	None
Adjustable Belt	Standard Front

^Warning feature does not meet government standards.
*Backup camera does not meet government standards.

Audi Q3

Specifications

Drive	AWD
Engine	2.0-liter I4
Transmission	6-sp. Automatic
Tow Rating (lbs.)	—
Head/Leg Room (in.)	Very Cramped-37/40
Interior Space (cu. ft.)	Very Cramped-84
Cargo Space (cu. ft.)	Cramped-16.7
Wheelbase/Length (in.)	102.5/172.6

Ratings—10 Best, 1 Worst

Combo Crash Tests	2
Safety Features	6
Rollover	5
Preventive Maintenance	4
Repair Costs	4
Warranty	7
Fuel Economy	4
Complaints	10
Insurance Costs	5
OVERALL RATING	**5**

Audi Q5

Audi Q5

At-a-Glance

Status/Year Series Started. Unchanged/2009
Twins . . . . –
Body Styles . . . . SUV
Seating. 5
Anti-Theft Device . . . . . . Std. Pass. Immobil. & Alarm
Parking Index Rating . . . . Average
Where Made. . . . . .Ingolstadt, Germany
Fuel Factor:
  MPG Rating (city/hwy). Poor-20/28
  Driving Range (mi.) Long-454.4
  Fuel Type. . . . . .Premium
  Annual Fuel Cost . . . . High-$1,536
  Gas Guzzler Tax . . . . .No
  Greenhouse Gas Emissions (tons/yr.). . Average-6.5
  Barrels of Oil Used per year High-14.3

How the Competition Rates

Competitors	Rating	Pg.
BMW X3	7	100
Lexus RX	–	197
Mercedes-Benz GLC-Class	–	211

Price Range

Price Range	Retail	Markup
2.0T Premium	$40,900	8%
3.0T Premium Plus	$46,000	8%
Prestige Hybird	$52,500	8%
3.0 Prestige TDI	$55,600	8%

Safety Checklist

Crash Tests:
  Frontal. . . . . .Very Poor
  Side. . . . . .Poor
Airbags:
  Torso Std. Fr. & Opt. Rr. Pelvis/Torso from Seat
  Pelvis Std. Fr. & Opt. Rr. Pelvis/Torso from Seat
  Roll Sensing. . . . . .Yes
  Knee Bolster . . . . None
Crash Avoidance:
  Collision Avoidance . . . . . . Optional CIB & DBS
  Blind Spot Detection . . . . Optional
  Lane Keeping Assist . . .Warning Only Optional^
  Backup Camera. . . . . .Optional*
  Pedestrian Crash Avoidance . . . . None
General:
  Auto. Crash Notification. . . . . None
  Day Running Lamps . . . . Standard
Safety Belt/Restraint:
  Dynamic Head Restraints . . . . None
  Adjustable Belt. . . . . .Standard Front

^Warning feature does not meet government standards.
*Backup camera does not meet government standards.

Audi Q5

Specifications

Drive. . . . . AWD
Engine 2.0-liter I4
Transmission . . . . .8-sp. Automatic
Tow Rating (lbs.) . . . . –
Head/Leg Room (in.) . . . . . Very Cramped-38.1/41
Interior Space (cu. ft.). –
Cargo Space (cu. ft.) Roomy-29.1
Wheelbase/Length (in.) 110.5/182.6

Ratings—10 Best, 1 Worst

Combo Crash Tests	—
Safety Features	3
Rollover	—
Preventive Maintenance	3
Repair Costs	1
Warranty	7
Fuel Economy	—
Complaints	—
Insurance Costs	5
OVERALL RATING	**—**

Audi Q7

Audi Q7

At-a-Glance

Status/Year Series Started. . . . . All New/2016
Twins . . . . –
Body Styles . . . . SUV
Seating 7
Anti-Theft Device . . . . . . Std. Pass. Immobil. & Alarm
Parking Index Rating . . . . .Very Hard
Where Made. . . . . Bratislava, Slovakia
Fuel Factor:
  MPG Rating (city/hwy) . . . . .Very Poor-0/0
  Driving Range (mi.) . . . . –
  Fuel Type . . . . .Premium
  Annual Fuel Cost . . . . –
  Gas Guzzler Tax . . . . .No
  Greenhouse Gas Emissions (tons/yr.). . . . . –
  Barrels of Oil Used per year . . . . –

How the Competition Rates

Competitors	Rating	Pg.
BMW X5	6	101
Infiniti QX60	3	170
Mercedes-Benz GL-Class	–	212

Price Range	Retail	Markup
3.0 Premium	$48,300	8%
3.0 Premium Plus	$54,800	8%
3.0 Prestige S-Line	$61,900	8%
3.0 Prestige TDI	$65,400	8%

Safety Checklist

Crash Tests:
  Frontal. . . . .–
  Side. . . . .–
Airbags:
  Torso Std. Fr. & Opt. Rr. Pelvis/Torso from Seat
  Pelvis Std. Fr. & Opt. Rr. Pelvis/Torso from Seat
  Roll Sensing. . . . . .Yes
  Knee Bolster . . . . None
Crash Avoidance:
  Collision Avoidance . . . . None
  Blind Spot Detection . . . . Standard
  Lane Keeping Assist . . . Warning Only Optional^
  Backup Camera . . . . .Standard*
  Pedestrian Crash Avoidance . . . . None
General:
  Auto. Crash Notification . . . . None
  Day Running Lamps . . . . Standard
Safety Belt/Restraint:
  Dynamic Head Restraints . . . . None
  Adjustable Belt. . . . . Standard

^Warning feature does not meet government standards.
*Backup camera does not meet government standards.

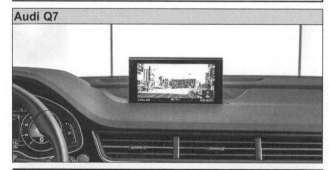

Audi Q7

Specifications

Drive. . . . . AWD
Engine 3.0-liter V6
Transmission . . . . .8-sp. Automatic
Tow Rating (lbs.) High-7700
Head/Leg Room (in.) Cramped-38.4/41.7
Interior Space (cu. ft.). . . . . –
Cargo Space (cu. ft.) Cramped-14.8
Wheelbase/Length (in.) 117.9/199.6

Ratings—10 Best, 1 Worst	
Combo Crash Tests	—
Safety Features	4
Rollover	—
Preventive Maintenance	4
Repair Costs	3
Warranty	8
Fuel Economy	6
Complaints	10
Insurance Costs	5
OVERALL RATING	**—**

BMW 2 Series

BMW 2 Series

At-a-Glance

Status/Year Series Started	Unchanged/2014
Twins	—
Body Styles	Coupe
Seating	4
Anti-Theft Device	Std. Passive Alarm Only
Parking Index Rating	Easy
Where Made	Leipzig, Germany

Fuel Factor:

MPG Rating (city/hwy)	Average-23/35
Driving Range (mi.)	Very Short-372.6
Fuel Type	Premium
Annual Fuel Cost	Average-$1,296
Gas Guzzler Tax	No
Greenhouse Gas Emissions (tons/yr.)	Average-6.4
Barrels of Oil Used per year	Average-12.2

How the Competition Rates

Competitors	Rating	Pg.
Acura ILX	9	81
Audi A3	5	85
Mercedes-Benz CLA-Class	—	208

Price Range	Retail	Markup
228i	$32,850	7%
228xi	$34,850	7%
M235i	$44,150	7%
M235xi	$46,150	7%

Safety Checklist

Crash Tests:
Frontal	—
Side	—

Airbags:
Torso	Front Torso from Seat
Pelvis	None
Roll Sensing	Yes
Knee Bolster	Standard Front

Crash Avoidance:
Collision Avoidance	Optional CIB & DBS
Blind Spot Detection	None
Lane Keeping Assist	Warning Only Optional^
Backup Camera	Standard
Pedestrian Crash Avoidance	Optional

General:
Auto. Crash Notif.	Oper. Assist. & Crash Info-Fee
Day Running Lamps	Standard

Safety Belt/Restraint:
Dynamic Head Restraints	None
Adjustable Belt	None

^Warning feature does not meet government standards.
*Backup camera does not meet government standards.

BMW 2 Series

Specifications

Drive	RWD
Engine	2.0-liter I4
Transmission	8-sp. Automatic
Tow Rating (lbs.)	—
Head/Leg Room (in.)	Average-40.1/41.5
Interior Space (cu. ft.)	Very Cramped-90
Cargo Space (cu. ft.)	Cramped-13.8
Wheelbase/Length (in.)	105.9/174.7

Ratings—10 Best, 1 Worst

Combo Crash Tests	7
Safety Features	6
Rollover	10
Preventive Maintenance	5
Repair Costs	3
Warranty	8
Fuel Economy	6
Complaints	6
Insurance Costs	5
OVERALL RATING	**8**

BMW 3 Series

BMW 3 Series

At-a-Glance

Status/Year Series Started Appearance Change/2013
Twins . . . . –
Body Styles . . . . .Sedan, Wagon, Convertible
Seating 5
Anti-Theft Device . . . . Std. Passive Alarm Only
Parking Index Rating . . . . Average
Where Made. . . . . .Munich, Germany
Fuel Factor:
  MPG Rating (city/hwy) Average-23/36
  Driving Range (mi.) Long-433.9
  Fuel Type. . . . . .Premium
  Annual Fuel Cost . . . . Average-$1,284
  Gas Guzzler Tax . . . . .No
  Greenhouse Gas Emissions (tons/yr.) Low-5.3
  Barrels of Oil Used per year Average-11.8

How the Competition Rates

Competitors	Rating	Pg.
Audi A4	8	86
Lexus IS	7	194
Mercedes-Benz C-Class	3	207

Price Range	Retail	Markup
320i	$33,150	7%
328d	$39,850	7%
335xi	$40,350	7%
340i	$45,800	7%

Safety Checklist

Crash Tests:
  Frontal. . . . . Average
  Side. . . . . Good
Airbags:
  Torso . . . . Front Torso from Seat
  Pelvis . . . . None
  Roll Sensing. . . . . .Yes
  Knee Bolster . . . . .Standard Front
Crash Avoidance:
  Collision Avoidance . . . . . .Optional CIB & DBS^
  Blind Spot Detection . . . . Optional
  Lane Keeping Assist . . .Warning Only Optional^
  Backup Camera . . . . Optional*
  Pedestrian Crash Avoidance . . . . Optional
General:
  Auto. Crash Notif.. Oper. Assist. & Crash Info-Free
  Day Running Lamps . . . . Standard
Safety Belt/Restraint:
  Dynamic Head Restraints . . . . None
  Adjustable Belt. None

^Warning feature does not meet government standards.
*Backup camera does not meet government standards.

BMW 3 Series

Specifications

Drive. . . . . RWD
Engine 2.0-liter I4
Transmission . . . . .8-sp. Automatic
Tow Rating (lbs.) . . . . –
Head/Leg Room (in.) Average-40.3/42
Interior Space (cu. ft.). Cramped-96
Cargo Space (cu. ft.) Average-17
Wheelbase/Length (in.) 110.6/182.4

BMW 4 Series Compact

Ratings—10 Best, 1 Worst

Combo Crash Tests	—
Safety Features	6
Rollover	—
Preventive Maintenance	5
Repair Costs	3
Warranty	8
Fuel Economy	6
Complaints	8
Insurance Costs	5

OVERALL RATING —

BMW 4 Series

BMW 4 Series

At-a-Glance

Status/Year Series Started. Unchanged/2014
Twins . . . . —
Body Styles . . . . Coupe, Convertible
Seating 4
Anti-Theft Device . . . . Std. Passive Alarm Only
Parking Index Rating . . . . Average
Where Made. . . . . .Munich, Germany
Fuel Factor:
  MPG Rating (city/hwy) Average-23/35
  Driving Range (mi.) Long-429.7
  Fuel Type . . . . .Premium
  Annual Fuel Cost . . . . Average-$1,296
  Gas Guzzler Tax . . . . .No
  Greenhouse Gas Emissions (tons/yr.). . Average-6.7
  Barrels of Oil Used per year Average-12.2

How the Competition Rates

Competitors	Rating	Pg.
Audi A5	—	87
Lexus RC		196
Mercedes-Benz C-Class	3	207

Price Range

Price Range	Retail	Markup
428i Coupe	$41,850	7%
435i Gran Coupe	$48,150	7%
435i Convertible	$56,950	8%
435xi Convertible	$58,950	8%

Safety Checklist

Crash Tests:
  Frontal. . . . . —
  Side. . . . . —
Airbags:
  Torso . . . . Front Torso from Seat
  Pelvis . . . . None
  Roll Sensing. . . . . .Yes
  Knee Bolster . . . . .Standard Front
Crash Avoidance:
  Collision Avoidance . . . . . .Optional CIB & DBS^
  Blind Spot Detection . . . . Optional
  Lane Keeping Assist . . .Warning Only Optional^
  Backup Camera . . . . Optional*
  Pedestrian Crash Avoidance . . . . Optional
General:
  Auto. Crash Notif.. Oper. Assist. & Crash Info-Free
  Day Running Lamps . . . . Standard
Safety Belt/Restraint:
  Dynamic Head Restraints . . . . None
  Adjustable Belt. . . . . None

^Warning feature does not meet government standards.
*Backup camera does not meet government standards.

BMW 4 Series

Specifications

Drive. . . . . RWD
Engine 2.0-liter I4
Transmission . . . . .8-sp. Automatic
Tow Rating (lbs.) . . . . —
Head/Leg Room (in.) Average-39.8/42.2
Interior Space (cu. ft.) . . . . Very Cramped-90
Cargo Space (cu. ft.) Cramped-15.7
Wheelbase/Length (in.) 110.6/182.6

Ratings—10 Best, 1 Worst	
Combo Crash Tests	5
Safety Features	7
Rollover	10
Preventive Maintenance	9
Repair Costs	1
Warranty	8
Fuel Economy	6
Complaints	5
Insurance Costs	5
OVERALL RATING	**8**

BMW 5 Series

Safety Checklist

Crash Tests:
Frontal . . . . Very Poor
Side . . . . Very Good
Airbags:
Torso . . . . Front Torso from Seat
Pelvis . . . . None
Roll Sensing . . . . Yes
Knee Bolster . . . . Standard Front
Crash Avoidance:
Collision Avoidance . . . . . . Optional CIB & DBS^
Blind Spot Detection . . . . Optional
Lane Keeping Assist . . . Warning Only Optional^
Backup Camera . . . . Optional*
Pedestrian Crash Avoidance . . . . Optional
General:
Auto. Crash Notif.. Oper. Assist. & Crash Info-Free
Day Running Lamps . . . . Standard
Safety Belt/Restraint:
Dynamic Head Restraints . . . . . . Standard Front
Adjustable Belt . . . . None

^Warning feature does not meet government standards.
*Backup camera does not meet government standards.

BMW 5 Series

At-a-Glance

Status/Year Series Started Unchanged/2011
Twins . . . . –
Body Styles . . . . Sedan, Wagon
Seating 5
Anti-Theft Device . . . . Std. Passive Alarm Only
Parking Index Rating . . . . Very Hard
Where Made . . . . Dingolfing, Germany
Fuel Factor:
MPG Rating (city/hwy) Average-23/34
Driving Range (mi.) . . . . Very Long-498.0
Fuel Type . . . . Premium
Annual Fuel Cost . . . . Average-$1,309
Gas Guzzler Tax . . . . No
Greenhouse Gas Emissions (tons/yr.) . . Average-6.6
Barrels of Oil Used per year Average-12.2

How the Competition Rates

Competitors	Rating	Pg.
Audi A6	8	88
Infiniti Q70	–	169
Mercedes-Benz E-Class	5	209

Price Range	Retail	Markup
528i	$50,200	8%
535i	$55,850	8%
550xi	$58,150	8%
535i Hybrid	$62,100	8%

BMW 5 Series

Specifications

Drive . . . . RWD
Engine 2.0-liter I4
Transmission . . . . 8-sp. Automatic
Tow Rating (lbs.) . . . . –
Head/Leg Room (in.) Average-40.5/41.4
Interior Space (cu. ft.) Average-102
Cargo Space (cu. ft.) Average-18.4
Wheelbase/Length (in.) 116.9/193.4

Ratings—10 Best, 1 Worst

Combo Crash Tests	—
Safety Features	5
Rollover	—
Preventive Maintenance	2
Repair Costs	1
Warranty	8
Fuel Economy	2
Complaints	9
Insurance Costs	5

OVERALL RATING — —

BMW 6 Series

BMW 6 Series

At-a-Glance

Status/Year Series Started........ Unchanged/2012
Twins . . . .—
Body Styles . . . . Coupe, Convertible
Seating 4
Anti-Theft Device . . . . Std. Passive Alarm Only
Parking Index Rating . . . . Hard
Where Made. . . . . Dingolfing, Germany
Fuel Factor:
 MPG Rating (city/hwy) . . . . .Very Poor-17/25
 Driving Range (mi.) . . . . Very Short-367.4
 Fuel Type . . . . .Premium
 Annual Fuel Cost . . . . .Very High-$1,774
 Gas Guzzler Tax . . . . .No
 Greenhouse Gas Emissions (tons/yr.) Very High-9.0
 Barrels of Oil Used per year High-16.5

How the Competition Rates

Competitors	Rating	Pg.
Audi A5	—	87
Cadillac CTS	8	108
Mercedes-Benz E-Class	5	209

Price Range	Retail	Markup
640i Coupe	$76,600	8%
640xi Convertible	$87,100	8%
650xi Convertible	$98,400	8%
650xi Gran Coupe	$98,400	8%

Safety Checklist

Crash Tests:
 Frontal. . . . .—
 Side. . . . .—
Airbags:
 Torso . . . . Front Head/Torso from Seat
 Pelvis . . . . None
 Roll Sensing. . . . . No
 Knee Bolster . . . . .Standard Front
Crash Avoidance:
 Collision Avoidance . . . . . .Optional CIB & DBS^
 Blind Spot Detection . . . . Optional
 Lane Keeping Assist . . .Warning Only Optional^
 Backup Camera . . . . .Standard*
 Pedestrian Crash Avoidance . . . . Optional
General:
 Auto. Crash Notif.. Oper. Assist. & Crash Info-Free
 Day Running Lamps . . . . Standard
Safety Belt/Restraint:
 Dynamic Head Restraints . . . . . .Standard Front
 Adjustable Belt . . . . None

^Warning feature does not meet government standards.
*Backup camera does not meet government standards.

BMW 6 Series

Specifications

Drive. . . . . RWD
Engine 4.4-liter V8
Transmission . . . . .8-sp. Automatic
Tow Rating (lbs.) . . . . —
Head/Leg Room (in.) Average-40.3/42.1
Interior Space (cu. ft.). . . . . Very Cramped-88
Cargo Space (cu. ft.) . . . . .Very Cramped-12.4
Wheelbase/Length (in.) 112.4/192.8

Ratings—10 Best, 1 Worst	
Combo Crash Tests	—
Safety Features	9
Rollover	—
Preventive Maintenance	9
Repair Costs	1
Warranty	8
Fuel Economy	4
Complaints	—
Insurance Costs	5

OVERALL RATING —

BMW 7 Series

BMW 7 Series

At-a-Glance

Status/Year Series Started	All New/2016
Twins	—
Body Styles	Sedan
Seating	5
Anti-Theft Device	Std. Passive Alarm Only
Parking Index Rating	Very Hard
Where Made	Dingolfing, Germany

Fuel Factor:

MPG Rating (city/hwy)	Poor-21/29
Driving Range (mi.)	Very Long-493.9
Fuel Type	Premium
Annual Fuel Cost	High-$1,470
Gas Guzzler Tax	No
Greenhouse Gas Emissions (tons/yr.)	Average-6.1
Barrels of Oil Used per year	High-13.7

How the Competition Rates

Competitors	Rating	Pg.
Cadillac XTS	9	110
Infiniti Q50	5	168
Mercedes-Benz S-Class	—	214

Price Range	Retail	Markup
740i	$81,300	8%
750i	$94,400	8%
750i xDrive	$97,400	8%

Safety Checklist

Crash Tests:

Frontal	−
Side	−

Airbags:

Torso	Front Torso from Seat
Pelvis	None
Roll Sensing	Yes
Knee Bolster	Standard Front

Crash Avoidance:

Collision Avoidance	Optional CIB & DBS^
Blind Spot Detection	Optional
Lane Keeping Assist	Warning Only Optional^
Backup Camera	Standard*
Pedestrian Crash Avoidance	Optional

General:

Auto. Crash Notif.. Oper. Assist. & Crash Info	Free
Day Running Lamps	Standard

Safety Belt/Restraint:

Dynamic Head Restraints	Standard Front
Adjustable Belt	None

^Warning feature does not meet government standards.
*Backup camera does not meet government standards.

BMW 7 Series

Specifications

Drive	RWD
Engine	6.0-liter V8
Transmission	8-sp. Automatic
Tow Rating (lbs.)	—
Head/Leg Room (in.)	Average-39.9/41.4
Interior Space (cu. ft.)	Roomy-107
Cargo Space (cu. ft.)	Average-18.2
Wheelbase/Length (in.)	126.4/206.6

Ratings—10 Best, 1 Worst

Combo Crash Tests	—
Safety Features	1
Rollover	—
Preventive Maintenance	—
Repair Costs	10
Warranty	8
Fuel Economy	10
Complaints	—
Insurance Costs	5
OVERALL RATING	**—**

BMW i3

BMW i3

At-a-Glance

Status/Year Series Started. Unchanged/2014
Twins . . . .—
Body Styles . . . . .Coupe
Seating 4
Anti-Theft Device . . . . Standard Pass. Alarm Only
Parking Index Rating . . . . .Very Easy
Where Made. . . . . Leipzig, Germany
Fuel Factor:
  MPG Rating (city/hwy) . . . . Very Good-137/111
  Driving Range (mi.) Short–150.0
  Fuel Type. . . . . .Premium
  Annual Fuel Cost . . . . .Very Low-$254
  Gas Guzzler Tax . . . . .No
  Greenhouse Gas Emissions (tons/yr.). Very Low-0.0
  Barrels of Oil Used per year . . . . Very Low-0.2

How the Competition Rates

Competitors	Rating	Pg.
Ford C-MAX	5	135
Nissan Leaf	4	226
Toyota Prius C	6	252

Price Range

Price Range	Retail	Markup
Hatchback	$42,400	7%
Hbk w/Range Ext	$46,250	7%

Safety Checklist

Crash Tests:
  Frontal. . . . .−
  Side. . . . .−
Airbags:
  Torso . . . . .Standard*
  Pelvis . . . . None
  Roll Sensing. . . . . No
  Knee Bolster . . . . Standard
Crash Avoidance:
  Collision Avoidance . . . . . .Optional CIB & DBS^
  Blind Spot Detection . . . . None
  Lane Keeping Assist . . . . No
  Backup Camera . . . . Optional*
  Pedestrian Crash Avoidance . . . . Optional
General:
  Auto. Crash Notification . . . . Standard
  Day Running Lamps . . . . Standard
Safety Belt/Restraint:
  Dynamic Head Restraints . . . . None
  Adjustable Belt. . . . . None

^Warning feature does not meet government standards.
*Backup camera does not meet government standards.

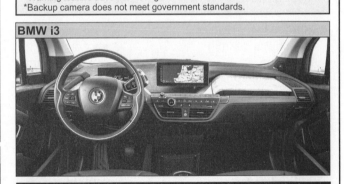
BMW i3

Specifications

Drive. . . . . .RWD
Engine.All Electric (w/opt. Gas Recharging Generator)
Transmission . . . . .CVT
Tow Rating (lbs.) . . . . −
Head/Leg Room (in.) Cramped-39.6/40.5
Interior Space (cu. ft.). . . . . .Very Cramped-83.1
Cargo Space (cu. ft.) . . . . .Very Cramped-11.8
Wheelbase/Length (in.) 101/157

See page 274 for more details.

Ratings—10 Best, 1 Worst

Combo Crash Tests	—
Safety Features	4
Rollover	—
Preventive Maintenance	7
Repair Costs	2
Warranty	8
Fuel Economy	5
Complaints	—
Insurance Costs	5

OVERALL RATING   —

BMW X1

BMW X1

At-a-Glance

Status/Year Series Started	All New/2016
Twins	—
Body Styles	SUV
Seating	5
Anti-Theft Device	Std. Passive Alarm Only
Parking Index Rating	Easy
Where Made	Leipzig, Germany

Fuel Factor:

MPG Rating (city/hwy)	Average-22/32
Driving Range (mi.)	Average-412.2
Fuel Type	Premium
Annual Fuel Cost	High-$1,376
Gas Guzzler Tax	No
Greenhouse Gas Emissions (tons/yr.)	Low-5.7
Barrels of Oil Used per year	Average-12.7

How the Competition Rates

Competitors	Rating	Pg.
Lexus NX	5	195
Mercedes-Benz GLA-Class	—	210
Porsche Macan	—	235

Price Range

	Retail	Markup
sDrive28i	$31,200	7%
XDrive28i	$33,000	7%
XDrive35i	$39,100	7%

Safety Checklist

Crash Tests:
Frontal	—
Side	—

Airbags:
Torso	Front Torso from Seat
Pelvis	None
Roll Sensing	Yes
Knee Bolster	Standard Driver

Crash Avoidance:
Collision Avoidance	None
Blind Spot Detection	None
Lane Keeping Assist	None
Backup Camera	Standard
Pedestrian Crash Avoidance	None

General:
Auto. Crash Notif.. Oper. Assist. & Crash Info	Free
Day Running Lamps	Standard

Safety Belt/Restraint:
Dynamic Head Restraints	None
Adjustable Belt	None

^Warning feature does not meet government standards.
*Backup camera does not meet government standards.

BMW X1

Specifications

Drive	RWD
Engine	2.0-liter I4
Transmission	8-sp. Automatic
Tow Rating (lbs.)	—
Head/Leg Room (in.)	Average-41.9/40.4
Interior Space (cu. ft.)	—
Cargo Space (cu. ft.)	Roomy-27.1
Wheelbase/Length (in.)	105.1/174.8

Ratings—10 Best, 1 Worst

Combo Crash Tests	6
Safety Features	7
Rollover	4
Preventive Maintenance	2
Repair Costs	5
Warranty	8
Fuel Economy	4
Complaints	7
Insurance Costs	5
OVERALL RATING	**7**

BMW X3

BMW X3

At-a-Glance

Status/Year Series Started........ Unchanged/2011
Twins . . . .–
Body Styles . . . . SUV
Seating 5
Anti-Theft Device . . . . Std. Passive Alarm Only
Parking Index Rating . . . . Hard
Where Made. . . . . Spartanburg, SC

Fuel Factor:
  MPG Rating (city/hwy) Poor-21/28
  Driving Range (mi.) Average-418.8
  Fuel Type . . . . Premium
  Annual Fuel Cost . . . . High-$1,490
  Gas Guzzler Tax . . . . .No
  Greenhouse Gas Emissions (tons/yr.) High-7.5
  Barrels of Oil Used per year High-13.7

How the Competition Rates

Competitors	Rating	Pg.
Audi Q5	5	90
Mercedes-Benz GLC-Class	–	211
Volvo XC60	10	269

Price Range	Retail	Markup
sDrive28i	$38,600	7%
XDrive28i	$40,600	7%
XDrive28d	$42,100	7%
XDrive35i	$46,350	7%

Safety Checklist

Crash Tests:
  Frontal. . . . . Average
  Side. . . . . .Poor
Airbags:
  Torso . . . . Front Torso from Seat
  Pelvis . . . . None
  Roll Sensing. . . . . .Yes
  Knee Bolster . . . . Standard Driver
Crash Avoidance:
  Collision Avoidance . . . . . . Optional CIB & DBS^
  Blind Spot Detection . . . . Optional
  Lane Keeping Assist . . . Warning Only Optional^
  Backup Camera . . . . Optional*
  Pedestrian Crash Avoidance . . . . Optional
General:
  Auto. Crash Notif.. Oper. Assist. & Crash Info-Free
  Day Running Lamps . . . . Standard
Safety Belt/Restraint:
  Dynamic Head Restraints . . . . . .Standard Front
  Adjustable Belt . . . . None

^Warning feature does not meet government standards.
*Backup camera does not meet government standards.

BMW X3

Specifications

Drive. . . . . AWD
Engine 3.0-liter I6
Transmission . . . . 8-sp. Automatic
Tow Rating (lbs.) . . . . –
Head/Leg Room (in.) Cramped-40.7/39.9
Interior Space (cu. ft.). . . . . . . .Very Cramped-90.1
Cargo Space (cu. ft.) Roomy-27.6
Wheelbase/Length (in.) 110.6/183.8

Ratings—10 Best, 1 Worst

Combo Crash Tests	8
Safety Features	9
Rollover	3
Preventive Maintenance	3
Repair Costs	1
Warranty	8
Fuel Economy	3
Complaints	9
Insurance Costs	3
OVERALL RATING	**6**

BMW X5

BMW X5

At-a-Glance

Status/Year Series Started	Unchanged/2014
Twins	–
Body Styles	SUV
Seating	5
Anti-Theft Device	Std. Passive Alarm Only
Parking Index Rating	Very Hard
Where Made	Spartanburg, SC

Fuel Factor:

MPG Rating (city/hwy)	Poor-18/27
Driving Range (mi.)	Very Long-474.4
Fuel Type	Premium
Annual Fuel Cost	Very High-$1,664
Gas Guzzler Tax	No
Greenhouse Gas Emissions (tons/yr.)	High-8.5
Barrels of Oil Used per year	High-15.7

How the Competition Rates

Competitors	Rating	Pg.
Cadillac SRX	6	109
Infiniti QX70	–	171
Lexus RX	–	197

Price Range

	Retail	Markup
sDrive35i	$53,900	8%
XDrive35i	$56,200	8%
XDrive35d	$57,700	8%
XDrive50i	$70,100	8%

Safety Checklist

Crash Tests:
Frontal	Good
Side	Average

Airbags:
Torso	Front Torso from Seat
Pelvis	None
Roll Sensing	Yes
Knee Bolster	Standard Front

Crash Avoidance:
Collision Avoidance	Optional CIB & DBS^
Blind Spot Detection	Optional
Lane Keeping Assist	Warning Only Optional^
Backup Camera	Optional*
Pedestrian Crash Avoidance	Optional

General:
Auto. Crash Notif.. Oper. Assist. & Crash Info-Free	
Day Running Lamps	Standard

Safety Belt/Restraint:
Dynamic Head Restraints	Standard Front
Adjustable Belt	None

^Warning feature does not meet government standards.
*Backup camera does not meet government standards.

Specifications

Drive	AWD
Engine	3.0-liter V6
Transmission	8-sp. Automatic
Tow Rating (lbs.)	–
Head/Leg Room (in.)	Cramped-40.5/40.4
Interior Space (cu. ft.)	–
Cargo Space (cu. ft.)	Roomy-23
Wheelbase/Length (in.)	115.5/193.2

Ratings—10 Best, 1 Worst

Combo Crash Tests	7
Safety Features	4
Rollover	4
Preventive Maintenance	2
Repair Costs	3
Warranty	7
Fuel Economy	2
Complaints	5
Insurance Costs	10
OVERALL RATING	**5**

Buick Enclave

At-a-Glance

Status/Year Series Started........ Unchanged/2008
Twins . . . . –
Body Styles . . . . SUV
Seating 7/8
Anti-Theft Device . . . . . . Std. Pass. Immobil. & Alarm
Parking Index Rating . . . . .Very Hard
Where Made. . . . . .Lansing, MI
Fuel Factor:
  MPG Rating (city/hwy) . . . . .Very Poor-17/24
  Driving Range (mi.) Long-430.5
  Fuel Type . . . . .Regular
  Annual Fuel Cost . . . . .Very High-$1,609
  Gas Guzzler Tax . . . . .No
  Greenhouse Gas Emissions (tons/yr.) Very High-9.5
  Barrels of Oil Used per year . . . . . . .Very High-17.3

How the Competition Rates

Competitors	Rating	Pg.
Audi Q7	–	91
Infiniti QX60	3	170
Lexus GX	–	193

Price Range

Price Range	Retail	Markup
Convenience FWD	$39,065	5%
Leather FWD	$43,660	5%
Leather AWD	$45,660	5%
Premium AWD	$49,515	5%

Buick Enclave

Safety Checklist

Crash Tests:
  Frontal. . . . . Good
  Side. . . . . Good
Airbags:
  Torso . . . . .Standard*
  Pelvis . . . . .Front Pelvis/Torso from Seat
  Roll Sensing. . . . . .Yes
  Knee Bolster . . . . None
Crash Avoidance:
  Collision Avoidance . . . . .Warning Only Optional
  Blind Spot Detection . . . . Optional
  Lane Keeping Assist . . . .Warning Only Optional
  Backup Camera . . . . .Standard*
  Pedestrian Crash Avoidance . . . . None
General:
  Auto. Crash Notif.Oper. Assist. And Crash Info-Fee
  Day Running Lamps . . . . Standard
Safety Belt/Restraint:
  Dynamic Head Restraints . . . . None
  Adjustable Belt. None

^Warning feature does not meet government standards.
*Backup camera does not meet government standards.

Buick Enclave

Specifications

Drive. . . . . FWD
Engine 3.6-liter V6
Transmission . . . . .6-sp. Automatic
Tow Rating (lbs.) Low-4500
Head/Leg Room (in.) Average-40.4/41.3
Interior Space (cu. ft.). Roomy-151.1
Cargo Space (cu. ft.) Roomy-23.3
Wheelbase/Length (in.) 119/201.9

Ratings—10 Best, 1 Worst

Combo Crash Tests	8
Safety Features	9
Rollover	2
Preventive Maintenance	7
Repair Costs	8
Warranty	7
Fuel Economy	5
Complaints	8
Insurance Costs	5
OVERALL RATING	**10**

Buick Encore

Buick Encore

At-a-Glance

Status/Year Series Started	Unchanged/2013
Twins	Chevrolet Trax
Body Styles	SUV
Seating	5
Anti-Theft Device	Std. Pass. Immobil. & Alarm
Parking Index Rating	Easy
Where Made	Bupyeong, South Korea

Fuel Factor:

MPG Rating (city/hwy)	Average-23/30
Driving Range (mi.)	Very Short-359.8
Fuel Type	Regular
Annual Fuel Cost	Average-$1,225
Gas Guzzler Tax	No
Greenhouse Gas Emissions (tons/yr.)	Average-6.9
Barrels of Oil Used per year	Average-12.7

How the Competition Rates

Competitors	Rating	Pg.
BMW X1	–	99
Ford Escape	5	137
Lincoln MKC	4	198

Price Range

	Retail	Markup
Base FWD	$24,065	4%
Convenience FWD	$26,355	4%
Leather AWD	$29,800	4%
Premium AWD	$31,285	4%

Safety Checklist

Crash Tests:
Frontal...................... Very Good
Side........................... Average

Airbags:
Torso .... Fr. & Rr. Pelvis/Torso from Seat
Pelvis .... Fr. & Rr. Pelvis/Torso from Seat
Roll Sensing.......................Yes
Knee Bolster ....Standard Front

Crash Avoidance:
Collision Avoidance .....Warning Only Optional
Blind Spot Detection .... Optional
Lane Keeping Assist ....Warning Only Optional
Backup Camera..................Standard*
Pedestrian Crash Avoidance .... None

General:
Auto. Crash Notif.Oper. Assist. And Crash Info-Fee
Day Running Lamps .... Standard

Safety Belt/Restraint:
Dynamic Head Restraints .... None
Adjustable Belt..............Standard Front

^Warning feature does not meet government standards.
*Backup camera does not meet government standards.

Specifications

Drive	AWD
Engine	1.4-liter I4
Transmission	6-sp. Automatic
Tow Rating (lbs.)	–
Head/Leg Room (in.)	Cramped-39.6/40.8
Interior Space (cu. ft.)	Cramped-92.8
Cargo Space (cu. ft.)	Average-18.8
Wheelbase/Length (in.)	100.6/168.4

Buick LaCrosse

Ratings—10 Best, 1 Worst

Combo Crash Tests	8
Safety Features	8
Rollover	7
Preventive Maintenance	2
Repair Costs	3
Warranty	7
Fuel Economy	3
Complaints	8
Insurance Costs	5
OVERALL RATING	**8**

Buick LaCrosse

Buick LaCrosse

Safety Checklist

Crash Tests:
Frontal........................ Very Good
Side............................. Average
Airbags:
Torso .... Fr. & Rr. Pelvis/Torso from Seat
Pelvis .... Fr. & Rr. Pelvis/Torso from Seat
Roll Sensing............................Yes
Knee Bolster .... None
Crash Avoidance:
Collision Avoidance .... Optional CIB
Blind Spot Detection .... Optional
Lane Keeping Assist ....Warning Only Optional
Backup Camera..................Standard*
Pedestrian Crash Avoidance .... None
General:
Auto. Crash Nofit.Oper. Assist. And Crash Info-Fee
Day Running Lamps .... Standard
Safety Belt/Restraint:
Dynamic Head Restraints .... None
Adjustable Belt...............Standard Front

^Warning feature does not meet government standards.
*Backup camera does not meet government standards.

At-a-Glance

Status/Year Series Started........ Unchanged/2010
Twins ....Cadillac XTS, Chevrolet Impala
Body Styles ....Sedan
Seating 5
Anti-Theft Device ...... Std. Pass. Immobil. & Alarm
Parking Index Rating .... Hard
Where Made......................... Fairfax, KS
Fuel Factor:
MPG Rating (city/hwy) Poor-18/28
Driving Range (mi.) Short-396.8
Fuel Type........................Regular
Annual Fuel Cost .... High-$1,468
Gas Guzzler Tax ....No
Greenhouse Gas Emissions (tons/yr.)..... High-8.6
Barrels of Oil Used per year High-15.7

How the Competition Rates

Competitors	Rating	Pg.
Cadillac XTS	9	110
Chevrolet Impala	6	116
Toyota Avalon	8	247

Price Range	Retail	Markup
Base FWD	$33,810	4%
Leather FWD	$35,900	4%
Premium II FWD	$40,145	4%
Premium I AWD	$40,675	4%

Buick LaCrosse

Specifications

Drive................................... FWD
Engine 3.6-liter V6
Transmission ....6-sp. Automatic
Tow Rating (lbs.) .... Very Low-1000
Head/Leg Room (in.) .... Very Cramped-38/41.7
Interior Space (cu. ft.)............... Average-99
Cargo Space (cu. ft.) Cramped-13.3
Wheelbase/Length (in.) 111.7/197

Ratings—10 Best, 1 Worst

Combo Crash Tests	5
Safety Features	5
Rollover	8
Preventive Maintenance	2
Repair Costs	4
Warranty	7
Fuel Economy	4
Complaints	8
Insurance Costs	5
OVERALL RATING	**5**

Buick Regal

At-a-Glance

Status/Year Series Started	Unchanged/2011
Twins	–
Body Styles	Sedan
Seating	5
Anti-Theft Device	Std. Pass. Immobil. & Alarm
Parking Index Rating	Hard
Where Made	Oshawa, Ontario

Fuel Factor:

MPG Rating (city/hwy)	Poor-19/31
Driving Range (mi.)	Very Short-363.5
Fuel Type	Regular
Annual Fuel Cost	Average-$1,369
Gas Guzzler Tax	No
Greenhouse Gas Emissions (tons/yr.)	High-7.9
Barrels of Oil Used per year	High-14.3

How the Competition Rates

Competitors	Rating	Pg.
Acura TLX	10	84
Cadillac CTS	8	108
Lincoln MKZ	6	200

Price Range	Retail	Markup
Base FWD	$28,990	4%
Premium I FWD	$31,900	4%
Premium II AWD	$33,990	4%
GS AWD	$36,490	4%

Buick Regal

Safety Checklist

Crash Tests:
Frontal	Average
Side	Average

Airbags:
Torso	Front Pelvis/Torso from Seat
Pelvis	Opt. Rear Torso
Roll Sensing	Yes
Knee Bolster	None

Crash Avoidance:
Collision Avoidance	Optional CIB
Blind Spot Detection	Optional
Lane Keeping Assist	Warning Only Optional
Backup Camera	Standard*
Pedestrian Crash Avoidance	None

General:
Auto. Crash Notif.Oper. Assist. And Crash Info-Fee	
Day Running Lamps	Standard

Safety Belt/Restraint:
Dynamic Head Restraints	Standard Front
Adjustable Belt	Standard Front

^Warning feature does not meet government standards.
*Backup camera does not meet government standards.

Buick Regal

Specifications

Drive	FWD
Engine	2.4-liter I4
Transmission	6-sp. Automatic
Tow Rating (lbs.)	–
Head/Leg Room (in.)	Cramped-38.8/42.1
Interior Space (cu. ft.)	Cramped-96.8
Cargo Space (cu. ft.)	Very Cramped-11.1
Wheelbase/Length (in.)	107.8/190.2

Ratings—10 Best, 1 Worst

Combo Crash Tests	10
Safety Features	8
Rollover	8
Preventive Maintenance	7
Repair Costs	7
Warranty	7
Fuel Economy	5
Complaints	—
Insurance Costs	3
OVERALL RATING	**10**

Buick Verano

Buick Verano

At-a-Glance

Status/Year Series Started. . . . . All New/2016
Twins . . . . .Chevrolet Cruze
Body Styles . . . . .Sedan
Seating 5
Anti-Theft Device . . . . . . Std. Pass. Immobil. & Alarm
Parking Index Rating .Easy
Where Made. . . . . Orion Township, MI
Fuel Factor:
  MPG Rating (city/hwy) Average-21/32
  Driving Range (mi.) Short-387.5
  Fuel Type. . . . . .Regular
  Annual Fuel Cost . . . . Average-$1,268
  Gas Guzzler Tax . . . . .No
  Greenhouse Gas Emissions (tons/yr.). . Average-6.0
  Barrels of Oil Used per year High-13.2

How the Competition Rates

Competitors	Rating	Pg.
Acura ILX	9	81
Dodge Dart	6	131
Lexus IS	7	194

Price Range	Retail	Markup
Base	$23,480	4%
Convenience	$24,475	4%
Leather	$26,505	4%
Turbo	$28,670	4%

Safety Checklist

Crash Tests:
  Frontal. . . . . Very Good
  Side. . . . . Very Good
Airbags:
  Torso . . . . Fr. & Rr. Pelvis/Torso from Seat
  Pelvis . . . . Fr. & Rr. Pelvis/Torso from Seat
  Roll Sensing. . . . . .Yes
  Knee Bolster . . . . .Standard Front
Crash Avoidance:
  Collision Avoidance . . . . .Warning Only Optional
  Blind Spot Detection . . . . Optional
  Lane Keeping Assist . . . .Warning Only Optional
  Backup Camera . . . . Optional*
  Pedestrian Crash Avoidance . . . . None
General:
  Auto. Crash Notif. Oper. Assist. And Crash Info-Fee
  Day Running Lamps . . . . Standard
Safety Belt/Restraint:
  Dynamic Head Restraints . . . . None
  Adjustable Belt. . . . . .Standard Front

^Warning feature does not meet government standards.
*Backup camera does not meet government standards.

Buick Verano

Specifications

Drive. . . . . FWD
Engine 2.4-liter I4
Transmission . . . . .6-sp. Automatic
Tow Rating (lbs.) . . . . Very Low-1000
Head/Leg Room (in.) Cramped-38.3/42
Interior Space (cu. ft.). Cramped-95
Cargo Space (cu. ft.) Cramped-14.3
Wheelbase/Length (in.) 105.7/183.9

Cadillac ATS

Ratings—10 Best, 1 Worst

Combo Crash Tests	8
Safety Features	8
Rollover	9
Preventive Maintenance	2
Repair Costs	5
Warranty	9
Fuel Economy	5
Complaints	3
Insurance Costs	5
OVERALL RATING	**8**

Cadillac ATS

Cadillac ATS

Cadillac ATS

At-a-Glance

Status/Year Series Started Unchanged/2013
Twins . . . . –
Body Styles . . . . Sedan, Coupe
Seating 5
Anti-Theft Device . . . . . . Std. Pass. Immobil. & Alarm
Parking Index Rating . . . . Easy
Where Made. .Lansing, MI
Fuel Factor:
  MPG Rating (city/hwy) Average-21/33
  Driving Range (mi.) Average-401.7
  Fuel Type . . . . .Regular
  Annual Fuel Cost . . . . Average-$1,255
  Gas Guzzler Tax . . . . .No
  Greenhouse Gas Emissions (tons/yr.) . . Average-7.2
  Barrels of Oil Used per year High-13.2

How the Competition Rates

Competitors	Rating	Pg.
Acura ILX	9	81
Infiniti Q50	5	168
Mercedes-Benz C-Class	3	207

Price Range

Price Range	Retail	Markup
Base 2.5L Sedan	$33,215	6%
Luxury 2.0T Sedan AWD	$39,340	6%
Performance 3.6L Sedan RWD	$45,155	7%
Premium 3.6L Coupe AWD	$49,210	7%

Safety Checklist

Crash Tests:
  Frontal . . . . Very Good
  Side . . . . .Poor
Airbags:
  Torso . . . . .Front Pelvis/Torso from Seat
  Pelvis .Opt. Rear Torso
  Roll Sensing. . . . . .Yes
  Knee Bolster . . . . .Standard Front
Crash Avoidance:
  Collision Avoidance . . . . . . Optional CIB & DBS
  Blind Spot Detection . . . . Optional
  Lane Keeping Assist . . . . Optional
  Backup Camera . . . . Optional*
  Pedestrian Crash Avoidance . . . . None
General:
  Auto. Crash Notif.Oper. Assist. And Crash Info-Fee
  Day Running Lamps . . . . Standard
Safety Belt/Restraint:
  Dynamic Head Restraints . . . . None
  Adjustable Belt . . . . .Optional Rear

^Warning feature does not meet government standards.
*Backup camera does not meet government standards.

Cadillac ATS

Specifications

Drive . . . . RWD
Engine 2.5-liter I4
Transmission . . . . .6-sp. Automatic
Tow Rating (lbs.) . . . . –
Head/Leg Room (in.) Cramped-38.6/42.5
Interior Space (cu. ft.). Cramped-90.9
Cargo Space (cu. ft.) . . . . .Very Cramped-10.4
Wheelbase/Length (in.) 109.3/182.8

Cadillac CTS

Ratings—10 Best, 1 Worst

Combo Crash Tests	7
Safety Features	9
Rollover	9
Preventive Maintenance	2
Repair Costs	4
Warranty	9
Fuel Economy	3
Complaints	5
Insurance Costs	5
OVERALL RATING	**8**

Cadillac CTS

Cadillac CTS

At-a-Glance

Status/Year Series Started........ Unchanged/2014
Twins .... –
Body Styles ....Sedan, Coupe, Wagon
Seating 5
Anti-Theft Device ...... Std. Pass. Immobil. & Alarm
Parking Index Rating .... Hard
Where Made........................Lansing, MI
Fuel Factor:
MPG Rating (city/hwy)............ Poor-18/29
Driving Range (mi.) Average-412.4
Fuel Type.................................Regular
Annual Fuel Cost .... High-$1,451
Gas Guzzler Tax ....No
Greenhouse Gas Emissions (tons/yr.)..... High-8.2
Barrels of Oil Used per year High-15.0

How the Competition Rates

Competitors	Rating	Pg.
Acura TLX	10	84
Lexus ES	8	191
Mercedes-Benz E-Class	5	209

Price Range

Price Range	Retail	Markup
2.0T Base RWD	$45,560	6%
3.6L Luxury AWD	$53,285	6%
Vsport Premium RWD	$59,955	7%
3.6L Premium AWD	$64,685	7%

Safety Checklist

Crash Tests:
Frontal............................. Good
Side............................... Good
Airbags:
Torso ....Front Pelvis/Torso from Seat
Pelvis ....Opt. Rear Torso
Roll Sensing............................Yes
Knee Bolster ....Standard Front
Crash Avoidance:
Collision Avoidance ...... Optional CIB & DBS
Blind Spot Detection .... Optional
Lane Keeping Assist .... Optional
Backup Camera................. Optional*
Pedestrian Crash Avoidance .... None
General:
Auto. Crash Notif.Oper. Assist. And Crash Info-Fee
Day Running Lamps .... Standard
Safety Belt/Restraint:
Dynamic Head Restraints .... None
Adjustable Belt.......Standard Front and Rear

^Warning feature does not meet government standards.
*Backup camera does not meet government standards.

Cadillac CTS

Specifications

Drive..................................... RWD
Engine 3.6-liter V6
Transmission .... 6-sp. Automatic
Tow Rating (lbs.) .... Very Low-1000
Head/Leg Room (in.) Average-42.6/39.2
Interior Space (cu. ft.)........... Cramped-97
Cargo Space (cu. ft.) Cramped-13.7
Wheelbase/Length (in.) 114.6/195.5

Ratings—10 Best, 1 Worst

Combo Crash Tests	6
Safety Features	6
Rollover	3
Preventive Maintenance	2
Repair Costs	5
Warranty	9
Fuel Economy	2
Complaints	7
Insurance Costs	10
OVERALL RATING	**6**

Cadillac SRX

Cadillac SRX

At-a-Glance

Status/Year Series Started	Unchanged/2010
Twins	–
Body Styles	SUV
Seating	5
Anti-Theft Device	Std. Pass. Immobil. & Alarm
Parking Index Rating	Very Hard
Where Made	Ramos Arizpe, Mexico

Fuel Factor:

MPG Rating (city/hwy)	Very Poor-17/24
Driving Range (mi.)	Average-410.9
Fuel Type	Regular
Annual Fuel Cost	Very High-$1,609
Gas Guzzler Tax	No
Greenhouse Gas Emissions (tons/yr.)	Very High-9.4
Barrels of Oil Used per year	Very High-17.3

How the Competition Rates

Competitors	Rating	Pg.
Acura RDX	10	83
Lexus RX	–	197
Volvo XC60	10	269

Price Range

Price Range	Retail	Markup
Base FWD	$37,605	6%
Luxury FWD	$43,640	6%
Performance AWD	$48,840	7%
Premium AWD	$51,730	7%

Safety Checklist

Crash Tests:
- Frontal .... Average
- Side .... Average

Airbags:
- Torso .... Front Pelvis/Torso from Seat
- Pelvis .... Front Pelvis/Torso from Seat
- Roll Sensing .... Yes
- Knee Bolster .... None

Crash Avoidance:
- Collision Avoidance .... Optional CIB
- Blind Spot Detection .... Optional
- Lane Keeping Assist ....Warning Only Optional
- Backup Camera .... Optional*
- Pedestrian Crash Avoidance .... None

General:
- Auto. Crash Notif.Oper. Assist. And Crash Info-Fee
- Day Running Lamps .... Standard

Safety Belt/Restraint:
- Dynamic Head Restraints .... None
- Adjustable Belt....... Standard Front and Rear

^Warning feature does not meet government standards.
*Backup camera does not meet government standards.

Cadillac SRX

Specifications

Drive	FWD
Engine	3.6-liter V6
Transmission	6-sp. Automatic
Tow Rating (lbs.)	Low-3500
Head/Leg Room (in.)	Cramped-39.7/41.2
Interior Space (cu. ft.)	Average-100.6
Cargo Space (cu. ft.)	Roomy-29.9
Wheelbase/Length (in.)	110.5/190.3

Ratings—10 Best, 1 Worst

Combo Crash Tests	10
Safety Features	9
Rollover	7
Preventive Maintenance	2
Repair Costs	2
Warranty	9
Fuel Economy	3
Complaints	7
Insurance Costs	5
OVERALL RATING	**9**

Cadillac XTS

Cadillac XTS

At-a-Glance

Status/Year Series Started........ Unchanged/2013
Twins ....Buick LaCrosse, Chevrolet Impala
Body Styles ....Sedan
Seating 5
Anti-Theft Device . Std. Pass. Immobil. & Active Alarm
Parking Index Rating .... Hard
Where Made.................. Oshawa, Ontario
Fuel Factor:
  MPG Rating (city/hwy)............... Poor-18/28
  Driving Range (mi.) Average-407.5
  Fuel Type........................Regular
  Annual Fuel Cost .... High-$1,468
  Gas Guzzler Tax ....No
  Greenhouse Gas Emissions (tons/yr.)..... High-8.6
  Barrels of Oil Used per year High-15.7

How the Competition Rates

Competitors	Rating	Pg.
BMW 7 Series	–	97
Chrysler 300	4	127
Lincoln MKS	5	199

Price Range	Retail	Markup
Base	$45,295	6%
Luxury AWD	$51,250	6%
Platinum	$64,550	7%
Platinum Vsport AWD	$72,320	7%

Safety Checklist

Crash Tests:
  Frontal........................ Very Good
  Side.............................. Good
Airbags:
  Torso ....Front Pelvis/Torso from Seat
  Pelvis .... Rear Torso from Seat
  Roll Sensing.........................Yes
  Knee Bolster ....Standard Front
Crash Avoidance:
  Collision Avoidance ...... Optional CIB & DBS
  Blind Spot Detection .... Optional
  Lane Keeping Assist .... Optional
  Backup Camera.................. Optional*
  Pedestrian Crash Avoidance .... None
General:
  Auto. Crash Notif.Oper. Assist. And Crash Info-Fee
  Day Running Lamps .... Standard
Safety Belt/Restraint:
  Dynamic Head Restraints .... None
  Adjustable Belt...............Standard Front

^Warning feature does not meet government standards.
*Backup camera does not meet government standards.

Cadillac XTS

Specifications

Drive................................... FWD
Engine 3.6-liter V6
Transmission ....6-sp. Automatic
Tow Rating (lbs.) .... Very Low-1000
Head/Leg Room (in.) ....Very Roomy-39/45.8
Interior Space (cu. ft.)..............Roomy-104.2
Cargo Space (cu. ft.) Average-18
Wheelbase/Length (in.) 111.7/202

Chevrolet Camaro Intermediate

Ratings—10 Best, 1 Worst

Combo Crash Tests	—
Safety Features	3
Rollover	—
Preventive Maintenance	2
Repair Costs	7
Warranty	6
Fuel Economy	3
Complaints	—
Insurance Costs	1
OVERALL RATING	**—**

Chevrolet Camaro

Chevrolet Camaro

At-a-Glance

Status/Year Series Started . . . . All New/2016
Twins . . . . –
Body Styles . . . . Coupe, Convertible
Seating 4
Anti-Theft Device . . Standard Pass. Immobil. & Alarm
Parking Index Rating . . . . -'
Where Made . . . . Lansing, MI
Fuel Factor:
  MPG Rating (city/hwy) Poor-19/28
  Driving Range (mi.) . . . . –
  Fuel Type . . . . Premium
  Annual Fuel Cost . . . . Very High-$1,587
  Gas Guzzler Tax . . . . No
  Greenhouse Gas Emissions (tons/yr.) . . Average-6.5
  Barrels of Oil Used per year High-14.3

How the Competition Rates

Competitors	Rating	Pg.
Dodge Challenger	5	129
Ford Mustang	–	146
Nissan 370Z	–	221

Price Range

Price Range	Retail	Markup
1LT Coupe	$25,700	4%
2LT Coupe	$29,800	4%
1SS Coupe	$36,300	4%
2SS Coupe	$41,300	4%

Safety Checklist

Crash Tests:
  Frontal . . . . –
  Side . . . . –
Airbags:
  Torso . . . . Front Pelvis/Torso from Seat
  Pelvis . . . . Front Pelvis/Torso from Seat
  Roll Sensing . . . . Yes
  Knee Bolster . . . . None
Crash Avoidance:
  Collision Avoidance . . . . None
  Blind Spot Detection . . . . Optional
  Lane Keeping Assist . . . . None
  Backup Camera . . . . Standard*
  Pedestrian Crash Avoidance . . . . None
General:
  Auto. Crash Notif. Oper. Assist. And Crash Info-Fee
  Day Running Lamps . . . . Standard
Safety Belt/Restraint:
  Dynamic Head Restraints . . . . None
  Adjustable Belt . . . . Optional Rear

^Warning feature does not meet government standards.
*Backup camera does not meet government standards.

Chevrolet Camaro

Specifications

Drive . . . . RWD
Engine 3.6-liter
Transmission . . . . 6-sp. Automatic
Tow Rating (lbs.) . . . . –
Head/Leg Room (in.) . . . . . Very Cramped-36.6/42.6
Interior Space (cu. ft.) . . . . –
Cargo Space (cu. ft.) . . . . Very Cramped-9.1
Wheelbase/Length (in.) 110.7/188.3

Ratings—10 Best, 1 Worst

Combo Crash Tests	4
Safety Features	4
Rollover	2
Preventive Maintenance	2
Repair Costs	6
Warranty	6
Fuel Economy	3
Complaints	3
Insurance Costs	10
OVERALL RATING	**3**

Chevrolet Colorado

Chevrolet Colorado

Chevrolet Colorado

At-a-Glance

Status/Year Series Started. Unchanged/2015
Twins . . . . GMC Canyon
Body Styles . . . . Pickup
Seating 5
Anti-Theft Device Std. Pass. Immob. & Opt. Pass. Alarm
Parking Index Rating . . . . .Very Hard
Where Made. . . . . .Wentzville, MO

Fuel Factor:
MPG Rating (city/hwy) Poor-20/27
Driving Range (mi.) . . . . .Very Long-475.5
Fuel Type. . . . . .Regular
Annual Fuel Cost . . . . High-$1,391
Gas Guzzler Tax . . . . .No
Greenhouse Gas Emissions (tons/yr.). High-8.2
Barrels of Oil Used per year High-15.0

How the Competition Rates

Competitors	Rating	Pg.
Nissan Frontier	–	224
Toyota Tacoma	–	257

Price Range

	Retail	Markup
Base Ext. Cab 2WD	$20,100	0%
W/T Crew Cab 4WD	$30,005	5%
LT Crew Cab 4WD	$32,535	5%
Z71 Crew Cab 4WD	$34,640	5%

Safety Checklist

Crash Tests:
  Frontal. . . . . Average
  Side. . . . . .Poor

Airbags:
  Torso . . . . .Front Pelvis/Torso from Seat
  Pelvis . . . . .Front Pelvis/Torso from Seat
  Roll Sensing. . . . . .Yes
  Knee Bolster . . . . None

Crash Avoidance:
  Collision Avoidance . . . . .Warning Only Optional
  Blind Spot Detection . . . . None
  Lane Keeping Assist . . . .Warning Only Optional
  Backup Camera . . . . .Standard*
  Pedestrian Crash Avoidance . . . . None

General:
  Auto. Crash Notif.Oper. Assist. And Crash Info-Fee
  Day Running Lamps . . . . Standard

Safety Belt/Restraint:
  Dynamic Head Restraints . . . . None
  Adjustable Belt. . . . . .Standard Front

^Warning feature does not meet government standards.
*Backup camera does not meet government standards.

Chevrolet Colorado

Specifications

Drive. . . . . .RWD
Engine 2.5-liter I4
Transmission . . . . .6-sp. Automatic
Tow Rating (lbs.) Low-3500
Head/Leg Room (in.) . . . . . . .Very Roomy-41.4/45
Interior Space (cu. ft.). . . . . –
Cargo Space (cu. ft.) . . . . Very Roomy-49.9
Wheelbase/Length (in.) 128.3/212.7

Ratings—10 Best, 1 Worst

Combo Crash Tests	—
Safety Features	1
Rollover	—
Preventive Maintenance	3
Repair Costs	1
Warranty	6
Fuel Economy	2
Complaints	7
Insurance Costs	10

OVERALL RATING   —

Chevrolet Corvette

At-a-Glance

Status/Year Series Started Unchanged/2014
Twins . . . .—
Body Styles . . . . Coupe, Convertible
Seating 2
Anti-Theft Device . . . . . . Std. Pass. Immobil. & Alarm
Parking Index Rating . . . . Average
Where Made . . . . .Bowling Green, KY

Fuel Factor:
  MPG Rating (city/hwy) . . . . .Very Poor-16/29
  Driving Range (mi.) . . . . Very Short-370.8
  Fuel Type . . . . .Premium
  Annual Fuel Cost . . . . .Very High-$1,759
  Gas Guzzler Tax . . . . .No
  Greenhouse Gas Emissions (tons/yr.) Very High-9.0
  Barrels of Oil Used per year High-16.5

How the Competition Rates

Competitors	Rating	Pg.
Dodge Challenger	5	129
Ford Mustang	–	146
Nissan 370Z	–	221

Price Range

Price Range	Retail	Markup
Base Coupe	$55,400	8%
Base Convertible	$59,400	8%
Z51 Coupe	$60,400	8%
Z51 Convertible	$64,400	8%

Chevrolet Corvette

Safety Checklist

Crash Tests:
  Frontal . . . .—
  Side . . . .—
Airbags:
  Torso . . . . .Front Head/Torso from Seat
  Pelvis . . . . None
  Roll Sensing . . . . No
  Knee Bolster . . . . None
Crash Avoidance:
  Collision Avoidance . . . . None
  Blind Spot Detection . . . . None
  Lane Keeping Assist . . . . None
  Backup Camera . . . . Optional*
  Pedestrian Crash Avoidance . . . . None
General:
  Auto. Crash Notif. Oper. Assist. And Crash Info-Fee
  Day Running Lamps . . . . Standard
Safety Belt/Restraint:
  Dynamic Head Restraints . . . . None
  Adjustable Belt . . . . None

^Warning feature does not meet government standards.
*Backup camera does not meet government standards.

Chevrolet Corvette

Specifications

Drive . . . . RWD
Engine 6.2-liter V8
Transmission . . . . .8-sp. Automatic
Tow Rating (lbs.) . . . . —
Head/Leg Room (in.) Cramped-38/43
Interior Space (cu. ft.) . . . . Very Cramped-52
Cargo Space (cu. ft.) Cramped-15
Wheelbase/Length (in.) 106.7/176.9

Ratings—10 Best, 1 Worst

Combo Crash Tests	—
Safety Features	8
Rollover	—
Preventive Maintenance	4
Repair Costs	8
Warranty	6
Fuel Economy	8
Complaints	—
Insurance Costs	1
OVERALL RATING	—

Chevrolet Cruze

Chevrolet Cruze

At-a-Glance

Status/Year Series Started. . . . . All New/2016
Twins . . . . Buick Verano
Body Styles . . . . .Sedan
Seating 5
Anti-Theft Device . . . . . . Std. Pass. Immobil. & Alarm
Parking Index Rating . . . . Easy
Where Made. . . . . .Lordstown, OH

Fuel Factor:
MPG Rating (city/hwy) Good-26/38
Driving Range (mi.) . . . . .Very Long-472.8
Fuel Type . . . . .Regular
Annual Fuel Cost . . . . Low-$1,039
Gas Guzzler Tax . . . . .No
Greenhouse Gas Emissions (tons/yr.). Low-4.9
Barrels of Oil Used per year Average-11.0

How the Competition Rates

Competitors	Rating	Pg.
Ford Focus	6	143
Honda Civic	—	149
Toyota Corolla	9	249

Price Range

Price Range	Retail	Markup
LS MT	$17,845	4%
1LT AT	$20,195	4%
Eco AT	$21,470	4%
LTZ	$24,370	5%

Safety Checklist

Crash Tests:
Frontal. . . . .–
Side. . . . .–

Airbags:
Torso . . . . Fr. & Rr. Pelvis/Torso from Seat
Pelvis . . . . Fr. & Rr. Pelvis/Torso from Seat
Roll Sensing. . . . . .Yes
Knee Bolster . . . . .Standard Front

Crash Avoidance:
Collision Avoidance . . . . Warning Only Optional^
Blind Spot Detection . . . . Optional
Lane Keeping Assist . . . Warning Only Optional^
Backup Camera . . . . .Standard*
Pedestrian Crash Avoidance . . . . None

General:
Auto. Crash Notif. Oper. Assist. And Crash Info-Fee
Day Running Lamps . . . . Standard

Safety Belt/Restraint:
Dynamic Head Restraints . . . . None
Adjustable Belt. . . . . . .Standard Front and Rear

^Warning feature does not meet government standards.
*Backup camera does not meet government standards.

Chevrolet Cruze

Specifications

Drive. . . . . FWD
Engine 1.8-liter I4
Transmission . . . . 6-sp. Autonatic
Tow Rating (lbs.) . . . . –
Head/Leg Room (in.) Average-39.3/42.28
Interior Space (cu. ft.). Cramped-94.6
Cargo Space (cu. ft.) Cramped-15
Wheelbase/Length (in.) 105.7/181

Ratings—10 Best, 1 Worst

Combo Crash Tests	2
Safety Features	5
Rollover	3
Preventive Maintenance	2
Repair Costs	6
Warranty	6
Fuel Economy	5
Complaints	5
Insurance Costs	5
OVERALL RATING	**2**

Chevrolet Equinox

Chevrolet Equinox

At-a-Glance

Status/Year Series Started	Unchanged/2005
Twins	GMC Terrain
Body Styles	SUV
Seating	5
Anti-Theft Device	Std. Pass. Immobil. & Alarm
Parking Index Rating	Very Hard
Where Made	Oshawa, Ontario / Spring Hill, TN

Fuel Factor:

MPG Rating (city/hwy)	Average-22/32
Driving Range (mi.)	Very Long-481.3
Fuel Type	Regular
Annual Fuel Cost	Average-$1,230
Gas Guzzler Tax	No
Greenhouse Gas Emissions (tons/yr.)	Average-6.9
Barrels of Oil Used per year	Average-12.7

How the Competition Rates

Competitors	Rating	Pg.
Dodge Journey	1	132
Ford Explorer	3	139
Honda Pilot	9	158

Price Range

Price Range	Retail	Markup
LS FWD	$25,210	5%
LT FWD	$26,450	5%
LT AWD	$28,200	5%
LTZ AWD	$31,490	5%

Safety Checklist

Crash Tests:

Frontal	Poor
Side	Very Poor

Airbags:

Torso	Front Pelvis/Torso from Seat
Pelvis	Front Pelvis/Torso from Seat
Roll Sensing	Yes
Knee Bolster	None

Crash Avoidance:

Collision Avoidance	Warning Only Optional
Blind Spot Detection	Optional
Lane Keeping Assist	Warning Only Optional
Backup Camera	Standard*
Pedestrian Crash Avoidance	None

General:

Auto. Crash Notif. Oper. Assist. And Crash Info-Fee
Day Running Lamps	Standard

Safety Belt/Restraint:

Dynamic Head Restraints	None
Adjustable Belt	Standard Front and Rear

^Warning feature does not meet government standards.
*Backup camera does not meet government standards.

Chevrolet Equinox

Specifications

Drive	FWD
Engine	2.4-liter I4
Transmission	6-sp. Automatic
Tow Rating (lbs.)	Very Low-1500
Head/Leg Room (in.)	Average-40.9/41.2
Interior Space (cu. ft.)	Average-99.7
Cargo Space (cu. ft.)	Roomy-31.5
Wheelbase/Length (in.)	112.5/187.8

Ratings—10 Best, 1 Worst

Combo Crash Tests	7
Safety Features	4
Rollover	7
Preventive Maintenance	2
Repair Costs	7
Warranty	6
Fuel Economy	3
Complaints	5
Insurance Costs	5
OVERALL RATING	**6**

Chevrolet Impala

Chevrolet Impala

At-a-Glance

Status/Year Series Started. Unchanged/2014
Twins . . . . .Buick LaCrosse, Cadillac XTS
Body Styles . . . . .Sedan
Seating 5
Anti-Theft Device . . . . . . Std. Pass. Immobil. & Alarm
Parking Index Rating . . . . Hard
Where Made. . . . . Detroit, MI / Oshawa, Ontario

Fuel Factor:
MPG Rating (city/hwy) Poor-18/28
Driving Range (mi.) Short-396.8
Fuel Type. . . . . .Regular
Annual Fuel Cost . . . . High-$1,468
Gas Guzzler Tax . . . . .No
Greenhouse Gas Emissions (tons/yr.). High-8.6
Barrels of Oil Used per year High-15.7

How the Competition Rates

Competitors	Rating	Pg.
Buick LaCrosse	8	104
Ford Taurus	4	147
Toyota Avalon	8	247

Price Range	Retail	Markup
LS	$27,095	4%
2LT	$30,435	5%
2LZ	$35,540	6%
3LT	$40,810	5%

Safety Checklist

Crash Tests:
Frontal. . . . . Good
Side. . . . . .Poor

Airbags:
Torso . . . . .Front Pelvis/Torso from Seat
Pelvis . . . . Rear Torso from Seat
Roll Sensing. . . . . .Yes
Knee Bolster . . . . .Standard Front

Crash Avoidance:
Collision Avoidance . . . . Optional CIB
Blind Spot Detection . . . . Optional
Lane Keeping Assist . . . .Warning Only Optional
Backup Camera . . . . Optional*
Pedestrian Crash Avoidance . . . . None

General:
Auto. Crash Notification. . . . . Standard
Day Running Lamps . . . . Standard

Safety Belt/Restraint:
Dynamic Head Restraints . . . . None
Adjustable Belt. . . . . . .Standard Front and Rear

^Warning feature does not meet government standards.
*Backup camera does not meet government standards.

Chevrolet Impala

Specifications

Drive. . . . . FWD
Engine 3.6-liter V6
Transmission . . . . .6-sp. Automatic
Tow Rating (lbs.) . . . . Very Low-1000
Head/Leg Room (in.) . . . . . . Very Roomy-39.9/45.8
Interior Space (cu. ft.). Roomy-105
Cargo Space (cu. ft.) Average-18.8
Wheelbase/Length (in.) 111.7/201.3

Ratings—10 Best, 1 Worst

Combo Crash Tests	6
Safety Features	9
Rollover	8
Preventive Maintenance	8
Repair Costs	7
Warranty	6
Fuel Economy	8
Complaints	—
Insurance Costs	3

OVERALL RATING —

Chevrolet Malibu

Chevrolet Malibu

At-a-Glance

Status/Year Series Started	All New/2016
Twins	—
Body Styles	Sedan
Seating	5
Anti-Theft Device	Std. Pass. Immobil. & Alarm
Parking Index Rating	—'
Where Made	Fairfax, KS

Fuel Factor:

MPG Rating (city/hwy)	Good-27/37
Driving Range (mi.)	Short-399.6
Fuel Type	Regular
Annual Fuel Cost	Low-$1,024
Gas Guzzler Tax	No
Greenhouse Gas Emissions (tons/yr.)	Low-4.8
Barrels of Oil Used per year	Low-10.6

How the Competition Rates

Competitors	Rating	Pg.
Ford Fusion	7	144
Honda Accord	10	148
Toyota Camry	7	248

Price Range	Retail	Markup
LS	$23,120	4%
LT	$25,020	4%
2LT	$28,620	4%
2LZ	$30,920	4%

Safety Checklist

Crash Tests:
- Frontal . . . . Average
- Side . . . . Good

Airbags:
- Torso . . . . Front Pelvis/Torso from Seat
- Pelvis . . . . Rear Torso from Seat
- Roll Sensing . . . . Yes
- Knee Bolster . . . . Standard Front

Crash Avoidance:
- Collision Avoidance . . . . . . Optional CIB & DBS
- Blind Spot Detection . . . . Optional
- Lane Keeping Assist . . . . Optional
- Backup Camera . . . . Optional*
- Pedestrian Crash Avoidance . . . . Optional

General:
- Auto. Crash Notif. Oper. Assist. And Crash Info-Fee
- Day Running Lamps . . . . Standard

Safety Belt/Restraint:
- Dynamic Head Restraints . . . . None
- Adjustable Belt . . . . Standard Front and Rear

^Warning feature does not meet government standards.
*Backup camera does not meet government standards.

Chevrolet Malibu

Specifications

Drive	FWD
Engine	1.5-liter I4
Transmission	8-sp. Auto
Tow Rating (lbs.)	—
Head/Leg Room (in.)	Cramped-39.1/42
Interior Space (cu. ft.)	Average-102.9
Cargo Space (cu. ft.)	Cramped-15.8
Wheelbase/Length (in.)	111.4/193.8

Ratings—10 Best, 1 Worst

Combo Crash Tests	9
Safety Features	4
Rollover	3
Preventive Maintenance	2
Repair Costs	6
Warranty	6
Fuel Economy	1
Complaints	7
Insurance Costs	5
OVERALL RATING	**5**

Chevrolet Silverado

Chevrolet Silverado

At-a-Glance

Status/Year Series Started........ Unchanged/2014
Twins . . . . GMC Sierra
Body Styles . . . . Pickup
Seating 5/6
Anti-Theft DeviceStd. Pass. Immobil. & Opt. Pass. Alarm
Parking Index Rating . . . . Very Hard
Where Made. Fort Wayne, IN

Fuel Factor:
MPG Rating (city/hwy) . . . . .Very Poor-16/22
Driving Range (mi.) . . . . .Very Long-474.2
Fuel Type. . . . . .Regular
Annual Fuel Cost . . . . Very High-$1,727
Gas Guzzler Tax . . . . .No
Greenhouse Gas Emissions (tons/yr.)Very High-10.0
Barrels of Oil Used per year . . . . . . .Very High-18.3

How the Competition Rates

Competitors	Rating	Pg.
Ford F-150	9	140
Ram 1500	4	236
Toyota Tundra	–	258

Price Range

Price Range	Retail	Markup
W/T Reg. Cab 2WD	$26,170	4%
LT Dbl. Cab 4WD	$38,120	8%
LTZ Crew Cab 4WD	$45,510	8%
High Country Crew Cab 4WD	$51,240	8%

Safety Checklist

Crash Tests:
  Frontal. . . . . Very Good
  Side. . . . . .Poor
Airbags:
  Torso . . . . Front Pelvis/Torso
  Pelvis . . . . Front Torso/Pelvis
  Roll Sensing. . . . . .Yes
  Knee Bolster . . . . None
Crash Avoidance:
  Collision Avoidance . . . . .Warning Only Optional
  Blind Spot Detection . . . . None
  Lane Keeping Assist . . . .Warning Only Optional
  Backup Camera. . . . . Optional*
  Pedestrian Crash Avoidance . . . . None
General:
  Auto. Crash Notif. Oper. Assist. And Crash Info-Fee
  Day Running Lamps . . . . Standard
Safety Belt/Restraint:
  Dynamic Head Restraints . . . . None
  Adjustable Belt. . . . . . .Standard Front and Rear

^Warning feature does not meet government standards.
*Backup camera does not meet government standards.

Chevrolet Silverado

Specifications

Drive. 4WD
Engine 5.3-liter V8
Transmission . . . . 6-sp. Automatic
Tow Rating (lbs.) . . . . Very High-9200
Head/Leg Room (in.) . . . . . . Very Roomy-42.8/45.2
Interior Space (cu. ft.). –
Cargo Space (cu. ft.) . . . . Very Roomy-61
Wheelbase/Length (in.) 143.5/230

Chevrolet Sonic   Subcompact

Ratings—10 Best, 1 Worst

Combo Crash Tests	8
Safety Features	8
Rollover	7
Preventive Maintenance	9
Repair Costs	10
Warranty	6
Fuel Economy	7
Complaints	6
Insurance Costs	1
OVERALL RATING	**10**

Chevrolet Sonic

Chevrolet Sonic

At-a-Glance

Status/Year Series Started Unchanged/2012
Twins . . . . –
Body Styles . . . . Sedan, Hatchback
Seating 5
Anti-Theft Device . . . . . . Std. Pass. Immobil. & Alarm
Parking Index Rating . . . . .Very Easy
Where Made. . . . . Orion Township, MI
Fuel Factor:
  MPG Rating (city/hwy) Good-25/35
  Driving Range (mi.) . . . . Very Short-350.0
  Fuel Type. . . . . .Regular
  Annual Fuel Cost . . . . Low-$1,098
  Gas Guzzler Tax . . . . .No
  Greenhouse Gas Emissions (tons/yr.). . Average-6.5
  Barrels of Oil Used per year Average-11.8

How the Competition Rates

Competitors	Rating	Pg.
Ford Fiesta	1	141
Nissan Versa	3	234
Toyota Yaris	6	259

Price Range	Retail	Markup
LS Sedan MT	$14,345	3%
LT Hatchback AT	$18,145	4%
LTZ Sedan AT	$19,780	5%
RS Hatchback AT	$21,495	5%

Safety Checklist

Crash Tests:
  Frontal. . . . . Very Good
  Side. . . . . Average
Airbags:
  Torso . . . . Fr. & Rr. Pelvis/Torso from Seat
  Pelvis . . . . Fr. & Rr. Pelvis/Torso from Seat
  Roll Sensing. . . . . .Yes
  Knee Bolster . . . . .Standard Front
Crash Avoidance:
  Collision Avoidance . . . . .Warning Only Optional
  Blind Spot Detection . . . . None
  Lane Keeping Assist . . . .Warning Only Optional
  Backup Camera . . . . Optional*
  Pedestrian Crash Avoidance . . . . None
General:
  Auto. Crash Notif. Oper. Assist. And Crash Info-Fee
  Day Running Lamps . . . . Standard
Safety Belt/Restraint:
  Dynamic Head Restraints . . . . None
  Adjustable Belt. . . . . . .Standard Front and Rear

^Warning feature does not meet government standards.
*Backup camera does not meet government standards.

Chevrolet Sonic

Specifications

Drive . . . . FWD
Engine 1.8-liter I4
Transmission . . . . .6-sp. Automatic
Tow Rating (lbs.) . . . . –
Head/Leg Room (in.) Cramped-38.7/41.8
Interior Space (cu. ft.). Cramped-90.6
Cargo Space (cu. ft.) Average-19
Wheelbase/Length (in.) 99.4/159

Ratings—10 Best, 1 Worst

Combo Crash Tests	—
Safety Features	8
Rollover	—
Preventive Maintenance	9
Repair Costs	9
Warranty	6
Fuel Economy	9
Complaints	—
Insurance Costs	1
OVERALL RATING	**—**

Chevrolet Spark

At-a-Glance

Status/Year Series Started. . . . . All New/2016
Twins . . . .–
Body Styles . . . . Hatchback
Seating 4
Anti-Theft DeviceStd. Pass. Immobil. & Opt. Pass. Alarm
Parking Index Rating . . . . .Very Easy
Where Made. . . . . Changwon, South Korea
Fuel Factor:
  MPG Rating (city/hwy) . . . . Very Good-31/41
  Driving Range (mi.) . . . . Very Short-313.4
  Fuel Type. . . . . .Regular
  Annual Fuel Cost . . . . .Very Low-$904
  Gas Guzzler Tax . . . . .No
  Greenhouse Gas Emissions (tons/yr.). Very Low-4.2
  Barrels of Oil Used per year Low-9.4

How the Competition Rates

Competitors	Rating	Pg.
Fiat 500	4	133
Kia Rio	6	182
Smart ForTwo	–	239

Price Range

Price Range	Retail	Markup
LS MT	$12,660	3%
1LT AT	$15,785	4%
2LT AT	$17,460	4%
2LT EV	$25,560	4%

Chevrolet Spark

Safety Checklist

Crash Tests:
  Frontal. . . . .–
  Side. . . . .–
Airbags:
  Torso . . . . Fr. & Rr. Pelvis/Torso from Seat
  Pelvis . . . . Fr. & Rr. Pelvis/Torso from Seat
  Roll Sensing. . . . . .Yes
  Knee Bolster . . . . .Standard Front
Crash Avoidance:
  Collision Avoidance . . . . None
  Blind Spot Detection . . . . Optional
  Lane Keeping Assist . . . .Warning Only Optional
  Backup Camera . . . . .Standard*
  Pedestrian Crash Avoidance . . . . None
General:
  Auto. Crash Notif. . . .Oper. Assist. & Crash Info-Fee
  Day Running Lamps . . . . Standard
Safety Belt/Restraint:
  Dynamic Head Restraints . . . . None
  Adjustable Belt. . . . . . .Standard Front and Rear

^Warning feature does not meet government standards.
*Backup camera does not meet government standards.

Chevrolet Spark

Specifications

Drive. . . . . FWD
Engine 1.4-liter I4
Transmission . . . . .CVT
Tow Rating (lbs.) . . . .–
Head/Leg Room (in.) Cramped-39/41.7
Interior Space (cu. ft.). . . . . Very Cramped-83
Cargo Space (cu. ft.) . . . . .Very Cramped-11.1
Wheelbase/Length (in.) 93.9/143.1

Ratings—10 Best, 1 Worst	Suburban	Yukon XL	Escalade ESV
Combo Crash Tests	5	5	—
Safety Features	5	4	6
Rollover	2	2	2
Preventive Maintenance	2	2	2
Repair Costs	8	1	2
Warranty	6	5	9
Fuel Economy	1	1	1
Complaints	1	9	5
Insurance Costs	10	10	5

OVERALL RATING 3

Chevrolet Suburban

GMC Yukon XL

At-a-Glance

Status/Year Series Started. Unchanged/2015
Twins . . . . . .Cadillac Escalade ESV, GMC Yukon XL
Body Styles . . . . SUV
Seating 6/9
Anti-Theft Device . . . . . . Std. Pass. Immobil. & Alarm
Parking Index Rating . . . . .Very Hard
Where Made. Arlington, TX

Fuel Factor:
  MPG Rating (city/hwy). . . . .Very Poor-15/22
  Driving Range (mi.) . . . . .Very Long-542.7
  Fuel Type. . . . . .Regular
  Annual Fuel Cost . . . . Very High-$1,799
  Gas Guzzler Tax . . . . .No
  Greenhouse Gas Emissions (tons/yr.)Very High-10.0
  Barrels of Oil Used per year . . . . . . .Very High-18.3

How the Competition Rates

Competitors	Rating	Pg.
Ford Expedition	7	138
Nissan Armada	–	223
Toyota Sequoia	–	255

Price Range	Retail	Markup
1500 LS 2WD	$49,700	8%
1500 LT 2WD	$54,730	8%
1500 LT 4WD	$57,730	8%
1500 LTZ 4WD	$67,310	8%

Safety Checklist

Crash Tests:
  Frontal. . . . . Average
  Side. . . . . Average
Airbags:
  Torso . . . . .Front Pelvis/Torso from Seat
  Pelvis . . . . .Front Pelvis/Torso from Seat
  Roll Sensing. .Yes
  Knee Bolster . . . . None
Crash Avoidance:
  Collision Avoidance . . . . Optional CIB
  Blind Spot Detection . . . . Optional
  Lane Keeping Assist . . . .Warning Only Optional
  Backup Camera. . . . . .Standard*
  Pedestrian Crash Avoidance . . . . None
General:
  Auto. Crash Notif.. .Oper. Assist. & Crash Info-Fee
  Day Running Lamps . . . . Standard
Safety Belt/Restraint:
  Dynamic Head Restraints . . . . None
  Adjustable Belt. . . . . . .Standard Front and Rear

^Warning feature does not meet government standards.
*Backup camera does not meet government standards.

Cadillac Escalade ESV

Specifications

Drive. 4WD
Engine .5.3-liter V8
Transmission . . . . .6-sp. Automatic
Tow Rating (lbs.) High-8000
Head/Leg Room (in.) . . . . . . Very Roomy-42.8/45.3
Interior Space (cu. ft.). Roomy-122.4
Cargo Space (cu. ft.) . . . . Very Roomy-39.3
Wheelbase/Length (in.) 130/224.4

Chevrolet Tahoe, GMC Yukon, Cad. Escalade   Large SUV

Ratings—10 Best, 1 Worst

	Tahoe	Yukon	Escalade
Combo Crash Tests	8	8	—
Safety Features	6	5	6
Rollover	1	1	1
Preventive Maintenance	2	2	2
Repair Costs	5	5	2
Warranty	6	5	9
Fuel Economy	1	1	1
Complaints	2	7	6
Insurance Costs	10	10	5
OVERALL RATING			**4**

Chevrolet Tahoe

Safety Checklist

Crash Tests:
Frontal . . . . Good
Side . . . . Very Good

Airbags:
Torso . . . . Front Pelvis/Torso from Seat
Pelvis . . . . Front Pelvis/Torso from Seat
Roll Sensing . . . . Yes
Knee Bolster . . . . None

Crash Avoidance:
Collision Avoidance . . . . Optional CIB
Blind Spot Detection . . . . Optional
Lane Keeping Assist . . . . Optional
Backup Camera . . . . Standard*
Pedestrian Crash Avoidance . . . . None

General:
Auto. Crash Notif.. . Oper. Assist.& Crash Info-Fee
Day Running Lamps . . . . Standard

Safety Belt/Restraint:
Dynamic Head Restraints . . . . None
Adjustable Belt . . . . . . Standard Front and Rear

^Warning feature does not meet government standards.
*Backup camera does not meet government standards.

GMC Yukon

At-a-Glance

Status/Year Series Started Unchanged/2015
Twins . . . . .Cadillac Escalade, GMC Yukon
Body Styles . . . . SUV
Seating 6/9
Anti-Theft Device . . . . . . Std. Pass. Immobil. & Alarm
Parking Index Rating . . . . Very Hard
Where Made. . . . . Arlington, TX
Fuel Factor:
MPG Rating (city/hwy) . . . . .Very Poor-16/22
Driving Range (mi.) . . . . .Very Long-474.2
Fuel Type . . . . .Regular
Annual Fuel Cost . . . . Very High-$1,727
Gas Guzzler Tax . . . . .No
Greenhouse Gas Emissions (tons/yr.)Very High-10.0
Barrels of Oil Used per year . . . . Very High-18.3

How the Competition Rates

Competitors	Rating	Pg.
Ford Expedition	7	138
Nissan Armada	–	223
Toyota Sequoia	–	255

Price Range

Price Range	Retail	Markup
LS FWD	$47,000	8%
LT 2WD	$52,030	8%
LT4WD	$55,030	8%
LTZ 4WD	$64,610	8%

Cadillac Escalade

Specifications

Drive 4WD
Engine 5.3-liter V8
Transmission . . . . .6-sp. Automatic
Tow Rating (lbs.) . . . . Very High-8400
Head/Leg Room (in.) . . . . Very Roomy-42.8/45.3
Interior Space (cu. ft.) Roomy-120.8
Cargo Space (cu. ft.) Cramped-15.3
Wheelbase/Length (in.) 116/204

Chevrolet Traverse

Ratings—10 Best, 1 Worst	
Combo Crash Tests	7
Safety Features	5
Rollover	4
Preventive Maintenance	2
Repair Costs	5
Warranty	6
Fuel Economy	2
Complaints	5
Insurance Costs	10
OVERALL RATING	**4**

Chevrolet Traverse

Chevrolet Traverse

At-a-Glance

Status/Year Series Started	Unchanged/2009
Twins	GMC Acadia
Body Styles	SUV
Seating	7/8
Anti-Theft Device	Std. Pass. Immobil. & Alarm
Parking Index Rating	Very Hard
Where Made	Lansing, MI

Fuel Factor:

MPG Rating (city/hwy)	Very Poor-17/24
Driving Range (mi.)	Long-430.5
Fuel Type	Regular
Annual Fuel Cost	Very High-$1,610
Gas Guzzler Tax	No
Greenhouse Gas Emissions (tons/yr.)	Very High-9.5
Barrels of Oil Used per year	Very High-17.3

How the Competition Rates

Competitors	Rating	Pg.
Buick Enclave	5	102
Ford Flex	–	142
Toyota Highlander	7	250

Price Range	Retail	Markup
LS FWD	$31,205	4%
LT FWD	$34,005	5%
2LT AWD	$38,505	5%
LTZ AWD	$44,145	6%

Safety Checklist

Crash Tests:

Frontal	Good
Side	Good

Airbags:

Torso	Front Pelvis/Torso from Seat
Pelvis	Front Pelvis/Torso from Seat
Roll Sensing	Yes
Knee Bolster	None

Crash Avoidance:

Collision Avoidance	Warning Only Optional
Blind Spot Detection	Optional
Lane Keeping Assist	Warning Only Optional
Backup Camera	Optional*
Pedestrian Crash Avoidance	None

General:

Auto. Crash Notif.	Oper. Assist. & Crash Info-Fee
Day Running Lamps	Standard

Safety Belt/Restraint:

Dynamic Head Restraints	None
Adjustable Belt	Standard Front and Rear

^Warning feature does not meet government standards.
*Backup camera does not meet government standards.

Chevrolet Traverse

Specifications

Drive	FWD
Engine	3.6-liter V6
Transmission	6-sp. Automatic
Tow Rating (lbs.)	Low-5200
Head/Leg Room (in.)	Average-40.4/41.3
Interior Space (cu. ft.)	Roomy-150.8
Cargo Space (cu. ft.)	Roomy-24.4
Wheelbase/Length (in.)	118.9/203.7

Ratings—10 Best, 1 Worst

Combo Crash Tests	8
Safety Features	6
Rollover	2
Preventive Maintenance	—
Repair Costs	5
Warranty	6
Fuel Economy	6
Complaints	10
Insurance Costs	5
OVERALL RATING	**9**

Chevrolet Trax

Chevrolet Trax

At-a-Glance

Status/Year Series Started Unchanged/2015
Twins . . . . Buick Encore
Body Styles . . . . SUV
Seating 5
Anti-Theft Device . . . . . . Std. Pass. Immobil. & Alarm
Parking Index Rating . . . . Easy
Where Made . . . . South Korea / Mexico
Fuel Factor:
  MPG Rating (city/hwy) Average-24/31
  Driving Range (mi.) Short-374.0
  Fuel Type . . . . .Regular
  Annual Fuel Cost . . . . Low-$1,179
  Gas Guzzler Tax . . . . .No
  Greenhouse Gas Emissions (tons/yr.) . . Average-6.7
  Barrels of Oil Used per year Average-12.2

How the Competition Rates

Competitors	Rating	Pg.
Ford Escape	5	137
Honda CR-V	7	154
Jeep Compass	4	174

Price Range

Price Range	Retail	Markup
LS FWD	$20,300	4%
LT FWD	$22,645	4%
LT AWD	$24,145	4%
LTZ AWD	$26,730	4%

Safety Checklist

Crash Tests:
  Frontal . . . . Very Good
  Side . . . . Average
Airbags:
  Torso . . . . Fr. & Rr. Pelvis/Torso from Seat
  Pelvis . . . . Fr. & Rr. Pelvis/Torso from Seat
  Roll Sensing . . . . .Yes
  Knee Bolster . . . . .Standard Front
Crash Avoidance:
  Collision Avoidance . . . . None
  Blind Spot Detection . . . . None
  Lane Keeping Assist . . . . None
  Backup Camera . . . . .Standard*
  Pedestrian Crash Avoidance . . . . None
General:
  Auto. Crash Notif . . . .Oper. Assist. & Crash Info-Fee
  Day Running Lamps . . . . Standard
Safety Belt/Restraint:
  Dynamic Head Restraints . . . . None
  Adjustable Belt . . . . . . .Standard Front and Rear

^Warning feature does not meet government standards.
*Backup camera does not meet government standards.

Chevrolet Trax

Specifications

Drive . . . . AWD
Engine 1.4-liter I4
Transmission . . . . .6-sp. Automatic
Tow Rating (lbs.) . . . . —
Head/Leg Room (in.) Cramped-39.6/40.8
Interior Space (cu. ft.) Cramped-92.8
Cargo Space (cu. ft.) Average-18.7
Wheelbase/Length (in.) 100.6/168.5

Ratings—10 Best, 1 Worst	
Combo Crash Tests	—
Safety Features	7
Rollover	—
Preventive Maintenance	3
Repair Costs	7
Warranty	6
Fuel Economy	10
Complaints	—
Insurance Costs	10
OVERALL RATING	**—**

Chevrolet Volt

Chevrolet Volt

At-a-Glance

Status/Year Series Started	All New/2016
Twins	—
Body Styles	Sedan
Seating	5
Anti-Theft Device	Std. Pass. Immobil. & Alarm
Parking Index Rating	Easy
Where Made	Detroit, MI

Fuel Factor:

MPG Rating (city/hwy)	Very Good-43/42
Driving Range (mi.)	Short-378.6
Fuel Type	Regular
Annual Fuel Cost	Very Low-$740
Gas Guzzler Tax	No
Greenhouse Gas Emissions (tons/yr.)	Very Low-0.8
Barrels of Oil Used per year	Very Low-2.0

How the Competition Rates

Competitors	Rating	Pg.
Ford C-MAX	5	135
Nissan Leaf	4	226
Toyota Prius	—	251

Price Range

	Retail	Markup
LT	$33,170	4%
Premier	$37,520	4%

Safety Checklist

Crash Tests:
Frontal	—
Side	—

Airbags:
Torso	Front Pelvis/Torso from Seat
Pelvis	Front Pelvis/Torso from Seat
Roll Sensing	Yes
Knee Bolster	Standard Front

Crash Avoidance:
Collision Avoidance	Warning Only Optional
Blind Spot Detection	Optional
Lane Keeping Assist	Warning Only Optional
Backup Camera	Standard*
Pedestrian Crash Avoidance	None

General:
Auto. Crash Notif.	Oper. Assist. & Crash Info-Fee
Day Running Lamps	Standard

Safety Belt/Restraint:
Dynamic Head Restraints	None
Adjustable Belt	Standard Rear

^Warning feature does not meet government standards.
*Backup camera does not meet government standards.

Chevrolet Volt

Specifications

Drive	FWD
Engine	Electric and Gas Power the Wheels
Transmission	CVT
Tow Rating (lbs.)	—
Head/Leg Room (in.)	Cramped-37.8/42.1
Interior Space (cu. ft.)	Very Cramped-90
Cargo Space (cu. ft.)	Very Cramped-10.6
Wheelbase/Length (in.)	106.1/180.4

See page 275 for more detail.

Ratings—10 Best, 1 Worst

Combo Crash Tests	8
Safety Features	9
Rollover	9
Preventive Maintenance	9
Repair Costs	9
Warranty	4
Fuel Economy	6
Complaints	1
Insurance Costs	5
OVERALL RATING	**10**

Chrysler 200

Chrysler 200

At-a-Glance

Status/Year Series Started........ Unchanged/2015
Twins . . . . —
Body Styles . . . . .Sedan
Seating. 5
Anti-Theft Device . . . . . . Std. Pass. Immobil. & Alarm
Parking Index Rating . . . . Hard
Where Made. . . . . Sterling Heights, MI

Fuel Factor:
MPG Rating (city/hwy) Average-23/36
Driving Range (mi.) Long-433.9
Fuel Type. . . . . .Regular
Annual Fuel Cost . . . . Low-$1,147
Gas Guzzler Tax . . . . .No
Greenhouse Gas Emissions (tons/yr.) . . Average-6.4
Barrels of Oil Used per year Average-11.8

How the Competition Rates

Competitors	Rating	Pg.
Chevrolet Malibu	9	117
Ford Fusion	7	144
Kia Optima	9	181

Price Range	Retail	Markup
LX	$21,995	0%
Limited	$24,145	2%
S AWD	$29,545	3%
C AWD	$31,425	3%

Safety Checklist

Crash Tests:
Frontal. . . . . Good
Side. . . . . Average

Airbags:
Torso . . . . .Front Pelvis/Torso from Seat
Pelvis . . . . .Front Pelvis/Torso from Seat
Roll Sensing. . . . . .Yes
Knee Bolster . . . . .Standard Front

Crash Avoidance:
Collision Avoidance . . . . . . Optional CIB & DBS
Blind Spot Detection . . . . Optional
Lane Keeping Assist . . . . Optional
Backup Camera . . . . Optional*
Pedestrian Crash Avoidance . . . . None

General:
Auto. Crash Notification . . . . None
Day Running Lamps . . . . None

Safety Belt/Restraint:
Dynamic Head Restraints . . . . . .Standard Front
Adjustable Belt. . . . . .Standard Front

^Warning feature does not meet government standards.
*Backup camera does not meet government standards.

Chrysler 200

Specifications

Drive. . . . . FWD
Engine 2.4-liter I4
Transmission . . . . .9-sp. Automatic
Tow Rating (lbs.) . . . . Very Low-0
Head/Leg Room (in.) Cramped-37.7/42.2
Interior Space (cu. ft.). Average-101.4
Cargo Space (cu. ft.) Cramped-16
Wheelbase/Length (in.) 108/192.3

Ratings—10 Best, 1 Worst	
Combo Crash Tests	4
Safety Features	7
Rollover	8
Preventive Maintenance	8
Repair Costs	5
Warranty	4
Fuel Economy	4
Complaints	3
Insurance Costs	1
OVERALL RATING	**4**

Chrysler 300

Chrysler 300

At-a-Glance

Status/Year Series Started........ Unchanged/2011
Twins .... –
Body Styles .... Sedan
Seating 5
Anti-Theft Device ...... Std. Pass. Immobil. & Alarm
Parking Index Rating .... Very Hard
Where Made.................... Brampton, Ontario

Fuel Factor:
  MPG Rating (city/hwy) Poor-19/31
  Driving Range (mi.) Average-425.6
  Fuel Type........................... Regular
  Annual Fuel Cost .... Average-$1,369
  Gas Guzzler Tax .... No
  Greenhouse Gas Emissions (tons/yr.)..... High-7.8
  Barrels of Oil Used per year High-14.3

How the Competition Rates

Competitors	Rating	Pg.
Buick LaCrosse	8	104
Cadillac XTS	9	110
Toyota Avalon	8	247

Price Range	Retail	Markup
S V6	$35,350	3%
S V6 AWD	$37,850	4%
C V8	$41,300	4%
C Platinum V8	$45,445	5%

Safety Checklist

Crash Tests:
  Frontal........................... Good
  Side............................. Poor
Airbags:
  Torso .... Front Pelvis/Torso from Seat
  Pelvis .... Front Pelvis/Torso from Seat
  Roll Sensing........................ Yes
  Knee Bolster .... Standard Driver
Crash Avoidance:
  Collision Avoidance ...... Optional CIB & DBS
  Blind Spot Detection .... Optional
  Lane Keeping Assist .... Optional
  Backup Camera .... Optional*
  Pedestrian Crash Avoidance .... None
General:
  Auto. Crash Notification .... None
  Day Running Lamps .... Optional
Safety Belt/Restraint:
  Dynamic Head Restraints ......Standard Front
  Adjustable Belt.............. Standard Front

^Warning feature does not meet government standards.
*Backup camera does not meet government standards.

Chrysler 300

Specifications

Drive........................... RWD
Engine 3.6-liter V6
Transmission .... 8-sp. Automatic
Tow Rating (lbs.) .... –
Head/Leg Room (in.) Cramped-38.6/41.8
Interior Space (cu. ft.)........ Roomy-106.3
Cargo Space (cu. ft.) Cramped-16.3
Wheelbase/Length (in.) 120.2/198.6

Ratings—10 Best, 1 Worst

Combo Crash Tests	2
Safety Features	4
Rollover	4
Preventive Maintenance	9
Repair Costs	7
Warranty	4
Fuel Economy	2
Complaints	2
Insurance Costs	5
OVERALL RATING	**3**

Chrysler Town and Country

Chrysler Town and Country

At-a-Glance

Status/Year Series Started........ Unchanged/2008
Twins . . . . –
Body Styles . . . . .Minivan
Seating 7
Anti-Theft Device . . . . . . Std. Pass. Immobil. & Alarm
Parking Index Rating . . . . .Very Hard
Where Made. . . . . Windsor, Ontario
Fuel Factor:
  MPG Rating (city/hwy) . . . . .Very Poor-17/25
  Driving Range (mi.) Short-397.2
  Fuel Type . . . . .Regular
  Annual Fuel Cost . . . . .Very High-$1,586
  Gas Guzzler Tax . . . . .No
  Greenhouse Gas Emissions (tons/yr.) Very High-9.0
  Barrels of Oil Used per year High-16.5

How the Competition Rates

Competitors	Rating	Pg.
Honda Odyssey	8	157
Nissan Quest	–	230
Toyota Sienna	3	256

Price Range

Price Range	Retail	Markup
LX	$29,995	1%
Touring	$31,580	3%
S	$33,695	3%
Limited	$37,995	4%

Safety Checklist

Crash Tests:
  Frontal. . . . . .Poor
  Side. . . . . .Very Poor
Airbags:
  Torso . . . . .Front Pelvis/Torso from Seat
  Pelvis . . . . .Front Pelvis/Torso from Seat
  Roll Sensing. . . . . .Yes
  Knee Bolster . . . . Standard Driver
Crash Avoidance:
  Collision Avoidance . . . . None
  Blind Spot Detection . . . . Optional
  Lane Keeping Assist . . . . None
  Backup Camera . . . . Optional*
  Pedestrian Crash Avoidance . . . . None
General:
  Auto. Crash Notification . . . . None
  Day Running Lamps . . . . None
Safety Belt/Restraint:
  Dynamic Head Restraints . . . . . .Standard Front
  Adjustable Belt . . . . . . .Standard Front and Rear

^Warning feature does not meet government standards.
*Backup camera does not meet government standards.

Chrysler Town and Country

Specifications

Drive. . . . . FWD
Engine 3.6-liter V6
Transmission . . . . .6-sp. Automatic
Tow Rating (lbs.) Low-3600
Head/Leg Room (in.) Cramped-39.8/40.7
Interior Space (cu. ft.). Roomy-163.5
Cargo Space (cu. ft.) . . . . .Very Roomy-33
Wheelbase/Length (in.) 121.2/202.8

Ratings—10 Best, 1 Worst

Combo Crash Tests	7
Safety Features	3
Rollover	8
Preventive Maintenance	8
Repair Costs	9
Warranty	4
Fuel Economy	3
Complaints	4
Insurance Costs	1
OVERALL RATING	**5**

Dodge Challenger

At-a-Glance

Status/Year Series Started........ Unchanged/2015
Twins . . . . –
Body Styles . . . . .Coupe
Seating 5
Anti-Theft Device . . . . . . Std. Pass. Immobil. & Alarm
Parking Index Rating . . . . Hard
Where Made. . . . . Brampton, Ontario
Fuel Factor:
  MPG Rating (city/hwy) Poor-19/30
  Driving Range (mi.) Average-421.0
  Fuel Type . . . . .Regular
  Annual Fuel Cost . . . . High-$1,384
  Gas Guzzler Tax . . . . .No
  Greenhouse Gas Emissions (tons/yr.) High-7.8
  Barrels of Oil Used per year High-14.3

How the Competition Rates

Competitors	Rating	Pg.
Chevrolet Camaro	–	111
Ford Mustang	–	146
Nissan 370Z	–	221

Price Range

	Retail	Markup
SXT	$26,995	1%
R/T	$31,995	2%
SCAT PACK	$37,995	4%
SRT Hellcat	$62,495	4%

Dodge Challenger

Safety Checklist

Crash Tests:
  Frontal. . . . . .Poor
  Side. . . . . Very Good
Airbags:
  Torso . . . . .Front Pelvis/Torso from Seat
  Pelvis . . . . .Front Pelvis/Torso from Seat
  Roll Sensing. . . . . .Yes
  Knee Bolster . . . . None
Crash Avoidance:
  Collision Avoidance . . . . .Warning Only Optional
  Blind Spot Detection . . . . Optional
  Lane Keeping Assist . . . . None
  Backup Camera . . . . Optional*
  Pedestrian Crash Avoidance . . . . None
General:
  Auto. Crash Notification . . . . None
  Day Running Lamps . . . . None
Safety Belt/Restraint:
  Dynamic Head Restraints . . . . . .Standard Front
  Adjustable Belt. None

^Warning feature does not meet government standards.
*Backup camera does not meet government standards.

Dodge Challenger

Specifications

Drive. . . . . RWD
Engine 3.6-liter V6
Transmission . . . . .8-sp. Automatic
Tow Rating (lbs.) . . . . Very Low-1000
Head/Leg Room (in.) Average-39.3/42
Interior Space (cu. ft.). Cramped-93.9
Cargo Space (cu. ft.) Cramped-16.2
Wheelbase/Length (in.) 116.2/197.9

Ratings—10 Best, 1 Worst

Combo Crash Tests	6
Safety Features	9
Rollover	9
Preventive Maintenance	8
Repair Costs	8
Warranty	4
Fuel Economy	4
Complaints	2
Insurance Costs	1
OVERALL RATING	**5**

Dodge Charger

Dodge Charger

At-a-Glance

Status/Year Series Started........ Unchanged/2011
Twins . . . . –
Body Styles . . . . .Sedan
Seating 5
Anti-Theft Device . . . . . . Std. Pass. Immobil. & Alarm
Parking Index Rating . . . . Hard
Where Made. . . . . Brampton, Ontario
Fuel Factor:
  MPG Rating (city/hwy) Poor-19/31
  Driving Range (mi.) Average-425.6
  Fuel Type. . . . . .Regular
  Annual Fuel Cost . . . . Average-$1,369
  Gas Guzzler Tax . . . . .No
  Greenhouse Gas Emissions (tons/yr.) High-7.8
  Barrels of Oil Used per year High-14.3

How the Competition Rates

Competitors	Rating	Pg.
Chevrolet Impala	6	116
Ford Taurus	4	147
Kia Cadenza	–	179

Price Range	Retail	Markup
SE	$27,995	2%
SXT	$29,995	2%
R/T	$33,695	3%
SRT Hellcat	$65,948	4%

Safety Checklist

Crash Tests:
  Frontal. . . . . Average
  Side. . . . . Average
Airbags:
  Torso . . . . .Front Pelvis/Torso from Seat
  Pelvis . . . . .Front Pelvis/Torso from Seat
  Roll Sensing. . . . . .Yes
  Knee Bolster . . . . Standard Driver
Crash Avoidance:
  Collision Avoidance . . . . . . Optional CIB & DBS
  Blind Spot Detection . . . . Optional
  Lane Keeping Assist . . . . Optional
  Backup Camera . . . . Optional*
  Pedestrian Crash Avoidance . . . . None
General:
  Auto. Crash Notification . . . . None
  Day Running Lamps . . . . Optional
Safety Belt/Restraint:
  Dynamic Head Restraints . . . . . .Standard Front
  Adjustable Belt. . . . . .Standard Front

^Warning feature does not meet government standards.
*Backup camera does not meet government standards.

Dodge Charger

Specifications

Drive. . . . . RWD
Engine 3.6-liter V6
Transmission . . . . .8-sp. Automatic
Tow Rating (lbs.) . . . . Very Low-1000
Head/Leg Room (in.) Cramped-38.6/41.8
Interior Space (cu. ft.). Roomy-104.7
Cargo Space (cu. ft.) Cramped-16.1
Wheelbase/Length (in.) 120.2/198.4

Ratings—10 Best, 1 Worst

Combo Crash Tests	8
Safety Features	2
Rollover	9
Preventive Maintenance	8
Repair Costs	6
Warranty	4
Fuel Economy	6
Complaints	—
Insurance Costs	1
OVERALL RATING	**6**

Dodge Dart

Dodge Dart

At-a-Glance

```
Status/Year Series Started........ Unchanged/2013
Twins .......................................... –
Body Styles .............................Sedan
Seating ...........................................5
Anti-Theft Device ...... Std. Pass. Immobil. & Alarm
Parking Index Rating ...................... Easy
Where Made...................... Belvedere, IL
Fuel Factor:
  MPG Rating (city/hwy)........... Average-24/34
  Driving Range (mi.) .............. Short-392.8
  Fuel Type.............................Regular
  Annual Fuel Cost.................. Low-$1,139
  Gas Guzzler Tax .........................No
  Greenhouse Gas Emissions (tons/yr.).. Average-6.7
  Barrels of Oil Used per year ........ Average-12.2
```

How the Competition Rates

Competitors	Rating	Pg.
Acura ILX	9	81
Chevrolet Cruze	–	114
Ford Focus	6	143

Price Range

	Retail	Markup
SE	$16,695	0%
SXT	$19,000	1%
GT	$21,995	1%
Limited	$23,795	2%

Safety Checklist

Crash Tests:
```
  Frontal......................... Average
  Side......................... Very Good
```
Airbags:
```
  Torso ...........Front Pelvis/Torso from Seat
  Pelvis ................ Rear Pelvis from Seat
  Roll Sensing......................... No
  Knee Bolster ...............Standard Front
```
Crash Avoidance:
```
  Collision Avoidance ................. None
  Blind Spot Detection .............. Optional
  Lane Keeping Assist ................ None
  Backup Camera................... Optional*
  Pedestrian Crash Avoidance .......... None
```
General:
```
  Auto. Crash Notification............. None
  Day Running Lamps ................ None
```
Safety Belt/Restraint:
```
  Dynamic Head Restraints ............ None
  Adjustable Belt...............Standard Front
```

^Warning feature does not meet government standards.
*Backup camera does not meet government standards.

Dodge Dart

Specifications

```
Drive...................................... FWD
Engine .......................... 2.0-liter I4
Transmission ...................6-sp. Automatic
Tow Rating (lbs.) .............. Very Low-1000
Head/Leg Room (in.) ........Cramped-38.6/42.2
Interior Space (cu. ft.).............Average-97.2
Cargo Space (cu. ft.) .........Very Cramped-13.1
Wheelbase/Length (in.) ............ 106.4/183.9
```

Ratings—10 Best, 1 Worst

Combo Crash Tests	2
Safety Features	4
Rollover	3
Preventive Maintenance	10
Repair Costs	4
Warranty	4
Fuel Economy	2
Complaints	1
Insurance Costs	3
OVERALL RATING	**1**

Dodge Journey

Dodge Journey

At-a-Glance

Status/Year Series Started........ Unchanged/2009
Twins ....–
Body Styles .... SUV
Seating 5/7
Anti-Theft Device ...... Std. Pass. Immobil. & Alarm
Parking Index Rating .... Hard
Where Made..................... Toluca, Mexico

Fuel Factor:
MPG Rating (city/hwy)...........Very Poor-17/25
Driving Range (mi.) Average-407.1
Fuel Type............................Regular
Annual Fuel Cost .... Very High-$1,586
Gas Guzzler Tax ....No
Greenhouse Gas Emissions (tons/yr.) Very High-9.4
Barrels of Oil Used per year .... Very High-17.3

How the Competition Rates

Competitors	Rating	Pg.
Chevrolet Equinox	2	115
Ford Edge	9	136
Nissan Murano	5	228

Price Range	Retail	Markup
SE FWD	$20,895	0%
SXT FWD	$24,395	3%
Crossroad AWD	$29,495	4%
R/T AWD	$33,295	4%

Safety Checklist

Crash Tests:
Frontal..........................Very Poor
Side...............................Very Poor
Airbags:
Torso ....Front Pelvis/Torso from Seat
Pelvis ....Front Pelvis/Torso from Seat
Roll Sensing...........................Yes
Knee Bolster .... Standard Driver
Crash Avoidance:
Collision Avoidance .... None
Blind Spot Detection .... None
Lane Keeping Assist .... None
Backup Camera .... Optional*
Pedestrian Crash Avoidance .... None
General:
Auto. Crash Notification.............. None
Day Running Lamps .... None
Safety Belt/Restraint:
Dynamic Head Restraints ......Standard Front
Adjustable Belt................Standard Front

^Warning feature does not meet government standards.
*Backup camera does not meet government standards.

Dodge Journey

Specifications

Drive.................................. FWD
Engine 3.6-liter V6
Transmission ....6-sp. Automatic
Tow Rating (lbs.) .... Very Low-2500
Head/Leg Room (in.) Average-40.8/40.8
Interior Space (cu. ft.)............. Roomy-123.7
Cargo Space (cu. ft.) ....Very Cramped-10.7
Wheelbase/Length (in.) 113.8/192.4

Ratings—10 Best, 1 Worst

Combo Crash Tests	2
Safety Features	2
Rollover	6
Preventive Maintenance	8
Repair Costs	9
Warranty	4
Fuel Economy	8
Complaints	2
Insurance Costs	5
OVERALL RATING	**4**

Fiat 500

Fiat 500

At-a-Glance

Status/Year Series Started Unchanged/2012
Twins . . . . –
Body Styles . . . . Hatchback
Seating 4
Anti-Theft Device . . . . . . Std. Pass. Immobil. & Alarm
Parking Index Rating . . . . .Very Easy
Where Made .Toluca, Mexico

Fuel Factor:
MPG Rating (city/hwy) Good-27/34
Driving Range (mi.) . . . . Very Short-312.4
Fuel Type . . . . .Regular
Annual Fuel Cost . . . . Low-$1,059
Gas Guzzler Tax . . . . .No
Greenhouse Gas Emissions (tons/yr.) . . Average-6.0
Barrels of Oil Used per year Average-11.0

How the Competition Rates

Competitors	Rating	Pg.
Chevrolet Sonic	10	119
Mini Cooper	–	215
Volkswagen Beetle	3	260

Price Range

	Retail	Markup
Pop Hatchback	$16,945	1%
Sport Hatchback	$17,700	2%
Lounge Hatchback	$20,300	2%
Abarth Cabriolet	$22,495	3%

Safety Checklist

Crash Tests:
Frontal . . . . .Very Poor
Side . . . . .Poor

Airbags:
Torso . . . . .Front Pelvis/Torso from Seat
Pelvis . . . . .Front Pelvis/Torso from Seat
Roll Sensing . . . . No
Knee Bolster . . . . Standard Driver

Crash Avoidance:
Collision Avoidance . . . . None
Blind Spot Detection . . . . None
Lane Keeping Assist . . . . None
Backup Camera . . . . None
Pedestrian Crash Avoidance . . . . None

General:
Auto. Crash Notification . . . . None
Day Running Lamps . . . . None

Safety Belt/Restraint:
Dynamic Head Restraints . . . . . .Standard Front
Adjustable Belt . . . . None

^Warning feature does not meet government standards.
*Backup camera does not meet government standards.

Fiat 500

Specifications

Drive . . . . FWD
Engine 1.4-liter I4
Transmission . . . . .6-sp. Automatic
Tow Rating (lbs.) . . . . Very Low-0
Head/Leg Room (in.) . . . . .Very Cramped-38.9/40.7
Interior Space (cu. ft.) . . . . .Very Cramped-75.5
Cargo Space (cu. ft.) . . . . .Very Cramped-9.5
Wheelbase/Length (in.) 90.6/139.6

Ratings—10 Best, 1 Worst

Combo Crash Tests	—
Safety Features	3
Rollover	—
Preventive Maintenance	8
Repair Costs	9
Warranty	4
Fuel Economy	5
Complaints	1
Insurance Costs	5
OVERALL RATING	—

Fiat 500L

Fiat 500L

At-a-Glance

Status/Year Series Started. Unchanged/2014
Twins . . . .—
Body Styles . . . . Hatchback
Seating. 5
Anti-Theft Device . . . . . . Std. Pass. Immobil. & Alarm
Parking Index Rating . . . . .Very Easy
Where Made. . . . . .Kragujevac, Serbia

Fuel Factor:
MPG Rating (city/hwy) Average-22/30
Driving Range (mi.) . . . . Very Short-330.0
Fuel Type. . . . . .Regular
Annual Fuel Cost . . . . Average-$1,260
Gas Guzzler Tax . . . . .No
Greenhouse Gas Emissions (tons/yr.). . Average-7.2
Barrels of Oil Used per year High-13.2

How the Competition Rates

Competitors	Rating	Pg.
Ford Focus	6	143
Kia Forte	5	180
Volkswagen Golf	3	262

Price Range

Price Range	Retail	Markup
Pop	$19,495	0%
Easy	$20,795	2%
Trekking	$21,795	2%
Lounge	$24,795	3%

Safety Checklist

Crash Tests:
Frontal. . . . .—
Side. . . . .—

Airbags:
Torso . . . . .Front Pelvis/Torso from Seat
Pelvis . . . . .Front Pelvis/Torso from Seat
Roll Sensing. . . . . .Yes
Knee Bolster . . . . Standard Driver

Crash Avoidance:
Collision Avoidance . . . . None
Blind Spot Detection . . . . None
Lane Keeping Assist . . . . None
Backup Camera . . . . None
Pedestrian Crash Avoidance . . . . None

General:
Auto. Crash Notification. . . . . None
Day Running Lamps . . . . None

Safety Belt/Restraint:
Dynamic Head Restraints . . . . . .Standard Front
Adjustable Belt. None

^Warning feature does not meet government standards.
*Backup camera does not meet government standards.

Fiat 500L

Specifications

Drive. . . . . FWD
Engine 1.4-liter I4
Transmission . . . . 6-sp. Automatic
Tow Rating (lbs.) . . . . Very Low-0
Head/Leg Room (in.) Cramped-40.7/40
Interior Space (cu. ft.). Average-98.8
Cargo Space (cu. ft.) Average-21.3
Wheelbase/Length (in.) 102.8/167.3

Ford C-MAX   Compact

Ratings—10 Best, 1 Worst

Combo Crash Tests	3
Safety Features	4
Rollover	6
Preventive Maintenance	9
Repair Costs	10
Warranty	3
Fuel Economy	10
Complaints	2
Insurance Costs	3
OVERALL RATING	**5**

Ford C-MAX

Ford C-MAX

At-a-Glance

Status/Year Series Started Unchanged/2013
Twins . . . . –
Body Styles . . . . Hatchback
Seating 5
Anti-Theft Device . . . . . . Std. Pass. Immobil. & Alarm
Parking Index Rating . . . . Average
Where Made . . . . Wayne, MI

Fuel Factor:
  MPG Rating (city/hwy) . . . . Very Good-42/37
  Driving Range (mi.) . . . . .Very Long-534.5
  Fuel Type . . . . .Regular
  Annual Fuel Cost . . . . .Very Low-$795
  Gas Guzzler Tax . . . . .No
  Greenhouse Gas Emissions (tons/yr.) . Very Low-4.5
  Barrels of Oil Used per year . . . . Very Low-8.2

How the Competition Rates

Competitors	Rating	Pg.
Chevrolet Volt	–	125
Nissan Leaf	4	226
Toyota Prius	–	251

Price Range

	Retail	Markup
SE	$24,170	7%
SEL	$27,170	7%
SEL Energi	$31,770	8%

Ford C-MAX

Safety Checklist

Crash Tests:
  Frontal . . . . .Very Poor
  Side . . . . Average
Airbags:
  Torso . . . . Front Pelvis/Torso from Seat
  Pelvis . . . . .Front Pelvis/Torso from Seat
  Roll Sensing . . . . .Yes
  Knee Bolster . . . . Standard Driver
Crash Avoidance:
  Collision Avoidance . . . . None
  Blind Spot Detection . . . . None
  Lane Keeping Assist . . . . None
  Backup Camera . . . . Optional
  Pedestrian Crash Avoidance . . . . None
General:
  Auto. Crash Notification . . . . . . Dial Assist.-Free
  Day Running Lamps . . . . Standard
Safety Belt/Restraint:
  Dynamic Head Restraints . . . . None
  Adjustable Belt . . . . Standard Front

^Warning feature does not meet government standards.
*Backup camera does not meet government standards.

Ford C-MAX

Specifications

Drive . . . . FWD
Engine 2.0-liter I4
Transmission . . . . .CVT
Tow Rating (lbs.) . . . . Very Low-0
Head/Leg Room (in.) Average-41/40.4
Interior Space (cu. ft.) Average-99.7
Cargo Space (cu. ft.) Roomy-24.5
Wheelbase/Length (in.) 104.3/173.6

Ratings—10 Best, 1 Worst	
Combo Crash Tests	10
Safety Features	7
Rollover	5
Preventive Maintenance	7
Repair Costs	5
Warranty	3
Fuel Economy	4
Complaints	7
Insurance Costs	5
OVERALL RATING	**9**

Ford Edge

Ford Edge

At-a-Glance

Status/Year Series Started Unchanged/2015
Twins . . . . –
Body Styles . . . . SUV
Seating 5
Anti-Theft Device . . . . . . Std. Pass. Immobil. & Alarm
Parking Index Rating . . . . .Very Easy
Where Made . . . . .Oakville, Ontario

Fuel Factor:
MPG Rating (city/hwy) Poor-20/30
Driving Range (mi.) Long-430.6
Fuel Type . . . . .Regular
Annual Fuel Cost . . . . Average-$1,338
Gas Guzzler Tax . . . . .No
Greenhouse Gas Emissions (tons/yr.) . . Average-7.1
Barrels of Oil Used per year High-15.7

How the Competition Rates

Competitors	Rating	Pg.
Chevrolet Equinox	2	115
Dodge Journey	1	132
Nissan Murano	5	228

Price Range	Retail	Markup
SE FWD	$28,100	6%
SEL FWD	$31,500	7%
Titanium AWD	$37,595	7%
Sport AWD	$40,095	7%

Safety Checklist

Crash Tests:
Frontal . . . . Very Good
Side . . . . Good
Airbags:
Torso . . . . Front Pelvis/Torso from Seat
Pelvis . . . . .Front Pelvis/Torso from Seat
Roll Sensing . . . . .Yes
Knee Bolster . . . . .Standard Front
Crash Avoidance:
Collision Avoidance . . . . .Warning Only Optional
Blind Spot Detection . . . . Optional
Lane Keeping Assist . . . . Optional
Backup Camera . . . . Standard
Pedestrian Crash Avoidance . . . . None
General:
Auto. Crash Notification . . . . . . Dial Assist.-Free
Day Running Lamps . . . . Standard
Safety Belt/Restraint:
Dynamic Head Restraints . . . . None
Adjustable Belt . . . . .Standard Front

^Warning feature does not meet government standards.
*Backup camera does not meet government standards.

Ford Edge

Specifications

Drive . . . . FWD
Engine 3.5-liter V6
Transmission . . . . .6-sp. Automatic
Tow Rating (lbs.) . . . . Very Low-1500
Head/Leg Room (in.) Roomy-40.2/42.6
Interior Space (cu. ft.) Roomy-113.9
Cargo Space (cu. ft.) . . . . Very Roomy-39.2
Wheelbase/Length (in.) 112.2/188.1

Ratings—10 Best, 1 Worst

Combo Crash Tests	5
Safety Features	4
Rollover	3
Preventive Maintenance	6
Repair Costs	10
Warranty	3
Fuel Economy	5
Complaints	6
Insurance Costs	5
OVERALL RATING	**5**

Ford Escape

Ford Escape

Ford Escape

Safety Checklist

Crash Tests:
Frontal . . . . Poor
Side . . . . Good
Airbags:
Torso . . . . Front Pelvis/Torso from Seat
Pelvis . . . . Front Pelvis/Torso from Seat
Roll Sensing . . . . .Yes
Knee Bolster . . . . Standard Driver
Crash Avoidance:
Collision Avoidance . . . . None
Blind Spot Detection . . . . Optional
Lane Keeping Assist . . . . None
Backup Camera . . . . Standard
Pedestrian Crash Avoidance . . . . None
General:
Auto. Crash Notification . . . . . . Dial Assist.-Free
Day Running Lamps . . . . Standard
Safety Belt/Restraint:
Dynamic Head Restraints . . . . None
Adjustable Belt . . . . .Standard Front

^Warning feature does not meet government standards.
*Backup camera does not meet government standards.

At-a-Glance

Status/Year Series Started Unchanged/2013
Twins . . . . .Lincoln MKC
Body Styles . . . . SUV
Seating 5
Anti-Theft Device . . . . . . Std. Pass. Immobil. & Alarm
Parking Index Rating . . . . Average
Where Made . . . . Louisville, Kentucky
Fuel Factor:
MPG Rating (city/hwy) Average-22/31
Driving Range (mi.) Short-389.7
Fuel Type . . . . .Regular
Annual Fuel Cost . . . . Average-$1,244
Gas Guzzler Tax . . . . .No
Greenhouse Gas Emissions (tons/yr.) . . Average-7.2
Barrels of Oil Used per year High-13.2

How the Competition Rates

Competitors	Rating	Pg.
Honda CR-V	7	154
Jeep Cherokee	7	173
Toyota RAV4	5	254

Price Range	Retail	Markup
S FWD	$23,450	6%
SE FWD	$25,650	7%
SE 4WD	$27,400	7%
Titanium 4WD	$31,485	7%

Ford Escape

Specifications

Drive . . . . FWD
Engine 2.5-liter I4
Transmission . . . . .6-sp. Automatic
Tow Rating (lbs.) . . . . Very Low-1500
Head/Leg Room (in.) Roomy-39.9/43.1
Interior Space (cu. ft.) Average-98.1
Cargo Space (cu. ft.) . . . . . . Very Roomy-34.3
Wheelbase/Length (in.) 105.9/178.1

Ford Expedition   Large SUV

Ford Expedition

Ratings—10 Best, 1 Worst

Combo Crash Tests	10
Safety Features	3
Rollover	2
Preventive Maintenance	3
Repair Costs	8
Warranty	3
Fuel Economy	1
Complaints	7
Insurance Costs	10
OVERALL RATING	**7**

Ford Expedition

At-a-Glance

Status/Year Series Started........ Unchanged/2003
Twins . . . . Lincoln Navigator
Body Styles . . . . SUV
Seating 7/8
Anti-Theft Device . . . . . . Std. Pass. Immobil. & Alarm
Parking Index Rating . . . . Very Hard
Where Made. . . . . Louisville, Kentucky
Fuel Factor:
 MPG Rating (city/hwy) . . . . Very Poor-15/20
 Driving Range (mi.) . . . . Very Long-473.2
 Fuel Type . . . . Regular
 Annual Fuel Cost . . . . Very High-$1,863
 Gas Guzzler Tax . . . . No
 Greenhouse Gas Emissions (tons/yr.)Very High-10.6
 Barrels of Oil Used per year . . . . Very High-19.4

How the Competition Rates

Competitors	Rating	Pg.
Chevrolet Suburban	3	121
Nissan Armada	–	223
Toyota Sequoia	–	255

Price Range	Retail	Markup
XL 2WD	$40,795	7%
XLT 2WD	$45,095	6%
King Ranch 4WD	$61,955	7%
Platinum 4WD	$63,035	7%

Safety Checklist

Crash Tests:
 Frontal . . . . Very Good
 Side. . . . . Very Good
Airbags:
 Torso . . . . Front Torso from Seat
 Pelvis . . . . None
 Roll Sensing. . . . . Yes
 Knee Bolster . . . . None
Crash Avoidance:
 Collision Avoidance . . . . None
 Blind Spot Detection . . . . Optional
 Lane Keeping Assist . . . . None
 Backup Camera . . . . Standard
 Pedestrian Crash Avoidance . . . . None
General:
 Auto. Crash Notification . . . . . . Dial Assist.-Free
 Day Running Lamps . . . . None
Safety Belt/Restraint:
 Dynamic Head Restraints . . . . . .Standard Front
 Adjustable Belt . . . . .Standard Front

^Warning feature does not meet government standards.
*Backup camera does not meet government standards.

Ford Expedition

Specifications

Drive 4WD
Engine 3.5-liter V6
Transmission . . . . .6-sp. Automatic
Tow Rating (lbs.) . . . . Very High-9200
Head/Leg Room (in.) Roomy-39.63/43
Interior Space (cu. ft.). Roomy-160.3
Cargo Space (cu. ft.) Average-18.6
Wheelbase/Length (in.) 119/206

Ford Explorer

Ratings—10 Best, 1 Worst

Combo Crash Tests	7
Safety Features	4
Rollover	4
Preventive Maintenance	5
Repair Costs	2
Warranty	3
Fuel Economy	2
Complaints	4
Insurance Costs	5
OVERALL RATING	**3**

Ford Explorer

Ford Explorer

At-a-Glance

Status/Year Series Started........ Unchanged/2011
Twins . . . . –
Body Styles . . . . SUV
Seating 6/7
Anti-Theft Device . . . . . . Std. Pass. Immobil. & Alarm
Parking Index Rating . . . . Hard
Where Made. . . . . Chicago, IL

Fuel Factor:
MPG Rating (city/hwy) . . . . .Very Poor-17/23
Driving Range (mi.) . . . . Very Short-358.3
Fuel Type. . . . . .Regular
Annual Fuel Cost . . . . .Very High-$1,635
Gas Guzzler Tax . . . . .No
Greenhouse Gas Emissions (tons/yr.) Very High-9.5
Barrels of Oil Used per year . . . . Very High-17.3

How the Competition Rates

Competitors	Rating	Pg.
Dodge Journey	1	132
Honda Pilot	9	158
Toyota Highlander	7	250

Price Range	Retail	Markup
Base FWD	$30,700	6%
XLT FWD	$33,400	7%
Limited 4WD	$43,300	7%
Platinum 4WD	$52,600	7%

Safety Checklist

Crash Tests:
Frontal. . . . . Good
Side. . . . . Average

Airbags:
Torso Std. Fr. & Opt. Rear Pelvis/Torso from Seat
Pelvis Std. Fr. & Opt. Rr. Pelvis/Torso from Seat
Roll Sensing. . . . . .Yes
Knee Bolster . . . . Standard Passenger

Crash Avoidance:
Collision Avoidance . . . . .Warning Only Optional
Blind Spot Detection . . . . Optional
Lane Keeping Assist . . . . Optional
Backup Camera . . . . Standard
Pedestrian Crash Avoidance . . . . None

General:
Auto. Crash Notification . . . . . . Dial Assist.-Free
Day Running Lamps . . . . None

Safety Belt/Restraint:
Dynamic Head Restraints . . . . None
Adjustable Belt. . . . . .Standard Front

^Warning feature does not meet government standards.
*Backup camera does not meet government standards.

Ford Explorer

Specifications

Drive. . . . . AWD
Engine 3.5-liter V6
Transmission . . . . .6-sp. Automatic
Tow Rating (lbs.) Low-5000
Head/Leg Room (in.) Average-41.4/40.6
Interior Space (cu. ft.). Roomy-151.7
Cargo Space (cu. ft.) Average-21
Wheelbase/Length (in.) 112.6/197.1

Ratings—10 Best, 1 Worst

Combo Crash Tests	10
Safety Features	4
Rollover	3
Preventive Maintenance	8
Repair Costs	8
Warranty	3
Fuel Economy	2
Complaints	9
Insurance Costs	5
OVERALL RATING	**9**

Ford F-150

Ford F-150

At-a-Glance

Status/Year Series Started. Unchanged/2015
Twins . . . . –
Body Styles . . . . Pickup
Seating 5/6
Anti-Theft Device . . . . . Std. Pass. Immobil. & Alarm
Parking Index Rating . . . . .Very Hard
Where Made. Dearborn, MI

Fuel Factor:
  MPG Rating (city/hwy) . . . . .Very Poor-17/23
  Driving Range (mi.) . . . . .Very Long-693.4
  Fuel Type. . . . . .Regular
  Annual Fuel Cost . . . . Very High-$1,635
  Gas Guzzler Tax . . . . .No
  Greenhouse Gas Emissions (tons/yr.) Very High-9.5
  Barrels of Oil Used per year . . . . . . .Very High-17.3

How the Competition Rates

Competitors	Rating	Pg.
Chevrolet Silverado	5	118
Ram 1500	4	236
Toyota Tundra	–	258

Price Range

	Retail	Markup
XL Reg. Cab 2WD	$25,420	8%
XLT Supercab 2WD	$30,695	10%
Lariat Supercrew 4WD	$44,465	10%
Platinum Supercrew 4WD	$54,385	10%

Safety Checklist

Crash Tests:
  Frontal. . . . . Very Good
  Side. . . . . Very Good
Airbags:
  Torso . . . . .Front Pelvis/Torso from Seat
  Pelvis . . . . .Front Pelvis/Torso from Seat
  Roll Sensing. . . . . .Yes
  Knee Bolster . . . . None
Crash Avoidance:
  Collision Avoidance . . . . .Warning Only Optional
  Blind Spot Detection . . . . None
  Lane Keeping Assist . . . . Optional
  Backup Camera. . . . . Optional
  Pedestrian Crash Avoidance . . . . None
General:
  Auto. Crash Notification . . . . . . Dial Assist.-Free
  Day Running Lamps . . . . Standard
Safety Belt/Restraint:
  Dynamic Head Restraints . . . . None
  Adjustable Belt . . . . .Standard Front

^Warning feature does not meet government standards.
*Backup camera does not meet government standards.

Ford F-150

Specifications

Drive. 4WD
Engine 3.5-liter V6
Transmission . . . . .6-sp. Automatic
Tow Rating (lbs.) . . . . .Very High-10700
Head/Leg Room (in.) . . . . . Very Roomy-40.8/43.9
Interior Space (cu. ft.). Roomy-116
Cargo Space (cu. ft.) . . . . Very Roomy-49.4
Wheelbase/Length (in.) 145/231.9

Ratings—10 Best, 1 Worst

Combo Crash Tests	3
Safety Features	2
Rollover	6
Preventive Maintenance	1
Repair Costs	10
Warranty	3
Fuel Economy	8
Complaints	1
Insurance Costs	1
OVERALL RATING	**1**

Ford Fiesta

Ford Fiesta

At-a-Glance

Status/Year Series Started........ Unchanged/2011
Twins . . . . –
Body Styles . . . . Sedan, Hatchback
Seating 5
Anti-Theft Device . . . . . . Std. Pass. Immobil. & Alarm
Parking Index Rating . . . . .Very Easy
Where Made. . . . . Cuautitlán, Mexico

Fuel Factor:
MPG Rating (city/hwy) Good-27/37
Driving Range (mi.) Short-381.2
Fuel Type. . . . . .Regular
Annual Fuel Cost . . . . Low-$1,024
Gas Guzzler Tax . . . . .No
Greenhouse Gas Emissions (tons/yr.). Low-5.8
Barrels of Oil Used per year Low-10.6

How the Competition Rates

Competitors	Rating	Pg.
Chevrolet Sonic	10	119
Hyundai Accent	6	159
Toyota Yaris	6	259

Price Range

Price Range	Retail	Markup
S Sedan	$14,580	4%
SE Hatchback	$16,110	4%
Titanium Sedan	$18,530	4%
ST Hatchback	$21,460	4%

Safety Checklist

Crash Tests:
Frontal. . . . . Average
Side. . . . . .Very Poor
Airbags:
Torso . . . . .Front Pelvis/Torso from Seat
Pelvis . . . . .Front Pelvis/Torso from Seat
Roll Sensing. . . . . No
Knee Bolster . . . . Standard Driver
Crash Avoidance:
Collision Avoidance . . . . None
Blind Spot Detection . . . . None
Lane Keeping Assist . . . . None
Backup Camera . . . . Optional
Pedestrian Crash Avoidance . . . . None
General:
Auto. Crash Notification . . . . . . Dial Assist.-Free
Day Running Lamps . . . . None
Safety Belt/Restraint:
Dynamic Head Restraints . . . . None
Adjustable Belt. . . . . .Standard Front

^Warning feature does not meet government standards.
*Backup camera does not meet government standards.

Specifications

Drive. . . . . FWD
Engine 1.6-liter I4
Transmission . . . . .6-sp. Automatic
Tow Rating (lbs.) . . . . Very Low-0
Head/Leg Room (in.) Average-39.1/42.2
Interior Space (cu. ft.). . . . . . . .Very Cramped-85.1
Cargo Space (cu. ft.) Cramped-14.9
Wheelbase/Length (in.) 98/159.7

Ratings—10 Best, 1 Worst

Combo Crash Tests	—
Safety Features	3
Rollover	—
Preventive Maintenance	6
Repair Costs	3
Warranty	3
Fuel Economy	2
Complaints	4
Insurance Costs	5

OVERALL RATING —

Ford Flex

Ford Flex

At-a-Glance

Status/Year Series Started. Unchanged/2009
Twins . . . . –
Body Styles . . . . SUV
Seating 6/7
Anti-Theft Device . . . . . . Std. Pass. Immobil. & Alarm
Parking Index Rating . . . . .Very Hard
Where Made. . . . . .Oakville, Ontario

Fuel Factor:
MPG Rating (city/hwy) . . . . .Very Poor-18/25
Driving Range (mi.) Short-383.1
Fuel Type. . . . . .Regular
Annual Fuel Cost . . . . High-$1,530
Gas Guzzler Tax . . . . .No
Greenhouse Gas Emissions (tons/yr.) Very High-9.0
Barrels of Oil Used per year High-16.5

How the Competition Rates

Competitors	Rating	Pg.
Chevrolet Traverse	4	123
Dodge Journey	1	132
Honda Pilot	9	158

Price Range	Retail	Markup
SE FWD	$29,100	6%
SEL AWD	$34,050	7%
Limited FWD	$37,700	7%
Limited Ecoboost AWD	$42,400	7%

Safety Checklist

Crash Tests:
Frontal. . . . .–
Side. . . . .–

Airbags:
Torso Std. Fr. & Opt. Rr. Pelvis/Torso from Seat
Pelvis Std. Fr. & Opt. Rr. Pelvis/Torso from Seat
Roll Sensing. . . . . .Yes
Knee Bolster . . . . None

Crash Avoidance:
Collision Avoidance . . . . .Warning Only Optional
Blind Spot Detection . . . . Optional
Lane Keeping Assist . . . . None
Backup Camera . . . . Standard
Pedestrian Crash Avoidance . . . . None

General:
Auto. Crash Notification . . . . . . Dial Assist.-Free
Day Running Lamps . . . . None

Safety Belt/Restraint:
Dynamic Head Restraints . . . . None
Adjustable Belt . . . . .Standard Front

^Warning feature does not meet government standards.
*Backup camera does not meet government standards.

Specifications

Drive. . . . . FWD
Engine 3.5-liter V6
Transmission . . . . .6-sp. Automatic
Tow Rating (lbs.) Low-4500
Head/Leg Room (in.) Roomy-41.8/40.8
Interior Space (cu. ft.). Roomy-155.8
Cargo Space (cu. ft.) Average-20
Wheelbase/Length (in.) 117.9/201.8

Ratings—10 Best, 1 Worst

Combo Crash Tests	7
Safety Features	5
Rollover	8
Preventive Maintenance	6
Repair Costs	9
Warranty	3
Fuel Economy	9
Complaints	1
Insurance Costs	1
OVERALL RATING	**6**

Ford Focus

Ford Focus

At-a-Glance

Status/Year Series Started........ Unchanged/2012
Twins .... –
Body Styles .... Sedan, Hatchback
Seating 5
Anti-Theft Device ...... Std. Pass. Immobil. & Alarm
Parking Index Rating .... Easy
Where Made........................ Wayne, MI

Fuel Factor:
  MPG Rating (city/hwy) .... Very Good-27/40
  Driving Range (mi.) Short-392.2
  Fuel Type............................... Regular
  Annual Fuel Cost .... Very Low-$996
  Gas Guzzler Tax .... No
  Greenhouse Gas Emissions (tons/yr.)..... Low-5.8
  Barrels of Oil Used per year Low-10.6

How the Competition Rates

Competitors	Rating	Pg.
Honda Civic	–	149
Kia Forte	5	180
Mazda Mazda3	8	204

Price Range

Price Range	Retail	Markup
S Sedan	$17,170	6%
Titanum Sedan	$23,170	7%
ST Hatchback	$24,370	7%
Electric Hatchback	$29,170	7%

Safety Checklist

Crash Tests:
  Frontal.......................... Average
  Side.............................. Good

Airbags:
  Torso ....Front Pelvis/Torso from Seat
  Pelvis ....Front Pelvis/Torso from Seat
  Roll Sensing....................... Yes
  Knee Bolster .... Standard Driver

Crash Avoidance:
  Collision Avoidance .... None
  Blind Spot Detection .... None
  Lane Keeping Assist .... Optional
  Backup Camera................... Standard
  Pedestrian Crash Avoidance .... None

General:
  Auto. Crash Notification...... Dial Assist.-Free
  Day Running Lamps .... Optional

Safety Belt/Restraint:
  Dynamic Head Restraints .... None
  Adjustable Belt............... Standard Front

^Warning feature does not meet government standards.
*Backup camera does not meet government standards.

Ford Focus

Specifications

Drive..................................... FWD
Engine 2.0-liter I4
Transmission .... 6-sp. Automatic
Tow Rating (lbs.) .... Very Low-0
Head/Leg Room (in.) Average-38.3/43.7
Interior Space (cu. ft.)...................... –
Cargo Space (cu. ft.) ....Very Cramped-13.2
Wheelbase/Length (in.) 104.3/178.5

Ratings—10 Best, 1 Worst	
Combo Crash Tests	6
Safety Features	5
Rollover	8
Preventive Maintenance	8
Repair Costs	10
Warranty	3
Fuel Economy	6
Complaints	4
Insurance Costs	5
OVERALL RATING	**7**

Ford Fusion

Ford Fusion

At-a-Glance

Status/Year Series Started........ Unchanged/2013
Twins ....Lincoln MKZ
Body Styles ....Sedan
Seating 5
Anti-Theft Device ...... Std. Pass. Immobil. & Alarm
Parking Index Rating .... Hard
Where Made..... Flat Rock, MI / Hermosillo, Mexico
Fuel Factor:
  MPG Rating (city/hwy)............ Average-22/34
  Driving Range (mi.) Long-431.5
  Fuel Type...........................Regular
  Annual Fuel Cost .... Low-$1,204
  Gas Guzzler Tax ....No
  Greenhouse Gas Emissions (tons/yr.). . Average-6.9
  Barrels of Oil Used per year Average-12.7

How the Competition Rates

Competitors	Rating	Pg.
Chevrolet Malibu	9	117
Hyundai Sonata	10	165
Toyota Camry	7	248

Price Range	Retail	Markup
S	$22,600	7%
SE	$24,135	8%
Titanium Hybrid	$31,430	8%
Titanium AWD	$32,880	8%

Safety Checklist

Crash Tests:
  Frontal............................. Good
  Side............................Very Poor
Airbags:
  Torso Std. Fr. & Opt. Rr. Pelvis/Torso from Seat
  Pelvis Std. Fr. & Opt. Rr. Pelvis/Torso from Seat
  Roll Sensing.......................... No
  Knee Bolster .... Standard
Crash Avoidance:
  Collision Avoidance ..... Warning Only Optional
  Blind Spot Detection .... Optional
  Lane Keeping Assist .... Optional
  Backup Camera................... Standard
  Pedestrian Crash Avoidance .... None
General:
  Auto. Crash Notification...... Dial Assist.-Free
  Day Running Lamps .... Standard
Safety Belt/Restraint:
  Dynamic Head Restraints .... None
  Adjustable Belt...............Standard Front

^Warning feature does not meet government standards.
*Backup camera does not meet government standards.

Ford Fusion

Specifications

Drive................................... FWD
Engine 2.5-liter I4
Transmission .... 6-sp. Automatic
Tow Rating (lbs.) .... −
Head/Leg Room (in.) Roomy-39.2/44.3
Interior Space (cu. ft.)...........Roomy-118.8
Cargo Space (cu. ft.) Cramped-16
Wheelbase/Length (in.) 112.2/191.7

Ratings—10 Best, 1 Worst

Combo Crash Tests	8
Safety Features	5
Rollover	—
Preventive Maintenance	6
Repair Costs	—
Warranty	3
Fuel Economy	10
Complaints	—
Insurance Costs	5
OVERALL RATING	**8**

Ford Fusion Energi

Ford Fusion Energi

At-a-Glance

Status/Year Series Started. Unchanged/2013
Twins . . . . –
Body Styles . . . . Sedan
Seating 5
Anti-Theft Device . . . . .Std. Pass. Immobil. & Alarm
Parking Index Rating . . . . .Average
Where Made. . . . . Hermosillo, Mexico
Fuel Factor:
MPG Rating (city/hwy) . . . . .Very Good-40/36
Driving Range (mi.) . . . . Very Long-533.3
Fuel Type . . . . Regular
Annual Fuel Cost . . . . Very Low-$827
Gas Guzzler Tax . . . . No
Greenhouse Gas Emissions (tons/yr.). . . .Very Low-2.1
Barrels of Oil Used per year . . . . .Very Low-4.9

How the Competition Rates

Competitors	Rating	Pg.
Chevrolet Volt	–	125
Mercedes-Benz C-Class	3	207
Toyota Prius	–	251

Price Range	Retail	Markup
SE Luxury	$33,900	8%
Titanium	$35,730	8%

Safety Checklist

Crash Tests:
Frontal. . . . . .Very Good
Side. . . . . .Poor
Airbags:
Torso . . . . . Std. Fr. & Opt. Rr. Pelvis/Torso from Seat
Pelvis . . . . . Std. Fr. & Opt. Rr. Pelvis/Torso from Seat
Roll Sensing. . . . . No
Knee Bolster . . . . Standard Front
Crash Avoidance:
Collision Avoidance . . . . Warning Only Optional
Blind Spot Detection . . . . .Optional
Lane Keeping Assist . . . . .Optional
Backup Camera . . . . Standard
Pedestrian Crash Avoidance . . . . None
General:
Auto. Crash Notification . . . . Dial Assist.-Free
Day Running Lamps . . . . Standard
Safety Belt/Restraint:
Dynamic Head Restraints . . . . None
Adjustable Belt. . . . . Standard Front

^Warning feature does not meet government standards.
*Backup camera does not meet government standards.

Ford Fusion Energi

Specifications

Drive. . . . . .FWD
Engine . . . . Electric and Gas Power the Wheels
Transmission . . . . CVT
Tow Rating (lbs.) . . . . –
Head/Leg Room (in.) Roomy-39.2/44.3
Interior Space (cu. ft.). Roomy-111
Cargo Space (cu. ft.) . . . . Very Cramped-8.2
Wheelbase/Length (in.) 112.2/191.8

Ford Mustang

Ratings—10 Best, 1 Worst

Combo Crash Tests	—
Safety Features	5
Rollover	—
Preventive Maintenance	8
Repair Costs	10
Warranty	3
Fuel Economy	3
Complaints	2
Insurance Costs	5
OVERALL RATING	**—**

Ford Mustang

At-a-Glance

Status/Year Series Started. Unchanged/2015
Twins . . . . —
Body Styles .Coupe, Convertible
Seating 4
Anti-Theft Device . . . . .Std. Pass. Immobil. & Alarm
Parking Index Rating . . . . Easy
Where Made. . . . . .Flat Rock, MI

Fuel Factor:
  MPG Rating (city/hwy). Poor-19/28
  Driving Range (mi.) . . . . .Very Short-355.4
  Fuel Type. . . . . Regular
  Annual Fuel Cost . . . . .High-$1,418
  Gas Guzzler Tax . . . . No
  Greenhouse Gas Emissions (tons/yr.). High-8.1
  Barrels of Oil Used per year High-15.0

How the Competition Rates

Competitors	Rating	Pg.
Chevrolet Camaro	—	111
Chevrolet Corvette	—	113
Dodge Challenger	5	129

Price Range

Price Range	Retail	Markup
Base Coupe	$23,800	6%
Eco Premium Coupe	$29,300	8%
GT Premium Convertible	$36,300	8%
GT 50 yr LTD Ed.	$47,870	8%

Safety Checklist

Crash Tests:
  Frontal. . . . . −
  Side. . . . . −

Airbags:
  Torso . . . . Front Pelvis/Torso from Seat
  Pelvis . . . . Front Pelvis/Torso from Seat
  Roll Sensing. . . . . Yes
  Knee Bolster . . . . Standard Front

Crash Avoidance:
  Collision Avoidance . . . . Warning Only Optional
  Blind Spot Detection . . . . .Optional
  Lane Keeping Assist . . . . None
  Backup Camera . . . . Standard
  Pedestrian Crash Avoidance . . . . None

General:
  Auto. Crash Notification. . . . . Dial Assist.-Free
  Day Running Lamps . . . . None

Safety Belt/Restraint:
  Dynamic Head Restraints . . . . None
  Adjustable Belt. . . . . None

^Warning feature does not meet government standards.
*Backup camera does not meet government standards.

Ford Mustang

Specifications

Drive. . . . . .RWD
Engine 3.7-liter V6
Transmission . . . . 6-sp. Automatic
Tow Rating (lbs.) . . . . −
Head/Leg Room (in.) Average-37.6/44.5
Interior Space (cu. ft.). . . . . Very Cramped-84.5
Cargo Space (cu. ft.) Cramped-13.5
Wheelbase/Length (in.) 107.1/188.3

Ratings—10 Best, 1 Worst

Combo Crash Tests	7
Safety Features	5
Rollover	8
Preventive Maintenance	5
Repair Costs	4
Warranty	3
Fuel Economy	3
Complaints	7
Insurance Costs	1
OVERALL RATING	**4**

Ford Taurus

Ford Taurus

At-a-Glance

Status/Year Series Started Unchanged/2010
Twins . . . . –
Body Styles . . . . Sedan
Seating 5
Anti-Theft Device . . . . .Std. Pass. Immobil. & Alarm
Parking Index Rating . . . . Very Hard
Where Made. . . . . Chicago, IL

Fuel Factor:
MPG Rating (city/hwy) Poor-19/29
Driving Range (mi.) Long-427.3
Fuel Type . . . . Regular
Annual Fuel Cost .High-$1,401
Gas Guzzler Tax . . . . No
Greenhouse Gas Emissions (tons/yr.) High-7.8
Barrels of Oil Used per year High-14.3

How the Competition Rates

Competitors	Rating	Pg.
Buick LaCrosse	8	104
Chevrolet Impala	6	116
Toyota Avalon	8	247

Price Range

Price Range	Retail	Markup
SE	$26,790	8%
SEL	$29,370	8%
Limited AWD	$36,140	8%
SHO AWD	$40,105	8%

Safety Checklist

Crash Tests:
Frontal. . . . . .Very Good
Side. . . . . .Poor

Airbags:
Torso . . . . . Std. Fr. & Opt. Rr. Pelvis/Torso from Seat
Pelvis . . . . . Std. Fr. & Opt. Rr. Pelvis/Torso from Seat
Roll Sensing. . . . . Yes
Knee Bolster . . . . .Standard Driver

Crash Avoidance:
Collision Avoidance . . . . Warning Only Optional
Blind Spot Detection . . . . .Optional
Lane Keeping Assist . . . . .Optional
Backup Camera . . . . Standard
Pedestrian Crash Avoidance . . . . None

General:
Auto. Crash Notification . . . . .Optional
Day Running Lamps . . . . None

Safety Belt/Restraint:
Dynamic Head Restraints . . . . None
Adjustable Belt. . . . . Standard Front

^Warning feature does not meet government standards.
*Backup camera does not meet government standards.

Ford Taurus

Specifications

Drive. . . . . .FWD
Engine 3.5-liter V6
Transmission . . . . 6-sp. Automatic
Tow Rating (lbs.) . . . . .Very Low-1000
Head/Leg Room (in.) Cramped-39/41.9
Interior Space (cu. ft.). Average-102.2
Cargo Space (cu. ft.) Average-20.1
Wheelbase/Length (in.) 112/202.9

Ratings—10 Best, 1 Worst

Combo Crash Tests	7
Safety Features	4
Rollover	4
Preventive Maintenance	2
Repair Costs	3
Warranty	5
Fuel Economy	2
Complaints	4
Insurance Costs	10
OVERALL RATING	**4**

GMC Acadia

GMC Acadia

At-a-Glance

Status/Year Series Started	Unchanged/2007
Twins	Chevrolet Traverse
Body Styles	SUV
Seating	7/8
Anti-Theft Device	Std. Pass. Immobil. & Alarm
Parking Index Rating	Very Hard
Where Made	Lansing, MI

Fuel Factor:

MPG Rating (city/hwy)	Very Poor-17/24
Driving Range (mi.)	Long-430.5
Fuel Type	Regular
Annual Fuel Cost	Very High-$1,610
Gas Guzzler Tax	17.3
Greenhouse Gas Emissions (tons/yr.)	High-7.7
Barrels of Oil Used per year	Very Low-0.0

How the Competition Rates

Competitors	Rating	Pg.
Buick Enclave	5	102
Ford Flex	–	142
Toyota Highlander	7	250

Price Range

Price Range	Retail	Markup
SLE1 FWD	$34,175	5%
SLT1 FWD	$41,020	5%
SLT2 AWD	$44,295	5%
Denali AWD	$49,890	5%

Safety Checklist

Crash Tests:

Frontal	Good
Side	Good

Airbags:

Torso	Front Pelvis/Torso from Seat
Pelvis	Front Pelvis/Torso from Seat
Roll Sensing	Yes
Knee Bolster	None

Crash Avoidance:

Collision Avoidance	Warning Only Optional
Blind Spot Detection	Optional
Lane Keeping Assist	Warning Only Optional
Backup Camera	Standard*
Pedestrian Crash Avoidance	None

General:

Auto. Crash Notif.	Oper. Assist. & Crash Info-Fee
Day Running Lamps	Standard

Safety Belt/Restraint:

Dynamic Head Restraints	None
Adjustable Belt	Standard Front and Rear

^Warning feature does not meet government standards.
*Backup camera does not meet government standards.

GMC Acadia

Specifications

Drive	FWD
Engine	3.6-liter V6
Transmission	6-sp. Automatic
Tow Rating (lbs.)	Low-5200
Head/Leg Room (in.)	Average-40.3/41.3
Interior Space (cu. ft.)	Roomy-151.8
Cargo Space (cu. ft.)	Roomy-24.1
Wheelbase/Length (in.)	118.9/200.8

Ratings—10 Best, 1 Worst

Combo Crash Tests	4
Safety Features	4
Rollover	2
Preventive Maintenance	2
Repair Costs	6
Warranty	5
Fuel Economy	2
Complaints	1
Insurance Costs	5
OVERALL RATING	**1**

GMC Canyon

GMC Canyon

At-a-Glance

Status/Year Series Started Unchanged/2015
Twins . . . . Chevrolet Colorado
Body Styles . . . . Pickup
Seating 4
Anti-Theft Device .Std. Pass. Immob. & Opt. Pass. Alarm
Parking Index Rating . . . . Very Hard
Where Made. . . . . Wentzville, MO

Fuel Factor:
MPG Rating (city/hwy) . . . . Very Poor-17/24
Driving Range (mi.) Average-410.9
Fuel Type. . . . . Regular
Annual Fuel Cost . . . . Very High-$1,610
Gas Guzzler Tax . . . . No
Greenhouse Gas Emissions (tons/yr.). . . Very High-9.0
Barrels of Oil Used per year High-16.5

How the Competition Rates

Competitors	Rating	Pg.
Nissan Frontier	–	224
Toyota Tacoma	–	257

Price Range

	Retail	Markup
SL Ext. Cab 2WD	$20,955	1%
Base Ext. Cab 2WD	$22,950	4%
SLE Crew Cab 4WD	$34,360	5%
SLT Crew Cab 4WD	$37,450	5%

Safety Checklist

Crash Tests:
Frontal. . . . . .Average
Side. . . . . .Poor

Airbags:
Torso . . . . Front Pelvis/Torso from Seat
Pelvis . . . . Front Pelvis/Torso from Seat
Roll Sensing. . . . . Yes
Knee Bolster . . . . None

Crash Avoidance:
Collision Avoidance . . . . Warning Only Optional
Blind Spot Detection . . . . None
Lane Keeping Assist . . . . Warning Only Optional
Backup Camera . . . . Standard*
Pedestrian Crash Avoidance . . . . None

General:
Auto. Crash Notif.. . . . . .Oper. Assist. & Crash Info-Fee
Day Running Lamps . . . . Standard

Safety Belt/Restraint:
Dynamic Head Restraints . . . . None
Adjustable Belt. . . . . Standard Front

^Warning feature does not meet government standards.
*Backup camera does not meet government standards.

GMC Canyon

Specifications

Drive 4WD
Engine 3.6-liter V6
Transmission . . . . 6-sp. Automatic
Tow Rating (lbs.) Average-6700
Head/Leg Room (in.) Average-40/41.7
Interior Space (cu. ft.). . . . . –
Cargo Space (cu. ft.) . . . . Very Roomy-49.9
Wheelbase/Length (in.) 128.3/212.4

GMC Sierra — Standard Pickup

Ratings—10 Best, 1 Worst

Combo Crash Tests	9
Safety Features	3
Rollover	3
Preventive Maintenance	2
Repair Costs	8
Warranty	5
Fuel Economy	1
Complaints	4
Insurance Costs	5
OVERALL RATING	**5**

GMC Sierra

GMC Sierra

At-a-Glance

Status/Year Series Started Unchanged/2014
Twins . . . . .Chevrolet Silverado
Body Styles . . . . Pickup
Seating 5/6
Anti-Theft Device Std. Pass. Immobil. & Opt. Pass. Alarm
Parking Index Rating . . . . Very Hard
Where Made. . . . . Fort Wayne, IN

Fuel Factor:
MPG Rating (city/hwy) . . . . Very Poor-16/22
Driving Range (mi.) . . . . Very Long-474.2
Fuel Type . . . . Regular
Annual Fuel Cost . . . . Very High-$1,727
Gas Guzzler Tax . . . . No
Greenhouse Gas Emissions (tons/yr.). . Very High-10.0
Barrels of Oil Used per year . . . . Very High-18.3

How the Competition Rates

Competitors	Rating	Pg.
Ford F-150	9	140
Ram 1500	4	236
Toyota Tundra	–	258

Price Range

Price Range	Retail	Markup
Base Reg. Cab 2WD	$26,605	4%
SLE Dbl. Cab 2WD	$35,540	8%
SLT Dbl. Cab 4WD	$43,490	8%
Denali Crew Cab 4WD	$52,855	8%

Safety Checklist

Crash Tests:
Frontal. . . . . .Very Good
Side. . . . . .Poor

Airbags:
Torso . . . . Front Pelvis/Torso from Seat
Pelvis . . . . Front Pelvis/Torso from Seat
Roll Sensing. . . . . Yes
Knee Bolster . . . . None

Crash Avoidance:
Collision Avoidance . . . . Warning Only Optional^
Blind Spot Detection . . . . None
Lane Keeping Assist . . . . Warning Only Optional
Backup Camera . . . . Optional*
Pedestrian Crash Avoidance . . . . None

General:
Auto. Crash Notif.. . . . . .Oper. Assist. & Crash Info-Fee
Day Running Lamps . . . . Standard

Safety Belt/Restraint:
Dynamic Head Restraints . . . . None
Adjustable Belt. . . . . Standard Front

^Warning feature does not meet government standards.
*Backup camera does not meet government standards.

GMC Sierra

Specifications

Drive. 4WD
Engine 5.3-liter V8
Transmission . . . . 6-sp. Automatic
Tow Rating (lbs.) Average-6200
Head/Leg Room (in.) . . . . Very Roomy-42.8/45.2
Interior Space (cu. ft.). . . . . –
Cargo Space (cu. ft.) . . . . Very Roomy-61
Wheelbase/Length (in.) 143.5/229.5

GMC Terrain — Medium SUV

GMC Terrain

Ratings—10 Best, 1 Worst

Combo Crash Tests	2
Safety Features	4
Rollover	3
Preventive Maintenance	2
Repair Costs	6
Warranty	5
Fuel Economy	5
Complaints	8
Insurance Costs	5
OVERALL RATING	**3**

GMC Terrain

At-a-Glance

Status/Year Series Started. Unchanged/2010
Twins . . . . .Chevrolet Equinox
Body Styles . . . . .SUV
Seating 5
Anti-Theft Device . . . . .Std. Pass. Immobil. & Alarm
Parking Index Rating . . . . Hard
Where Made. . . . . .Ingersoll, Ontario

Fuel Factor:
MPG Rating (city/hwy). Average-22/32
Driving Range (mi.) Long-460.8
Fuel Type. . . . . –
Annual Fuel Cost . . . . .Average-$1,230
Gas Guzzler Tax . . . . No
Greenhouse Gas Emissions (tons/yr.) Low-5.7
Barrels of Oil Used per year Average-12.7

How the Competition Rates

Competitors	Rating	Pg.
Dodge Journey	1	132
Ford Explorer	3	139
Honda Pilot	9	158

Price Range

	Retail	Markup
SLE1 FWD	$26,800	5%
SLE2 FWD	$28,300	5%
SLT1 AWD	$30,620	5%
Denali AWD	$35,725	5%

Safety Checklist

Crash Tests:
Frontal. . . . . .Poor
Side. . . . . Very Poor

Airbags:
Torso . . . . Front Pelvis/Torso from Seat
Pelvis . . . . Front Pelvis/Torso from Seat
Roll Sensing. . . . . Yes
Knee Bolster . . . . None

Crash Avoidance:
Collision Avoidance . . . . Warning Only Optional
Blind Spot Detection . . . . .Optional
Lane Keeping Assist . . . . Warning Only Optional
Backup Camera . . . . Standard*
Pedestrian Crash Avoidance . . . . None

General:
Auto. Crash Notif. . . . . .Oper. Assist. & Crash Info-Fee
Day Running Lamps . . . . Standard

Safety Belt/Restraint:
Dynamic Head Restraints . . . . None
Adjustable Belt. . . . . Standard Front and Rear

^Warning feature does not meet government standards.
*Backup camera does not meet government standards.

GMC Terrain

Specifications

Drive. . . . . .FWD
Engine 2.4-liter I4
Transmission . . . . 6-sp. Automatic
Tow Rating (lbs.) . . . . .Very Low-1500
Head/Leg Room (in.) Cramped-39.8/41.2
Interior Space (cu. ft.). Average-99.6
Cargo Space (cu. ft.) Roomy-31.6
Wheelbase/Length (in.) 112.5/185.3

Honda Accord

Ratings—10 Best, 1 Worst

Combo Crash Tests	9
Safety Features	7
Rollover	10
Preventive Maintenance	9
Repair Costs	7
Warranty	1
Fuel Economy	8
Complaints	6
Insurance Costs	5
OVERALL RATING	**10**

Honda Accord

At-a-Glance

Status/Year Series Started. Unchanged/2013
Twins . . . . .Acura TLX
Body Styles . . . . .Sedan, Coupe
Seating 5
Anti-Theft Device . . . . .Std. Pass. Immobil. & Alarm
Parking Index Rating . . . . Hard
Where Made. .Marysville, OH

Fuel Factor:
MPG Rating (city/hwy) Good-27/36
Driving Range (mi.) . . . . Very Long-523.3
Fuel Type . . . . Regular
Annual Fuel Cost . . . . Low-$1,035
Gas Guzzler Tax . . . . No
Greenhouse Gas Emissions (tons/yr.). Low-5.8
Barrels of Oil Used per year Low-10.6

How the Competition Rates

Competitors	Rating	Pg.
Ford Fusion	7	144
Nissan Altima	7	222
Toyota Camry	7	248

Price Range

Price Range	Retail	Markup
LX Sedan MT	$22,105	9%
EX Sedan AT	$25,480	9%
EX-L Coupe V6 AT	$30,925	9%
Touring Sedan V6 AT	$34,580	9%

Safety Checklist

Crash Tests:
Frontal. . . . . .Very Good
Side. . . . . .Good
Airbags:
Torso . . . . Front Pelvis/Torso from Seat
Pelvis . . . . Front Pelvis/Torso from Seat
Roll Sensing. . . . . Yes
Knee Bolster . . . . None
Crash Avoidance:
Collision Avoidance . . . . Optional CIB & DBS
Blind Spot Detection . . . . None
Lane Keeping Assist . . . . Warning Only Optional
Backup Camera . . . . Standard
Pedestrian Crash Avoidance . . . . .Optional
General:
Auto. Crash Notification . . . . Dial Assist.-Free
Day Running Lamps . . . . Standard
Safety Belt/Restraint:
Dynamic Head Restraints . . . . None
Adjustable Belt. . . . . Standard Front

^Warning feature does not meet government standards.
*Backup camera does not meet government standards.

Honda Accord

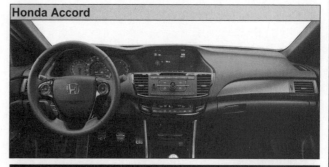

Specifications

Drive. . . . . .FWD
Engine 2.4-liter I4
Transmission . . . . CVT
Tow Rating (lbs.) . . . . –
Head/Leg Room (in.) Average-39.1/42.5
Interior Space (cu. ft.). Average-103.2
Cargo Space (cu. ft.) Cramped-15.8
Wheelbase/Length (in.) 109.3/191.4

Ratings—10 Best, 1 Worst

Combo Crash Tests	—
Safety Features	8
Rollover	—
Preventive Maintenance	10
Repair Costs	9
Warranty	1
Fuel Economy	9
Complaints	—
Insurance Costs	5
OVERALL RATING	—

Honda Civic

Honda Civic

At-a-Glance

Status/Year Series Started . . . . .All New/2016
Twins . . . . —
Body Styles . . . . Coupe
Seating 5
Anti-Theft Device . . . . .Std. Pass. Immobil. & Alarm
Parking Index Rating . . . . Easy
Where Made . . . . .Greensburg, IN / Alliston, Ontario

Fuel Factor:
MPG Rating (city/hwy) . . . . .Very Good-31/41
Driving Range (mi.) Long-431.8
Fuel Type . . . . Regular
Annual Fuel Cost . . . . Very Low-$905
Gas Guzzler Tax . . . . No
Greenhouse Gas Emissions (tons/yr.) . . . .Very Low-4.2
Barrels of Oil Used per year Low-9.4

How the Competition Rates

Competitors	Rating	Pg.
Nissan Sentra	6	232
Subaru Impreza	5	241
Volkswagen Jetta	7	263

Price Range

	Retail	Markup
LX Coupe MT	$18,290	8%
LX Sedan AT	$19,290	8%
EX-L Sedan w/Nav	$24,340	8%
Si Sedan w/Nav	$24,950	9%

Safety Checklist

Crash Tests:
Frontal . . . . −
Side . . . . −

Airbags:
Torso . . . . Front Pelvis/Torso from Seat
Pelvis . . . . Front Pelvis/Torso from Seat
Roll Sensing . . . . Yes
Knee Bolster . . . . None

Crash Avoidance:
Collision Avoidance . . . . Optional CIB & DBS
Blind Spot Detection . . . . None
Lane Keeping Assist . . . . .Optional
Backup Camera . . . . Standard
Pedestrian Crash Avoidance . . . . .Optional

General:
Auto. Crash Notification . . . . Dial Assist.-Free
Day Running Lamps . . . . Standard

Safety Belt/Restraint:
Dynamic Head Restraints . . . . None
Adjustable Belt . . . . Standard Front

^Warning feature does not meet government standards.
*Backup camera does not meet government standards.

Honda Civic

Specifications

Drive . . . . .FWD
Engine 1.8-liter I4
Transmission . . . . CVT
Tow Rating (lbs.) . . . . −
Head/Leg Room (in.) Average-39.3/42.3
Interior Space (cu. ft.) Cramped-94.8
Cargo Space (cu. ft.) Cramped-15.1
Wheelbase/Length (in.) 106.3/179.4

Ratings—10 Best, 1 Worst	
Combo Crash Tests	6
Safety Features	7
Rollover	4
Preventive Maintenance	9
Repair Costs	9
Warranty	1
Fuel Economy	7
Complaints	3
Insurance Costs	10
OVERALL RATING	**7**

Honda CR-V

Honda CR-V

At-a-Glance

Status/Year Series Started. . . Appearance Change/2012
Twins . . . . –
Body Styles . . . . .SUV
Seating 5
Anti-Theft Device .Std. Pass. Immob. & Opt. Pass. Alarm
Parking Index Rating . . . . Easy
Where Made. East Liberty, OH

Fuel Factor:
MPG Rating (city/hwy) Good-26/33
Driving Range (mi.) Long-439.8
Fuel Type . . . . Regular
Annual Fuel Cost .Low-$1,096
Gas Guzzler Tax . . . . No
Greenhouse Gas Emissions (tons/yr.). Low-5.1
Barrels of Oil Used per year Average-11.4

How the Competition Rates

Competitors	Rating	Pg.
Ford Escape	5	137
Jeep Cherokee	7	173
Toyota RAV4	5	254

Price Range	Retail	Markup
LX 2WD	$23,320	6%
EX 2WD	$25,420	6%
EX-L AWD	$29,270	7%
Touring AWD	$32,770	7%

Safety Checklist

Crash Tests:
Frontal . . . . .Average
Side . . . . .Poor
Airbags:
Torso .Front Torso from Seat
Pelvis . . . . None
Roll Sensing. . . . . Yes
Knee Bolster . . . . None
Crash Avoidance:
Collision Avoidance . . . . Optional CIB & DBS
Blind Spot Detection . . . . None
Lane Keeping Assist . . . . .Optional
Backup Camera . . . . Standard
Pedestrian Crash Avoidance . . . . .Optional
General:
Auto. Crash Notification . . . . Dial Assist.-Free
Day Running Lamps . . . . Standard
Safety Belt/Restraint:
Dynamic Head Restraints . . . . None
Adjustable Belt. . . . . Standard Front

^Warning feature does not meet government standards.
*Backup camera does not meet government standards.

Honda CR-V

Specifications

Drive. . . . . -
Engine 185.0-liter I4
Transmission . . . . CVT
Tow Rating (lbs.) . . . . .Very Low-1500
Head/Leg Room (in.) Cramped-39.9/41.3
Interior Space (cu. ft.). Roomy-104.1
Cargo Space (cu. ft.) . . . . .Very Roomy-37.2
Wheelbase/Length (in.) 103.1/179.4

Ratings—10 Best, 1 Worst

Combo Crash Tests	9
Safety Features	3
Rollover	5
Preventive Maintenance	10
Repair Costs	8
Warranty	1
Fuel Economy	9
Complaints	2
Insurance Costs	5
OVERALL RATING	**7**

Honda Fit

Honda Fit

At-a-Glance

Status/Year Series Started. Unchanged/2015
Twins . . . . –
Body Styles .Sedan, Hatchback
Seating. 5
Anti-Theft Device .Std. Pass. Immob. & Opt. Pass. Alarm
Parking Index Rating . . . . Very Easy
Where Made. . . . . Celaya, Mexico
Fuel Factor:
MPG Rating (city/hwy) . . . . .Very Good-33/41
Driving Range (mi.) Short-383.5
Fuel Type . . . . Regular
Annual Fuel Cost . . . . Very Low-$871
Gas Guzzler Tax . . . . No
Greenhouse Gas Emissions (tons/yr.) Low-5.0
Barrels of Oil Used per year Low-9.1

How the Competition Rates

Competitors	Rating	Pg.
Chevrolet Sonic	10	119
Nissan Versa	3	234
Toyota Yaris	6	259

Price Range

Price Range	Retail	Markup
LX MT	$15,790	8
EX MT	$17,700	8
EX AT	$18,500	8
EX-L AT w/Nav	$21,065	8

Safety Checklist

Crash Tests:
Frontal. . . . . .Good
Side. . . . . .Very Good
Airbags:
Torso . . . . Front Pelvis/Torso from Seat
Pelvis . . . . Front Pelvis/Torso from Seat
Roll Sensing. . . . . Yes
Knee Bolster . . . . None
Crash Avoidance:
Collision Avoidance . . . . None
Blind Spot Detection . . . . None
Lane Keeping Assist . . . . None
Backup Camera. . . . . Standard
Pedestrian Crash Avoidance . . . . None
General:
Auto. Crash Notification . . . . Dial Assist.-Free
Day Running Lamps . . . . Standard
Safety Belt/Restraint:
Dynamic Head Restraints . . . . None
Adjustable Belt. . . . . Standard Front

^Warning feature does not meet government standards.
*Backup camera does not meet government standards.

Honda Fit

Specifications

Drive. . . . . .FWD
Engine 1.5-liter I4
Transmission . . . . CVT
Tow Rating (lbs.) . . . . –
Head/Leg Room (in.) Cramped-39.5/41.4
Interior Space (cu. ft.). Cramped-95.7
Cargo Space (cu. ft.) Cramped-16.6
Wheelbase/Length (in.) 99.6/160

Ratings—10 Best, 1 Worst

Combo Crash Tests	4
Safety Features	3
Rollover	5
Preventive Maintenance	7
Repair Costs	9
Warranty	1
Fuel Economy	8
Complaints	—
Insurance Costs	5
OVERALL RATING	**5**

Honda HR-V

Honda HR-V

At-a-Glance

Status/Year Series Started . . . . .All New/2016
Twins . . . . –
Body Styles . . . . .SUV
Seating 5
Anti-Theft Device .Std. Pass. Immob. & Opt. Pass. Alarm
Parking Index Rating . . . . Easy
Where Made. . . . . Celaya, Mexico

Fuel Factor:
MPG Rating (city/hwy) Good-28/35
Driving Range (mi.) Average-406.2
Fuel Type . . . . Regular
Annual Fuel Cost . . . . .Very Low-$1,024
Gas Guzzler Tax . . . . No
Greenhouse Gas Emissions (tons/yr.). Low-4.7
Barrels of Oil Used per year Low-10.6

How the Competition Rates

Competitors	Rating	Pg.
Chevrolet Trax	9	124
Jeep Renegade	2	177
Nissan Juke	2	225

Price Range

Price Range	Retail	Markup
LX 2WD MT	$19,115	3%
LX 2WD AT	$19,915	3%
EX AWD AT	$23,215	3%
EX-L AWD w/Nav	$25,840	3%

Safety Checklist

Crash Tests:
Frontal. . . . . .Poor
Side. . . . . .Average

Airbags:
Torso . . . . Front Pelvis/Torso from Seat
Pelvis . . . . Front Pelvis/Torso from Seat
Roll Sensing. . . . . Yes
Knee Bolster . . . . None

Crash Avoidance:
Collision Avoidance . . . . None
Blind Spot Detection . . . . .Optional
Lane Keeping Assist . . . . None
Backup Camera . . . . Standard
Pedestrian Crash Avoidance . . . . None

General:
Auto. Crash Notification . . . . Dial Assist.-Free
Day Running Lamps . . . . Standard

Safety Belt/Restraint:
Dynamic Head Restraints . . . . None
Adjustable Belt. . . . . Standard Front

^Warning feature does not meet government standards.
*Backup camera does not meet government standards.

Honda HR-V

Specifications

Drive. 2WD
Engine 1.8-liter I4
Transmission . . . . CVT
Tow Rating (lbs.) . . . .–
Head/Leg Room (in.) Cramped-39.5/41.2
Interior Space (cu. ft.). Average-100.1
Cargo Space (cu. ft.) Roomy-24.3
Wheelbase/Length (in.) 102.8/169.1

Ratings—10 Best, 1 Worst

Combo Crash Tests	7
Safety Features	6
Rollover	7
Preventive Maintenance	9
Repair Costs	9
Warranty	1
Fuel Economy	3
Complaints	6
Insurance Costs	10
OVERALL RATING	**8**

Honda Odyssey

Honda Odyssey

At-a-Glance

Status/Year Series Started Unchanged/2005
Twins . . . . –
Body Styles . . . . Minivan
Seating 7/8
Anti-Theft Device . . . . .Standard Pass. Immobil.
Parking Index Rating . . . . Hard
Where Made. . . . . Lincoln, AL

Fuel Factor:
MPG Rating (city/hwy) Poor-19/28
Driving Range (mi.) . . . . Very Long-466.5
Fuel Type . . . . Regular
Annual Fuel Cost .High-$1,418
Gas Guzzler Tax . . . . No
Greenhouse Gas Emissions (tons/yr.) Average-7.1
Barrels of Oil Used per year High-15.0

How the Competition Rates

Competitors	Rating	Pg.
Chrysler Town and Country	3	128
Nissan Quest	–	230
Toyota Sienna	3	256

Price Range	Retail	Markup
LX	$29,275	9%
EX	$32,425	9%
EX-L w/Nav	$37,925	9%
Touring Elite	$44,750	9%

Safety Checklist

Crash Tests:
Frontal . . . . .Average
Side . . . . Good
Airbags:
Torso . . . . Front Pelvis/Torso from Seat
Pelvis . . . . Front Pelvis/Torso from Seat
Roll Sensing. . . . . Yes
Knee Bolster . . . . None
Crash Avoidance:
Collision Avoidance . . . . Warning Only Optional
Blind Spot Detection . . . . .Optional
Lane Keeping Assist . . . . Warning Only Optional
Backup Camera . . . . Standard
Pedestrian Crash Avoidance . . . . None
General:
Auto. Crash Notification . . . . Dial Assist.-Free
Day Running Lamps . . . . Standard
Safety Belt/Restraint:
Dynamic Head Restraints . . . . Standard Front
Adjustable Belt. . . . . Standard Front and Rear

^Warning feature does not meet government standards.
*Backup camera does not meet government standards.

Honda Odyssey

Specifications

Drive. . . . . .FWD
Engine 3.5-liter V6
Transmission . . . . 5-sp. Automatic
Tow Rating (lbs.) Low-3500
Head/Leg Room (in.) Cramped-39.7/40.9
Interior Space (cu. ft.). Roomy-172.6
Cargo Space (cu. ft.) . . . . Very Roomy-38.4
Wheelbase/Length (in.) 118.1/202.9

Honda Pilot

Honda Pilot

Ratings—10 Best, 1 Worst

Combo Crash Tests	8
Safety Features	10
Rollover	4
Preventive Maintenance	9
Repair Costs	8
Warranty	1
Fuel Economy	3
Complaints	—
Insurance Costs	10
OVERALL RATING	**9**

Honda Pilot

Safety Checklist

Crash Tests:
Frontal . . . . .Average
Side . . . . .Very Good

Airbags:
Torso . . . . Front Pelvis/Torso from Seat
Pelvis . . . . Front Pelvis/Torso from Seat
Roll Sensing . . . . Yes
Knee Bolster . . . . None

Crash Avoidance:
Collision Avoidance . . . . Optional CIB & DBS
Blind Spot Detection . . . . .Optional
Lane Keeping Assist . . . . .Optional
Backup Camera . . . . Standard
Pedestrian Crash Avoidance . . . . .Optional

General:
Auto. Crash Notification . . . . Dial Assist.-Free
Day Running Lamps . . . . Standard

Safety Belt/Restraint:
Dynamic Head Restraints . . . . Standard Front
Adjustable Belt . . . . Standard Front and Rear

^Warning feature does not meet government standards.
*Backup camera does not meet government standards.

At-a-Glance

Status/Year Series Started . . . . .All New/2016
Twins . . . . –
Body Styles . . . . .SUV
Seating 8
Anti-Theft Device . . . . .Standard Pass. Immobil.
Parking Index Rating . . . . Hard
Where Made . . . . Lincoln, AL

Fuel Factor:
MPG Rating (city/hwy) Poor-19/27
Driving Range (mi.) Long-427.5
Fuel Type . . . . Regular
Annual Fuel Cost . . . . .High-$1,436
Gas Guzzler Tax . . . . No
Greenhouse Gas Emissions (tons/yr.) Average-6.4
Barrels of Oil Used per year High-14.3

Honda Pilot

How the Competition Rates

Competitors	Rating	Pg.
Chevrolet Equinox	2	115
Ford Explorer	3	139
Toyota 4Runner	3	246

Specifications

Drive . . . . .AWD
Engine 3.5-liter V6
Transmission . . . . 6-sp. Automatic
Tow Rating (lbs.) Low-3500
Head/Leg Room (in.) Cramped-40.1/40.9
Interior Space (cu. ft.) Roomy-152.9
Cargo Space (cu. ft.) Cramped-16.5
Wheelbase/Length (in.) 111/194.5

Price Range

	Retail	Markup
LX 2WD	$29,995	9%
EX 2WD	$32,430	9%
EX-L AWD	$37,705	9%
Touring Elite AWD	$46,420	9%

Ratings—10 Best, 1 Worst

Combo Crash Tests	2
Safety Features	2
Rollover	7
Preventive Maintenance	6
Repair Costs	10
Warranty	10
Fuel Economy	8
Complaints	9
Insurance Costs	1
OVERALL RATING	**6**

Hyundai Accent

Hyundai Accent

At-a-Glance

Status/Year Series Started. Unchanged/2012
Twins . . . . Kia Rio
Body Styles .Sedan, Hatchback
Seating 5
Anti-Theft Device . . . . None
Parking Index Rating . . . . Very Easy
Where Made. . . . . .Ulsan, South Korea

Fuel Factor:
MPG Rating (city/hwy) Good-26/37
Driving Range (mi.) . . . . .Very Short-342.2
Fuel Type . . . . Regular
Annual Fuel Cost . . . . .Low-$1,049
Gas Guzzler Tax . . . . No
Greenhouse Gas Emissions (tons/yr.) Average-6.0
Barrels of Oil Used per year Average-11.0

How the Competition Rates

Competitors	Rating	Pg.
Ford Fiesta	1	141
Nissan Versa	3	234
Toyota Yaris	6	259

Price Range

	Retail	Markup
SE Sedan MT	$14,745	3%
SE Hatchback AT	$16,195	3%
Sport Hatchback MT	$16,495	3%
Sport Hatchback AT	$17,495	3%

Safety Checklist

Crash Tests:
Frontal. . . . . .Poor
Side. . . . . Very Poor

Airbags:
Torso . . . . Front Pelvis/Torso from Seat
Pelvis . . . . Front Pelvis/Torso from Seat
Roll Sensing. . . . . Yes
Knee Bolster . . . . None

Crash Avoidance:
Collision Avoidance . . . . None
Blind Spot Detection . . . . None
Lane Keeping Assist . . . . None
Backup Camera . . . . None
Pedestrian Crash Avoidance . . . . None

General:
Auto. Crash Notification . . . . None
Day Running Lamps . . . . None

Safety Belt/Restraint:
Dynamic Head Restraints . . . . None
Adjustable Belt. . . . . Standard Front

^Warning feature does not meet government standards.
*Backup camera does not meet government standards.

Specifications

Drive. . . . . .FWD
Engine 1.6-liter I4
Transmission . . . . 6-sp. Automatic
Tow Rating (lbs.) . . . . –
Head/Leg Room (in.) Average-39.9/41.8
Interior Space (cu. ft.). . . . . Very Cramped-90.1
Cargo Space (cu. ft.) Average-21.2
Wheelbase/Length (in.) 101.2/162

Ratings—10 Best, 1 Worst

Combo Crash Tests	—
Safety Features	4
Rollover	—
Preventive Maintenance	4
Repair Costs	10
Warranty	10
Fuel Economy	4
Complaints	4
Insurance Costs	5
OVERALL RATING	**—**

Hyundai Azera

Hyundai Azera

At-a-Glance

Status/Year Series Started Unchanged/2012
Twins . . . . Kia Cadenza
Body Styles . . . . Sedan
Seating 5
Anti-Theft Device . . . Std. Pass. Immobil. & Active Alarm
Parking Index Rating .Average
Where Made. . . . . Asan, South Korea
Fuel Factor:
  MPG Rating (city/hwy) Poor-20/29
  Driving Range (mi.) Long-430.1
  Fuel Type . . . . Regular
  Annual Fuel Cost . . . . .Average-$1,355
  Gas Guzzler Tax . . . . No
  Greenhouse Gas Emissions (tons/yr.). High-7.8
  Barrels of Oil Used per year High-14.3

How the Competition Rates

Competitors	Rating	Pg.
Chevrolet Impala	6	116
Kia Cadenza	–	179
Nissan Maxima	5	227

Price Range

Price Range	Retail	Markup
Sedan	$34,000	7%
Sedan Limited	$38,200	7%

Safety Checklist

Crash Tests:
  Frontal . . . . −
  Side . . . . −
Airbags:
  Torso . . . . Front Pelvis/Torso from Seat
  Pelvis . . . . Rear Torso from Seat
  Roll Sensing. . . . . Yes
  Knee Bolster .Standard Driver
Crash Avoidance:
  Collision Avoidance . . . . Warning Only Optional
  Blind Spot Detection . . . . Standard
  Lane Keeping Assist . . . . Warning Only Optional
  Backup Camera . . . . Standard*
  Pedestrian Crash Avoidance . . . . None
General:
  Auto. Crash Notification . . . . .Operator Assist.-Fee
  Day Running Lamps . . . . Standard
Safety Belt/Restraint:
  Dynamic Head Restraints . . . . None
  Adjustable Belt. . . . . Standard Front

^Warning feature does not meet government standards.
*Backup camera does not meet government standards.

Hyundai Azera

Specifications

Drive. . . . . .FWD
Engine 3.3-liter V6
Transmission . . . . 6-sp. Automatic
Tow Rating (lbs.) . . . . −
Head/Leg Room (in.) . . . . Very Roomy-40.3/45.5
Interior Space (cu. ft.). Roomy-107
Cargo Space (cu. ft.) Cramped-16.3
Wheelbase/Length (in.) 112/193.3

Ratings—10 Best, 1 Worst

Combo Crash Tests	4
Safety Features	1
Rollover	8
Preventive Maintenance	4
Repair Costs	10
Warranty	10
Fuel Economy	9
Complaints	7
Insurance Costs	1
OVERALL RATING	**7**

Hyundai Elantra

Hyundai Elantra

At-a-Glance

Status/Year Series Started	Unchanged/2011
Twins	Kia Forte
Body Styles	Sedan, Coupe, Hatchback
Seating	5
Anti-Theft Device	Std. Pass. Immobil. & Active Alarm
Parking Index Rating	Easy
Where Made	Montgomery, AL

Fuel Factor:

MPG Rating (city/hwy)	Very Good-28/38
Driving Range (mi.)	Average-406.5
Fuel Type	Regular
Annual Fuel Cost	Very Low-$992
Gas Guzzler Tax	No
Greenhouse Gas Emissions (tons/yr.)	Low-5.6
Barrels of Oil Used per year	Low-10.3

How the Competition Rates

Competitors	Rating	Pg.
Honda Civic	–	149
Nissan Sentra	6	232
Toyota Corolla	9	249

Price Range

	Retail	Markup
SE MT	$17,250	3%
GT AT	$19,800	4%
Sport AT	$21,250	4%
Limited AT	$21,700	4%

Safety Checklist

Crash Tests:

Frontal	Average
Side	Poor

Airbags:

Torso	Front Pelvis/Torso from Seat
Pelvis	Rear Torso from Seat
Roll Sensing	No
Knee Bolster	None

Crash Avoidance:

Collision Avoidance	None
Blind Spot Detection	None
Lane Keeping Assist	None
Backup Camera	Optional*
Pedestrian Crash Avoidance	None

General:

Auto. Crash Notification	Operator Assist.-Fee
Day Running Lamps	Standard

Safety Belt/Restraint:

Dynamic Head Restraints	None
Adjustable Belt	Standard Front

^Warning feature does not meet government standards.
*Backup camera does not meet government standards.

Hyundai Elantra

Specifications

Drive	FWD
Engine	1.8-liter I4
Transmission	6-sp. Automatic
Tow Rating (lbs.)	–
Head/Leg Room (in.)	Roomy-40/43.6
Interior Space (cu. ft.)	Cramped-95.6
Cargo Space (cu. ft.)	Cramped-14.8
Wheelbase/Length (in.)	106.3/179.1

Ratings—10 Best, 1 Worst

Combo Crash Tests	9
Safety Features	8
Rollover	10
Preventive Maintenance	3
Repair Costs	4
Warranty	10
Fuel Economy	3
Complaints	1
Insurance Costs	3
OVERALL RATING	**7**

Hyundai Genesis

Hyundai Genesis

At-a-Glance

Status/Year Series Started Unchanged/2015
Twins . . . . –
Body Styles . . . . Sedan
Seating 5
Anti-Theft Device . . . Std. Pass. Immobil. & Active Alarm
Parking Index Rating . . . . Average
Where Made . . . . Ulsan, South Korea
Fuel Factor:
  MPG Rating (city/hwy) Poor-18/29
  Driving Range (mi.) Long-440.6
  Fuel Type . . . . Regular
  Annual Fuel Cost . . . . High-$1,451
  Gas Guzzler Tax . . . . No
  Greenhouse Gas Emissions (tons/yr.) High-8.2
  Barrels of Oil Used per year High-15.0

How the Competition Rates

Competitors	Rating	Pg.
Acura TLX	10	84
Lexus ES	8	191
Volkswagen CC	–	261

Price Range	Retail	Markup
3.8 L V6 Coupe	$26,750	5%
3.8L V6 Sedan FWD	$38,000	7%
3.8L V6 Sedan AWD	$40,500	7%
5.0L V8 Sedan FWD	$51,500	8%

Safety Checklist

Crash Tests:
  Frontal . . . . Very Good
  Side . . . . Good
Airbags:
  Torso . . . . Front Pelvis/Torso from Seat
  Pelvis . . . . Rear Torso from Seat
  Roll Sensing . . . . Yes
  Knee Bolster . . . . Standard Driver
Crash Avoidance:
  Collision Avoidance . . . . Optional CIB & DBS
  Blind Spot Detection . . . . Optional
  Lane Keeping Assist . . . . Optional
  Backup Camera . . . . Standard*
  Pedestrian Crash Avoidance . . . . None
General:
  Auto. Crash Notification . . . . None
  Day Running Lamps . . . . Standard
Safety Belt/Restraint:
  Dynamic Head Restraints . . . . None
  Adjustable Belt . . . . Standard Front

^Warning feature does not meet government standards.
*Backup camera does not meet government standards.

Hyundai Genesis

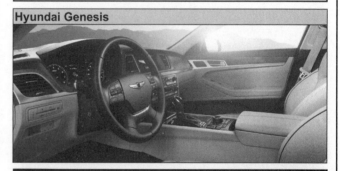

Specifications

Drive . . . . RWD
Engine 3.8-liter V6
Transmission . . . . 8-sp. Automatic
Tow Rating (lbs.) . . . . –
Head/Leg Room (in.) . . . . Very Roomy-41.1/45.7
Interior Space (cu. ft.) Roomy-107.7
Cargo Space (cu. ft.) Cramped-15.3
Wheelbase/Length (in.) 118.5/196.5

Hyundai Santa Fe | Medium SUV

Ratings—10 Best, 1 Worst

Combo Crash Tests	—
Safety Features	4
Rollover	—
Preventive Maintenance	4
Repair Costs	8
Warranty	10
Fuel Economy	2
Complaints	3
Insurance Costs	5
OVERALL RATING	—

Hyundai Santa Fe

Hyundai Santa Fe

At-a-Glance

Status/Year Series Started. Unchanged/2013
Twins . . . . –
Body Styles . . . . .SUV
Seating 6/7
Anti-Theft Device . . . Std. Pass. Immobil. & Active Alarm
Parking Index Rating .Average
Where Made. . . . . West Point, GA
Fuel Factor:
MPG Rating (city/hwy) . . . . Very Poor-18/25
Driving Range (mi.) Short-387.2
Fuel Type . . . . Regular
Annual Fuel Cost . . . . .High-$1,530
Gas Guzzler Tax . . . . No
Greenhouse Gas Emissions (tons/yr.). High-8.5
Barrels of Oil Used per year High-15.7

How the Competition Rates

Competitors	Rating	Pg.
Acura MDX	6	82
Mitsubishi Outlander	4	219
Nissan Pathfinder	1	229

Price Range

	Retail	Markup
SE FWD	$30,400	5%
SE AWD	$32,150	5%
Limited FWD	$34,500	6%
Limited AWD	$36,250	6%

Safety Checklist

Crash Tests:
Frontal. . . . . –
Side. . . . . –
Airbags:
Torso . . . . Front Pelvis/Torso from Seat
Pelvis . . . . Front Pelvis/Torso from Seat
Roll Sensing. . . . . Yes
Knee Bolster . . . . .Driver
Crash Avoidance:
Collision Avoidance . . . . None
Blind Spot Detection . . . . .Optional
Lane Keeping Assist . . . . None
Backup Camera. . . . . Standard*
Pedestrian Crash Avoidance . . . . None
General:
Auto. Crash Notification . . . . .Operator Assist.-Fee
Day Running Lamps . . . . Standard
Safety Belt/Restraint:
Dynamic Head Restraints . . . . None
Adjustable Belt. . . . . Standard Front

^Warning feature does not meet government standards.
*Backup camera does not meet government standards.

Hyundai Santa Fe

Specifications

Drive. . . . . .FWD
Engine 3.3-liter V6
Transmission . . . . 6-sp. Automatic
Tow Rating (lbs.) Low-5000
Head/Leg Room (in.) Cramped-39.6/41.3
Interior Space (cu. ft.). Roomy-146.6
Cargo Space (cu. ft.) Cramped-13.5
Wheelbase/Length (in.) 110.2/193.1

Ratings—10 Best, 1 Worst

Combo Crash Tests	7
Safety Features	4
Rollover	5
Preventive Maintenance	4
Repair Costs	5
Warranty	10
Fuel Economy	3
Complaints	—
Insurance Costs	5
OVERALL RATING	**5**

Hyundai Santa Fe Sport

At-a-Glance

Status/Year Series Started. Unchanged/2014
Twins . . . . –
Body Styles . . . . .SUV
Seating 5
Anti-Theft Device . . . Std. Pass. Immobil. & Active Alarm
Parking Index Rating . . . . Easy
Where Made. . . . . West Point, GA

Fuel Factor:
MPG Rating (city/hwy) Poor-20/27
Driving Range (mi.) Short-394.0
Fuel Type . . . . Regular
Annual Fuel Cost . . . . .High-$1,391
Gas Guzzler Tax . . . . No
Greenhouse Gas Emissions (tons/yr.). High-7.9
Barrels of Oil Used per year High-14.3

How the Competition Rates

Competitors	Rating	Pg.
Kia Sorento	5	184
Mitsubishi Outlander Sport	3	220

Price Range	Retail	Markup
2.4L FWD	$24,950	4%
2.4L AWD	$26,700	4%
2.0T Turbo FWD	$31,250	6%
2.0T Turbo AWD	$33,000	6%

Hyundai Santa Fe Sport

Safety Checklist

Crash Tests:
Frontal. . . . . .Good
Side. . . . . .Average

Airbags:
Torso . . . . Front Pelvis/Torso from Seat
Pelvis . . . . Front Pelvis/Torso from Seat
Roll Sensing. . . . . Yes
Knee Bolster . . . . .Standard Driver

Crash Avoidance:
Collision Avoidance . . . . None
Blind Spot Detection . . . . .Optional
Lane Keeping Assist . . . . None
Backup Camera . . . . Optional*
Pedestrian Crash Avoidance . . . . None

General:
Auto. Crash Notification . . . . .Operator Assist.-Fee
Day Running Lamps . . . . Standard

Safety Belt/Restraint:
Dynamic Head Restraints . . . . None
Adjustable Belt. . . . . Standard Front

^Warning feature does not meet government standards.
*Backup camera does not meet government standards.

Hyundai Santa Fe Sport

Specifications

Drive. . . . . .FWD
Engine 2.4-liter I4
Transmission . . . . 6-sp. Automatic
Tow Rating (lbs.) . . . . .Very Low-2000
Head/Leg Room (in.) Cramped-39.6/41.3
Interior Space (cu. ft.). Roomy-108
Cargo Space (cu. ft.) . . . . Very Roomy-35.4
Wheelbase/Length (in.) 106.3/184.6

Ratings—10 Best, 1 Worst

Combo Crash Tests	9
Safety Features	8
Rollover	9
Preventive Maintenance	5
Repair Costs	10
Warranty	10
Fuel Economy	7
Complaints	3
Insurance Costs	3
OVERALL RATING	**10**

Hyundai Sonata

Hyundai Sonata

At-a-Glance

Status/Year Series Started Unchanged/2015
Twins . . . . –
Body Styles . . . . Sedan
Seating 5
Anti-Theft Device . . . Std. Pass. Immobil. & Active Alarm
Parking Index Rating . . . . Easy
Where Made . . . . Montgomery, AL
Fuel Factor:
  MPG Rating (city/hwy) Good-25/37
  Driving Range (mi.) . . . . Very Long-541.5
  Fuel Type . . . . Regular
  Annual Fuel Cost . . . . Low-$1,076
  Gas Guzzler Tax . . . . No
  Greenhouse Gas Emissions (tons/yr.) Average-6.2
  Barrels of Oil Used per year Average-11.4

How the Competition Rates

Competitors	Rating	Pg.
Mazda Mazda6	8	205
Toyota Camry	7	248
Volkswagen Passat	7	264

Price Range

Price Range	Retail	Markup
SE 2.4L	$21,150	4%
Sport 2.4L	$23,175	5%
Sedan Hybrid	$26,000	5%
Sport 2.0L Turbo	$26,525	6%

Safety Checklist

Crash Tests:
  Frontal . . . . Very Good
  Side . . . . Average
Airbags:
  Torso . . . . Front Pelvis/Torso from Seat
  Pelvis . . . . Front Pelvis/Torso from Seat
  Roll Sensing . . . . Yes
  Knee Bolster . . . . Standard Driver
Crash Avoidance:
  Collision Avoidance . . . . Optional CIB & DBS
  Blind Spot Detection . . . . Optional
  Lane Keeping Assist . . . . Warning Only Optional
  Backup Camera . . . . Standard*
  Pedestrian Crash Avoidance . . . . None
General:
  Auto. Crash Notification . . . . Operator Assist.-Fee
  Day Running Lamps . . . . Standard
Safety Belt/Restraint:
  Dynamic Head Restraints . . . . None
  Adjustable Belt . . . . Standard Front

^Warning feature does not meet government standards.
*Backup camera does not meet government standards.

Hyundai Sonata

Specifications

Drive . . . . FWD
Engine 2.4-liter I4
Transmission . . . . 6-sp. Automatic
Tow Rating (lbs.) . . . . Very Low-0
Head/Leg Room (in.) . . . . Very Roomy-40.4/45.5
Interior Space (cu. ft.) Roomy-106.1
Cargo Space (cu. ft.) Cramped-16.3
Wheelbase/Length (in.) 110.4/191.1

Hyundai Tucson

Ratings—10 Best, 1 Worst

Combo Crash Tests	4
Safety Features	8
Rollover	3
Preventive Maintenance	4
Repair Costs	10
Warranty	10
Fuel Economy	5
Complaints	—
Insurance Costs	5
OVERALL RATING	**7**

Hyundai Tucson

Hyundai Tucson

At-a-Glance

Status/Year Series Started. . . . . .All New/2016
Twins . . . . —
Body Styles . . . . .SUV
Seating. 5
Anti-Theft Device . . . Std. Pass. Immobil. & Active Alarm
Parking Index Rating . . . . Very Easy
Where Made. . . . . .Ulsan, South Korea
Fuel Factor:
MPG Rating (city/hwy). Average-24/28
Driving Range (mi.) Average-420.6
Fuel Type. . . . . Regular
Annual Fuel Cost . . . . .Average-$1,228
Gas Guzzler Tax . . . . No
Greenhouse Gas Emissions (tons/yr.). Low-5.8
Barrels of Oil Used per year Average-12.7

How the Competition Rates

Competitors	Rating	Pg.
Ford Escape	5	137
Honda CR-V	7	154
Toyota RAV4	5	254

Price Range	Retail	Markup
SE FWD	$22,700	4%
SE AWD	$24,100	4%
Sport AWD	$27,550	5%
Limited AWD	$31,300	5%

Safety Checklist

Crash Tests:
Frontal. . . . . Poor
Side. . . . . .Average
Airbags:
Torso . . . . Front Pelvis/Torso from Seat
Pelvis . . . . Front Pelvis/Torso from Seat
Roll Sensing. . . . . Yes
Knee Bolster . . . . None
Crash Avoidance:
Collision Avoidance . . . . Optional CIB & DBS
Blind Spot Detection . . . . .Optional
Lane Keeping Assist . . . . Warning Only Optional
Backup Camera. . . . . Standard
Pedestrian Crash Avoidance . . . . .Optional
General:
Auto. Crash Notification . . . . .Operator Assist.-Fee
Day Running Lamps . . . . .Optional
Safety Belt/Restraint:
Dynamic Head Restraints . . . . Standard Front
Adjustable Belt. . . . . Standard Front

^Warning feature does not meet government standards.
*Backup camera does not meet government standards.

Hyundai Tucson

Specifications

Drive. . . . . .FWD
Engine 2.0-liter I4
Transmission . . . . 6-sp. Automatic
Tow Rating (lbs.) . . . . —
Head/Leg Room (in.) Cramped-39.6/41.5
Interior Space (cu. ft.). Average-102.2
Cargo Space (cu. ft.) Roomy-31
Wheelbase/Length (in.) 105.1/176.2

Ratings—10 Best, 1 Worst

Combo Crash Tests	4
Safety Features	2
Rollover	9
Preventive Maintenance	6
Repair Costs	9
Warranty	10
Fuel Economy	8
Complaints	—
Insurance Costs	1
OVERALL RATING	**6**

Hyundai Veloster

Hyundai Veloster

At-a-Glance

Status/Year Series Started. . . . . .All New/2016
Twins . . . . –
Body Styles . . . . Coupe
Seating 5
Anti-Theft Device . . . Std. Pass. Immobil. & Active Alarm
Parking Index Rating . . . . Very Easy
Where Made. . . . . .Ulsan, South Korea
Fuel Factor:
  MPG Rating (city/hwy). Good-28/36
  Driving Range (mi.) Average-410.7
  Fuel Type. . . . . Regular
  Annual Fuel Cost . . . . .Very Low-$1,013
  Gas Guzzler Tax . . . . No
  Greenhouse Gas Emissions (tons/yr.). . Very High-10.6
  Barrels of Oil Used per year . . . . .Very Low-4.7

How the Competition Rates

Competitors	Rating	Pg.
Chevrolet Sonic	10	119
Mini Cooper	–	215
Scion tC	5	238

Price Range

Price Range	Retail	Markup
Base MT	$18,000	4%
Base AT	$19,100	4%
Turbo MT	$22,600	5%
Turbo AT	$23,800	5%

Safety Checklist

Crash Tests:
  Frontal. . . . . .Poor
  Side. . . . . .Average
Airbags:
  Torso . . . . Front Pelvis/Torso from Seat
  Pelvis . . . . Front Pelvis/Torso from Seat
  Roll Sensing. . . . . No
  Knee Bolster . . . . None
Crash Avoidance:
  Collision Avoidance . . . . None
  Blind Spot Detection . . . . None
  Lane Keeping Assist . . . . None
  Backup Camera. . . . . Standard*
  Pedestrian Crash Avoidance . . . . None
General:
  Auto. Crash Notification . . . . Dial Assist.-Free
  Day Running Lamps . . . . Standard
Safety Belt/Restraint:
  Dynamic Head Restraints . . . . None
  Adjustable Belt. . . . . None

^Warning feature does not meet government standards.
*Backup camera does not meet government standards.

Hyundai Veloster

Specifications

Drive. . . . . .FWD
Engine 1.6-liter I4
Transmission . . . . 6-dp. Automatic
Tow Rating (lbs.) . . . . –
Head/Leg Room (in.) Roomy-39/43.9
Interior Space (cu. ft.). . . . . Very Cramped-89.8
Cargo Space (cu. ft.) Cramped-15.5
Wheelbase/Length (in.) 104.3/166.1

Ratings—10 Best, 1 Worst

Combo Crash Tests	4
Safety Features	5
Rollover	10
Preventive Maintenance	1
Repair Costs	2
Warranty	8
Fuel Economy	4
Complaints	9
Insurance Costs	5
OVERALL RATING	**5**

Infiniti Q50

Infiniti Q50

At-a-Glance

Status/Year Series Started Unchanged/2014
Twins . . . . –
Body Styles . . . . Sedan
Seating 5
Anti-Theft Device . . . . Std. Pass. Immobil. & Alarm
Parking Index Rating . . . . Average
Where Made . . . . Tochigi, Japan

Fuel Factor:
MPG Rating (city/hwy) Poor-20/29
Driving Range (mi.) Long-464.9
Fuel Type . . . . Premium
Annual Fuel Cost . . . . .High-$1,516
Gas Guzzler Tax . . . . No
Greenhouse Gas Emissions (tons/yr.) High-7.8
Barrels of Oil Used per year High-14.3

How the Competition Rates

Competitors	Rating	Pg.
BMW 3 Series	8	93
Lexus IS	7	194
Lincoln MKZ	6	200

Price Range

	Retail	Markup
Base RWD	$37,150	8%
Premium RWD	$40,000	8%
S AWD	$45,450	8%
Hybrid AWD	$46,200	8%

Safety Checklist

Crash Tests:
Frontal . . . . Very Poor
Side . . . . .Very Good

Airbags:
Torso . . . . Front Pelvis/Torso from Seat
Pelvis . . . . Front Pelvis/Torso from Seat
Roll Sensing . . . . No
Knee Bolster . . . . None

Crash Avoidance:
Collision Avoidance . . . . Optional CIB & DBS
Blind Spot Detection . . . . .Optional
Lane Keeping Assist . . . . .Optional
Backup Camera . . . . Standard*
Pedestrian Crash Avoidance . . . . None

General:
Auto. Crash Notification . . . . .Operator Assist.-Fee
Day Running Lamps . . . . Standard

Safety Belt/Restraint:
Dynamic Head Restraints . . . . None
Adjustable Belt . . . . Standard Front

^Warning feature does not meet government standards.
*Backup camera does not meet government standards.

Infiniti Q50

Specifications

Drive . . . . .RWD
Engine 3.7-liter V6
Transmission . . . . 7-sp. Automatic
Tow Rating (lbs.) . . . . –
Head/Leg Room (in.) Roomy-39.5/44.5
Interior Space (cu. ft.) Average-100
Cargo Space (cu. ft.) Cramped-13.5
Wheelbase/Length (in.) 112.2/188.3

Ratings—10 Best, 1 Worst	
Combo Crash Tests	—
Safety Features	6
Rollover	—
Preventive Maintenance	8
Repair Costs	2
Warranty	8
Fuel Economy	2
Complaints	3
Insurance Costs	5
OVERALL RATING	—

Infiniti Q70

Infiniti Q70

At-a-Glance

Status/Year Series Started	Unchanged/2011
Twins	—
Body Styles	Sedan
Seating	5
Anti-Theft Device	Std. Pass. Immobil. & Alarm
Parking Index Rating	Hard
Where Made	Tochigi, Japan

Fuel Factor:

MPG Rating (city/hwy)	Very Poor-18/24
Driving Range (mi.)	Average-405.6
Fuel Type	Premium
Annual Fuel Cost	Very High-$1,738
Gas Guzzler Tax	No
Greenhouse Gas Emissions (tons/yr.)	Very High-9.0
Barrels of Oil Used per year	High-16.5

How the Competition Rates

Competitors	Rating	Pg.
BMW 5 Series	8	95
Lexus ES	8	191
Mercedes-Benz S-Class	—	214

Price Range	Retail	Markup
3.7L	$49,850	8%
3.7L AWD	$52,000	8%
Hybrid	$55,900	8%
5.6L AWD	$67,050	8%

Safety Checklist

Crash Tests:

Frontal	—
Side	—

Airbags:

Torso	Front Pelvis/Torso from Seat
Pelvis	Front Pelvis/Torso from Seat
Roll Sensing	No
Knee Bolster	None

Crash Avoidance:

Collision Avoidance	Optional CIB & DBS
Blind Spot Detection	Optional
Lane Keeping Assist	Warning Only Optional
Backup Camera	Standard*
Pedestrian Crash Avoidance	None

General:

Auto. Crash Notification	Operator Assist.-Fee
Day Running Lamps	Standard

Safety Belt/Restraint:

Dynamic Head Restraints	Standard Front
Adjustable Belt	Standard Front

^Warning feature does not meet government standards.
*Backup camera does not meet government standards.

Infiniti Q70

Specifications

Drive	AWD
Engine	3.7-liter V6
Transmission	7-sp. Automatic
Tow Rating (lbs.)	—
Head/Leg Room (in.)	Roomy-39.1/44.4
Interior Space (cu. ft.)	Average-103.6
Cargo Space (cu. ft.)	Cramped-14.9
Wheelbase/Length (in.)	114.2/196.1

Ratings—10 Best, 1 Worst

Combo Crash Tests	5
Safety Features	7
Rollover	4
Preventive Maintenance	1
Repair Costs	1
Warranty	8
Fuel Economy	3
Complaints	2
Insurance Costs	5
OVERALL RATING	**3**

Infiniti QX60

Infiniti QX60

At-a-Glance

Status/Year Series Started	Unchanged/2013
Twins	Nissan Pathfinder
Body Styles	SUV
Seating	7
Anti-Theft Device	Std. Pass. Immobil. & Alarm
Parking Index Rating	Hard
Where Made	Smyrna, TN

Fuel Factor:

MPG Rating (city/hwy)	Poor-19/26
Driving Range (mi.)	Average-421.6
Fuel Type	Premium
Annual Fuel Cost	Very High-$1,630
Gas Guzzler Tax	No
Greenhouse Gas Emissions (tons/yr.)	High-8.2
Barrels of Oil Used per year	High-15.0

How the Competition Rates

Competitors	Rating	Pg.
Acura MDX	6	82
Buick Enclave	5	102
Hyundai Santa Fe	–	163

Price Range

	Retail	Markup
Base FWD	$42,400	8
Base AWD	$43,800	8
Hybrid FWD	$45,400	8
Hybrid AWD	$46,800	8

Safety Checklist

Crash Tests:

Frontal	Average
Side	Average

Airbags:

Torso	Front Pelvis/Torso from Seat
Pelvis	Front Pelvis/Torso from Seat
Roll Sensing	Yes
Knee Bolster	None

Crash Avoidance:

Collision Avoidance	Optional CIB & DBS
Blind Spot Detection	Optional
Lane Keeping Assist	Optional
Backup Camera	Standard*
Pedestrian Crash Avoidance	Optional

General:

Auto. Crash Notification	Operator Assist.-Fee
Day Running Lamps	None

Safety Belt/Restraint:

Dynamic Head Restraints	None
Adjustable Belt	Standard Front and Rear

^Warning feature does not meet government standards.
*Backup camera does not meet government standards.

Infiniti QX60

Specifications

Drive	AWD
Engine	3.5-liter V6
Transmission	7-sp. Automatic
Tow Rating (lbs.)	Low-5000
Head/Leg Room (in.)	Roomy-40.7/42.3
Interior Space (cu. ft.)	Roomy-149.8
Cargo Space (cu. ft.)	Cramped-15.8
Wheelbase/Length (in.)	114.2/196.4

Ratings—10 Best, 1 Worst

Combo Crash Tests	—
Safety Features	6
Rollover	—
Preventive Maintenance	8
Repair Costs	1
Warranty	8
Fuel Economy	1
Complaints	9
Insurance Costs	5
OVERALL RATING	**—**

Infiniti QX70

At-a-Glance

Status/Year Series Started Unchanged/2009
Twins . . . . —
Body Styles . . . . .SUV
Seating 5
Anti-Theft Device . . . . Std. Pass. Immobil. & Alarm
Parking Index Rating . . . . .Average
Where Made. . . . . .Tochigi, Japan

Fuel Factor:
MPG Rating (city/hwy) . . . . Very Poor-16/22
Driving Range (mi.) Long-434.1
Fuel Type. . . . . Premium
Annual Fuel Cost . . . . Very High-$1,933
Gas Guzzler Tax . . . . No
Greenhouse Gas Emissions (tons/yr.). . Very High-10.0
Barrels of Oil Used per year . . . . Very High-18.3

How the Competition Rates

Competitors	Rating	Pg.
Acura MDX	6	82
BMW X3	7	100
Mercedes-Benz GLE-Class	–	213

Price Range	Retail	Markup
V6 RWD	$45,850	8%
V6 AWD	$47,300	8%

Infiniti QX70

Safety Checklist

Crash Tests:
  Frontal. . . . . −
  Side. . . . . −
Airbags:
  Torso . . . . Front Pelvis/Torso from Seat
  Pelvis . . . . Front Pelvis/Torso from Seat
  Roll Sensing. . . . . Yes
  Knee Bolster . . . . None
Crash Avoidance:
  Collision Avoidance . . . . Optional CIB
  Blind Spot Detection . . . . None
  Lane Keeping Assist . . . . Warning Only Optional
  Backup Camera . . . . Standard*
  Pedestrian Crash Avoidance . . . . None
General:
  Auto. Crash Notification. . . . . . . .Operator Assist.-Fee
  Day Running Lamps . . . . None
Safety Belt/Restraint:
  Dynamic Head Restraints . . . . Standard Front
  Adjustable Belt. . . . . Standard Front

^Warning feature does not meet government standards.
*Backup camera does not meet government standards.

Infiniti QX70

Specifications

Drive. . . . . .AWD
Engine 3.5-liter V6
Transmission . . . . 7-sp. Automatic
Tow Rating (lbs.) . . . . .Very Low-2000
Head/Leg Room (in.) Roomy-39.3/44.7
Interior Space (cu. ft.). Average-102.5
Cargo Space (cu. ft.) Roomy-24.8
Wheelbase/Length (in.) 113.6/191.3

Ratings—10 Best, 1 Worst

Combo Crash Tests	—
Safety Features	7
Rollover	—
Preventive Maintenance	3
Repair Costs	3
Warranty	8
Fuel Economy	1
Complaints	5
Insurance Costs	5

OVERALL RATING   —

Infiniti QX80

Infiniti QX80

At-a-Glance

Status/Year Series Started. Unchanged/2011
Twins . . . . —
Body Styles . . . . .SUV
Seating. 7/8
Anti-Theft Device . . . . .Std. Pass. Immobil. & Alarm
Parking Index Rating . . . . Very Hard
Where Made. . . . . Kyushu, Japan

Fuel Factor:
  MPG Rating (city/hwy) . . . . Very Poor-14/20
  Driving Range (mi.) Average-420.8
  Fuel Type. . . . . Premium
  Annual Fuel Cost . . . . Very High-$2,178
  Gas Guzzler Tax . . . . No
  Greenhouse Gas Emissions (tons/yr.). . Very High-11.2
  Barrels of Oil Used per year . . . . Very High-20.6

How the Competition Rates

Competitors	Rating	Pg.
Audi Q7	—	91
Lexus GX	—	193
Mercedes-Benz GL-Class	—	212

Price Range

Price Range	Retail	Markup
2WD	$63,250	8
AWD	$66,350	8

Safety Checklist

Crash Tests:
  Frontal. . . . . –
  Side. . . . . –

Airbags:
  Torso . . . . Front Pelvis/Torso from Seat
  Pelvis . . . . Front Pelvis/Torso from Seat
  Roll Sensing. . . . . Yes
  Knee Bolster . . . . None

Crash Avoidance:
  Collision Avoidance . . . . Optional CIB & DBS
  Blind Spot Detection . . . . .Optional
  Lane Keeping Assist . . . . Warning Only Optional
  Backup Camera. Standard*
  Pedestrian Crash Avoidance . . . . None

General:
  Auto. Crash Notification . . . . .Operator Assist.-Fee
  Day Running Lamps . . . . None

Safety Belt/Restraint:
  Dynamic Head Restraints . . . . Standard Front
  Adjustable Belt. . . . . Standard Front and Rear

^Warning feature does not meet government standards.
*Backup camera does not meet government standards.

Infiniti QX80

Specifications

Drive. . . . . .AWD
Engine 5.6-liter V8
Transmission . . . . 7-sp. Automatic
Tow Rating (lbs.) . . . . Very High-8500
Head/Leg Room (in.) . . . . Very Cramped-39.9/39.6
Interior Space (cu. ft.). Roomy-151.3
Cargo Space (cu. ft.) Cramped-16.6
Wheelbase/Length (in.) 121.1/208.9

Ratings—10 Best, 1 Worst

Combo Crash Tests	5
Safety Features	9
Rollover	4
Preventive Maintenance	10
Repair Costs	7
Warranty	7
Fuel Economy	4
Complaints	1
Insurance Costs	5
OVERALL RATING	**7**

Jeep Cherokee

Jeep Cherokee

At-a-Glance

Status/Year Series Started. Unchanged/2014
Twins . . . . –
Body Styles . . . . .SUV
Seating 5
Anti-Theft Device . . . . .Std. Pass. Immobil. & Alarm
Parking Index Rating .Average
Where Made. . . . . Toldeo, OH

Fuel Factor:
MPG Rating (city/hwy) Poor-21/28
Driving Range (mi.) Short-376.2
Fuel Type . . . . Regular
Annual Fuel Cost . . . . .Average-$1,331
Gas Guzzler Tax . . . . No
Greenhouse Gas Emissions (tons/yr.). High-7.5
Barrels of Oil Used per year High-13.7

How the Competition Rates

Competitors	Rating	Pg.
Ford Escape	5	137
Mazda CX-5	3	202
Toyota RAV4	5	254

Price Range	Retail	Markup
Sport FWD	$23,295	1%
Latitude FWD	$25,195	2%
Trailhawk 4WD	$30,595	2%
Limited 4WD	$30,895	2%

Safety Checklist

Crash Tests:
Frontal. . . . . Very Poor
Side. . . . . .Very Good

Airbags:
Torso . . . . Front Pelvis/Torso from Seat
Pelvis .Rear Pelvis from Seat
Roll Sensing. . . . . Yes
Knee Bolster . . . . Standard Front

Crash Avoidance:
Collision Avoidance . . . . Optional CIB & DBS
Blind Spot Detection . . . . .Optional
Lane Keeping Assist . . . . .Optional
Backup Camera . . . . .Optional*
Pedestrian Crash Avoidance . . . . None

General:
Auto. Crash Notification . . . . None
Day Running Lamps . . . . None

Safety Belt/Restraint:
Dynamic Head Restraints . . . . None
Adjustable Belt. . . . . Standard Front

^Warning feature does not meet government standards.
*Backup camera does not meet government standards.

Specifications

Drive. . . . . .AWD
Engine 2.4-liter I4
Transmission . . . . 9-sp. Automatic
Tow Rating (lbs.) . . . . .Very Low-2000
Head/Leg Room (in.) Cramped-39.4/41.1
Interior Space (cu. ft.). Average-103.4
Cargo Space (cu. ft.) Roomy-24.6
Wheelbase/Length (in.) 106.3/182

Ratings—10 Best, 1 Worst	
Combo Crash Tests	1
Safety Features	3
Rollover	3
Preventive Maintenance	10
Repair Costs	8
Warranty	7
Fuel Economy	3
Complaints	5
Insurance Costs	5
OVERALL RATING	**4**

Jeep Compass

Jeep Compass

Jeep Compass

Safety Checklist

Crash Tests:
Frontal.............................. Very Poor
Side.................................. Very Poor

Airbags:
Torso .... Front Pelvis/Torso from Seat
Pelvis .... Front Pelvis/Torso from Seat
Roll Sensing................................ Yes
Knee Bolster .... None

Crash Avoidance:
Collision Avoidance .... None
Blind Spot Detection .... None
Lane Keeping Assist .... None
Backup Camera........................Optional*
Pedestrian Crash Avoidance .... None

General:
Auto. Crash Notification .... None
Day Running Lamps .... None

Safety Belt/Restraint:
Dynamic Head Restraints .... Standard Front
Adjustable Belt.................. Standard Front

^Warning feature does not meet government standards.
*Backup camera does not meet government standards.

At-a-Glance

Status/Year Series Started...........Unchanged/2007
Twins .... –
Body Styles ....SUV
Seating 5
Anti-Theft Device ....Std. Pass. Immobil.
Parking Index Rating .... Easy
Where Made.......................Belvedere, IL
Fuel Factor:
MPG Rating (city/hwy)................. Poor-20/23
Driving Range (mi.) ....Very Short-286.8
Fuel Type............................. Regular
Annual Fuel Cost ....High-$1,483
Gas Guzzler Tax .... No
Greenhouse Gas Emissions (tons/yr.)........High-8.6
Barrels of Oil Used per year High-15.7

Jeep Compass

Jeep Compass

How the Competition Rates

Competitors	Rating	Pg.
Acura RDX	10	83
Ford Escape	5	137
Honda CR-V	7	154

Price Range	Retail	Markup
Sport FWD	$19,395	0%
Sport AWD	$21,395	1%
Latitude FWD	$23,595	2%
Latitude 4WD	$25,595	2%

Specifications

Drive...................................... 4WD
Engine 2.4-liter I4
Transmission .... CVT
Tow Rating (lbs.) ....Very Low-2000
Head/Leg Room (in.) Average-40.7/40.6
Interior Space (cu. ft.)................. Average-101.3
Cargo Space (cu. ft.) Average-22.7
Wheelbase/Length (in.) 103.7/175.1

Ratings—10 Best, 1 Worst

Combo Crash Tests	6
Safety Features	7
Rollover	2
Preventive Maintenance	8
Repair Costs	7
Warranty	7
Fuel Economy	1
Complaints	1
Insurance Costs	5
OVERALL RATING	**5**

Jeep Grand Cherokee

At-a-Glance

Status/Year Series Started	Unchanged/2011
Twins	–
Body Styles	SUV
Seating	5
Anti-Theft Device	Std. Pass. Immobil. & Alarm
Parking Index Rating	Average
Where Made	Detroit, MI

Fuel Factor:

MPG Rating (city/hwy)	Very Poor-14/20
Driving Range (mi.)	Short-398.2
Fuel Type	Regular
Annual Fuel Cost	Very High-$1,946
Gas Guzzler Tax	No
Greenhouse Gas Emissions (tons/yr.)	Very High-11.3
Barrels of Oil Used per year	Very High-20.6

How the Competition Rates

Competitors	Rating	Pg.
Chevrolet Equinox	2	115
Ford Explorer	3	139
Honda Pilot	9	158

Price Range

Price Range	Retail	Markup
Laredo 2WD	$29,995	5%
Limited 2WD	$36,895	5%
Overland 4WD	$46,295	5%
SRT 4WD	$64,595	5%

Jeep Grand Cherokee

Safety Checklist

Crash Tests:

Frontal	Good
Side	Poor

Airbags:

Torso	Front Pelvis/Torso from Seat
Pelvis	Front Pelvis/Torso from Seat
Roll Sensing	Yes
Knee Bolster	Standard Driver

Crash Avoidance:

Collision Avoidance	Optional CIB & DBS
Blind Spot Detection	Standard
Lane Keeping Assist	None
Backup Camera	Standard
Pedestrian Crash Avoidance	None

General:

Auto. Crash Notification	None
Day Running Lamps	None

Safety Belt/Restraint:

Dynamic Head Restraints	Standard Front
Adjustable Belt	Standard Front

^Warning feature does not meet government standards.
*Backup camera does not meet government standards.

Jeep Grand Cherokee

Specifications

Drive	4WD
Engine	5.7-liter V8
Transmission	8-sp. Automatic
Tow Rating (lbs.)	Average-7200
Head/Leg Room (in.)	Cramped-39.9/40.3
Interior Space (cu. ft.)	Roomy-103.9
Cargo Space (cu. ft.)	Very Roomy-36.3
Wheelbase/Length (in.)	114.8/189.8

Ratings—10 Best, 1 Worst

Combo Crash Tests	1
Safety Features	3
Rollover	2
Preventive Maintenance	10
Repair Costs	10
Warranty	7
Fuel Economy	3
Complaints	3
Insurance Costs	5
OVERALL RATING	**3**

Jeep Patriot

At-a-Glance

Status/Year Series Started Unchanged/2007
Twins . . . . –
Body Styles . . . . .SUV
Seating 5
Anti-Theft Device . . . . Std. Pass. Immobil
Parking Index Rating . . . . Easy
Where Made. . . . . .Belvedere, IL

Fuel Factor:
 MPG Rating (city/hwy) Poor-20/23
 Driving Range (mi.) . . . . .Very Short-286.8
 Fuel Type . . . . Regular
 Annual Fuel Cost .High-$1,483
 Gas Guzzler Tax . . . . No
 Greenhouse Gas Emissions (tons/yr.). High-8.6
 Barrels of Oil Used per year High-15.7

How the Competition Rates

Competitors	Rating	Pg.
Ford Escape	5	137
Mitsubishi Outlander Sport	3	220
Toyota RAV4	5	254

Price Range

	Retail	Markup
Sport FWD	$17,295	0%
Sport AWD	$19,395	1%
Latitude 4WD	$21,895	2%
Latitude FWD	$25,195	3%

Jeep Patriot

Safety Checklist

Crash Tests:
 Frontal. . . . . Very Poor
 Side. . . . . Very Poor

Airbags:
 Torso . . . . Front Pelvis/Torso from Seat
 Pelvis . . . . Front Pelvis/Torso from Seat
 Roll Sensing. . . . . Yes
 Knee Bolster . . . . None

Crash Avoidance:
 Collision Avoidance . . . . None
 Blind Spot Detection . . . . None
 Lane Keeping Assist . . . . None
 Backup Camera .Optional*
 Pedestrian Crash Avoidance . . . . None

General:
 Auto. Crash Notification . . . . None
 Day Running Lamps . . . . None

Safety Belt/Restraint:
 Dynamic Head Restraints . . . . Standard Front
 Adjustable Belt . . . . Standard Front

^Warning feature does not meet government standards.
*Backup camera does not meet government standards.

Jeep Patriot

Specifications

Drive 4WD
Engine 2.4-liter I4
Transmission . . . . CVT
Tow Rating (lbs.) . . . . .Very Low-2000
Head/Leg Room (in.) Average-41/40.6
Interior Space (cu. ft.). Roomy-104.4
Cargo Space (cu. ft.) Roomy-23
Wheelbase/Length (in.) 103.7/173.8

Jeep Renegade

Small SUV

Ratings—10 Best, 1 Worst	
Combo Crash Tests	3
Safety Features	5
Rollover	3
Preventive Maintenance	2
Repair Costs	10
Warranty	7
Fuel Economy	4
Complaints	1
Insurance Costs	5
OVERALL RATING	**2**

Jeep Renegade

Jeep Renegade

At-a-Glance

Status/Year Series Started	Unchanged/2015
Twins	–
Body Styles	SUV
Seating	5
Anti-Theft Device	Std. Pass. Immobil
Parking Index Rating	Easy
Where Made	Melfi, Italy

Fuel Factor:

MPG Rating (city/hwy)	Poor-21/29
Driving Range (mi.)	Very Short-304.5
Fuel Type	Premium
Annual Fuel Cost	High-$1,470
Gas Guzzler Tax	No
Greenhouse Gas Emissions (tons/yr.)	Average-6.1
Barrels of Oil Used per year	Very Low-0.0

How the Competition Rates

Competitors	Rating	Pg.
Chevrolet Trax	9	124
Ford Edge	9	136
Nissan Juke	2	225

Price Range	Retail	Markup
Sport FWD	$17,995	0%
Latitude FWD	$21,345	2%
Trailhawk 4WD	$26,145	2%
Limited 4WD	$26,895	2%

Safety Checklist

Crash Tests:

Frontal	–
Side	–

Airbags:

Torso	Front Pelvis/Torso from Seat
Pelvis	Front Pelvis/Torso from Seat
Roll Sensing	Yes
Knee Bolster	Standard Driver

Crash Avoidance:

Collision Avoidance	Warning Only Optional
Blind Spot Detection	None
Lane Keeping Assist	None
Backup Camera	None
Pedestrian Crash Avoidance	None

General:

Auto. Crash Notification	None
Day Running Lamps	None

Safety Belt/Restraint:

Dynamic Head Restraints	Standard Front
Adjustable Belt	Standard Front

^Warning feature does not meet government standards.
*Backup camera does not meet government standards.

Jeep Renegade

Specifications

Drive	FWD
Engine	1.4-liter I4
Transmission	6-sp. Automatic
Tow Rating (lbs.)	Very Low-2000
Head/Leg Room (in.)	Average-41.1/41.2
Interior Space (cu. ft.)	Average-100.1
Cargo Space (cu. ft.)	Very Roomy-50.8
Wheelbase/Length (in.)	101.2/166.6

Ratings—10 Best, 1 Worst	
Combo Crash Tests	—
Safety Features	1
Rollover	—
Preventive Maintenance	10
Repair Costs	9
Warranty	7
Fuel Economy	2
Complaints	2
Insurance Costs	5

OVERALL RATING — —

Jeep Wrangler

Jeep Wrangler

At-a-Glance

Status/Year Series Started	Unchanged/2007
Twins	—
Body Styles	SUV
Seating	4
Anti-Theft Device	None
Parking Index Rating	Very Easy
Where Made	Toldeo, OH

Fuel Factor:

MPG Rating (city/hwy)	Very Poor-17/21
Driving Range (mi.)	Very Short-345.8
Fuel Type	Regular
Annual Fuel Cost	Very High-$1,694
Gas Guzzler Tax	No
Greenhouse Gas Emissions (tons/yr.)	Very High-10.0
Barrels of Oil Used per year	Very High-18.3

How the Competition Rates

Competitors	Rating	Pg.
Mazda CX-5	3	202
Mitsubishi Outlander Sport	3	220
Subaru Forester	4	240

Price Range	Retail	Markup
Sport	$23,195	2%
Rubicon	$32,395	5%
Unlimited Sahara	$32,995	5%
Unlimited Rubicon	$36,195	5%

Safety Checklist

Crash Tests:
- Frontal .... −
- Side .... −

Airbags:
- Torso .... Opt. Front Head/ Torso from Seat
- Pelvis .... None
- Roll Sensing .... No
- Knee Bolster .... None

Crash Avoidance:
- Collision Avoidance .... None
- Blind Spot Detection .... None
- Lane Keeping Assist .... None
- Backup Camera .... None
- Pedestrian Crash Avoidance .... None

General:
- Auto. Crash Notification .... None
- Day Running Lamps .... None

Safety Belt/Restraint:
- Dynamic Head Restraints .... None
- Adjustable Belt .... Standard Front

^Warning feature does not meet government standards.
*Backup camera does not meet government standards.

Jeep Wrangler

Specifications

Drive	4WD
Engine	3.6-liter V6
Transmission	5-sp. Automatic
Tow Rating (lbs.)	Very Low-2000
Head/Leg Room (in.)	Average-41.3/41
Interior Space (cu. ft.)	Very Cramped-88.4
Cargo Space (cu. ft.)	Very Cramped-12.8
Wheelbase/Length (in.)	95.4/152.8

Ratings—10 Best, 1 Worst

Combo Crash Tests	—
Safety Features	2
Rollover	—
Preventive Maintenance	4
Repair Costs	1
Warranty	9
Fuel Economy	3
Complaints	2
Insurance Costs	5
OVERALL RATING	**—**

Kia Cadenza

Kia Cadenza

At-a-Glance

Status/Year Series Started	Unchanged/2014
Twins	Hyundai Azera
Body Styles	Sedan
Seating	5
Anti-Theft Device	Std. Pass. Immobil. & Alarm
Parking Index Rating	Average
Where Made	Hwasung, South Korea

Fuel Factor:

MPG Rating (city/hwy)	Poor-19/28
Driving Range (mi.)	Average-410.9
Fuel Type	Regular
Annual Fuel Cost	High-$1,418
Gas Guzzler Tax	No
Greenhouse Gas Emissions (tons/yr.)	High-8.2
Barrels of Oil Used per year	High-15.0

How the Competition Rates

Competitors	Rating	Pg.
Acura TLX	10	84
Honda Accord	10	148
Lexus ES	8	191

Price Range

Price Range	Retail	Markup
Premium	$34,900	8%
Limited	$43,800	8%

Safety Checklist

Crash Tests:
Frontal . . . . –
Side . . . . –

Airbags:
Torso . . . . Front Pelvis/Torso from Seat
Pelvis . . . . Rear Torso from Seat
Roll Sensing . . . . No
Knee Bolster . . . . None

Crash Avoidance:
Collision Avoidance . . . . None
Blind Spot Detection . . . . Optional
Lane Keeping Assist . . . . Warning Only Optional
Backup Camera . . . . Optional*
Pedestrian Crash Avoidance . . . . None

General:
Auto. Crash Notification . . . . Dial Assist.-Free
Day Running Lamps . . . . None

Safety Belt/Restraint:
Dynamic Head Restraints . . . . None
Adjustable Belt . . . . Standard Front

^Warning feature does not meet government standards.
*Backup camera does not meet government standards.

Kia Cadenza

Specifications

Drive	FWD
Engine	3.3-liter V6
Transmission	6-sp. Automatic
Tow Rating (lbs.)	–
Head/Leg Room (in.)	Very Roomy-40/45.5
Interior Space (cu. ft.)	Roomy-106.8
Cargo Space (cu. ft.)	Cramped-15.9
Wheelbase/Length (in.)	112/195.5

Kia Forte

Compact

Ratings—10 Best, 1 Worst	
Combo Crash Tests	3
Safety Features	1
Rollover	9
Preventive Maintenance	9
Repair Costs	10
Warranty	9
Fuel Economy	7
Complaints	3
Insurance Costs	1
OVERALL RATING	**5**

Kia Forte

Kia Forte

At-a-Glance

Status/Year Series Started	Unchanged/2014
Twins	Hyundai Elantra
Body Styles	Sedan, Hatchback
Seating	5
Anti-Theft Device	Std. Pass. Immobil. & Active Alarm
Parking Index Rating	Easy
Where Made	Hwasung, South Korea

Fuel Factor:

MPG Rating (city/hwy)	Good-25/36
Driving Range (mi.)	Short-382.6
Fuel Type	Regular
Annual Fuel Cost	Low-$1,087
Gas Guzzler Tax	No
Greenhouse Gas Emissions (tons/yr.)	Average-6.2
Barrels of Oil Used per year	Average-11.4

How the Competition Rates

Competitors	Rating	Pg.
Chevrolet Cruze	–	114
Honda Civic	–	149
Subaru Impreza	5	241

Price Range	Retail	Markup
LX Sedan MT	$15,990	2%
LX Hatchback AT	$19,400	4%
EX Sedan AT	$19,990	5%
SX Hatchback AT	$21,990	6%

Safety Checklist

Crash Tests:

Frontal	Poor
Side	Poor

Airbags:

Torso	Front Pelvis/Torso from Seat
Pelvis	Front Pelvis/Torso from Seat
Roll Sensing	No
Knee Bolster	None

Crash Avoidance:

Collision Avoidance	None
Blind Spot Detection	None
Lane Keeping Assist	None
Backup Camera	Optional*
Pedestrian Crash Avoidance	None

General:

Auto. Crash Notification	Dial Assist.-Free
Day Running Lamps	None

Safety Belt/Restraint:

Dynamic Head Restraints	None
Adjustable Belt	Standard Front

^Warning feature does not meet government standards.
*Backup camera does not meet government standards.

Kia Forte

Specifications

Drive	FWD
Engine	2.0-liter I4
Transmission	6-sp. Automatic
Tow Rating (lbs.)	–
Head/Leg Room (in.)	Average-39.1/42.2
Interior Space (cu. ft.)	Cramped-96.2
Cargo Space (cu. ft.)	Cramped-14.9
Wheelbase/Length (in.)	106.3/179.5

Kia Optima Intermediate

Ratings—10 Best, 1 Worst

Combo Crash Tests	6
Safety Features	5
Rollover	10
Preventive Maintenance	6
Repair Costs	10
Warranty	9
Fuel Economy	6
Complaints	7
Insurance Costs	1
OVERALL RATING	**9**

Kia Optima

Kia Optima

At-a-Glance

Status/Year Series Started. Unchanged/2011
Twins . . . . –
Body Styles . . . . Sedan
Seating 5
Anti-Theft Device . . . Std. Pass. Immobil. & Active Alarm
Parking Index Rating . . . . Easy
Where Made. West Point, GA

Fuel Factor:
MPG Rating (city/hwy) Average-23/34
Driving Range (mi.) . . . . Very Long-498.0
Fuel Type . . . . Regular
Annual Fuel Cost . . . . Low-$1,170
Gas Guzzler Tax . . . . No
Greenhouse Gas Emissions (tons/yr.) Average-6.7
Barrels of Oil Used per year Average-12.2

How the Competition Rates

Competitors	Rating	Pg.
Honda Accord	10	148
Nissan Altima	7	222
Toyota Camry	7	248

Price Range	Retail	Markup
LX	$21,840	5%
SX	$25,790	7%
EX Hybrid	$32,150	8%
SXL Turbo	$35,500	7%

Safety Checklist

Crash Tests:
Frontal. . . . . .Good
Side. . . . . Very Poor
Airbags:
Torso . . . . Front Pelvis/Torso from Seat
Pelvis . . . . Front Pelvis/Torso from Seat
Roll Sensing. . . . . No
Knee Bolster . . . . None
Crash Avoidance:
Collision Avoidance . . . . Optional CIB & DBS
Blind Spot Detection . . . . .Optional
Lane Keeping Assist . . . . Warning Only Optional
Backup Camera . . . . .Optional
Pedestrian Crash Avoidance . . . . Optonal
General:
Auto. Crash Notification . . . . Dial Assist.-Free
Day Running Lamps . . . . .Optional
Safety Belt/Restraint:
Dynamic Head Restraints . . . . None
Adjustable Belt. . . . . Standard Front

^Warning feature does not meet government standards.
*Backup camera does not meet government standards.

Kia Optima

Specifications

Drive. . . . . .FWD
Engine 2.4-liter I4
Transmission . . . . 6-sp. Automatic
Tow Rating (lbs.) . . . . –
Head/Leg Room (in.) . . . . Very Roomy-40/45.5
Interior Space (cu. ft.). Roomy-117.6
Cargo Space (cu. ft.) Cramped-15.4
Wheelbase/Length (in.) 110/190.7

Kia Rio
Subcompact

Ratings—10 Best, 1 Worst

Combo Crash Tests	2
Safety Features	1
Rollover	8
Preventive Maintenance	7
Repair Costs	10
Warranty	9
Fuel Economy	8
Complaints	9
Insurance Costs	1
OVERALL RATING	**6**

Kia Rio

Kia Rio

At-a-Glance

Status/Year Series Started. . . Appearance Change/2012
Twins . . . . .Hyundai Accent
Body Styles .Sedan, Hatchback
Seating 5
Anti-Theft Device . . . Std. Pass. Immobil. & Active Alarm
Parking Index Rating . . . . Very Easy
Where Made. . . . . Gwanmyeong, South Korea
Fuel Factor:
  MPG Rating (city/hwy) Good-27/37
  Driving Range (mi.) . . . . .Very Short-350.4
  Fuel Type. . . . . Regular
  Annual Fuel Cost .Low-$1,025
  Gas Guzzler Tax . . . . No
  Greenhouse Gas Emissions (tons/yr.). Low-5.8
  Barrels of Oil Used per year Low-10.6

How the Competition Rates

Competitors	Rating	Pg.
Chevrolet Sonic	10	119
Ford Focus	6	143
Nissan Versa	3	234

Price Range

Price Range	Retail	Markup
LX Sedan MT	$14,165	2%
LX Hatchback AT	$15,495	3%
EX Sedan AT	$17,755	5%
SX Hatchback AT	$20,905	6%

Safety Checklist

Crash Tests:
  Frontal. . . . . Very Poor
  Side. . . . . Very Poor
Airbags:
  Torso . . . . Front Pelvis/Torso from Seat
  Pelvis . . . . Front Pelvis/Torso from Seat
  Roll Sensing. . . . . No
  Knee Bolster . . . . None
Crash Avoidance:
  Collision Avoidance . . . . None
  Blind Spot Detection . . . . None
  Lane Keeping Assist . . . . None
  Backup Camera . . . . Optional*
  Pedestrian Crash Avoidance . . . . None
General:
  Auto. Crash Notification . . . . None
  Day Running Lamps . . . . None
Safety Belt/Restraint:
  Dynamic Head Restraints . . . . None
  Adjustable Belt. . . . . Standard Front

^Warning feature does not meet government standards.
*Backup camera does not meet government standards.

Kia Rio

Specifications

Drive. . . . . .FWD
Engine 1.6-liter I4
Transmission . . . . 6-sp. Automatic
Tow Rating (lbs.) . . . . –
Head/Leg Room (in.) Roomy-40/43.8
Interior Space (cu. ft.). . . . . Very Cramped-88.4
Cargo Space (cu. ft.) Cramped-13.7
Wheelbase/Length (in.) 101.2/171.9

Kia Sedona Minivan

Kia Sedona

Ratings—10 Best, 1 Worst

Combo Crash Tests	7
Safety Features	4
Rollover	6
Preventive Maintenance	4
Repair Costs	8
Warranty	9
Fuel Economy	2
Complaints	6
Insurance Costs	5
OVERALL RATING	**7**

Kia Sedona

At-a-Glance

Status/Year Series Started	Unchanged/2015
Twins	–
Body Styles	Minivan
Seating	7/8
Anti-Theft Device	Opt. Pass. Immobil. & Active Alarm
Parking Index Rating	Hard
Where Made	West Point, GA

Fuel Factor:

MPG Rating (city/hwy)	Very Poor-18/24
Driving Range (mi.)	Long-427.9
Fuel Type	Regular
Annual Fuel Cost	High-$1,553
Gas Guzzler Tax	No
Greenhouse Gas Emissions (tons/yr.)	Very High-9.0
Barrels of Oil Used per year	High-16.5

How the Competition Rates

Competitors	Rating	Pg.
Honda Odyssey	8	157
Nissan Quest	–	230
Toyota Sequoia	–	255

Price Range

	Retail	Markup
L	$26,400	3%
EX	$32,700	6%
SX	$36,400	7%
SXL	$39,900	7%

Safety Checklist

Crash Tests:

Frontal	Very Good
Side	Very Poor

Airbags:

Torso	Front Pelvis/Torso from Seat
Pelvis	Front Pelvis/Torso from Seat
Roll Sensing	Yes
Knee Bolster	None

Crash Avoidance:

Collision Avoidance	Warning Only Optional
Blind Spot Detection	Optional
Lane Keeping Assist	Warning Only Optional
Backup Camera	Optional*
Pedestrian Crash Avoidance	None

General:

Auto. Crash Notification	Dial Assist.-Free
Day Running Lamps	None

Safety Belt/Restraint:

Dynamic Head Restraints	None
Adjustable Belt	Standard Front

^Warning feature does not meet government standards.
*Backup camera does not meet government standards.

Kia Sedona

Specifications

Drive	FWD
Engine	3.3-liter V6
Transmission	6-sp. Automatic
Tow Rating (lbs.)	Low-3500
Head/Leg Room (in.)	Roomy-39.8/43.1
Interior Space (cu. ft.)	–
Cargo Space (cu. ft.)	Very Roomy-33.9
Wheelbase/Length (in.)	120.5/201.4

Ratings—10 Best, 1 Worst	
Combo Crash Tests	6
Safety Features	5
Rollover	5
Preventive Maintenance	5
Repair Costs	4
Warranty	9
Fuel Economy	4
Complaints	—
Insurance Costs	5
OVERALL RATING	**5**

Kia Sorento

Kia Sorento

At-a-Glance

Status/Year Series Started	All New/2016
Twins	–
Body Styles	SUV
Seating	5
Anti-Theft Device	Std. Pass. Immobil. & Active Alarm
Parking Index Rating	Very Easy
Where Made	West Point, GA

Fuel Factor:

MPG Rating (city/hwy)	Poor-21/29
Driving Range (mi.)	Long-450.8
Fuel Type	Regular
Annual Fuel Cost	Average-$1,314
Gas Guzzler Tax	No
Greenhouse Gas Emissions (tons/yr.)	Average-6.2
Barrels of Oil Used per year	High-13.7

How the Competition Rates

Competitors	Rating	Pg.
Ford Edge	9	136
Jeep Grand Cherokee	5	175
Nissan Rogue	2	231

Price Range	Retail	Markup
LX FWD	$26,200	4%
LX AWD V6	$30,300	4%
SX AWD	$39,900	6%
Limited AWD	$43,100	6%

Safety Checklist

Crash Tests:

Frontal	Good
Side	Poor

Airbags:

Torso	Front Pelvis/Torso from Seat
Pelvis	Front Pelvis/Torso from Seat
Roll Sensing	Yes
Knee Bolster	None

Crash Avoidance:

Collision Avoidance	Warning Only Optional
Blind Spot Detection	Optional
Lane Keeping Assist	Warning Only Optional
Backup Camera	Optional*
Pedestrian Crash Avoidance	None

General:

Auto. Crash Notification	Dial Assist.-Free
Day Running Lamps	None

Safety Belt/Restraint:

Dynamic Head Restraints	Standard Front
Adjustable Belt	Standard Front

^Warning feature does not meet government standards.
*Backup camera does not meet government standards.

Kia Sorento

Specifications

Drive	FWD
Engine	2.4-liter I4
Transmission	6-sp. Automatic
Tow Rating (lbs.)	Very Low-2000
Head/Leg Room (in.)	Roomy-39.5/44.1
Interior Space (cu. ft.)	Roomy-146.4
Cargo Space (cu. ft.)	Very Roomy-38.8
Wheelbase/Length (in.)	109.4/187.4

Ratings—10 Best, 1 Worst

Combo Crash Tests	9
Safety Features	3
Rollover	5
Preventive Maintenance	5
Repair Costs	9
Warranty	9
Fuel Economy	5
Complaints	3
Insurance Costs	1
OVERALL RATING	**7**

Kia Soul

Kia Soul

At-a-Glance

Status/Year Series Started. Unchanged/2014
Twins . . . . –
Body Styles . . . . .Wagon
Seating 5
Anti-Theft Device . . . . Std. Pass. Immobil & Alarm
Parking Index Rating . . . . Very Easy
Where Made. . . . . West Point, GA

Fuel Factor:
MPG Rating (city/hwy) Average-23/31
Driving Range (mi.) . . . . .Very Short-369.5
Fuel Type . . . . Regular
Annual Fuel Cost . . . . .Average-$1,211
Gas Guzzler Tax . . . . No
Greenhouse Gas Emissions (tons/yr.) Average-6.9
Barrels of Oil Used per year Average-12.7

How the Competition Rates

Competitors	Rating	Pg.
Chevrolet Sonic	10	119
Mini Countryman	–	216
Volkswagen Golf	3	262

Price Range

Price Range	Retail	Markup
EV e	$31,950	7%
EV	$33,950	7%
EV+	$35,950	8%

Safety Checklist

Crash Tests:
Frontal. . . . . Good
Side. . . . . .Very Good

Airbags:
Torso . . . . Front Pelvis/Torso from Seat
Pelvis . . . . Front Pelvis/Torso from Seat
Roll Sensing. . . . . Yes
Knee Bolster . . . . None

Crash Avoidance:
Collision Avoidance . . . . Warning Only Optional
Blind Spot Detection . . . . None
Lane Keeping Assist . . . . Warning Only Optional^
Backup Camera . . . . .Optional*
Pedestrian Crash Avoidance . . . . None

General:
Auto. Crash Notification . . . . Dial Assist.-Free
Day Running Lamps . . . . None

Safety Belt/Restraint:
Dynamic Head Restraints . . . . None
Adjustable Belt. . . . . Standard Front

^Warning feature does not meet government standards.
*Backup camera does not meet government standards.

Kia Soul

Specifications

Drive. . . . . .FWD
Engine 2.0-liter I4
Transmission . . . . 6-sp. Automatic
Tow Rating (lbs.) . . . . –
Head/Leg Room (in.) Cramped-39.6/40.9
Interior Space (cu. ft.). Average-101
Cargo Space (cu. ft.) Roomy-24.2
Wheelbase/Length (in.) 101.2/163

Ratings—10 Best, 1 Worst

Combo Crash Tests	6
Safety Features	2
Rollover	4
Preventive Maintenance	5
Repair Costs	5
Warranty	9
Fuel Economy	4
Complaints	9
Insurance Costs	5
OVERALL RATING	**5**

Kia Sportage

Kia Sportage

At-a-Glance

Status/Year Series Started Unchanged/2011
Twins . . . . –
Body Styles . . . . .SUV
Seating 5
Anti-Theft Device . . . Std. Pass. Immobil. & Active Alarm
Parking Index Rating . . . . Very Easy
Where Made . . . . Gwangju, South Korea
Fuel Factor:
  MPG Rating (city/hwy) Poor-21/28
  Driving Range (mi.) . . . . .Very Short-343.1
  Fuel Type . . . . Regular
  Annual Fuel Cost . . . . .Average-$1,331
  Gas Guzzler Tax . . . . No
  Greenhouse Gas Emissions (tons/yr.) High-7.5
  Barrels of Oil Used per year High-13.7

How the Competition Rates

Competitors	Rating	Pg.
Ford Escape	5	137
Honda CR-V	7	154
Toyota RAV4	5	254

Price Range	Retail	Markup
LX FWD	$22,150	4%
EX FWD	$25,350	5%
EX AWD	$26,850	5%
SX AWD	$31,490	6%

Safety Checklist

Crash Tests:
  Frontal . . . . .Good
  Side . . . . Very Poor
Airbags:
  Torso . . . . Front Pelvis/Torso from Seat
  Pelvis . . . . Front Pelvis/Torso from Seat
  Roll Sensing . . . . No
  Knee Bolster . . . . None
Crash Avoidance:
  Collision Avoidance . . . . None
  Blind Spot Detection . . . . None
  Lane Keeping Assist . . . . None
  Backup Camera . . . . .Optional*
  Pedestrian Crash Avoidance . . . . None
General:
  Auto. Crash Notification . . . . Dial Assist.-Free
  Day Running Lamps . . . . .Optional
Safety Belt/Restraint:
  Dynamic Head Restraints . . . . Standard Front
  Adjustable Belt . . . . Standard Front

^Warning feature does not meet government standards.
*Backup camera does not meet government standards.

Kia Sportage

Specifications

Drive . . . . .FWD
Engine 2.4-liter I4
Transmission . . . . 6-sp. Automaitc
Tow Rating (lbs.) . . . . .Very Low-2000
Head/Leg Room (in.) Cramped-39.1/41.4
Interior Space (cu. ft.) Average-100
Cargo Space (cu. ft.) Roomy-26.1
Wheelbase/Length (in.) 103.9/174.8

Land Rover Range Rover

Large SUV

Ratings—10 Best, 1 Worst

Combo Crash Tests	—
Safety Features	6
Rollover	—
Preventive Maintenance	6
Repair Costs	2
Warranty	3
Fuel Economy	1
Complaints	3
Insurance Costs	5
OVERALL RATING	**—**

Land Rover Range Rover

Land Rover Range Rover

At-a-Glance

Status/Year Series Started. Unchanged/2013
Twins . . . . —
Body Styles . . . . SUV
Seating 5
Anti-Theft Device . . . . Std. Pass. Immobil. & Alarm
Parking Index Rating . . . . Very Hard
Where Made. . . . . Solihull, England
Fuel Factor:
MPG Rating (city/hwy) . . . . Very Poor-14/19
Driving Range (mi.) Long-439.9
Fuel Type. . . . . Premium
Annual Fuel Cost . . . . Very High-$2,220
Gas Guzzler Tax . . . . No
Greenhouse Gas Emissions (tons/yr.). . Very High-11.3
Barrels of Oil Used per year . . . . Very High-20.6

How the Competition Rates

Competitors	Rating	Pg.
Audi Q7	—	91
Lexus GX	—	193
Mercedes-Benz GL-Class	—	212

Price Range

Price Range	Retail	Markup
Base	$83,495	10%
HSE	$89,995	10%
Supercharged	$101,995	10%
Autobiography	$137,995	10%

Safety Checklist

Crash Tests:
Frontal. . . . . −
Side. . . . . −
Airbags:
Torso . . . . Front Torso from Seat
Pelvis . . . . None
Roll Sensing. . . . . Yes
Knee Bolster . . . . None
Crash Avoidance:
Collision Avoidance . . . . Std. DBS & Opt. CIB^
Blind Spot Detection . . . . Optional
Lane Keeping Assist . . . . Warning Only Optional^
Backup Camera. Standard*
Pedestrian Crash Avoidance . . . . None
General:
Auto. Crash Notification. . . . . Dial Assist.-Free
Day Running Lamps . . . . Standard
Safety Belt/Restraint:
Dynamic Head Restraints . . . . None
Adjustable Belt. . . . . Standard Front

^Warning feature does not meet government standards.
*Backup camera does not meet government standards.

Land Rover Range Rover

Specifications

Drive. 4WD
Engine 5.0-liter V8
Transmission . . . . 6-sp. Automatic
Tow Rating (lbs.) High-7716
Head/Leg Room (in.) Average-42.5/39.1
Interior Space (cu. ft.). . . . . −
Cargo Space (cu. ft.) Roomy-32.1
Wheelbase/Length (in.) 115/196.8

Ratings—10 Best, 1 Worst

Combo Crash Tests	—
Safety Features	7
Rollover	—
Preventive Maintenance	10
Repair Costs	6
Warranty	3
Fuel Economy	4
Complaints	6
Insurance Costs	5
OVERALL RATING	**—**

Land Rover Range Rover Evoque

Land Rover Range Rover Evoque

At-a-Glance

Status/Year Series Started. . . Appearance Change/2012
Twins . . . . —
Body Styles . . . . .SUV
Seating 5
Anti-Theft Device . . . . .Std. Pass. Immobil. & Alarm
Parking Index Rating . . . . Easy
Where Made. . . . . .Halewood, England
Fuel Factor:
  MPG Rating (city/hwy). Poor-21/30
  Driving Range (mi.) Long-448.9
  Fuel Type. . . . . Premium
  Annual Fuel Cost . . . . .High-$1,452
  Gas Guzzler Tax . . . . No
  Greenhouse Gas Emissions (tons/yr.). High-7.5
  Barrels of Oil Used per year High-13.7

How the Competition Rates

Competitors	Rating	Pg.
Audi Q3	—	89
Lexus NX	5	195
Mercedes-Benz GLA-Class	—	210

Price Range

Price Range	Retail	Markup
Pure	$41,100	10%
Pure Premium 2 Door	$49,900	10%
Prestige	$55,700	10%
Dynamic 2 Door	$56,600	10%

Safety Checklist

Crash Tests:
  Frontal. . . . . −
  Side. . . . . −
Airbags:
  Torso . . . . .Front Torso from Seat
  Pelvis . . . . None
  Roll Sensing. . . . . Yes
  Knee Bolster . . . . .Standard Driver
Crash Avoidance:
  Collision Avoidance . . . . .Std. DBS & Opt. CIB^
  Blind Spot Detection . . . . .Optional
  Lane Keeping Assist . . . . Warning Only Optional^
  Backup Camera . . . . Standard*
  Pedestrian Crash Avoidance . . . . None
General:
  Auto. Crash Notification . . . . Dial Assist.-Free
  Day Running Lamps . . . . Standard
Safety Belt/Restraint:
  Dynamic Head Restraints . . . . None
  Adjustable Belt. . . . . Standard Front

^Warning feature does not meet government standards.
*Backup camera does not meet government standards.

Land Rover Range Rover Evoque

Specifications

Drive. 4WD
Engine 2.0-liter I4
Transmission . . . . 9-sp. Automatic
Tow Rating (lbs.) . . . . −
Head/Leg Room (in.) Cramped-40.3/40.1
Interior Space (cu. ft.). . . . . −
Cargo Space (cu. ft.) Average-20.3
Wheelbase/Length (in.) 104.8/171.5

Ratings—10 Best, 1 Worst

Combo Crash Tests	—
Safety Features	6
Rollover	—
Preventive Maintenance	1
Repair Costs	2
Warranty	3
Fuel Economy	1
Complaints	5
Insurance Costs	3
OVERALL RATING	**—**

Land Rover Range Rover Sport

Land Rover Range Rover Sport

Safety Checklist

Crash Tests:
- Frontal . . . . −
- Side . . . . −

Airbags:
- Torso . . . . Front Torso from Seat
- Pelvis . . . . None
- Roll Sensing . . . . Yes
- Knee Bolster . . . . None

Crash Avoidance:
- Collision Avoidance . . . . Std. DBS & Opt. CIB^
- Blind Spot Detection . . . . .Optional
- Lane Keeping Assist . . . . Warning Only Optional^
- Backup Camera . . . . Standard*
- Pedestrian Crash Avoidance . . . . None

General:
- Auto. Crash Notification . . . . Dial Assist.-Free
- Day Running Lamps . . . . Standard

Safety Belt/Restraint:
- Dynamic Head Restraints . . . . None
- Adjustable Belt . . . . Standard Front

^Warning feature does not meet government standards.
*Backup camera does not meet government standards.

At-a-Glance

- Status/Year Series Started Unchanged/2014
- Twins . . . . −
- Body Styles . . . . .SUV
- Seating 5
- Anti-Theft Device . . . . Std. Pass. Immobil. & Alarm
- Parking Index Rating . . . . Very Hard
- Where Made. Solihull, England

Fuel Factor:
- MPG Rating (city/hwy) . . . . Very Poor-14/19
- Driving Range (mi.) Long-439.9
- Fuel Type . . . . Premium
- Annual Fuel Cost . . . . Very High-$2,220
- Gas Guzzler Tax . . . . No
- Greenhouse Gas Emissions (tons/yr.) . . Very High-11.2
- Barrels of Oil Used per year . . . . Very High-20.6

Land Rover Range Rover Sport

How the Competition Rates

Competitors	Rating	Pg.
Acura MDX	6	82
Audi Q5	5	90
BMW X5	6	101

Specifications

- Drive 4WD
- Engine 5.0-liter V8
- Transmission . . . . 8-sp. Automatic
- Tow Rating (lbs.) High-7716
- Head/Leg Room (in.) Average-39.4/42.2
- Interior Space (cu. ft.). −
- Cargo Space (cu. ft.) Roomy-27.7
- Wheelbase/Length (in.) 115.1/191.8

Price Range

	Retail	Markup
SE	$63,350	10%
HSE	$68,495	10%
Supercharged	$79,995	10%
Autobiography	$92,495	10%

Ratings—10 Best, 1 Worst

Combo Crash Tests	—
Safety Features	5
Rollover	—
Preventive Maintenance	9
Repair Costs	2
Warranty	6
Fuel Economy	10
Complaints	6
Insurance Costs	3

OVERALL RATING —

Lexus CT

Lexus CT

At-a-Glance

Status/Year Series Started	Unchanged/2011
Twins	–
Body Styles	Hatchback
Seating	5
Anti-Theft Device	Std. Pass. Immobil. & Alarm
Parking Index Rating	Easy
Where Made	Kyushu, Japan

Fuel Factor:

MPG Rating (city/hwy)	Very Good-43/40
Driving Range (mi.)	Very Long-495.0
Fuel Type	Regular
Annual Fuel Cost	Very Low-$757
Gas Guzzler Tax	No
Greenhouse Gas Emissions (tons/yr.)	Very Low-4.3
Barrels of Oil Used per year	Very Low-7.8

How the Competition Rates

Competitors	Rating	Pg.
Chevrolet Volt	—	125
Ford C-MAX	5	135
Toyota Prius	—	251

Price Range

	Retail	Markup
Hybrid	$31,250	5%

Safety Checklist

Crash Tests:

Frontal	−
Side	−

Airbags:

Torso	Front Pelvis/Torso from Seat
Pelvis	Front Pelvis/Torso from Seat
Roll Sensing	No
Knee Bolster	Standard Front

Crash Avoidance:

Collision Avoidance	Optional CIB & DBS
Blind Spot Detection	None
Lane Keeping Assist	None
Backup Camera	Optional*
Pedestrian Crash Avoidance	None

General:

Auto. Crash Notification	Operator Assist.-Fee
Day Running Lamps	Standard

Safety Belt/Restraint:

Dynamic Head Restraints	None
Adjustable Belt	Standard Front

^Warning feature does not meet government standards.
*Backup camera does not meet government standards.

Lexus CT

Specifications

Drive	FWD
Engine	1.8-liter I4
Transmission	CVT
Tow Rating (lbs.)	−
Head/Leg Room (in.)	Cramped-38.3/42.1
Interior Space (cu. ft.)	Very Cramped-86.1
Cargo Space (cu. ft.)	Cramped-14.3
Wheelbase/Length (in.)	102.4/171.2

Ratings—10 Best, 1 Worst

Combo Crash Tests	6
Safety Features	10
Rollover	8
Preventive Maintenance	6
Repair Costs	1
Warranty	6
Fuel Economy	5
Complaints	9
Insurance Costs	3
OVERALL RATING	**8**

Lexus ES

Lexus ES

At-a-Glance

Status/Year Series Started. Unchanged/2013
Twins . . . . .Toyota Avalon
Body Styles . . . . Sedan
Seating 5
Anti-Theft Device . . . . .Std. Pass. Immobil. & Alarm
Parking Index Rating . . . . .Average
Where Made. Kyushu, Japan
Fuel Factor:
  MPG Rating (city/hwy) Average-21/31
  Driving Range (mi.) Average-422.5
  Fuel Type . . . . Regular
  Annual Fuel Cost . . . . .Average-$1,282
  Gas Guzzler Tax . . . . No
  Greenhouse Gas Emissions (tons/yr.) High-7.5
  Barrels of Oil Used per year High-13.7

How the Competition Rates

Competitors	Rating	Pg.
Acura TLX	10	84
Infiniti Q70	–	169
Volkswagen Passat	7	264

Price Range

	Retail	Markup
Sedan	$38,000	7%
Hybrid	$40,920	7%

Safety Checklist

Crash Tests:
  Frontal. . . . . .Good
  Side. . . . . .Poor
Airbags:
  Torso . . . . .Fr. & Rr. Pelvis/Torso from Seat
  Pelvis . . . . .Fr. & Rr. Pelvis/Torso from Seat
  Roll Sensing. . . . . Yes
  Knee Bolster . . . . Standard Front
Crash Avoidance:
  Collision Avoidance . . . . .Optional CIB & DBS^
  Blind Spot Detection . . . . .Optional
  Lane Keeping Assist . . . . .Optional
  Backup Camera. Standard*
  Pedestrian Crash Avoidance . . . . .Optional
General:
  Auto. Crash Notification . . . . .Operator Assist.-Fee
  Day Running Lamps . . . . Standard
Safety Belt/Restraint:
  Dynamic Head Restraints . . . . None
  Adjustable Belt. . . . . Standard Front

^Warning feature does not meet government standards.
*Backup camera does not meet government standards.

Lexus ES

Specifications

Drive. . . . . .FWD
Engine 3.5-liter V6
Transmission . . . . 6-sp. Automatic
Tow Rating (lbs.) . . . . –
Head/Leg Room (in.) . . . . Very Cramped-37.5/41.9
Interior Space (cu. ft.). Average-100.1
Cargo Space (cu. ft.) Cramped-15.2
Wheelbase/Length (in.) 111/192.7

Ratings—10 Best, 1 Worst

Combo Crash Tests	—
Safety Features	9
Rollover	—
Preventive Maintenance	8
Repair Costs	1
Warranty	6
Fuel Economy	3
Complaints	10
Insurance Costs	1
OVERALL RATING	—

Lexus GS

Lexus GS

At-a-Glance

Status/Year Series Started	Unchanged/2012
Twins	—
Body Styles	Sedan
Seating	5
Anti-Theft Device	Std. Pass. Immobil. & Alarm
Parking Index Rating	Average
Where Made	Tahara, Japan

Fuel Factor:

MPG Rating (city/hwy)	Poor-19/29
Driving Range (mi.)	Short-391.3
Fuel Type	Premium
Annual Fuel Cost	High-$1,567
Gas Guzzler Tax	No
Greenhouse Gas Emissions (tons/yr.)	High-7.8
Barrels of Oil Used per year	High-14.3

How the Competition Rates

Competitors	Rating	Pg.
Acura TLX	10	84
Audi A6	8	88
Hyundai Genesis	7	162

Price Range

Price Range	Retail	Markup
Sedan	$48,600	8%
Sedan AWD	$50,850	8%
Hybrid	$61,330	8%

Safety Checklist

Crash Tests:
- Frontal.................................... –
- Side...................................... –

Airbags:
- Torso............Fr. & Rr. Pelvis/Torso from Seat
- Pelvis............Fr. & Rr. Pelvis/Torso from Seat
- Roll Sensing................................ No
- Knee Bolster .... Standard Front

Crash Avoidance:
- Collision Avoidance .... Optional CIB & DBS
- Blind Spot Detection ....Optional
- Lane Keeping Assist ....Optional
- Backup Camera..................... Standard
- Pedestrian Crash Avoidance ....Optional

General:
- Auto. Crash Notification........Operator Assist.-Fee
- Day Running Lamps .... Standard

Safety Belt/Restraint:
- Dynamic Head Restraints .... None
- Adjustable Belt................... Standard Front

^Warning feature does not meet government standards.
*Backup camera does not meet government standards.

Lexus GS

Specifications

Drive	RWD
Engine	3.5-liter V6
Transmission	8-sp. Automatic
Tow Rating (lbs.)	—
Head/Leg Room (in.)	Cramped-38/42.3
Interior Space (cu. ft.)	Average-99
Cargo Space (cu. ft.)	Cramped-14.1
Wheelbase/Length (in.)	112.2/190.7

Ratings—10 Best, 1 Worst

Combo Crash Tests	—
Safety Features	10
Rollover	—
Preventive Maintenance	6
Repair Costs	3
Warranty	6
Fuel Economy	1
Complaints	10
Insurance Costs	10
OVERALL RATING	**—**

Lexus GX

Lexus GX

At-a-Glance

Status/Year Series Started. Unchanged/2003
Twins . . . . Toyota 4Runner
Body Styles . . . . SUV
Seating 7
Anti-Theft Device . . . . Std. Pass. Immobil. & Alarm
Parking Index Rating . . . . Very Hard
Where Made. . . . . Tahara, Japan

Fuel Factor:
MPG Rating (city/hwy) . . . . Very Poor-15/20
Driving Range (mi.) Short-388.7
Fuel Type. . . . . Premium
Annual Fuel Cost . . . . Very High-$2,085
Gas Guzzler Tax . . . . No
Greenhouse Gas Emissions (tons/yr.). . Very High-10.6
Barrels of Oil Used per year . . . . Very High-19.4

How the Competition Rates

Competitors	Rating	Pg.
Audi Q7	–	91
Infiniti QX80	–	172
Mercedes-Benz GL-Class	–	212

Price Range

Price Range	Retail	Markup
4WD	$50,140	9%
4WD Luxury	$61,515	9%

Safety Checklist

Crash Tests:
Frontal. . . . . –
Side. . . . . –

Airbags:
Torso . . . . Fr. & Rr. Torso from Seat
Pelvis . . . . Front Pelvis/Torso from Seat
Roll Sensing. . . . . Yes
Knee Bolster . . . . Standard

Crash Avoidance:
Collision Avoidance . . . . Optional CIB & DBS
Blind Spot Detection . . . . .Optional
Lane Keeping Assist . . . . Warning Only Optional^
Backup Camera . . . . Standard
Pedestrian Crash Avoidance . . . . None

General:
Auto. Crash Notification . . . . .Operator Assist.-Fee
Day Running Lamps . . . . Standard

Safety Belt/Restraint:
Dynamic Head Restraints . . . . Standard Front
Adjustable Belt. . . . . Standard Front and Rear

^Warning feature does not meet government standards.
*Backup camera does not meet government standards.

Lexus GX

Specifications

Drive. 4WD
Engine 4.6-liter V8
Transmission . . . . 6-sp. Automatic
Tow Rating (lbs.) Average-6500
Head/Leg Room (in.) . . . . Very Cramped-38/41.7
Interior Space (cu. ft.). Roomy-129.7
Cargo Space (cu. ft.) . . . . Very Cramped-11.6
Wheelbase/Length (in.) 109.8/192.1

Lexus IS — Compact

Ratings—10 Best, 1 Worst

Combo Crash Tests	5
Safety Features	9
Rollover	10
Preventive Maintenance	7
Repair Costs	1
Warranty	6
Fuel Economy	4
Complaints	10
Insurance Costs	3
OVERALL RATING	**7**

Lexus IS

Lexus IS

At-a-Glance

Status/Year Series Started...........Unchanged/2014
Twins ....–
Body Styles ....Sedan, Convertible
Seating 5
Anti-Theft Device ....Std. Pass. Immobil. & Alarm
Parking Index Rating ....Easy
Where Made..........Kyushu, Japan / Tahara, Japan
Fuel Factor:
MPG Rating (city/hwy)................Poor-21/30
Driving Range (mi.)...............Average-422.4
Fuel Type................................Premium
Annual Fuel Cost...................High-$1,451
Gas Guzzler Tax...........................No
Greenhouse Gas Emissions (tons/yr.).......High-7.5
Barrels of Oil Used per year.............High-13.7

How the Competition Rates

Competitors	Rating	Pg.
Acura ILX	9	81
BMW 3 Series	8	93
Infiniti Q50	5	168

Price Range	Retail	Markup
250 Sedan FWD	$36,550	8%
300 Sedan AWD	$39,700	8%
350 Sedan AWD	$43,035	8%
250 Convertible	$43,360	8%

Safety Checklist

Crash Tests:
Frontal.............................. Very Poor
Side...............................Very Good
Airbags:
Torso ....Fr. & Rr. Pelvis/Torso from Seat
Pelvis ....Fr. & Rr. Pelvis/Torso from Seat
Roll Sensing...............................No
Knee Bolster ....Standard Front
Crash Avoidance:
Collision Avoidance ....Optional CIB & DBS
Blind Spot Detection ....Optional
Lane Keeping Assist ....Warning Only Optional
Backup Camera.......................Optional
Pedestrian Crash Avoidance.............Optional
General:
Auto. Crash Notification........Operator Assist.-Fee
Day Running Lamps ....Standard
Safety Belt/Restraint:
Dynamic Head Restraints ....None
Adjustable Belt..................Standard Front

^Warning feature does not meet government standards.
*Backup camera does not meet government standards.

Lexus IS

Specifications

Drive.......................................RWD
Engine 2.5-liter V6
Transmission ....6-sp. Automatic
Tow Rating (lbs.) ....–
Head/Leg Room (in.) Roomy-38.2/44.8
Interior Space (cu. ft.)............Very Cramped-90.2
Cargo Space (cu. ft.) Cramped-13.8
Wheelbase/Length (in.) 110.2/183.7

Ratings—10 Best, 1 Worst

Combo Crash Tests	8
Safety Features	9
Rollover	5
Preventive Maintenance	1
Repair Costs	2
Warranty	6
Fuel Economy	4
Complaints	5
Insurance Costs	5
OVERALL RATING	**5**

Lexus NX

Lexus NX

At-a-Glance

Status/Year Series Started. Unchanged/2015
Twins . . . . .Toyota RAV4
Body Styles . . . . .SUV
Seating. 5
Anti-Theft Device . . . . .Std. Pass. Immobil. & Alarm
Parking Index Rating . . . . Very Easy
Where Made. Kyushu, Japan
Fuel Factor:
  MPG Rating (city/hwy) Poor-22/28
  Driving Range (mi.) Short-387.1
  Fuel Type . . . . Premium
  Annual Fuel Cost . . . . .High-$1,448
  Gas Guzzler Tax . . . . No
  Greenhouse Gas Emissions (tons/yr.) . . . .Very Low-3.5
  Barrels of Oil Used per year High-13.7

How the Competition Rates

Competitors	Rating	Pg.
BMW X1	–	99
Lincoln MKC	4	198
Mercedes-Benz GLA-Class	–	210

Price Range

	Retail	Markup
Base 2WD	$34,480	7%
Base AWD	$35,880	7%
F Sport AWD	$37,980	7%
Utility AWD	$41,310	6%

Safety Checklist

Crash Tests:
  Frontal. . . . . .Very Good
  Side. . . . . Very Poor
Airbags:
  Torso . . . . Front Pelvis/Torso from Seat
  Pelvis . . . . Front Pelvis/Torso from Seat
  Roll Sensing. . . . . Yes
  Knee Bolster . . . . Standard Front
Crash Avoidance:
  Collision Avoidance . . . . Optional CIB & DBS
  Blind Spot Detection . . . . .Optional
  Lane Keeping Assist . . . . Warning Only Optional
  Backup Camera . . . . Standard
  Pedestrian Crash Avoidance . . . . None
General:
  Auto. Crash Notification . . . . .Operator Assist.-Fee
  Day Running Lamps . . . . Standard
Safety Belt/Restraint:
  Dynamic Head Restraints . . . . None
  Adjustable Belt. . . . . Standard Front

^Warning feature does not meet government standards.
*Backup camera does not meet government standards.

Lexus NX

Specifications

Drive. . . . . .AWD
Engine 2.0-liter I4
Transmission . . . . 6-sp. Automatic
Tow Rating (lbs.) . . . . .Very Low-2000
Head/Leg Room (in.) Cramped-38.2/42.8
Interior Space (cu. ft.). . . . . Very Cramped-71.6
Cargo Space (cu. ft.) Average-17.7
Wheelbase/Length (in.) 104.7/182.3

Ratings—10 Best, 1 Worst

Combo Crash Tests	—
Safety Features	2
Rollover	—
Preventive Maintenance	5
Repair Costs	2
Warranty	6
Fuel Economy	5
Complaints	—
Insurance Costs	5

OVERALL RATING —

Lexus RC

Lexus RC

At-a-Glance

Status/Year Series Started	Unchanged/2015
Twins	—
Body Styles	Coupe
Seating	4
Anti-Theft Device	Std. Pass. Immobil. & Alarm
Parking Index Rating	Easy
Where Made	Tahara, Japan

Fuel Factor:

MPG Rating (city/hwy)	Good-22/32
Driving Range (mi.)	Long-445
Fuel Type	Premium
Annual Fuel Cost	High-$1376
Gas Guzzler Tax	No
Greenhouse Gas Emissions (tons/yr.)	Low-5.7
Barrels of Oil Used per year	High-12.7

How the Competition Rates

Competitors	Rating	Pg.
Acura ILX	9	81
Audi A5	–	87
BMW 4 Series	–	94

Price Range

Price Range	Retail	Markup
Coupe	$42,790	8%
Coupe AWD	$45,025	8%
F Coupe	$62,400	8%

Safety Checklist

Crash Tests:

Frontal	–
Side	–

Airbags:

Torso	Front Pelvis/Torso from Seat
Pelvis	Front Pelvis/Torso from Seat
Roll Sensing	Front Pelvis/Torso from Seat
Knee Bolster	Standard Front

Crash Avoidance:

Collision Avoidance	Optional CIB & DBS
Blind Spot Detection	Standard
Lane Keeping Assist	Warning Only Optional
Backup Camera	Standard
Pedestrian Crash Avoidance	None

General:

Auto. Crash Notification	Operator Assist.-Fee
Day Running Lamps	Standard

Safety Belt/Restraint:

Dynamic Head Restraints	None
Adjustable Belt	Standard Front

^Warning feature does not meet government standards.
*Backup camera does not meet government standards.

Lexus RC

Specifications

Drive	RWD
Engine	2.0-liter I4
Transmission	8-sp. Automatic
Tow Rating (lbs.)	–
Head/Leg Room (in.)	Roomy-37.8/45.4
Interior Space (cu. ft.)	Very Cramped-82
Cargo Space (cu. ft.)	Very Cramped-10.4
Wheelbase/Length (in.)	107.5/184.8

Ratings—10 Best, 1 Worst

Combo Crash Tests	—
Safety Features	10
Rollover	—
Preventive Maintenance	5
Repair Costs	2
Warranty	6
Fuel Economy	4
Complaints	—
Insurance Costs	5
OVERALL RATING	—

Lexus RX

Lexus RX

At-a-Glance

Status/Year Series Started. . . . . .All New/2016
Twins . . . . —
Body Styles . . . . .SUV
Seating 5
Anti-Theft Device . . . . .Std. Pass. Immobil. & Alarm
Parking Index Rating . . . . Hard
Where Made. . . . . . Kyushu, Japan / Cambridge, Ontario

Fuel Factor:
MPG Rating (city/hwy) Poor-20/28
Driving Range (mi.) Long-440.7
Fuel Type. . . . . Regular
Annual Fuel Cost . . . . .Average-$1,373
Gas Guzzler Tax . . . . No
Greenhouse Gas Emissions (tons/yr.). Average-6.4
Barrels of Oil Used per year High-14.3

How the Competition Rates

Competitors	Rating	Pg.
Audi Q5	5	90
BMW X3	7	100
Mercedes-Benz GLC-Class	–	211

Price Range

	Retail	Markup
450 Hybrid AWD		
350 Base FWD	$40,970	7%
350 Base AWD	$42,370	7%
350 F Sport AWD	$48,710	7%

Safety Checklist

Crash Tests:
Frontal. . . . . –
Side. . . . . –

Airbags:
Torso . . . . Fr. & Rr. Torso from Seat
Pelvis . . . . Front Pelvis/Torso from Seat
Roll Sensing. . . . . Yes
Knee Bolster . . . . Standard Front

Crash Avoidance:
Collision Avoidance . . . . Optional CIB & DBS
Blind Spot Detection . . . . .Optional
Lane Keeping Assist . . . . .Optional
Backup Camera. . . . . Standard
Pedestrian Crash Avoidance . . . . .Optional

General:
Auto. Crash Notification . . . . .Operator Assist.-Fee
Day Running Lamps . . . . Standard

Safety Belt/Restraint:
Dynamic Head Restraints . . . . Standard Front
Adjustable Belt. . . . . Standard Front

^Warning feature does not meet government standards.
*Backup camera does not meet government standards.

Lexus RX

Specifications

Drive. . . . . .FWD
Engine 3.5-liter V6
Transmission . . . . 8-sp. Automatic
Tow Rating (lbs.) . . . . –
Head/Leg Room (in.) Roomy-39.4/44.4
Interior Space (cu. ft.). Roomy-139.7
Cargo Space (cu. ft.) Average-18.4
Wheelbase/Length (in.) 109.8/192.5

Lincoln MKC

Ratings—10 Best, 1 Worst

Combo Crash Tests	3
Safety Features	7
Rollover	4
Preventive Maintenance	6
Repair Costs	3
Warranty	8
Fuel Economy	3
Complaints	3
Insurance Costs	5
OVERALL RATING	**4**

Lincoln MKC

At-a-Glance

Status/Year Series Started	Unchanged/2015
Twins	Ford Escape
Body Styles	SUV
Seating	5
Anti-Theft Device	Std. Pass. Immobil. & Alarm
Parking Index Rating	Average
Where Made	Louisville, Kentucky

Fuel Factor:

MPG Rating (city/hwy)	Poor-19/26
Driving Range (mi.)	Very Short-335.1
Fuel Type	Regular
Annual Fuel Cost	High-$1,457
Gas Guzzler Tax	No
Greenhouse Gas Emissions (tons/yr.)	High-8.2
Barrels of Oil Used per year	High-15.0

How the Competition Rates

Competitors	Rating	Pg.
Audi Q3	–	89
BMW X1	–	99
Lexus NX	5	195

Price Range

	Retail	Markup
Premiere FWD	$33,260	5%
Select FWD	$37,090	6%
Reserve AWD	$42,955	6%
Black Label AWD	$48,950	7%

Safety Checklist

Crash Tests:

Frontal	Poor
Side	Poor

Airbags:

Torso	Front Pelvis/Torso from Seat
Pelvis	Front Pelvis/Torso from Seat
Roll Sensing	Yes
Knee Bolster	Standard Driver

Crash Avoidance:

Collision Avoidance	Warning Only Optional
Blind Spot Detection	Optional
Lane Keeping Assist	Optional
Backup Camera	Standard
Pedestrian Crash Avoidance	None

General:

Auto. Crash Notification	Dial Assist.-Free
Day Running Lamps	Standard

Safety Belt/Restraint:

Dynamic Head Restraints	None
Adjustable Belt	Standard Front

^Warning feature does not meet government standards.
*Backup camera does not meet government standards.

Lincoln MKC

Specifications

Drive	AWD
Engine	2.0-liter I5
Transmission	6-sp. Automatic
Tow Rating (lbs.)	Very Low-2000
Head/Leg Room (in.)	Average-39.6/42.8
Interior Space (cu. ft.)	Average-97.9
Cargo Space (cu. ft.)	Roomy-25.2
Wheelbase/Length (in.)	105.9/179.2

Ratings—10 Best, 1 Worst

Combo Crash Tests	7
Safety Features	4
Rollover	8
Preventive Maintenance	5
Repair Costs	2
Warranty	8
Fuel Economy	3
Complaints	7
Insurance Costs	3
OVERALL RATING	**5**

Lincoln MKS

Lincoln MKS

At-a-Glance

Status/Year Series Started..........Unchanged/2009
Twins . . . . –
Body Styles . . . . Sedan
Seating 5
Anti-Theft Device . . . . .Std. Pass. Immobil. & Alarm
Parking Index Rating . . . . Very Hard
Where Made. . . . . Chicago, IL
Fuel Factor:
  MPG Rating (city/hwy) Poor-19/28
  Driving Range (mi.) Average-422.0
  Fuel Type. . . . . Regular
  Annual Fuel Cost .High-$1,418
  Gas Guzzler Tax . . . . No
  Greenhouse Gas Emissions (tons/yr.). High-8.2
  Barrels of Oil Used per year High-15.0

How the Competition Rates

Competitors	Rating	Pg.
Chrysler 300	4	127
Hyundai Genesis	7	162
Lexus GS	–	192

Price Range

	Retail	Markup
FWD	$38,850	5%
AWD	$40,845	5%
Ecoboost AWD	$45,840	5%

Safety Checklist

Crash Tests:
  Frontal. . . . . .Very Good
  Side. . . . . .Poor
Airbags:
  Torso .Front Torso from Seat
  Pelvis . . . . None
  Roll Sensing. . . . . Yes
  Knee Bolster . . . . None
Crash Avoidance:
  Collision Avoidance . . . . Warning Only Optional
  Blind Spot Detection . . . . .Optional
  Lane Keeping Assist . . . . .Optional
  Backup Camera . . . . Standard
  Pedestrian Crash Avoidance . . . . None
General:
  Auto. Crash Notification . . . . Dial Assist.-Free
  Day Running Lamps . . . . None
Safety Belt/Restraint:
  Dynamic Head Restraints . . . . None
  Adjustable Belt. . . . . Standard Front

^Warning feature does not meet government standards.
*Backup camera does not meet government standards.

Lincoln MKS

Specifications

Drive. . . . . .FWD
Engine 3.7-liter V6
Transmission . . . . 6-sp. Automatic
Tow Rating (lbs.) . . . . –
Head/Leg Room (in.) Average-39.7/41.9
Interior Space (cu. ft.). Roomy-105.8
Cargo Space (cu. ft.) Average-19.2
Wheelbase/Length (in.) 112.9/205.6

Ratings—10 Best, 1 Worst	
Combo Crash Tests	6
Safety Features	5
Rollover	8
Preventive Maintenance	8
Repair Costs	1
Warranty	8
Fuel Economy	3
Complaints	7
Insurance Costs	3
OVERALL RATING	**6**

Lincoln MKZ

Lincoln MKZ

At-a-Glance

Status/Year Series Started Unchanged/2013
Twins . . . . .Ford Fusion
Body Styles . . . . Sedan
Seating. 5
Anti-Theft Device . . . . .Std. Pass. Immobil. & Alarm
Parking Index Rating . . . . Hard
Where Made. . . . . Hermosillo, Mexico
Fuel Factor:
  MPG Rating (city/hwy) Poor-18/27
  Driving Range (mi.) . . . . .Very Short-349.4
  Fuel Type. . . . . Regular
  Annual Fuel Cost . . . . .High-$1,487
  Gas Guzzler Tax . . . . No
  Greenhouse Gas Emissions (tons/yr.). High-8.1
  Barrels of Oil Used per year High-15.0

How the Competition Rates

Competitors	Rating	Pg.
BMW 3 Series	8	93
Buick Regal	5	105
Cadillac CTS	8	108

Price Range	Retail	Markup
Hybrid	$35,190	5%
Base FWD	$35,190	5%
Black Label Hybrid FWD	$45,605	6%
Black Label AWD	$47,495	6%

Safety Checklist

Crash Tests:
  Frontal. . . . . .Good
  Side. . . . . Very Poor
Airbags:
  Torso . . . . Front Pelvis/Torso from Seat
  Pelvis . . . . Front Pelvis/Torso from Seat
  Roll Sensing. . . . . No
  Knee Bolster . . . . Standard
Crash Avoidance:
  Collision Avoidance . . . . Warning Only Optional
  Blind Spot Detection . . . . .Optional
  Lane Keeping Assist . . . . .Optional
  Backup Camera . . . . Standard
  Pedestrian Crash Avoidance . . . . None
General:
  Auto. Crash Notification . . . . Dial Assist.-Free
  Day Running Lamps . . . . Standard
Safety Belt/Restraint:
  Dynamic Head Restraints . . . . None
  Adjustable Belt. . . . . Standard Front

^Warning feature does not meet government standards.
*Backup camera does not meet government standards.

Lincoln MKZ

Specifications

Drive. . . . . .FWD
Engine 3.7-liter V6
Transmission . . . . 6-sp. Automatic
Tow Rating (lbs.) . . . . .Very Low-1000
Head/Leg Room (in.) Average-37.9/44.3
Interior Space (cu. ft.). Cramped-96.5
Cargo Space (cu. ft.) Cramped-15.4
Wheelbase/Length (in.) 112.2/194.1

Ratings—10 Best, 1 Worst

Combo Crash Tests	10
Safety Features	4
Rollover	2
Preventive Maintenance	3
Repair Costs	8
Warranty	8
Fuel Economy	1
Complaints	10
Insurance Costs	10
OVERALL RATING	**9**

Lincoln Navigator

Lincoln Navigator

At-a-Glance

Status/Year Series Started	Unchanged/2007
Twins	Ford Expedition
Body Styles	SUV
Seating	8
Anti-Theft Device	Std. Pass. Immobil. & Alarm
Parking Index Rating	Very Easy
Where Made	Louisville, Kentucky

Fuel Factor:

MPG Rating (city/hwy)	Very Poor-15/20
Driving Range (mi.)	Very Long-473.2
Fuel Type	Premium
Annual Fuel Cost	Very High-$2,086
Gas Guzzler Tax	No
Greenhouse Gas Emissions (tons/yr.)	Very High-10.6
Barrels of Oil Used per year	Very High-19.4

How the Competition Rates

Competitors	Rating	Pg.
Chevrolet Suburban	3	121
Nissan Armada	–	223
Toyota Sequoia	–	255

Price Range	Retail	Markup
Select 2WD	$63,090	5%
Select 4WD	$66,665	5%
Reserve 4WD	$71,150	6%
Reserve 4WD	$74,150	6%

Safety Checklist

Crash Tests:

Frontal	Very Good
Side	Very Good

Airbags:

Torso	Front Torso from Seat
Pelvis	None
Roll Sensing	Yes
Knee Bolster	None

Crash Avoidance:

Collision Avoidance	None
Blind Spot Detection	Standard
Lane Keeping Assist	None
Backup Camera	Standard
Pedestrian Crash Avoidance	None

General:

Auto. Crash Notification	Dial Assist.-Free
Day Running Lamps	Optional

Safety Belt/Restraint:

Dynamic Head Restraints	Standard Front
Adjustable Belt	Standard Front

^Warning feature does not meet government standards.
*Backup camera does not meet government standards.

Lincoln Navigator

Specifications

Drive	4WD
Engine	3.5-liter V6
Transmission	6-sp. Automatic
Tow Rating (lbs.)	Very High-8600
Head/Leg Room (in.)	Average-39.5/43
Interior Space (cu. ft.)	Roomy-189.5
Cargo Space (cu. ft.)	Average-18.1
Wheelbase/Length (in.)	119/107.4

Ratings—10 Best, 1 Worst

Combo Crash Tests	3
Safety Features	6
Rollover	4
Preventive Maintenance	7
Repair Costs	10
Warranty	1
Fuel Economy	7
Complaints	3
Insurance Costs	3
OVERALL RATING	**3**

Mazda CX-5

Mazda CX-5

At-a-Glance

Status/Year Series Started. Unchanged/2013
Twins . . . . –
Body Styles . . . . .SUV
Seating 5
Anti-Theft Device . . . . Std. Pass. Immobil.
Parking Index Rating .Average
Where Made. . . . . Hiroshima, Japan
Fuel Factor:
  MPG Rating (city/hwy). Good-26/32
  Driving Range (mi.) Average-420.3
  Fuel Type. . . . . Regular
  Annual Fuel Cost . . . . Low-$1,109
  Gas Guzzler Tax . . . . No
  Greenhouse Gas Emissions (tons/yr.). Average-6.2
  Barrels of Oil Used per year Average-11.4

How the Competition Rates

Competitors	Rating	Pg.
Buick Encore	10	103
Honda CR-V	7	154
Mitsubishi Outlander Sport	3	220

Price Range	Retail	Markup
Sport FWD MT	$21,795	3%
Sport AWD AT	$24,445	3%
Touring AWD	$26,465	3%
Grand Touring AWD	$29,470	3%

Safety Checklist

Crash Tests:
  Frontal. . . . . Very Poor
  Side. . . . . .Average
Airbags:
  Torso . . . . Front Pelvis/Torso from Seat
  Pelvis . . . . Front Pelvis/Torso from Seat
  Roll Sensing. . . . . Yes
  Knee Bolster . . . . None
Crash Avoidance:
  Collision Avoidance . . . . Optional CIB & DBS
  Blind Spot Detection . . . . .Optional
  Lane Keeping Assist . . . . Warning Only Optional^
  Backup Camera .Optional*
  Pedestrian Crash Avoidance . . . . None
General:
  Auto. Crash Notification . . . . Dial Assist.-Free
  Day Running Lamps . . . . Standard
Safety Belt/Restraint:
  Dynamic Head Restraints . . . . None
  Adjustable Belt. . . . . Standard Front

^Warning feature does not meet government standards.
*Backup camera does not meet government standards.

Mazda CX-5

Specifications

Drive. . . . . .FWD
Engine 2.0-liter I4
Transmission . . . . 6-sp. Automatic
Tow Rating (lbs.) . . . . .Very Low-2000
Head/Leg Room (in.) Cramped-40.1/41
Interior Space (cu. ft.). Roomy-103.8
Cargo Space (cu. ft.) . . . . Very Roomy-34.1
Wheelbase/Length (in.) 106.3/178.7

Mazda CX-9 — Medium SUV

Ratings—10 Best, 1 Worst

Combo Crash Tests	1
Safety Features	6
Rollover	5
Preventive Maintenance	7
Repair Costs	4
Warranty	1
Fuel Economy	1
Complaints	6
Insurance Costs	5
OVERALL RATING	**2**

Mazda CX-9

Mazda CX-9

At-a-Glance

Status/Year Series Started Unchanged/2007
Twins . . . . –
Body Styles . . . . .SUV
Seating 7
Anti-Theft Device . . . . .Std. Pass. Immobil. & Alarm
Parking Index Rating . . . . Hard
Where Made. . . . . Hiroshima, Japan
Fuel Factor:
MPG Rating (city/hwy) . . . . Very Poor-16/22
Driving Range (mi.) . . . . .Very Short-366.6
Fuel Type . . . . Regular
Annual Fuel Cost . . . . Very High-$1,727
Gas Guzzler Tax . . . . No
Greenhouse Gas Emissions (tons/yr.) . . Very High-10.0
Barrels of Oil Used per year . . . . Very High-18.3

How the Competition Rates

Competitors	Rating	Pg.
Hyundai Santa Fe	–	163
Kia Sorento	5	184
Nissan Murano	5	228

Price Range

	Retail	Markup
Sport FWD	$29,985	6%
Touring FWD	$32,480	6%
Touring AWD	$34,070	6%
Grand Touring AWD	$36,625	6%

Safety Checklist

Crash Tests:
Frontal. . . . . Very Poor
Side. . . . . .Poor
Airbags:
Torso . . . . Front Pelvis/Torso from Seat
Pelvis . . . . Front Pelvis/Torso from Seat
Roll Sensing. . . . . Yes
Knee Bolster . . . . None
Crash Avoidance:
Collision Avoidance . . . . Optional CIB & DBS
Blind Spot Detection . . . . .Optional
Lane Keeping Assist . . . . .Optional
Backup Camera .Optional*
Pedestrian Crash Avoidance . . . . None
General:
Auto. Crash Notification . . . . Dial Assist.-Free
Day Running Lamps . . . . .Optional
Safety Belt/Restraint:
Dynamic Head Restraints . . . . None
Adjustable Belt. . . . . Standard Front

^Warning feature does not meet government standards.
*Backup camera does not meet government standards.

Mazda CX-9

Specifications

Drive. . . . . .AWD
Engine 3.7-liter V6
Transmission . . . . 6-sp. Automatic
Tow Rating (lbs.) Low-3500
Head/Leg Room (in.) Cramped-39.6/40.9
Interior Space (cu. ft.). Roomy-139.4
Cargo Space (cu. ft.) Average-17.2
Wheelbase/Length (in.) 113.2/200.6

Ratings—10 Best, 1 Worst

Combo Crash Tests	6
Safety Features	5
Rollover	9
Preventive Maintenance	7
Repair Costs	9
Warranty	1
Fuel Economy	9
Complaints	8
Insurance Costs	5
OVERALL RATING	**8**

Mazda Mazda3

Mazda Mazda3

At-a-Glance

Status/Year Series Started..........Unchanged/2014
Twins .... –
Body Styles ....Sedan, Hatchback
Seating.. 5
Anti-Theft Device ....Std. Pass. Immobil.
Parking Index Rating .... Easy
Where Made.........................Hofu, Japan

Fuel Factor:
MPG Rating (city/hwy).............Very Good-30/41
Driving Range (mi.) Long-450.4
Fuel Type........................... Regular
Annual Fuel Cost .... Very Low-$923
Gas Guzzler Tax .... No
Greenhouse Gas Emissions (tons/yr.)....... Low-5.3
Barrels of Oil Used per year Low-9.7

How the Competition Rates

Competitors	Rating	Pg.
Ford Focus	6	143
Mitsubishi Lancer	4	217
Volkswagen Jetta	7	263

Price Range

	Retail	Markup
i Sport MT	$17,845	4%
i Touring Sedan AT	$21,095	5%
s Touring Hatchback MT	$25,495	5%
s Grand Touring Hatchback AT	$25,650	5%

Safety Checklist

Crash Tests:
Frontal.................................Good
Side.................................Average

Airbags:
Torso ....Front Pelvis/Torso from Seat
Pelvis ....Front Pelvis/Torso from Seat
Roll Sensing........................... Yes
Knee Bolster .... None

Crash Avoidance:
Collision Avoidance ....Optional CIB^
Blind Spot Detection ....Optional
Lane Keeping Assist .... Warning Only Optional^
Backup Camera...................... Standard*
Pedestrian Crash Avoidance .... None

General:
Auto. Crash Notification.......... Dial Assist.-Free
Day Running Lamps .... Standard

Safety Belt/Restraint:
Dynamic Head Restraints .... None
Adjustable Belt................... Standard Front

^Warning feature does not meet government standards.
*Backup camera does not meet government standards.

Mazda Mazda3

Specifications

Drive....................................FWD
Engine 2.0-liter I4
Transmission .... 6-sp. Automatic
Tow Rating (lbs.) .... –
Head/Leg Room (in.) Cramped-38.6/42.2
Interior Space (cu. ft.)............. Cramped-96.3
Cargo Space (cu. ft.) .... Very Cramped-12.4
Wheelbase/Length (in.) 106.3/180.3

Ratings—10 Best, 1 Worst

Combo Crash Tests	8
Safety Features	5
Rollover	9
Preventive Maintenance	7
Repair Costs	9
Warranty	1
Fuel Economy	8
Complaints	4
Insurance Costs	—
OVERALL RATING	**8**

Mazda Mazda6

Mazda Mazda6

At-a-Glance

Status/Year Series Started. Unchanged/2014
Twins . . . . —
Body Styles . . . . Sedan
Seating. 5
Anti-Theft Device . . . . .Std. Pass. Immobil. & Alarm
Parking Index Rating .Average
Where Made. . . . . .Flat Rock, MI
Fuel Factor:
MPG Rating (city/hwy). Good-26/38
Driving Range (mi.) . . . . Very Long-497.0
Fuel Type. . . . . Regular
Annual Fuel Cost .Low-$1,039
Gas Guzzler Tax . . . . No
Greenhouse Gas Emissions (tons/yr.). Average-6.0
Barrels of Oil Used per year Average-11.0

How the Competition Rates

Competitors	Rating	Pg.
Kia Optima	9	181
Nissan Altima	7	222
Toyota Camry	7	248

Price Range	Retail	Markup
i Sport MT	$21,495	5%
i Sport AT	$22,995	5%
i Touring AT	$24,995	6%
i Grant Touring	$30,195	6%

Safety Checklist

Crash Tests:
Frontal. . . . . .Good
Side. . . . . .Good
Airbags:
Torso . . . . Front Pelvis/Torso from Seat
Pelvis . . . . Front Pelvis/Torso from Seat
Roll Sensing. . . . . No
Knee Bolster . . . . None
Crash Avoidance:
Collision Avoidance . . . . Optional CIB & DBS
Blind Spot Detection . . . . .Optional
Lane Keeping Assist . . . . Warning Only Optional
Backup Camera. . . . . .Optional*
Pedestrian Crash Avoidance . . . . None
General:
Auto. Crash Notification. . . . . Dial Assist.-Free
Day Running Lamps . . . . Standard
Safety Belt/Restraint:
Dynamic Head Restraints . . . . None
Adjustable Belt. . . . . Standard Front

^Warning feature does not meet government standards.
*Backup camera does not meet government standards.

Mazda Mazda6

Specifications

Drive. . . . . .FWD
Engine 2.5-liter I4
Transmission . . . . 6-sp. Automatic
Tow Rating (lbs.) . . . .—
Head/Leg Room (in.) Cramped-38.4/42.2
Interior Space (cu. ft.). Average-99.7
Cargo Space (cu. ft.) Cramped-14.8
Wheelbase/Length (in.) 111.4/191.5

Ratings—10 Best, 1 Worst

Combo Crash Tests	—
Safety Features	1
Rollover	—
Preventive Maintenance	6
Repair Costs	7
Warranty	1
Fuel Economy	8
Complaints	—
Insurance Costs	—
OVERALL RATING	**—**

Mazda MX-5

At-a-Glance

Status/Year Series Started . . . . All New/2016
Twins . . . . —
Body Styles . . . . Coupe, Convertible
Seating 2
Anti-Theft Device . . . . Std. Pass. Immobil. & Alarm
Parking Index Rating . . . . Very Easy
Where Made . . . . Hiroshima, Japan

Fuel Factor:
MPG Rating (city/hwy) Good-27/36
Driving Range (mi.) . . . . Very Short-361.7
Fuel Type . . . . Premium
Annual Fuel Cost . . . . Low-$1,158
Gas Guzzler Tax . . . . No
Greenhouse Gas Emissions (tons/yr.) Low-4.9
Barrels of Oil Used per year Average-11.0

How the Competition Rates

Competitors	Rating	Pg.
Hyundai Genesis	7	162
Nissan 370Z	—	221
Scion FR-S	3	237

Price Range

Price Range	Retail	Markup
Sport AT	$26,395	6%
Club AT	$29,330	6%
Grand Touring AT	$31,270	6%
Sport MT	$24,915	6%

Mazda MX-5

Safety Checklist

Crash Tests:
Frontal . . . . —
Side . . . . —
Airbags:
Torso . . . . Front Head/Torso
Pelvis . . . . None
Roll Sensing . . . . No
Knee Bolster . . . . None
Crash Avoidance:
Collision Avoidance . . . . None
Blind Spot Detection . . . . None
Lane Keeping Assist . . . . Warning Only Optional^
Backup Camera . . . . None
Pedestrian Crash Avoidance . . . . None
General:
Auto. Crash Notification . . . . None
Day Running Lamps . . . . None
Safety Belt/Restraint:
Dynamic Head Restraints . . . . None
Adjustable Belt . . . . None

^Warning feature does not meet government standards.
*Backup camera does not meet government standards.

Mazda MX-5

Specifications

Drive . . . . RWD
Engine 2.0-liter I4
Transmission . . . . 6-sp. Manual
Tow Rating (lbs.) . . . . —
Head/Leg Room (in.) Cramped-37.4/43.1
Interior Space (cu. ft.) . . . . —
Cargo Space (cu. ft.) . . . . Very Cramped-4.6
Wheelbase/Length (in.) 90.9/154.1

Mercedes-Benz C-Class

Ratings—10 Best, 1 Worst

Combo Crash Tests	3
Safety Features	10
Rollover	8
Preventive Maintenance	2
Repair Costs	3
Warranty	2
Fuel Economy	5
Complaints	4
Insurance Costs	5
OVERALL RATING	**3**

Mercedes-Benz C-Class

Mercedes-Benz C-Class

At-a-Glance

Status/Year Series Started Unchanged/2015
Twins . . . . –
Body Styles . . . . Sedan, Coupe, Wagon
Seating 5
Anti-Theft Device . . . Std. Active Immobil. & Pass. Alarm
Parking Index Rating .Average
Where Made . . . . Tuscaloosa, AL
Fuel Factor:
MPG Rating (city/hwy) Average-22/31
Driving Range (mi.) Long-455.5
Fuel Type . . . . Premium
Annual Fuel Cost . . . . .High-$1,393
Gas Guzzler Tax . . . . No
Greenhouse Gas Emissions (tons/yr.) Average-7.2
Barrels of Oil Used per year High-13.2

How the Competition Rates

Competitors	Rating	Pg.
Audi A4	8	86
BMW 3 Series	8	93
Lexus IS	7	194

Price Range	Retail	Markup
C250	$39,400	8%
C350	$44,050	8%
C350 4Matic	$46,050	8%
C60 AMG	$63,000	8%

Safety Checklist

Crash Tests:
Frontal . . . . .Poor
Side . . . . Very Poor
Airbags:
Torso . . . . Fr. & Rr. Torso from Seat
Pelvis . . . . None
Roll Sensing . . . . Yes
Knee Bolster . . . . .Standard Driver
Crash Avoidance:
Collision Avoidance . . . . Standard CIB & DBS
Blind Spot Detection . . . . .Optional
Lane Keeping Assist . . . . .Optional
Backup Camera . . . . Standard
Pedestrian Crash Avoidance . . . . .Optional
General:
Auto. Crash Notification . . . . .Operator Assist.-Fee
Day Running Lamps . . . . Standard
Safety Belt/Restraint:
Dynamic Head Restraints . . . . None
Adjustable Belt . . . . Standard Front

^Warning feature does not meet government standards.
*Backup camera does not meet government standards.

Mercedes-Benz C-Class

Specifications

Drive . . . . .RWD
Engine 2.0-liter I4
Transmission . . . . 7-sp. Automatic
Tow Rating (lbs.) . . . . –
Head/Leg Room (in.) . . . . Very Cramped-37.1/41.7
Interior Space (cu. ft.) . . . . .Very Cramped-81
Cargo Space (cu. ft.) . . . . Very Cramped-12.8
Wheelbase/Length (in.) 111.8/184.5

Ratings—10 Best, 1 Worst

Combo Crash Tests	—
Safety Features	10
Rollover	—
Preventive Maintenance	2
Repair Costs	3
Warranty	2
Fuel Economy	8
Complaints	2
Insurance Costs	3
OVERALL RATING	**—**

Mercedes-Benz CLA-Class

Mercedes-Benz CLA-Class

At-a-Glance

Status/Year Series Started. Unchanged/2014
Twins . . . . –
Body Styles . . . . Coupe
Seating 5
Anti-Theft Device . . . Std. Active Immobil. & Pass. Alarm
Parking Index Rating . . . . Easy
Where Made. . . . . .Kecskemet, Hungary
Fuel Factor:
  MPG Rating (city/hwy) Good-26/38
  Driving Range (mi.) Short-400.0
  Fuel Type . . . . Premium
  Annual Fuel Cost . . . . Low-$1,163
  Gas Guzzler Tax . . . . No
  Greenhouse Gas Emissions (tons/yr.). Average-6.1
  Barrels of Oil Used per year Average-11.0

How the Competition Rates

Competitors	Rating	Pg.
Acura ILX	9	81
Cadillac ATS	8	107
Infiniti Q50	5	168

Price Range	Retail	Markup
CLA250	$31,500	8
CLA250 4Matic	$33,500	8
CLA45 AMG	$48,500	8

Safety Checklist

Crash Tests:
  Frontal. . . . . –
  Side. . . . . –
Airbags:
  Torso . . . . .Fr. & Rr. Torso from Seat
  Pelvis . . . . None
  Roll Sensing. . . . . Yes
  Knee Bolster . . . . Standard Front
Crash Avoidance:
  Collision Avoidance . . . . Standard CIB & DBS
  Blind Spot Detection . . . . .Optional
  Lane Keeping Assist . . . . Warning Only Optional
  Backup Camera .Optional*
  Pedestrian Crash Avoidance . . . . .Optional
General:
  Auto. Crash Notification . . . . .Operator Assist.-Fee
  Day Running Lamps . . . . Standard
Safety Belt/Restraint:
  Dynamic Head Restraints . . . . None
  Adjustable Belt. . . . . Standard Front

^Warning feature does not meet government standards.
*Backup camera does not meet government standards.

Mercedes-Benz CLA-Class

Specifications

Drive . . . . .FWD
Engine 2.0-liter I4
Transmission . . . . 7-sp. Automatic
Tow Rating (lbs.) . . . . –
Head/Leg Room (in.) . . . . Very Cramped-38.2/40.2
Interior Space (cu. ft.). . . . . .Very Cramped-88
Cargo Space (cu. ft.) . . . . .Very Cramped-13
Wheelbase/Length (in.) 106.3/182.3

Ratings—10 Best, 1 Worst

Combo Crash Tests	3
Safety Features	10
Rollover	10
Preventive Maintenance	4
Repair Costs	2
Warranty	2
Fuel Economy	4
Complaints	9
Insurance Costs	5
OVERALL RATING	**5**

Mercedes-Benz E-Class

At-a-Glance

Status/Year Series Started Unchanged/2010
Twins . . . . –
Body Styles . . . . . . .Sedan, Coupe, Wagon, Convertible
Seating 5
Anti-Theft Device . . . Std. Active Immobil. & Pass. Alarm
Parking Index Rating . . . . .Average
Where Made . . . . Sindelfingen, Germany
Fuel Factor:
MPG Rating (city/hwy) Poor-20/29
Driving Range (mi.) . . . . Very Long-490.5
Fuel Type . . . . Premium
Annual Fuel Cost .High-$1,516
Gas Guzzler Tax . . . . No
Greenhouse Gas Emissions (tons/yr.) High-7.8
Barrels of Oil Used per year High-14.3

How the Competition Rates

Competitors	Rating	Pg.
Audi A6	8	88
BMW 5 Series	8	95
Lexus GS	–	192

Price Range

Price Range	Retail	Markup
E250 Sport	$52,650	8%
E350 Luxury 4Matic	$55,150	8%
E400 Sport Sedan	$63,100	8%
E63 AMG S 4Matic	$101,700	8%

Mercedes-Benz E-Class

Safety Checklist

Crash Tests:
Frontal . . . . Very Poor
Side . . . . .Average
Airbags:
Torso . . . . Fr. & Rr. Torso from Seat
Pelvis . . . . Front Pelvis from Seat
Roll Sensing . . . . Yes
Knee Bolster .Standard Driver
Crash Avoidance:
Collision Avoidance . . . . Standard CIB & DBS
Blind Spot Detection .Optional
Lane Keeping Assist . . . . .Optional
Backup Camera . . . . .Optional*
Pedestrian Crash Avoidance . . . . .Optional
General:
Auto. Crash Notification . . . . .Operator Assist.-Fee
Day Running Lamps . . . . Standard
Safety Belt/Restraint:
Dynamic Head Restraints . . . . Standard Front
Adjustable Belt . . . . Standard Front and Rear

^Warning feature does not meet government standards.
*Backup camera does not meet government standards.

Mercedes-Benz E-Class

Specifications

Drive . . . . .RWD
Engine 3.5-liter V6
Transmission . . . . 7-sp. Automatic
Tow Rating (lbs.) . . . .–
Head/Leg Room (in.) . . . . . Very Cramped-37.9/41.3
Interior Space (cu. ft.) Average-98
Cargo Space (cu. ft.) . . . . Very Cramped-12.9
Wheelbase/Length (in.) 113.2/192.1

Ratings—10 Best, 1 Worst

Combo Crash Tests	—
Safety Features	10
Rollover	—
Preventive Maintenance	10
Repair Costs	2
Warranty	2
Fuel Economy	6
Complaints	3
Insurance Costs	5
OVERALL RATING	—

Mercedes-Benz GLA-Class

Mercedes-Benz GLA-Class

At-a-Glance

Status/Year Series Started. Unchanged/2015
Twins . . . . –
Body Styles . . . . .SUV
Seating 5
Anti-Theft Device . . . Std. Active Immobil. & Pass. Alarm
Parking Index Rating .Average
Where Made. Rastatt, Germany

Fuel Factor:
MPG Rating (city/hwy) Average-24/32
Driving Range (mi.) Short-400.2
Fuel Type . . . . Premium
Annual Fuel Cost . . . . .Average-$1,304
Gas Guzzler Tax . . . . No
Greenhouse Gas Emissions (tons/yr.). Average-6.7
Barrels of Oil Used per year Average-12.2

How the Competition Rates

Competitors	Rating	Pg.
Audi Q3	–	89
Lexus NX	5	195
Porsche Macan	–	235

Price Range

Price Range	Retail	Markup
GLA250	$31,300	8%
GLA250 4Matic	$33,300	8%
GLA45 AMG 4Matic	$48,300	8%

Safety Checklist

Crash Tests:
Frontal. . . . . –
Side. . . . . –
Airbags:
Torso . . . . Fr. & Rr. Torso from Seat
Pelvis . . . . None
Roll Sensing. . . . . Yes
Knee Bolster . . . . Standard Front
Crash Avoidance:
Collision Avoidance . . . . Standard CIB & DBS
Blind Spot Detection . . . . .Optional
Lane Keeping Assist . . . . Warning Only Optional
Backup Camera . . . . .Optional*
Pedestrian Crash Avoidance . . . . None
General:
Auto. Crash Notification . . . . .Operator Assist.-Fee
Day Running Lamps . . . . Standard
Safety Belt/Restraint:
Dynamic Head Restraints . . . . None
Adjustable Belt. . . . . None

^Warning feature does not meet government standards.
*Backup camera does not meet government standards.

Mercedes-Benz GLA-Class

Specifications

Drive. . . . . .AWD
Engine 2.0-liter I4
Transmission . . . . 7-sp. Automatic
Tow Rating (lbs.) . . . . –
Head/Leg Room (in.) Cramped-38.3/41.9
Interior Space (cu. ft.). Average-91
Cargo Space (cu. ft.) Average-17.2
Wheelbase/Length (in.) 106.3/173.9

Mercedes-Benz GLC-Class

Small SUV

Ratings—10 Best, 1 Worst

Combo Crash Tests	—
Safety Features	10
Rollover	—
Preventive Maintenance	10
Repair Costs	3
Warranty	2
Fuel Economy	2
Complaints	—
Insurance Costs	8

OVERALL RATING —

Mercedes-Benz GLC-Class

Mercedes-Benz GLC-Class

At-a-Glance

Status/Year Series Started............All New/2016
Twins . . . . —
Body Styles . . . . .SUV
Seating 5
Anti-Theft Device . . . Std. Active Immobil. & Pass. Alarm
Parking Index Rating .Average
Where Made. .Tuscaloosa, AL

Fuel Factor:
  MPG Rating (city/hwy) . . . . Very Poor-18/25
  Driving Range (mi.) . . . . .Very Short-358.4
  Fuel Type. . . . . Premium
  Annual Fuel Cost . . . . Very High-$1,712
  Gas Guzzler Tax . . . . No
  Greenhouse Gas Emissions (tons/yr.). High-8.6
  Barrels of Oil Used per year . . . . Very High-45.7

How the Competition Rates

Competitors	Rating	Pg.
Audi Q5	5	90
BMW X3	7	100
Lexus RX	—	197

Price Range

Price Range	Retail	Markup
GLC300	$38,950	8%
GLC300 4Matic	$40,950	8%

Mercedes-Benz GLC-Class

Safety Checklist

Crash Tests:
  Frontal. . . . . −
  Side. . . . . −
Airbags:
  Torso . . . . Fr. & Rr. Torso from Seat
  Pelvis . . . . None
  Roll Sensing. . . . . Yes
  Knee Bolster . . . . Standard Front
Crash Avoidance:
  Collision Avoidance . . . . Standard CIB & DBS
  Blind Spot Detection . . . . .Optional
  Lane Keeping Assist . . . . Warning Only Optional
  Backup Camera . . . . Standard*
  Pedestrian Crash Avoidance . . . . .Optional
General:
  Auto. Crash Notification . . . . .Operator Assist.-Fee
  Day Running Lamps . . . . Standard
Safety Belt/Restraint:
  Dynamic Head Restraints . . . . None
  Adjustable Belt. . . . . None

^Warning feature does not meet government standards.
*Backup camera does not meet government standards.

Mercedes-Benz GLC-Class

Specifications

Drive. 4WD
Engine 2.1-liter I4
Transmission . . . . .7-sp. Auto
Tow Rating (lbs.) Low-3500
Head/Leg Room (in.) Cramped-39/41.4
Interior Space (cu. ft.). . . . . Very Cramped-79.5
Cargo Space (cu. ft.) Cramped-16.5
Wheelbase/Length (in.) 108.5/178.3

Mercedes-Benz GL-Class — Large SUV

Ratings—10 Best, 1 Worst

Combo Crash Tests	—
Safety Features	10
Rollover	—
Preventive Maintenance	3
Repair Costs	2
Warranty	2
Fuel Economy	3
Complaints	—
Insurance Costs	5
OVERALL RATING	**—**

Mercedes-Benz GL-Class

Mercedes-Benz GL-Class

At-a-Glance

Status/Year Series Started. . . . . .All New/2016
Twins . . . . –
Body Styles . . . . .SUV
Seating 5
Anti-Theft Device . . . Std. Active Immobil. & Pass. Alarm
Parking Index Rating . . . . Very Hard
Where Made. .Tuscaloosa, AL
Fuel Factor:
  MPG Rating (city/hwy) Poor-19/26
  Driving Range (mi.) . . . . Very Long-570.7
  Fuel Type . . . . Premium
  Annual Fuel Cost . . . . Very High-$1,630
  Gas Guzzler Tax . . . . No
  Greenhouse Gas Emissions (tons/yr.). Low-5.1
  Barrels of Oil Used per year . . . . .Very Low-0.0

How the Competition Rates

Competitors	Rating	Pg.
Audi Q7	–	91
Infiniti QX80	–	172
Lexus GX	–	193

Price Range

Price Range	Retail	Markup
GL350	$63,600	8%
GL450	$65,200	8%
GL550	$89,950	8%
GL63 AMG	$119,450	8%

Safety Checklist

Crash Tests:
  Frontal. . . . . –
  Side. . . . . –
Airbags:
  Torso . . . . .Fr. & Rr. Torso from Seat
  Pelvis . . . . None
  Roll Sensing. . . . . Yes
  Knee Bolster . . . . .Standard Driver
Crash Avoidance:
  Collision Avoidance . . . . .Std. DBS & Opt. CIB
  Blind Spot Detection . . . . .Optional
  Lane Keeping Assist . . . . .Optional
  Backup Camera . . . . Standard*
  Pedestrian Crash Avoidance . . . . .Optional
General:
  Auto. Crash Notification . . . . .Operator Assist.-Fee
  Day Running Lamps . . . . Standard
Safety Belt/Restraint:
  Dynamic Head Restraints . . . . None
  Adjustable Belt. . . . . Standard Front

^Warning feature does not meet government standards.
*Backup camera does not meet government standards.

Mercedes-Benz GL-Class

Specifications

Drive. 4WD
Engine 3.0-liter V6
Transmission . . . . 7-sp. Automatic
Tow Rating (lbs.) . . . .
Head/Leg Room (in.) Average-41.2/40.3
Interior Space (cu. ft.). . . . . –
Cargo Space (cu. ft.) Cramped-16
Wheelbase/Length (in.) 121.1/201.6

Ratings—10 Best, 1 Worst

Combo Crash Tests	—
Safety Features	10
Rollover	—
Preventive Maintenance	10
Repair Costs	2
Warranty	2
Fuel Economy	2
Complaints	—
Insurance Costs	5
OVERALL RATING	—

Mercedes-Benz GLE M-Class

Mercedes-Benz GLE M-Class

At-a-Glance

Status/Year Series Started... Appearance Change/2012
Twins . . . . –
Body Styles . . . . .SUV
Seating 5
Anti-Theft Device . . . Std. Active Immobil. & Pass. Alarm
Parking Index Rating . . . . Hard
Where Made. .Bremen, Germany
Fuel Factor:
  MPG Rating (city/hwy) . . . . Very Poor-18/24
  Driving Range (mi.) . . . . Very Long-498.9
  Fuel Type . . . . Premium
  Annual Fuel Cost . . . . Very High-$1,738
  Gas Guzzler Tax . . . . No
  Greenhouse Gas Emissions (tons/yr.). High-7.3
  Barrels of Oil Used per year High-16.5

How the Competition Rates

Competitors	Rating	Pg.
Audi Q5	5	90
BMW X5	6	101
Volvo XC60	10	269

Price Range

Price Range	Retail	Markup
GLE350	$51,100	8%
GLE350 4Matic	$53,600	8%
GLE400 4Matic	$64,600	8%
AMG GLE63	$99,950	8%

Safety Checklist

Crash Tests:
  Frontal. . . . . –
  Side. . . . . –
Airbags:
  Torso . . . . .Fr. & Rr. Pelvis/Torso from Seat
  Pelvis . . . . Front Pelvis/Torso from Seat
  Roll Sensing. . . . . Yes
  Knee Bolster . . . . .Standard Driver
Crash Avoidance:
  Collision Avoidance . . . . Std. DBS & Opt. CIB^
  Blind Spot Detection . . . . .Optional
  Lane Keeping Assist . . . . .Optional
  Backup Camera. Standard*
  Pedestrian Crash Avoidance . . . . None
General:
  Auto. Crash Notification. . . . . . . .Operator Assist.-Fee
  Day Running Lamps . . . . Standard
Safety Belt/Restraint:
  Dynamic Head Restraints . . . . None
  Adjustable Belt. . . . . Standard Front

^Warning feature does not meet government standards.
*Backup camera does not meet government standards.

Mercedes-Benz GLE M-Class

Specifications

Drive. . . . . .RWD
Engine 3.5-liter V6
Transmission . . . . 7-sp. Automatic
Tow Rating (lbs.) Average-6600
Head/Leg Room (in.) . . . . Very Cramped-38.9/40.3
Interior Space (cu. ft.). . . . . –
Cargo Space (cu. ft.) . . . . Very Roomy-38.2
Wheelbase/Length (in.) 114.8/189.1

Ratings—10 Best, 1 Worst

Combo Crash Tests	—
Safety Features	9
Rollover	—
Preventive Maintenance	4
Repair Costs	1
Warranty	2
Fuel Economy	2
Complaints	4
Insurance Costs	5
OVERALL RATING	—

Mercedes-Benz S-Class

At-a-Glance

Status/Year Series Started. Unchanged/2014
Twins . . . . –
Body Styles . . . . .Sedan, Coupe
Seating. 5
Anti-Theft Device . . . Std. Active Immobil. & Pass. Alarm
Parking Index Rating . . . . Very Hard
Where Made. . . . . Sindelfingen, Germany

Fuel Factor:
  MPG Rating (city/hwy) . . . . Very Poor-17/26
  Driving Range (mi.) Average-424.9
  Fuel Type. . . . . Premium
  Annual Fuel Cost . . . . Very High-$1,751
  Gas Guzzler Tax . . . . No
  Greenhouse Gas Emissions (tons/yr.). . . Very High-9.0
  Barrels of Oil Used per year High-16.5

How the Competition Rates

Competitors	Rating	Pg.
BMW 7 Series	–	97
Cadillac XTS	9	110
Infiniti Q50	5	168

Price Range

	Retail	Markup
S550	$94,400	8%
S550 4Matic	$119,900	8%
S600	$166,900	8%
S65 AMG	$222,000	8%

Mercedes-Benz S-Class

Safety Checklist

Crash Tests:
  Frontal. . . . . –
  Side. . . . . –
Airbags:
  Torso . . . . Fr. & Rr. Torso from Seat
  Pelvis . . . . None
  Roll Sensing. . . . . Yes
  Knee Bolster . . . . Standard Front
Crash Avoidance:
  Collision Avoidance . . . . Standard CIB & DBS
  Blind Spot Detection . . . . .Optional
  Lane Keeping Assist . . . . .Optional
  Backup Camera. . . . . Standard*
  Pedestrian Crash Avoidance . . . . .Optional
General:
  Auto. Crash Notification . . . . .Operator Assist.-Fee
  Day Running Lamps . . . . Standard
Safety Belt/Restraint:
  Dynamic Head Restraints . . . . None
  Adjustable Belt. . . . . Standard Front

^Warning feature does not meet government standards.
*Backup camera does not meet government standards.

Mercedes-Benz S-Class

Specifications

Drive. . . . . .RWD
Engine 4.7-liter V8
Transmission . . . . 7-sp. Automatic
Tow Rating (lbs.) . . . . –
Head/Leg Room (in.) Cramped-39.7/41.4
Interior Space (cu. ft.). Roomy-112
Cargo Space (cu. ft.) Cramped-16.5
Wheelbase/Length (in.) 124.6/206.5

Ratings—10 Best, 1 Worst

Combo Crash Tests	—
Safety Features	3
Rollover	—
Preventive Maintenance	1
Repair Costs	4
Warranty	9
Fuel Economy	7
Complaints	—
Insurance Costs	5

OVERALL RATING —

Mini Cooper

Mini Cooper

At-a-Glance

Status/Year Series Started	All New/2016
Twins	—
Body Styles	Sedan
Seating	4
Anti-Theft Device	Std. Passive Alarm Only
Parking Index Rating	Very Easy
Where Made	Oxford, England

Fuel Factor:

MPG Rating (city/hwy)	Good-27/32
Driving Range (mi.)	Very Short-336.9
Fuel Type	Premium
Annual Fuel Cost	Average-$1,214
Gas Guzzler Tax	No
Greenhouse Gas Emissions (tons/yr.)	Low-5.2
Barrels of Oil Used per year	Average-11.4

How the Competition Rates

Competitors	Rating	Pg.
Chevrolet Sonic	10	119
Kia Soul	7	185
Volkswagen Beetle	3	260

Price Range

	Retail	Markup
Base Hatchback	$20,700	5%
S Coupe	$24,100	9%
S Hatchback	$25,100	9%
John Cooper Works Hatchback	$30,600	12%

Safety Checklist

Crash Tests:

Frontal	—
Side	—

Airbags:

Torso	Front Head/Torso from Seat
Pelvis	None
Roll Sensing	Yes
Knee Bolster	Standard Driver

Crash Avoidance:

Collision Avoidance	Optional CIB & DBS^
Blind Spot Detection	None
Lane Keeping Assist	None
Backup Camera	Optional*
Pedestrian Crash Avoidance	Optional

General:

Auto. Crash Notification	None
Day Running Lamps	Standard

Safety Belt/Restraint:

Dynamic Head Restraints	None
Adjustable Belt	None

^Warning feature does not meet government standards.
*Backup camera does not meet government standards.

Mini Cooper

Specifications

Drive	FWD
Engine	1.5-liter I3
Transmission	6-sp. Automatic
Tow Rating (lbs.)	—
Head/Leg Room (in.)	Average-39.9/41.4
Interior Space (cu. ft.)	Very Cramped-84
Cargo Space (cu. ft.)	Very Cramped-9
Wheelbase/Length (in.)	101.1/157.4

Ratings—10 Best, 1 Worst

Combo Crash Tests	—
Safety Features	2
Rollover	—
Preventive Maintenance	1
Repair Costs	6
Warranty	9
Fuel Economy	8
Complaints	10
Insurance Costs	5
OVERALL RATING	**—**

Mini Countryman

Mini Countryman

At-a-Glance

Status/Year Series Started. Unchanged/2012
Twins . . . . –
Body Styles . . . . Hatchback
Seating 5
Anti-Theft Device . . . . Std. Passive Alarm Only
Parking Index Rating . . . . Easy
Where Made. . . . . Oxford, England
Fuel Factor:
  MPG Rating (city/hwy) Good-27/34
  Driving Range (mi.) . . . . Very Short-369.0
  Fuel Type. . . . . Premium
  Annual Fuel Cost . . . . Low-$1,185
  Gas Guzzler Tax . . . . No
  Greenhouse Gas Emissions (tons/yr.). Average-6.0
  Barrels of Oil Used per year Average-11.0

How the Competition Rates

Competitors	Rating	Pg.
Kia Soul	7	185
Nissan Juke	2	225
Subaru Impreza	5	241

Price Range	Retail	Markup
Base	$22,750	5%
S	$26,100	9%
S ALL4	$27,850	9%
John Cooper Works ALL4	$35,350	12%

Safety Checklist

Crash Tests:
  Frontal. . . . . –
  Side. . . . . –
Airbags:
  Torso .Front Torso from Seat
  Pelvis . . . . None
  Roll Sensing. . . . . Yes
  Knee Bolster . . . . .Standard Passenger
Crash Avoidance:
  Collision Avoidance . . . . None
  Blind Spot Detection . . . . None
  Lane Keeping Assist . . . . None
  Backup Camera. . . . . None
  Pedestrian Crash Avoidance . . . . None
General:
  Auto. Crash Notification . . . . None
  Day Running Lamps . . . . Standard
Safety Belt/Restraint:
  Dynamic Head Restraints . . . . None
  Adjustable Belt. . . . . None

^Warning feature does not meet government standards.
*Backup camera does not meet government standards.

Specifications

Drive. . . . . .FWD
Engine 1.6-liter I4
Transmission . . . . 6-sp. Manual
Tow Rating (lbs.) . . . . –
Head/Leg Room (in.) Cramped-39.9/40.4
Interior Space (cu. ft.). . . . . .Very Cramped-87
Cargo Space (cu. ft.). Average-17.5
Wheelbase/Length (in.) 102.2/162.2

Mitsubishi Lancer

Ratings—10 Best, 1 Worst

Combo Crash Tests	2
Safety Features	2
Rollover	7
Preventive Maintenance	9
Repair Costs	4
Warranty	10
Fuel Economy	7
Complaints	6
Insurance Costs	1
OVERALL RATING	**4**

Mitsubishi Lancer

Mitsubishi Lancer

At-a-Glance

Status/Year Series Started	Unchanged/2008
Twins	–
Body Styles	Sedan
Seating	5
Anti-Theft Device	Std. Pass. Immobil. & Alarm
Parking Index Rating	Very Easy
Where Made	Mizushima, Japan

Fuel Factor:

MPG Rating (city/hwy)	Good-26/34
Driving Range (mi.)	Long-450.7
Fuel Type	Regular
Annual Fuel Cost	Low-$1,083
Gas Guzzler Tax	No
Greenhouse Gas Emissions (tons/yr.)	Average-6.2
Barrels of Oil Used per year	Average-11.4

How the Competition Rates

Competitors	Rating	Pg.
Honda Civic	–	149
Mazda Mazda3	8	204
Subaru Impreza	5	241

Price Range

	Retail	Markup
ES MT	$16,660	
GT AT	$21,595	4%
Ralliart AWD	$29,495	4%
Evolution MR Touring AWD	$40,995	5%

Safety Checklist

Crash Tests:

Frontal	Poor
Side	Very Poor

Airbags:

Torso	Front Pelvis/Torso from Seat
Pelvis	Front Pelvis/Torso from Seat
Roll Sensing	No
Knee Bolster	Standard Driver

Crash Avoidance:

Collision Avoidance	None
Blind Spot Detection	None
Lane Keeping Assist	None
Backup Camera	Optional*
Pedestrian Crash Avoidance	None

General:

Auto. Crash Notification	None
Day Running Lamps	Optional

Safety Belt/Restraint:

Dynamic Head Restraints	None
Adjustable Belt	Standard Front

^Warning feature does not meet government standards.
*Backup camera does not meet government standards.

Mitsubishi Lancer

Specifications

Drive	FWD
Engine	2.0-liter I4
Transmission	CVT
Tow Rating (lbs.)	–
Head/Leg Room (in.)	Average-39.6/42.3
Interior Space (cu. ft.)	Cramped-93.5
Cargo Space (cu. ft.)	Very Cramped-12.3
Wheelbase/Length (in.)	103.7/180

Ratings—10 Best, 1 Worst

Combo Crash Tests	2
Safety Features	2
Rollover	4
Preventive Maintenance	8
Repair Costs	6
Warranty	10
Fuel Economy	10
Complaints	3
Insurance Costs	1
OVERALL RATING	**4**

Mitsubishi Mirage

Mitsubishi Mirage

At-a-Glance

Status/Year Series Started. . . . . On Hold/2014
Twins . . . . —
Body Styles . . . . Hatchback
Seating 5
Anti-Theft Device Standard Pass. Immobil. & Active Alarm
Parking Index Rating . . . . Very Easy
Where Made. . . . . Laem Chabang, Thailand
Fuel Factor:
MPG Rating (city/hwy) . . . . Very Good-37/44
Driving Range (mi.) . . . . Very Short-366.6
Fuel Type . . . . Regular
Annual Fuel Cost . . . . Very Low-$790
Gas Guzzler Tax . . . . No
Greenhouse Gas Emissions (tons/yr.) . . . . Very Low-4.5
Barrels of Oil Used per year . . . . Very Low-8.2

How the Competition Rates

Competitors	Rating	Pg.
Ford Fiesta	1	141
Nissan Versa	3	234
Toyota Yaris	6	259

Price Range	Retail	Markup
DE MT	$12,995	2%
DE AT	$14,095	2%
ES MT	$14,295	2%
ES AT	$15,395	2%

Safety Checklist

Crash Tests:
Frontal . . . . Poor
Side . . . . Very Poor
Airbags:
Torso . . . . Front Pelvis/Torso from Seat
Pelvis . . . . Front Pelvis/Torso from Seat
Roll Sensing . . . . No
Knee Bolster . . . . Standard Driver
Crash Avoidance:
Collision Avoidance . . . . None
Blind Spot Detection . . . . None
Lane Keeping Assist . . . . None
Backup Camera . . . . None
Pedestrian Crash Avoidance . . . . None
General:
Auto. Crash Notification . . . . None
Day Running Lamps . . . . None
Safety Belt/Restraint:
Dynamic Head Restraints . . . . None
Adjustable Belt . . . . Standard Front

^Warning feature does not meet government standards.
*Backup camera does not meet government standards.

Mitsubishi Mirage

Specifications

Drive. . . . . FWD
Engine 1.2-liter I3
Transmission . . . . CVT
Tow Rating (lbs.) . . . . —
Head/Leg Room (in.) Cramped-39.1/41.7
Interior Space (cu. ft.). . . . . Very Cramped-86.1
Cargo Space (cu. ft.) Average-17.2
Wheelbase/Length (in.) 96.5/148.8

Mitsubishi Outlander

Ratings—10 Best, 1 Worst

Combo Crash Tests	5
Safety Features	6
Rollover	4
Preventive Maintenance	4
Repair Costs	7
Warranty	10
Fuel Economy	5
Complaints	2
Insurance Costs	1
OVERALL RATING	**4**

Mitsubishi Outlander

Mitsubishi Outlander

At-a-Glance

Status/Year Series Started. . . Appearance Change/2014
Twins . . . . –
Body Styles . . . . .SUV
Seating 7
Anti-Theft Device . . . . .Std. Pass. Immobil. & Alarm
Parking Index Rating . . . . Easy
Where Made. . . . . . .Mizushima, Japan / Okazaki, Japan
Fuel Factor:
  MPG Rating (city/hwy) Average-24/29
  Driving Range (mi.) Average-411.1
  Fuel Type . . . . Regular
  Annual Fuel Cost . . . . .Average-$1,211
  Gas Guzzler Tax . . . . No
  Greenhouse Gas Emissions (tons/yr.) Average-6.9
  Barrels of Oil Used per year Average-12.7

How the Competition Rates

Competitors	Rating	Pg.
Hyundai Santa Fe	–	163
Nissan Pathfinder	1	229
Toyota Highlander	7	250

Price Range	Retail	Markup
ES 2WD	$22,995	3%
SE 2WD	$23,995	3%
SE AWD	$25,995	3%
GT AWD	$30,995	3%

Safety Checklist

Crash Tests:
  Frontal. . . . . .Average
  Side. . . . . .Poor
Airbags:
  Torso . . . . Front Pelvis/Torso from Seat
  Pelvis . . . . Front Pelvis/Torso from Seat
  Roll Sensing. . . . . Yes
  Knee Bolster . . . . .Standard Driver
Crash Avoidance:
  Collision Avoidance . . . . Optional CIB & DBS
  Blind Spot Detection . . . . None
  Lane Keeping Assist . . . . Warning Only Optional
  Backup Camera . . . . .Optional*
  Pedestrian Crash Avoidance . . . . None
General:
  Auto. Crash Notification. . . . . None
  Day Running Lamps . . . . None
Safety Belt/Restraint:
  Dynamic Head Restraints . . . . None
  Adjustable Belt. . . . . Standard Front

^Warning feature does not meet government standards.
*Backup camera does not meet government standards.

Mitsubishi Outlander

Specifications

Drive. 4WD
Engine 2.4-liter I4
Transmission . . . . CVT
Tow Rating (lbs.) . . . . .Very Low-1500
Head/Leg Room (in.) Average-40.6/40.9
Interior Space (cu. ft.). Roomy-128.2
Cargo Space (cu. ft.) . . . . Very Cramped-10.3
Wheelbase/Length (in.) 105.1/183.3

Ratings—10 Best, 1 Worst

Combo Crash Tests	4
Safety Features	3
Rollover	4
Preventive Maintenance	7
Repair Costs	3
Warranty	10
Fuel Economy	6
Complaints	5
Insurance Costs	1
OVERALL RATING	**3**

Mitsubishi Outlander Sport

Mitsubishi Outlander Sport

At-a-Glance

Status/Year Series Started... Appearance Change/2013
Twins . . . . –
Body Styles . . . . .SUV
Seating 5
Anti-Theft Device . . . . .Std. Pass. Immobil. & Alarm
Parking Index Rating . . . . Very Easy
Where Made. . . . . Normal, IL

Fuel Factor:
MPG Rating (city/hwy) Average-25/32
Driving Range (mi.) Average-424.3
Fuel Type . . . . Regular
Annual Fuel Cost .Low-$1,136
Gas Guzzler Tax . . . . No
Greenhouse Gas Emissions (tons/yr.) Average-6.4
Barrels of Oil Used per year Average-11.8

How the Competition Rates

Competitors	Rating	Pg.
Acura RDX	10	83
Hyundai Santa Fe Sport	5	164
Jeep Cherokee	7	173

Price Range

	Retail	Markup
ES2.0L 2WD MT	$19,595	3%
ES 2.4L 2WD AT	$21,295	3%
SE 2.0L 2WD AT	$24,195	3%
SE 4WD	$24,995	3%

Safety Checklist

Crash Tests:
Frontal. . . . . .Poor
Side. . . . . .Poor

Airbags:
Torso . . . . Front Pelvis/Torso from Seat
Pelvis . . . . Front Pelvis/Torso from Seat
Roll Sensing. . . . . Yes
Knee Bolster . . . . .Standard Driver

Crash Avoidance:
Collision Avoidance . . . . None
Blind Spot Detection . . . . None
Lane Keeping Assist . . . . None
Backup Camera .Optional*
Pedestrian Crash Avoidance . . . . None

General:
Auto. Crash Notification . . . . None
Day Running Lamps . . . . .Optional

Safety Belt/Restraint:
Dynamic Head Restraints . . . . None
Adjustable Belt. . . . . Standard Front

^Warning feature does not meet government standards.
*Backup camera does not meet government standards.

Mitsubishi Outlander Sport

Specifications

Drive. . . . . .FWD
Engine 2.0-liter I4
Transmission . . . . CVT
Tow Rating (lbs.) . . . . –
Head/Leg Room (in.) Cramped-39.4/41.6
Interior Space (cu. ft.). Average-97.5
Cargo Space (cu. ft.) Average-21.7
Wheelbase/Length (in.) 105.1/169.1

Nissan 370Z

Ratings—10 Best, 1 Worst

Combo Crash Tests	—
Safety Features	1
Rollover	—
Preventive Maintenance	9
Repair Costs	3
Warranty	1
Fuel Economy	3
Complaints	4
Insurance Costs	3

OVERALL RATING —

Nissan 370Z

Nissan 370Z

Safety Checklist

Crash Tests:
Frontal . . . . −
Side . . . . −

Airbags:
Torso . . . . Front Pelvis/Torso from Seat
Pelvis . . . . Front Pelvis/Torso from Seat
Roll Sensing . . . . No
Knee Bolster . . . . None

Crash Avoidance:
Collision Avoidance . . . . None
Blind Spot Detection . . . . None
Lane Keeping Assist . . . . None
Backup Camera . . . . Optional*
Pedestrian Crash Avoidance . . . . None

General:
Auto. Crash Notification . . . . None
Day Running Lamps . . . . Standard

Safety Belt/Restraint:
Dynamic Head Restraints . . . . Standard Front
Adjustable Belt . . . . None

^Warning feature does not meet government standards.
*Backup camera does not meet government standards.

At-a-Glance

Status/Year Series Started Unchanged/2010
Twins . . . . −
Body Styles . . . . Coupe, Convertible
Seating 2
Anti-Theft Device . . . . Std. Pass. Immobil. & Alarm
Parking Index Rating . . . . Very Easy
Where Made . . . . Tochigi, Japan

Fuel Factor:
MPG Rating (city/hwy) Poor-19/26
Driving Range (mi.) Average-410.8
Fuel Type . . . . Premium
Annual Fuel Cost . . . . Very High-$1,630
Gas Guzzler Tax . . . . No
Greenhouse Gas Emissions (tons/yr.) High-7.6
Barrels of Oil Used per year High-15.7

Nissan 370Z

How the Competition Rates

Competitors	Rating	Pg.
Hyundai Genesis	7	162
Mazda MX-5	—	206
Scion FR-S	3	237

Price Range

Price Range	Retail	Markup
Base Coupe MT	$29,990	8
Sport Coupe AT	$34,870	8
Nismo Tech Coupe AT	$46,790	8
Tourinhg Sport Roadster AT	$49,400	8

Specifications

Drive . . . . RWD
Engine 3.7-liter V6
Transmission . . . . 7-sp. Automatic
Tow Rating (lbs.) . . . . Very Low-0
Head/Leg Room (in.) Cramped-38.2/42.9
Interior Space (cu. ft.) . . . . Very Cramped-51.6
Cargo Space (cu. ft.) . . . . Very Cramped-6.9
Wheelbase/Length (in.) 100.4/167.5

Ratings—10 Best, 1 Worst

Combo Crash Tests	6
Safety Features	6
Rollover	9
Preventive Maintenance	5
Repair Costs	8
Warranty	1
Fuel Economy	8
Complaints	5
Insurance Costs	5
OVERALL RATING	**7**

Nissan Altima

Nissan Altima

At-a-Glance

Status/Year Series Started...	Appearance Change/2013
Twins	–
Body Styles	Sedan, Coupe
Seating	5
Anti-Theft Device	Std. Pass. Immobil. & Alarm
Parking Index Rating	Easy
Where Made	Smyrna, TN / Canton, MS

Fuel Factor:

MPG Rating (city/hwy)	Good-27/38
Driving Range (mi.)	Very Long-558.8
Fuel Type	Regular
Annual Fuel Cost	Very Low-$1,015
Gas Guzzler Tax	No
Greenhouse Gas Emissions (tons/yr.)	Low-5.8
Barrels of Oil Used per year	Low-10.6

How the Competition Rates

Competitors	Rating	Pg.
Honda Accord	10	148
Kia Optima	9	181
Toyota Camry	7	248

Price Range

Price Range	Retail	Markup
Base	$22,300	6%
S 2.5L	$22,560	8%
SV 3.5L	$29,830	8%
SL 3.5L	$31,950	8%

Safety Checklist

Crash Tests:
Frontal	Very Good
Side	Very Poor

Airbags:
Torso	Front Pelvis/Torso from Seat
Pelvis	Front Pelvis/Torso from Seat
Roll Sensing	Yes
Knee Bolster	*

Crash Avoidance:
Collision Avoidance	Optional CIB & DBS^
Blind Spot Detection	Optional
Lane Keeping Assist	Warning Only Optional
Backup Camera	Optional*
Pedestrian Crash Avoidance	None

General:
Auto. Crash Notification	None
Day Running Lamps	None

Safety Belt/Restraint:
Dynamic Head Restraints	None
Adjustable Belt	Standard Front

^Warning feature does not meet government standards.
*Backup camera does not meet government standards.

Nissan Altima

Specifications

Drive	FWD
Engine	2.5-liter I4
Transmission	6-sp. Automatic
Tow Rating (lbs.)	–
Head/Leg Room (in.)	Very Roomy-40/45
Interior Space (cu. ft.)	Average-101.9
Cargo Space (cu. ft.)	Cramped-15.4
Wheelbase/Length (in.)	109.3/191.5

Nissan Armada

Ratings—10 Best, 1 Worst

Combo Crash Tests	—
Safety Features	1
Rollover	—
Preventive Maintenance	3
Repair Costs	4
Warranty	1
Fuel Economy	1
Complaints	4
Insurance Costs	10

OVERALL RATING   —

Nissan Armada

At-a-Glance

Status/Year Series Started.......... Unchanged/2004
Twins . . . . –
Body Styles . . . . SUV
Seating 7/8
Anti-Theft Device . . . . Std. Pass. Immobil. & Alarm
Parking Index Rating . . . . Very Hard
Where Made. . . . . Canton, MS
Fuel Factor:
  MPG Rating (city/hwy) . . . . Very Poor-13/19
  Driving Range (mi.) Average-424.3
  Fuel Type . . . . Regular
  Annual Fuel Cost . . . . Very High-$2,079
  Gas Guzzler Tax . . . . No
  Greenhouse Gas Emissions (tons/yr.). . Very High-12.0
  Barrels of Oil Used per year . . . . Very High-22.0

How the Competition Rates

Competitors	Rating	Pg.
Chevrolet Suburban	3	121
Ford Expedition	7	138
Toyota Sequoia	–	255

Price Range

	Retail	Markup
SV 2WD	$38,410	10%
SL 2WD	$43,500	9%
SL 4WD	$46,400	9%
Platinum 4WD	$53,680	9%

Safety Checklist

Crash Tests:
  Frontal . . . . –
  Side . . . . –
Airbags:
  Torso . . . . Front Pelvis/Torso from Seat
  Pelvis . . . . Front Pelvis/Torso from Seat
  Roll Sensing. . . . . No
  Knee Bolster . . . . None
Crash Avoidance:
  Collision Avoidance . . . . None
  Blind Spot Detection . . . . None
  Lane Keeping Assist . . . . None
  Backup Camera . . . . None
  Pedestrian Crash Avoidance . . . . None
General:
  Auto. Crash Notification . . . . None
  Day Running Lamps . . . . None
Safety Belt/Restraint:
  Dynamic Head Restraints . . . . Standard Front
  Adjustable Belt. . . . . Standard Front and Rear

^Warning feature does not meet government standards.
*Backup camera does not meet government standards.

Nissan Armada

Specifications

Drive. . . . . .RWD
Engine 5.6-liter V8
Transmission . . . . 5-sp. Automatic
Tow Rating (lbs.) High-8200
Head/Leg Room (in.) Roomy-41/41.8
Interior Space (cu. ft.). . . . . –
Cargo Space (cu. ft.) Average-20
Wheelbase/Length (in.) 123.2/207.7

Ratings—10 Best, 1 Worst

Combo Crash Tests	—
Safety Features	2
Rollover	—
Preventive Maintenance	3
Repair Costs	8
Warranty	1
Fuel Economy	1
Complaints	6
Insurance Costs	5
OVERALL RATING	**—**

Nissan Frontier

Nissan Frontier

At-a-Glance

Status/Year Series Started. Unchanged/2005
Twins . . . . –
Body Styles . . . . Pickup
Seating 5
Anti-Theft Device . . . . .Std. Pass. Immobil. & Alarm
Parking Index Rating . . . . Very Hard
Where Made. . . . . .Canton, MS
Fuel Factor:
  MPG Rating (city/hwy) . . . . Very Poor-15/21
  Driving Range (mi.) . . . . .Very Short-363.2
  Fuel Type. . . . . Regular
  Annual Fuel Cost . . . . Very High-$1,830
  Gas Guzzler Tax . . . . No
  Greenhouse Gas Emissions (tons/yr.). . Very High-10.5
  Barrels of Oil Used per year . . . . Very High-19.4

How the Competition Rates

Competitors	Rating	Pg.
Chevrolet Colorado	3	112
GMC Canyon	1	149
Toyota Tacoma	–	257

Price Range

	Retail	Markup
S King Cab I4 2WD MT	$17,990	4%
SV Crew Cab V6 2WD AT	$24,630	4%
PRO-4X Crew Cab 4WD AT	$32,560	7%
SL Crew Cab 4WD AT	$34,010	7%

Safety Checklist

Crash Tests:
  Frontal. . . . . –
  Side. . . . . –
Airbags:
  Torso . . . . Front Pelvis/Torso from Seat
  Pelvis . . . . Front Pelvis/Torso from Seat
  Roll Sensing. . . . . Yes
  Knee Bolster . . . . None
Crash Avoidance:
  Collision Avoidance . . . . None
  Blind Spot Detection . . . . None
  Lane Keeping Assist . . . . None
  Backup Camera .Optional*
  Pedestrian Crash Avoidance . . . . None
General:
  Auto. Crash Notification . . . . None
  Day Running Lamps . . . . None
Safety Belt/Restraint:
  Dynamic Head Restraints . . . . Standard Front
  Adjustable Belt . . . . Standard Front

^Warning feature does not meet government standards.
*Backup camera does not meet government standards.

Nissan Frontier

Specifications

Drive. 4WD
Engine 4.0-liter V6
Transmission . . . . 5-sp. Automatic
Tow Rating (lbs.) Average-6300
Head/Leg Room (in.) Average-39.7/42.4
Interior Space (cu. ft.). . . . . Very Cramped-87.7
Cargo Space (cu. ft.) . . . . .Very Roomy-33.5
Wheelbase/Length (in.) 125.9/205.5

Ratings—10 Best, 1 Worst

Combo Crash Tests	1
Safety Features	2
Rollover	5
Preventive Maintenance	5
Repair Costs	7
Warranty	1
Fuel Economy	7
Complaints	8
Insurance Costs	5
OVERALL RATING	**2**

Nissan Juke

Nissan Juke

At-a-Glance

Status/Year Series Started. Unchanged/2011
Twins . . . . –
Body Styles . . . . .SUV
Seating 5
Anti-Theft Device . . . . .Std. Pass. Immobil. & Alarm
Parking Index Rating . . . . Very Easy
Where Made. . . . . Oppama, Japan
Fuel Factor:
　MPG Rating (city/hwy) Good-26/31
　Driving Range (mi.) . . . . .Very Short-330.8
　Fuel Type . . . . Premium
　Annual Fuel Cost . . . . .Average-$1,257
　Gas Guzzler Tax . . . . No
　Greenhouse Gas Emissions (tons/yr.) Average-6.5
　Barrels of Oil Used per year Average-11.8

How the Competition Rates

Competitors	Rating	Pg.
Ford Escape	5	137
Kia Soul	7	185
Mitsubishi Outlander Sport	3	220

Price Range

Price Range	Retail	Markup
S FWD	$20,250	4%
SV FWD	$22,300	4%
SL AWD	$26,740	4%
NISMO RS AWD	$30,020	4%

Safety Checklist

Crash Tests:
　Frontal. . . . . Very Poor
　Side. . . . . Very Poor
Airbags:
　Torso . . . . Front Pelvis/Torso from Seat
　Pelvis . . . . Front Pelvis/Torso from Seat
　Roll Sensing. . . . . No
　Knee Bolster . . . . None
Crash Avoidance:
　Collision Avoidance . . . . None
　Blind Spot Detection . . . . None
　Lane Keeping Assist . . . . None
　Backup Camera. . . . . Standard*
　Pedestrian Crash Avoidance . . . . None
General:
　Auto. Crash Notification . . . . None
　Day Running Lamps . . . . .Optional
Safety Belt/Restraint:
　Dynamic Head Restraints . . . . Standard Front
　Adjustable Belt. . . . . Standard Front

^Warning feature does not meet government standards.
*Backup camera does not meet government standards.

Nissan Juke

Specifications

Drive. . . . . .AWD
Engine 1.6-liter I4
Transmission . . . . CVT
Tow Rating (lbs.) . . . . –
Head/Leg Room (in.) Average-39.6/42.1
Interior Space (cu. ft.). . . . . .Very Cramped-87
Cargo Space (cu. ft.) . . . . Very Cramped-10.5
Wheelbase/Length (in.) 99.6/162.4

Nissan Leaf

Ratings—10 Best, 1 Worst

Combo Crash Tests	1
Safety Features	1
Rollover	8
Preventive Maintenance	8
Repair Costs	—
Warranty	1
Fuel Economy	10
Complaints	2
Insurance Costs	10
OVERALL RATING	**4**

Nissan Leaf

At-a-Glance

Status/Year Series Started Unchanged/2011
Twins . . . . –
Body Styles . . . . Hatchback
Seating 5
Anti-Theft Device . . . . Std. Pass. Immobil. & Alarm
Parking Index Rating . . . . Very Easy
Where Made . . . . Smyrna, TN
Fuel Factor:
MPG Rating (city/hwy) . . . . Very Good-126/101
Driving Range (mi.) Short-84
Fuel Type . . . . Electricity
Annual Fuel Cost . . . . Very Low-$370
Gas Guzzler Tax . . . . No
Greenhouse Gas Emissions (tons/yr.) . . . . Very Low-3.1
Barrels of Oil Used per year . . . . Very Low-0.2

How the Competition Rates

Competitors	Rating	Pg.
Chevrolet Volt	—	125
Ford C-MAX	5	135
Toyota Prius	—	251

Price Range

Price Range	Retail	Markup
S	$29,010	6%
SV	$32,100	6%
SL	$35,120	6%

Safety Checklist

Crash Tests:
Frontal . . . . Very Poor
Side . . . . Very Poor
Airbags:
Torso . . . . Front Pelvis/Torso from Seat
Pelvis . . . . Front Pelvis/Torso from Seat
Roll Sensing . . . . No
Knee Bolster . . . . None
Crash Avoidance:
Collision Avoidance . . . . None
Blind Spot Detection . . . . None
Lane Keeping Assist . . . . None
Backup Camera . . . . Standard*
Pedestrian Crash Avoidance . . . . None
General:
Auto. Crash Notification . . . . None
Day Running Lamps . . . . None
Safety Belt/Restraint:
Dynamic Head Restraints . . . . None
Adjustable Belt . . . . Standard Front

^Warning feature does not meet government standards.
*Backup camera does not meet government standards.

Nissan Leaf

Specifications

Drive . . . . FWD
Engine . . . . All Electric
Transmission . . . . —
Tow Rating (lbs.) . . . . Very Low-0
Head/Leg Room (in.) Roomy-41.2/42.1
Interior Space (cu. ft.) Cramped-92.4
Cargo Space (cu. ft.) Roomy-24
Wheelbase/Length (in.) 106.3/175

See page 277 for more detail.

Ratings—10 Best, 1 Worst

Combo Crash Tests	7
Safety Features	3
Rollover	10
Preventive Maintenance	6
Repair Costs	6
Warranty	1
Fuel Economy	5
Complaints	—
Insurance Costs	3
OVERALL RATING	**5**

Nissan Maxima

Nissan Maxima

At-a-Glance

Status/Year Series Started	All New/2016
Twins	–
Body Styles	Sedan
Seating	5
Anti-Theft Device	Std. Pass. Immobil. & Alarm
Parking Index Rating	Hard
Where Made	Smyrna, TN

Fuel Factor:

MPG Rating (city/hwy)	Average-22/30
Driving Range (mi.)	Long-450.0
Fuel Type	Premium
Annual Fuel Cost	High-$1,410
Gas Guzzler Tax	No
Greenhouse Gas Emissions (tons/yr.)	Average-6.0
Barrels of Oil Used per year	High-13.2

How the Competition Rates

Competitors	Rating	Pg.
Chevrolet Malibu	9	117
Ford Fusion	7	144
Honda Accord	10	148

Price Range	Retail	Markup
S	$32,410	8
SV	$34,390	8
SR	$37,670	8
Platinum	$39,860	8

Safety Checklist

Crash Tests:

Frontal	Good
Side	Good

Airbags:

Torso	Front Pelvis/Torso from Seat
Pelvis	Front Pelvis/Torso from Seat
Roll Sensing	No
Knee Bolster	None

Crash Avoidance:

Collision Avoidance	Optional CIB & DBS
Blind Spot Detection	Optional
Lane Keeping Assist	None
Backup Camera	Standard*
Pedestrian Crash Avoidance	None

General:

Auto. Crash Notification	None
Day Running Lamps	Standard

Safety Belt/Restraint:

Dynamic Head Restraints	None
Adjustable Belt	Standard Front

^Warning feature does not meet government standards.
*Backup camera does not meet government standards.

Nissan Maxima

Specifications

Drive	FWD
Engine	3.5-liter V6
Transmission	CVT
Tow Rating (lbs.)	–
Head/Leg Room (in.)	Roomy-39.4/45
Interior Space (cu. ft.)	Average-98.6
Cargo Space (cu. ft.)	Cramped-14.3
Wheelbase/Length (in.)	109.3/192.8

Ratings—10 Best, 1 Worst	
Combo Crash Tests	3
Safety Features	7
Rollover	5
Preventive Maintenance	8
Repair Costs	6
Warranty	1
Fuel Economy	4
Complaints	4
Insurance Costs	10
OVERALL RATING	**5**

Nissan Murano

Nissan Murano

At-a-Glance

Status/Year Series Started. Unchanged/2015
Twins . . . . –
Body Styles . . . . .SUV
Seating 5
Anti-Theft Device . . . . .Std. Pass. Immobil. & Alarm
Parking Index Rating . . . . Hard
Where Made. . . . . .Canton, MS
Fuel Factor:
  MPG Rating (city/hwy) Poor-21/28
  Driving Range (mi.) Long-449.6
  Fuel Type. . . . . Regular
  Annual Fuel Cost . . . . .Average-$1,331
  Gas Guzzler Tax . . . . No
  Greenhouse Gas Emissions (tons/yr.). High-7.5
  Barrels of Oil Used per year High-13.7

How the Competition Rates

Competitors	Rating	Pg.
Chevrolet Equinox	2	115
Ford Explorer	3	139
Honda Pilot	9	158

Price Range

Price Range	Retail	Markup
S FWD	$29,560	7%
SV FWD	$32,620	7%
SL AWD	$38,550	7%
Platinum AWD	$40,600	7%

Safety Checklist

Crash Tests:
  Frontal. . . . . Very Poor
  Side. . . . . .Average
Airbags:
  Torso . . . . Front Pelvis/Torso from Seat
  Pelvis . . . . Front Pelvis/Torso from Seat
  Roll Sensing. . . . . Yes
  Knee Bolster . . . . .Standard Driver
Crash Avoidance:
  Collision Avoidance . . . . Optional CIB & DBS
  Blind Spot Detection . . . . .Optional
  Lane Keeping Assist . . . . None
  Backup Camera . . . . Standard*
  Pedestrian Crash Avoidance . . . . None
General:
  Auto. Crash Notification . . . . None
  Day Running Lamps . . . . Standard
Safety Belt/Restraint:
  Dynamic Head Restraints . . . . None
  Adjustable Belt. . . . . Standard Front

^Warning feature does not meet government standards.
*Backup camera does not meet government standards.

Nissan Murano

Specifications

Drive. . . . . .AWD
Engine 3.5-liter V6
Transmission . . . . CVT
Tow Rating (lbs.) . . . . .Very Low-1500
Head/Leg Room (in.) Cramped-39.9/40.5
Interior Space (cu. ft.). Roomy-108.1
Cargo Space (cu. ft.) . . . . Very Roomy-39.6
Wheelbase/Length (in.) 111.2/192.4

Nissan Pathfinder

Ratings—10 Best, 1 Worst

Combo Crash Tests	5
Safety Features	3
Rollover	4
Preventive Maintenance	1
Repair Costs	5
Warranty	1
Fuel Economy	3
Complaints	2
Insurance Costs	10
OVERALL RATING	**1**

Nissan Pathfinder

Nissan Pathfinder

At-a-Glance

Status/Year Series Started. Unchanged/2013
Twins . . . . Infiniti QX60
Body Styles . . . . .SUV
Seating 7
Anti-Theft Device . . . . .Std. Pass. Immobil. & Alarm
Parking Index Rating . . . . Hard
Where Made. .Smyrna, TN

Fuel Factor:
MPG Rating (city/hwy) Poor-19/26
Driving Range (mi.) Average-421.6
Fuel Type. . . . . Regular
Annual Fuel Cost . . . . .High-$1,457
Gas Guzzler Tax . . . . No
Greenhouse Gas Emissions (tons/yr.). High-8.2
Barrels of Oil Used per year High-15.0

How the Competition Rates

Competitors	Rating	Pg.
Buick Enclave	5	102
Chevrolet Traverse	4	123
Toyota Highlander	7	250

Price Range	Retail	Markup
S 2WD	$29,510	8%
SV 2WD	$32,810	8%
SL 4WD	$37,750	8%
	$43,100	8%

Safety Checklist

Crash Tests:
Frontal. . . . . .Average
Side. . . . . .Average

Airbags:
Torso . . . . Front Pelvis/Torso from Seat
Pelvis . . . . Front Pelvis/Torso from Seat
Roll Sensing. . . . . Yes
Knee Bolster . . . . None

Crash Avoidance:
Collision Avoidance . . . . None
Blind Spot Detection . . . . .Optional
Lane Keeping Assist . . . . None
Backup Camera. . . . . Standard*
Pedestrian Crash Avoidance . . . . None

General:
Auto. Crash Notification . . . . None
Day Running Lamps . . . . None

Safety Belt/Restraint:
Dynamic Head Restraints . . . . None
Adjustable Belt. . . . . Standard Front and Rear

^Warning feature does not meet government standards.
*Backup camera does not meet government standards.

Nissan Pathfinder

Specifications

Drive. 4WD
Engine 3.5-liter V6
Transmission . . . . CVT
Tow Rating (lbs.) Low-5000
Head/Leg Room (in.) Roomy-41.1/42.3
Interior Space (cu. ft.). Roomy-157.8
Cargo Space (cu. ft.) Cramped-16
Wheelbase/Length (in.) 114.2/197.2

Ratings—10 Best, 1 Worst

Combo Crash Tests	—
Safety Features	2
Rollover	—
Preventive Maintenance	8
Repair Costs	6
Warranty	1
Fuel Economy	3
Complaints	6
Insurance Costs	5

OVERALL RATING   —

Nissan Quest

Nissan Quest

At-a-Glance

Status/Year Series Started Unchanged/2011
Twins . . . . –
Body Styles . . . . Minivan
Seating 7/8
Anti-Theft Device . . . . .Std. Pass. Immobil. & Alarm
Parking Index Rating . . . . .Average
Where Made. Kyushu, Japan

Fuel Factor:
MPG Rating (city/hwy) Poor-20/27
Driving Range (mi.) Long-452.8
Fuel Type . . . . Regular
Annual Fuel Cost . . . . .High-$1,391
Gas Guzzler Tax . . . . No
Greenhouse Gas Emissions (tons/yr.) High-8.2
Barrels of Oil Used per year High-15.0

How the Competition Rates

Competitors	Rating	Pg.
Chrysler Town and Country	3	128
Honda Odyssey	8	157
Toyota Sienna	3	256

Price Range

Price Range	Retail	Markup
S	$26,530	6%
SV	$30,280	7%
SL	$34,060	7%
Platinum	$43,180	8%

Safety Checklist

Crash Tests:
Frontal. . . . . –
Side. . . . . –

Airbags:
Torso . . . . Front Pelvis/Torso from Seat
Pelvis . . . . Front Pelvis/Torso from Seat
Roll Sensing. . . . . No
Knee Bolster . . . . None

Crash Avoidance:
Collision Avoidance . . . . None
Blind Spot Detection . . . . .Optional
Lane Keeping Assist . . . . None
Backup Camera . . . . .Optional*
Pedestrian Crash Avoidance . . . . None

General:
Auto. Crash Notification . . . . None
Day Running Lamps . . . . None

Safety Belt/Restraint:
Dynamic Head Restraints . . . . Standard Front
Adjustable Belt. . . . . Standard Front and Rear

^Warning feature does not meet government standards.
*Backup camera does not meet government standards.

Nissan Quest

Specifications

Drive. . . . . .FWD
Engine 3.5-liter V6
Transmission . . . . CVT
Tow Rating (lbs.) Low-3500
Head/Leg Room (in.) . . . . Very Roomy-42.1/43.8
Interior Space (cu. ft.). Roomy-177.8
Cargo Space (cu. ft.) . . . . Very Roomy-37.1
Wheelbase/Length (in.) 118.1/200.8

Nissan Rogue   Medium SUV

Ratings—10 Best, 1 Worst

Combo Crash Tests	1
Safety Features	6
Rollover	4
Preventive Maintenance	3
Repair Costs	4
Warranty	1
Fuel Economy	6
Complaints	8
Insurance Costs	5
OVERALL RATING	**2**

Nissan Rogue

Nissan Rogue

At-a-Glance

Status/Year Series Started. Unchanged/2014
Twins . . . . –
Body Styles . . . . .SUV
Seating. 5/7
Anti-Theft Device . . . . .Std. Pass. Immobil. & Alarm
Parking Index Rating . . . . .Average
Where Made. . . . . .Smyrna, TN
Fuel Factor:
  MPG Rating (city/hwy). Average-25/32
  Driving Range (mi.) Average-402.1
  Fuel Type. . . . . Regular
  Annual Fuel Cost . . . . .Low-$1,136
  Gas Guzzler Tax . . . . No
  Greenhouse Gas Emissions (tons/yr.). Average-6.4
  Barrels of Oil Used per year Average-11.8

How the Competition Rates

Competitors	Rating	Pg.
Kia Sorento	5	184
Mazda CX-5	3	202
Volvo XC60	10	269

Price Range

Price Range	Retail	Markup
S FWD	$23,040	6%
SV FWD	$24,490	6%
SV AWD	$25,840	6%
SL AWD	$29,630	6%

Safety Checklist

Crash Tests:
  Frontal. . . . . Very Poor
  Side. . . . . Very Poor
Airbags:
  Torso . . . . Front Pelvis/Torso from Seat
  Pelvis . . . . Front Pelvis/Torso from Seat
  Roll Sensing. . . . . Yes
  Knee Bolster . . . . None
Crash Avoidance:
  Collision Avoidance . . . . Optional CIB & DBS
  Blind Spot Detection . . . . .Optional
  Lane Keeping Assist . . . . Warning Only Optional
  Backup Camera. Standard*
  Pedestrian Crash Avoidance . . . . None
General:
  Auto. Crash Notification . . . . None
  Day Running Lamps . . . . Standard
Safety Belt/Restraint:
  Dynamic Head Restraints . . . . None
  Adjustable Belt. . . . . Standard Front

^Warning feature does not meet government standards.
*Backup camera does not meet government standards.

Nissan Rogue

Specifications

Drive. . . . . .AWD
Engine 2.5-liter I4
Transmission . . . . CVT
Tow Rating (lbs.) . . . . .Very Low-1000
Head/Leg Room (in.) . . . . Very Roomy-41.6/43
Interior Space (cu. ft.). Roomy-105.8
Cargo Space (cu. ft.) . . . . Very Cramped-9.4
Wheelbase/Length (in.) 106.5/182.3

Ratings—10 Best, 1 Worst	
Combo Crash Tests	3
Safety Features	3
Rollover	7
Preventive Maintenance	8
Repair Costs	9
Warranty	1
Fuel Economy	9
Complaints	8
Insurance Costs	5
OVERALL RATING	**6**

Nissan Sentra

Nissan Sentra

At-a-Glance

Status/Year Series Started... Appearance Change/2013
Twins . . . . –
Body Styles . . . . Sedan
Seating 5
Anti-Theft Device . . . . .Std. Pass. Immobil. & Alarm
Parking Index Rating . . . . Easy
Where Made. . .Aguascalientes, Mexico / Kyushu, Japan
Fuel Factor:
  MPG Rating (city/hwy) . . . . .Very Good-30/39
  Driving Range (mi.) Long-441.9
  Fuel Type . . . . Regular
  Annual Fuel Cost . . . . Very Low-$941
  Gas Guzzler Tax . . . . No
  Greenhouse Gas Emissions (tons/yr.). Low-5.3
  Barrels of Oil Used per year Low-9.7

How the Competition Rates

Competitors	Rating	Pg.
Chevrolet Cruze	–	114
Honda Civic	–	149
Toyota Corolla	9	249

Price Range	Retail	Markup
S MT	$16,480	3%
SV	$18,300	6%
SR	$19,910	6%
SL	$20,670	6%

Safety Checklist

Crash Tests:
  Frontal. . . . . Very Poor
  Side. . . . . .Average
Airbags:
  Torso . . . . Front Pelvis/Torso from Seat
  Pelvis . . . . Front Pelvis/Torso from Seat
  Roll Sensing. . . . . No
  Knee Bolster . . . . None
Crash Avoidance:
  Collision Avoidance . . . . Optional CIB & DBS^
  Blind Spot Detection . . . . .Optional
  Lane Keeping Assist . . . . None
  Backup Camera . . . . .Optional*
  Pedestrian Crash Avoidance . . . . None
General:
  Auto. Crash Notification . . . . .Optional
  Day Running Lamps . . . . None
Safety Belt/Restraint:
  Dynamic Head Restraints . . . . None
  Adjustable Belt. . . . . Standard Front

^Warning feature does not meet government standards.
*Backup camera does not meet government standards.

Nissan Sentra

Specifications

Drive. . . . . .FWD
Engine 2.0-liter I4
Transmission . . . . CVT
Tow Rating (lbs.) . . . . –
Head/Leg Room (in.) Average-39.4/42.5
Interior Space (cu. ft.). Cramped-95.9
Cargo Space (cu. ft.) Cramped-15.1
Wheelbase/Length (in.) 106.3/182.1

Ratings—10 Best, 1 Worst

Combo Crash Tests	—
Safety Features	3
Rollover	—
Preventive Maintenance	1
Repair Costs	6
Warranty	1
Fuel Economy	—
Complaints	—
Insurance Costs	5
OVERALL RATING	**—**

Nissan Titan

Nissan Titan

At-a-Glance

Status/Year Series Started	All New/2016
Twins	—
Body Styles	Pickup
Seating	6
Anti-Theft Device	Std. Pass. Immobil. & Alarm
Parking Index Rating	Very Hard
Where Made	Canton, MS

Fuel Factor:

MPG Rating (city/hwy)	—
Driving Range (mi.)	—
Fuel Type	—
Annual Fuel Cost	—
Gas Guzzler Tax	No
Greenhouse Gas Emissions (tons/yr.)	—
Barrels of Oil Used per year	—

How the Competition Rates

Competitors	Rating	Pg.
Chevrolet Silverado	5	118
Ford F-150	9	140
Toyota Tundra	—	258

Price Range

	Retail	Markup
S King Cab 2WD	$29,640	9%
SV King Cab 4WD	$34,790	9%
PRO-4X Crew Cab 4WD	$40,370	9%
SL Crew Cab 4WD	$43,860	9%

Safety Checklist

Crash Tests:

Frontal	—
Side	—

Airbags:

Torso	Front Pelvis/Torso from Seat
Pelvis	Front Pelvis/Torso from Seat
Roll Sensing	Yes
Knee Bolster	None

Crash Avoidance:

Collision Avoidance	None
Blind Spot Detection	Optional
Lane Keeping Assist	None
Backup Camera	Standard*
Pedestrian Crash Avoidance	None

General:

Auto. Crash Notification	None
Day Running Lamps	None

Safety Belt/Restraint:

Dynamic Head Restraints	Standard Front
Adjustable Belt	Standard Front

^Warning feature does not meet government standards.
*Backup camera does not meet government standards.

Specifications

Drive	4WD
Engine	5.0-liter V8
Transmission	6-sp. Automatic
Tow Rating (lbs.)	Very High-12038
Head/Leg Room (in.)	Roomy-41/41.8
Interior Space (cu. ft.)	—
Cargo Space (cu. ft.)	Very Roomy-58.1
Wheelbase/Length (in.)	151.6/242.7

Ratings—10 Best, 1 Worst

Combo Crash Tests	1
Safety Features	1
Rollover	6
Preventive Maintenance	9
Repair Costs	10
Warranty	1
Fuel Economy	9
Complaints	6
Insurance Costs	1
OVERALL RATING	**3**

Nissan Versa

Nissan Versa

At-a-Glance

Status/Year Series Started. Unchanged/2006
Twins . . . . –
Body Styles .Sedan, Hatchback
Seating 4
Anti-Theft Device . . . . .Std. Pass. Immobil.
Parking Index Rating . . . . Very Easy
Where Made. . .Aguascalientes, Mexico / Kyushu, Japan
Fuel Factor:
MPG Rating (city/hwy). . . . . .Very Good-31/40
Driving Range (mi.) . . . . .Very Short-372.5
Fuel Type. . . . . Regular
Annual Fuel Cost . . . . Very Low-$913
Gas Guzzler Tax . . . . No
Greenhouse Gas Emissions (tons/yr.). Low-5.1
Barrels of Oil Used per year Low-9.4

How the Competition Rates

Competitors	Rating	Pg.
Hyundai Accent	6	159
Kia Forte	5	180
Toyota Yaris	6	259

Price Range

	Retail	Markup
S MT	$11,990	8
S Plus	$13,990	8
SL Hatchback	$15,530	8
SL	$17,090	8

Safety Checklist

Crash Tests:
Frontal. . . . . Very Poor
Side. . . . . Very Poor
Airbags:
Torso . . . . Front Pelvis/Torso from Seat
Pelvis . . . . Front Pelvis/Torso from Seat
Roll Sensing. . . . . No
Knee Bolster . . . . None
Crash Avoidance:
Collision Avoidance . . . . None
Blind Spot Detection . . . . None
Lane Keeping Assist . . . . None
Backup Camera. Optional*
Pedestrian Crash Avoidance . . . . None
General:
Auto. Crash Notification . . . . None
Day Running Lamps . . . . None
Safety Belt/Restraint:
Dynamic Head Restraints . . . . None
Adjustable Belt. . . . . Standard Front

^Warning feature does not meet government standards.
*Backup camera does not meet government standards.

Nissan Versa

Specifications

Drive. . . . . .FWD
Engine 1.6-liter I4
Transmission . . . . .CVT
Tow Rating (lbs.) . . . . –
Head/Leg Room (in.) Average-39.8/41.8
Interior Space (cu. ft.). . . . . .Very Cramped-90.2
Cargo Space (cu. ft.) Cramped-14.9
Wheelbase/Length (in.). 102.4/175.4

Ratings—10 Best, 1 Worst

Combo Crash Tests	—
Safety Features	6
Rollover	—
Preventive Maintenance	—
Repair Costs	1
Warranty	6
Fuel Economy	2
Complaints	—
Insurance Costs	5
OVERALL RATING	—

Porsche Macan

Porsche Macan

At-a-Glance

Status/Year Series Started	Unchanged/2015
Twins	—
Body Styles	SUV
Seating	5
Anti-Theft Device	Std. Pass. Immobil. & Active Alarm
Parking Index Rating	Hard
Where Made	Leipzig, Germany

Fuel Factor:

MPG Rating (city/hwy)	Very Poor-17/23
Driving Range (mi.)	Short-381.4
Fuel Type	Premium
Annual Fuel Cost	Very High-$1,830
Gas Guzzler Tax	No
Greenhouse Gas Emissions (tons/yr.)	Very High-9.5
Barrels of Oil Used per year	Very High-17.3

How the Competition Rates

Competitors	Rating	Pg.
Audi Q3	—	89
BMW X1	—	99
Mercedes-Benz GLA-Class	—	210

Price Range	Retail	Markup
S	$49,900	10
Turbo	$72,300	10

Safety Checklist

Crash Tests:

Frontal	—
Side	—

Airbags:

Torso	Fr. & Rr. Torso from Seat
Pelvis	None
Roll Sensing	Yes
Knee Bolster	Standard Front

Crash Avoidance:

Collision Avoidance	Optional DBS^
Blind Spot Detection	Optional
Lane Keeping Assist	Optional
Backup Camera	Optional*
Pedestrian Crash Avoidance	None

General:

Auto. Crash Notification	None
Day Running Lamps	Standard

Safety Belt/Restraint:

Dynamic Head Restraints	None
Adjustable Belt	Standard Front

^Warning feature does not meet government standards.
*Backup camera does not meet government standards.

Porsche Macan

Specifications

Drive	AWD
Engine	3.0-liter V6
Transmission	7-sp. Automatic
Tow Rating (lbs.)	Low-4409
Head/Leg Room (in.)	—
Interior Space (cu. ft.)	—
Cargo Space (cu. ft.)	Average-17.7
Wheelbase/Length (in.)	110.51/184.29

Ratings—10 Best, 1 Worst

Combo Crash Tests	4
Safety Features	2
Rollover	2
Preventive Maintenance	9
Repair Costs	10
Warranty	4
Fuel Economy	1
Complaints	4
Insurance Costs	5
OVERALL RATING	**4**

Ram 1500

Ram 1500

At-a-Glance

Status/Year Series Started. Unchanged/2009
Twins . . . . –
Body Styles . . . . .Pickup
Seating 5/6
Anti-Theft Device . . . . Std. Pass. Immobil. & Alarm
Parking Index Rating . . . . Very Hard
Where Made. . . . . .Warren, MI / Saltillo, Mexico

Fuel Factor:
MPG Rating (city/hwy) . . . . Very Poor-13/19
Driving Range (mi.) Short-394.0
Fuel Type . . . . Regular
Annual Fuel Cost . . . . Very High-$2,079
Gas Guzzler Tax . . . . No
Greenhouse Gas Emissions (tons/yr.). . Very High-12.0
Barrels of Oil Used per year . . . . Very High-22.0

How the Competition Rates

Competitors	Rating	Pg.
Chevrolet Silverado	5	118
Ford F-150	9	140
Nissan Titan	–	233

Price Range

	Retail	Markup
Tradesman Reg. Cab 2WD	$25,965	4%
SLT Quad Cab 2WD	$33,995	6%
Sport Crew Cab 4WD	$44,850	9%
Laramie Longhorn Crew Cab 4WD	$50,895	10%

Safety Checklist

Crash Tests:
Frontal. . . . . .Poor
Side. . . . . .Good
Airbags:
Torso . . . . Front Pelvis/Torso from Seat
Pelvis . . . . Front Pelvis/Torso from Seat
Roll Sensing. . . . . Yes
Knee Bolster . . . . None
Crash Avoidance:
Collision Avoidance . . . . None
Blind Spot Detection . . . . None
Lane Keeping Assist . . . . None
Backup Camera . . . . Optional*
Pedestrian Crash Avoidance . . . . None
General:
Auto. Crash Notification . . . . None
Day Running Lamps . . . . None
Safety Belt/Restraint:
Dynamic Head Restraints . . . . None
Adjustable Belt . . . . Standard Front

^Warning feature does not meet government standards.
*Backup camera does not meet government standards.

Ram 1500

Specifications

Drive. 4WD
Engine 5.7-liter V8
Transmission . . . . 6-sp. Automatic
Tow Rating (lbs.) . . . . Very High-8807
Head/Leg Room (in.) Average-41/41
Interior Space (cu. ft.). Roomy-116.6
Cargo Space (cu. ft.) . . . . Very Roomy-57.5
Wheelbase/Length (in.) 140.5/229

Ratings—10 Best, 1 Worst	
Combo Crash Tests	4
Safety Features	1
Rollover	10
Preventive Maintenance	4
Repair Costs	5
Warranty	1
Fuel Economy	7
Complaints	7
Insurance Costs	1
OVERALL RATING	**3**

Scion FR-S

Scion FR-S

At-a-Glance

Status/Year Series Started	Unchanged/2013
Twins	–
Body Styles	Coupe
Seating	4
Anti-Theft Device	Std. Pass. Immobil.
Parking Index Rating	Very Easy
Where Made	Gunma, Japan

Fuel Factor:

MPG Rating (city/hwy)	Good-25/34
Driving Range (mi.)	Short-374.6
Fuel Type	Premium
Annual Fuel Cost	Average-$1,242
Gas Guzzler Tax	No
Greenhouse Gas Emissions (tons/yr.)	Average-6.4
Barrels of Oil Used per year	Average-11.8

How the Competition Rates

Competitors	Rating	Pg.
Hyundai Genesis	7	162
Mazda MX-5	–	206
Nissan 370Z	–	221

Price Range	Retail	Markup
Base MT	$25,305	5%
Base AT	$26,405	5%

Safety Checklist

Crash Tests:

Frontal	Average
Side	Very Poor

Airbags:

Torso	Front Pelvis/Torso from Seat
Pelvis	Front Pelvis/Torso from Seat
Roll Sensing	No
Knee Bolster	None

Crash Avoidance:

Collision Avoidance	None
Blind Spot Detection	None
Lane Keeping Assist	None
Backup Camera	None
Pedestrian Crash Avoidance	None

General:

Auto. Crash Notification	None
Day Running Lamps	Standard

Safety Belt/Restraint:

Dynamic Head Restraints	None
Adjustable Belt	None

^Warning feature does not meet government standards.
*Backup camera does not meet government standards.

Scion FR-S

Specifications

Drive	RWD
Engine	2.0-liter I4
Transmission	6-sp. Automatic
Tow Rating (lbs.)	–
Head/Leg Room (in.)	Very Cramped-37.1/41.9
Interior Space (cu. ft.)	Very Cramped-76.5
Cargo Space (cu. ft.)	Very Cramped-6.9
Wheelbase/Length (in.)	101.2/166.7

Ratings—10 Best, 1 Worst

Combo Crash Tests	6
Safety Features	2
Rollover	8
Preventive Maintenance	9
Repair Costs	6
Warranty	1
Fuel Economy	5
Complaints	10
Insurance Costs	1
OVERALL RATING	**5**

Scion tC

Scion tC

At-a-Glance

Status/Year Series Started. Unchanged/2011
Twins . . . . –
Body Styles . . . . Coupe
Seating 5
Anti-Theft Device . . . . Std. Pass. Immobil.
Parking Index Rating . . . . Easy
Where Made. . . . . Tsutsumi, Japan
Fuel Factor:
  MPG Rating (city/hwy) Average-23/31
  Driving Range (mi.) Short-377.3
  Fuel Type. . . . . Regular
  Annual Fuel Cost . . . . .Average-$1,211
  Gas Guzzler Tax . . . . No
  Greenhouse Gas Emissions (tons/yr.). Average-6.9
  Barrels of Oil Used per year Average-12.7

How the Competition Rates

Competitors	Rating	Pg.
Mazda Mazda3	8	204
Mitsubishi Lancer	4	217
Subaru Impreza	5	241

Price Range

	Retail	Markup
MT	$19,385	5%
AT	$20,535	5%

Safety Checklist

Crash Tests:
  Frontal. . . . . .Poor
  Side. . . . . Good
Airbags:
  Torso . . . . Front Pelvis/Torso from Seat
  Pelvis . . . . Front Pelvis/Torso from Seat
  Roll Sensing. . . . . No
  Knee Bolster . . . . Standard Front
Crash Avoidance:
  Collision Avoidance . . . . None
  Blind Spot Detection . . . . None
  Lane Keeping Assist . . . . None
  Backup Camera . . . . None
  Pedestrian Crash Avoidance . . . . None
General:
  Auto. Crash Notification . . . . None
  Day Running Lamps . . . . None
Safety Belt/Restraint:
  Dynamic Head Restraints . . . . Standard Front
  Adjustable Belt. . . . . None

^Warning feature does not meet government standards.
*Backup camera does not meet government standards.

Scion tC

Specifications

Drive. . . . . .FWD
Engine 2.5-liter I4
Transmission . . . . 6-sp. Automatic
Tow Rating (lbs.) . . . .–
Head/Leg Room (in.) . . . . Very Cramped-37.7/41.8
Interior Space (cu. ft.). . . . . Very Cramped-88.4
Cargo Space (cu. ft.) . . . . Very Roomy-34.5
Wheelbase/Length (in.) 106.3/176.6

Smart ForTwo

Ratings—10 Best, 1 Worst

Combo Crash Tests	—
Safety Features	3
Rollover	—
Preventive Maintenance	1
Repair Costs	4
Warranty	3
Fuel Economy	9
Complaints	—
Insurance Costs	5
OVERALL RATING	—

Smart ForTwo

At-a-Glance

Status/Year Series Started . . . . .All New/2016
Twins . . . . –
Body Styles . . . . Coupe
Seating 2
Anti-Theft Device . . . Std. Active Immobil. & Pass. Alarm
Parking Index Rating . . . . Very Easy
Where Made. Hambach, France
Fuel Factor:
 MPG Rating (city/hwy) . . . . .Very Good-34/39
 Driving Range (mi.) . . . . .Very Short-277.8
 Fuel Type . . . . Premium
 Annual Fuel Cost . . . . Very Low-$977
 Gas Guzzler Tax . . . . .No
 Greenhouse Gas Emissions (tons/yr.). . . .Very Low-4.1
 Barrels of Oil Used per year Low-9.1

How the Competition Rates

Competitors	Rating	Pg.
Fiat 500	4	133
Mini Cooper	–	215
Mitsubishi Mirage	4	218

Price Range

Price Range	Retail	Markup
pure	$13,270	8
passion Coupe	$14,930	8
passion Cabriolet	$17,930	8
Electric Coupe	$25,000	8

Safety Checklist

Crash Tests:
 Frontal . . . . –
 Side . . . . –
Airbags:
 Torso .Front Torso from Seat
 Pelvis . . . . None
 Roll Sensing. . . . . No
 Knee Bolster . . . . Standard Front
Crash Avoidance:
 Collision Avoidance . . . . Warning Only Optional
 Blind Spot Detection . . . . None
 Lane Keeping Assist . . . . .Optional
 Backup Camera .Optional*
 Pedestrian Crash Avoidance . . . . None
General:
 Auto. Crash Notification . . . . .Optional
 Day Running Lamps . . . . .Optional
Safety Belt/Restraint:
 Dynamic Head Restraints . . . . None
 Adjustable Belt. . . . . None

^Warning feature does not meet government standards.
*Backup camera does not meet government standards.

Smart ForTwo

Specifications

Drive. . . . . .RWD
Engine 1.0-liter I3
Transmission . . . . 5-sp. Automatic
Tow Rating (lbs.) . . . . –
Head/Leg Room (in.) Cramped-39.7/41.2
Interior Space (cu. ft.). . . . . Very Cramped-45.4
Cargo Space (cu. ft.). . . . . Very Cramped-7.8
Wheelbase/Length (in.) 73.5/106.1

Ratings—10 Best, 1 Worst

Combo Crash Tests	7
Safety Features	8
Rollover	4
Preventive Maintenance	4
Repair Costs	7
Warranty	2
Fuel Economy	6
Complaints	4
Insurance Costs	1
OVERALL RATING	**4**

Subaru Forester

Subaru Forester

At-a-Glance

Status/Year Series Started. Unchanged/2014
Twins . . . . –
Body Styles . . . . .SUV
Seating 5
Anti-Theft Device . . . Std. Pass. Immobil. & Active Alarm
Parking Index Rating . . . . Easy
Where Made. . . . . Lafayette, IN
Fuel Factor:
　MPG Rating (city/hwy) Average-24/32
　Driving Range (mi.) Long-430.0
　Fuel Type . . . . Regular
　Annual Fuel Cost . . . . Low-$1,165
　Gas Guzzler Tax . . . . No
　Greenhouse Gas Emissions (tons/yr.). Average-6.6
　Barrels of Oil Used per year Average-12.2

How the Competition Rates

Competitors	Rating	Pg.
Hyundai Tucson	7	166
Mazda CX-5	3	202
Toyota RAV4	5	254

Price Range	Retail	Markup
2.5i MT	$22,395	6%
2.5i Premium AT	$25,295	6%
2.5i Touring	$30,795	7%
2.0 XT Touring	$33,795	7%

Safety Checklist

Crash Tests:
　Frontal. . . . . .Poor
　Side. . . . . Good
Airbags:
　Torso . . . . Front Pelvis/Torso from Seat
　Pelvis . . . . Front Pelvis/Torso from Seat
　Roll Sensing. . . . . Yes
　Knee Bolster . . . . .Standard Driver
Crash Avoidance:
　Collision Avoidance . . . . Optional CIB & DBS
　Blind Spot Detection . . . . None
　Lane Keeping Assist . . . . Warning Only Optional
　Backup Camera . . . . Standard
　Pedestrian Crash Avoidance . . . . .Optional
General:
　Auto. Crash Notification . . . . .Optional
　Day Running Lamps . . . . Standard
Safety Belt/Restraint:
　Dynamic Head Restraints . . . . None
　Adjustable Belt. . . . . Standard Front

^Warning feature does not meet government standards.
*Backup camera does not meet government standards.

Subaru Forester

Specifications

Drive. . . . . .AWD
Engine 2.5-liter I4
Transmission . . . . CVT
Tow Rating (lbs.) . . . . .Very Low-1500
Head/Leg Room (in.) Roomy-41.4/43
Interior Space (cu. ft.). Roomy-113.1
Cargo Space (cu. ft.) . . . . Very Roomy-34.4
Wheelbase/Length (in.) 103.9/180.9

Subaru Impreza   Compact

Subaru Impreza

Ratings—10 Best, 1 Worst

Combo Crash Tests	4
Safety Features	6
Rollover	10
Preventive Maintenance	4
Repair Costs	8
Warranty	2
Fuel Economy	9
Complaints	7
Insurance Costs	1
OVERALL RATING	**5**

Subaru Impreza

At-a-Glance

Status/Year Series Started. Unchanged/2012
Twins . . . . –
Body Styles .Sedan, Hatchback
Seating 5
Anti-Theft Device . . . Std. Pass. Immobil. & Active Alarm
Parking Index Rating . . . . Very Easy
Where Made. . . . . Gunma, Japan
Fuel Factor:
  MPG Rating (city/hwy) . . . . .Very Good-28/37
  Driving Range (mi.) Long-455.9
  Fuel Type . . . . Regular
  Annual Fuel Cost . . . . .Very Low-$1,002
  Gas Guzzler Tax . . . . No
  Greenhouse Gas Emissions (tons/yr.) Low-5.8
  Barrels of Oil Used per year Low-10.6

How the Competition Rates

Competitors	Rating	Pg.
Dodge Dart	6	131
Honda Civic	–	149
Mitsubishi Lancer	4	217

Price Range

Price Range	Retail	Markup
2.0i Sedan MT	$18,295	5%
2.0i Premium Hatchback AT	$21,595	5%
2.0i Limited Sedan	$22,595	5%
2.0i Sport Limited Hatchback	$23,595	6%

Safety Checklist

Crash Tests:
  Frontal. . . . . Very Poor
  Side. . . . . .Good
Airbags:
  Torso . . . . Front Pelvis/Torso from Seat
  Pelvis . . . . Front Pelvis/Torso from Seat
  Roll Sensing. . . . . No
  Knee Bolster . . . . .Standard Driver
Crash Avoidance:
  Collision Avoidance . . . . Optional CIB & DBS
  Blind Spot Detection . . . . None
  Lane Keeping Assist . . . . Warning Only Optional
  Backup Camera . . . . Standard
  Pedestrian Crash Avoidance . . . . .Optional
General:
  Auto. Crash Notification . . . . .Optional
  Day Running Lamps . . . . Standard
Safety Belt/Restraint:
  Dynamic Head Restraints . . . . None
  Adjustable Belt. . . . . Standard Front

^Warning feature does not meet government standards.
*Backup camera does not meet government standards.

Subaru Impreza

Specifications

Drive. . . . . .AWD
Engine 2.0-liter I4
Transmission . . . . CVT
Tow Rating (lbs.) . . . . –
Head/Leg Room (in.) Roomy-39.8/43.5
Interior Space (cu. ft.). Cramped-96.9
Cargo Space (cu. ft.) . . . . .Very Cramped-12
Wheelbase/Length (in.) 104.1/180.5

Ratings—10 Best, 1 Worst

Combo Crash Tests	10
Safety Features	8
Rollover	9
Preventive Maintenance	1
Repair Costs	8
Warranty	2
Fuel Economy	8
Complaints	1
Insurance Costs	1
OVERALL RATING	**7**

Subaru Legacy

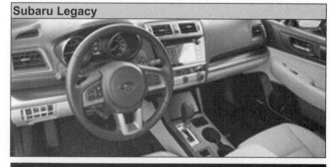

Subaru Legacy

At-a-Glance

Status/Year Series Started.........Unchanged/2015
Twins . . . . –
Body Styles . . . . Sedan
Seating. 5
Anti-Theft Device . . . Std. Pass. Immobil. & Active Alarm
Parking Index Rating .Average
Where Made. Lafayette, IN

Fuel Factor:
MPG Rating (city/hwy) Good-26/36
Driving Range (mi.) . . . . Very Long-549.7
Fuel Type. . . . . Regular
Annual Fuel Cost . . . . .Low-$1,060
Gas Guzzler Tax . . . . No
Greenhouse Gas Emissions (tons/yr.). Average-6.0
Barrels of Oil Used per year Average-11.0

Safety Checklist

Crash Tests:
Frontal. . . . . .Very Good
Side. . . . . .Very Good

Airbags:
Torso . . . . Front Pelvis/Torso from Seat
Pelvis . . . . Front Pelvis/Torso from Seat
Roll Sensing. . . . . Yes
Knee Bolster . . . . None

Crash Avoidance:
Collision Avoidance . . . . Optional CIB & DBS
Blind Spot Detection . . . . .Optional
Lane Keeping Assist . . . . .Optional
Backup Camera. . . . . Standard
Pedestrian Crash Avoidance . . . . .Optional

General:
Auto. Crash Notification . . . . None
Day Running Lamps . . . . Standard

Safety Belt/Restraint:
Dynamic Head Restraints . . . . None
Adjustable Belt. . . . . Standard Front

^Warning feature does not meet government standards.
*Backup camera does not meet government standards.

How the Competition Rates

Competitors	Rating	Pg.
Ford Fusion	7	144
Kia Optima	9	181
Mazda Mazda6	8	205

Price Range	Retail	Markup
Base	$21,745	6%
Premium	$23,845	6%
Limited	$26,845	6%
3.6R Limited	$29,945	7%

Specifications

Drive. . . . . .AWD
Engine 2.5-liter I4
Transmission . . . . 6-sp. Automatic
Tow Rating (lbs.) . . . . –
Head/Leg Room (in.) Roomy-40/42.9
Interior Space (cu. ft.). Roomy-104.6
Cargo Space (cu. ft.) Cramped-15
Wheelbase/Length (in.) 108.3/188.8

Subaru Outback

Ratings—10 Best, 1 Worst	
Combo Crash Tests	10
Safety Features	8
Rollover	4
Preventive Maintenance	1
Repair Costs	10
Warranty	2
Fuel Economy	7
Complaints	1
Insurance Costs	5
OVERALL RATING	**7**

Subaru Outback

Subaru Outback

At-a-Glance

Status/Year Series Started. Unchanged/2015
Twins . . . . –
Body Styles . . . . .Wagon
Seating 5
Anti-Theft Device . . . Std. Pass. Immobil. & Active Alarm
Parking Index Rating . . . . Easy
Where Made. . . . . Lafayette, IN

Fuel Factor:
MPG Rating (city/hwy) Good-25/33
Driving Range (mi.) . . . . Very Long-519.1
Fuel Type. . . . . Regular
Annual Fuel Cost . . . . .Low-$1,123
Gas Guzzler Tax . . . . No
Greenhouse Gas Emissions (tons/yr.) Average-6.4
Barrels of Oil Used per year Average-11.8

How the Competition Rates

Competitors	Rating	Pg.
Mazda CX-5	3	202
Volkswagen Jetta	7	263
Volvo V60	–	268

Price Range

Price Range	Retail	Markup
Base	$24,995	6%
Premium	$27,395	6%
Limited	$30,395	7%
3.6R Limited	$33,395	7%

Safety Checklist

Crash Tests:
Frontal. . . . . .Very Good
Side. . . . . Good

Airbags:
Torso . . . . Front Pelvis/Torso from Seat
Pelvis . . . . Front Pelvis/Torso from Seat
Roll Sensing. . . . . Yes
Knee Bolster . . . . None

Crash Avoidance:
Collision Avoidance . . . . Optional CIB & DBS
Blind Spot Detection . . . . .Optional
Lane Keeping Assist . . . . .Optional
Backup Camera . . . . Standard
Pedestrian Crash Avoidance . . . . .Optional

General:
Auto. Crash Notification . . . . None
Day Running Lamps . . . . Standard

Safety Belt/Restraint:
Dynamic Head Restraints . . . . None
Adjustable Belt. . . . . Standard Front

^Warning feature does not meet government standards.
*Backup camera does not meet government standards.

Subaru Outback

Specifications

Drive. . . . . .AWD
Engine 2.5-liter I4
Transmission . . . . 6-sp. Automatic
Tow Rating (lbs.) . . . . .Very Low-2700
Head/Leg Room (in.) Roomy-40.8/42.9
Interior Space (cu. ft.). Roomy-108.1
Cargo Space (cu. ft.) . . . . Very Roomy-35.5
Wheelbase/Length (in.) 108.1/189.6

Ratings—10 Best, 1 Worst

Combo Crash Tests	4
Safety Features	8
Rollover	5
Preventive Maintenance	4
Repair Costs	7
Warranty	2
Fuel Economy	7
Complaints	9
Insurance Costs	3
OVERALL RATING	**5**

Subaru XV Crosstrek

At-a-Glance

Status/Year Series Started. Unchanged/2013
Twins . . . . –
Body Styles . . . . .SUV
Seating. 5
Anti-Theft Device . . . Std. Pass. Immobil. & Active Alarm
Parking Index Rating . . . . Very Easy
Where Made. Gunma, Japan

Fuel Factor:
  MPG Rating (city/hwy) Good-26/34
  Driving Range (mi.) Long-462.4
  Fuel Type. . . . . Regular
  Annual Fuel Cost . . . . Low-$1,083
  Gas Guzzler Tax . . . . No
  Greenhouse Gas Emissions (tons/yr.). Average-6.2
  Barrels of Oil Used per year Average-11.4

How the Competition Rates

Competitors	Rating	Pg.
Jeep Renegade	2	177
Kia Soul	7	185
Nissan Juke	2	225

Price Range	Retail	Markup
Base	$21,595	5%
Premium MT	$22,395	5%
Limited	$25,095	6%
Hybrid Touring	$29,995	5%

Subaru XV Crosstrek

Safety Checklist

Crash Tests:
  Frontal. . . . . .Average
  Side. . . . . .Poor

Airbags:
  Torso . . . . Front Pelvis/Torso from Seat
  Pelvis . . . . Front Pelvis/Torso from Seat
  Roll Sensing. . . . . Yes
  Knee Bolster . . . . .Standard Driver

Crash Avoidance:
  Collision Avoidance . . . . Optional CIB & DBS
  Blind Spot Detection . . . . .Optional
  Lane Keeping Assist . . . . Warning Only Optional
  Backup Camera . . . . Standard
  Pedestrian Crash Avoidance . . . . .Optional

General:
  Auto. Crash Notification. . . . . None
  Day Running Lamps . . . . Standard

Safety Belt/Restraint:
  Dynamic Head Restraints . . . . None
  Adjustable Belt. . . . . Standard Front

^Warning feature does not meet government standards.
*Backup camera does not meet government standards.

Subaru XV Crosstrek

Specifications

Drive. . . . . .AWD
Engine 2.0-liter I4
Transmission . . . . CVT
Tow Rating (lbs.) . . . . –
Head/Leg Room (in.) Roomy-39.8/43.5
Interior Space (cu. ft.). Average-97.5
Cargo Space (cu. ft.) Average-22.3
Wheelbase/Length (in.) 103.7/175.2

Ratings—10 Best, 1 Worst

Combo Crash Tests	9
Safety Features	8
Rollover	10
Preventive Maintenance	—
Repair Costs	—
Warranty	10
Fuel Economy	10
Complaints	—
Insurance Costs	5
OVERALL RATING	**10**

Tesla Model S

Tesla Model S

At-a-Glance

Status/Year Series Started Unchanged/2012
Twins . . . . –
Body Styles . . . . Sedan
Seating 5
Anti-Theft Device . . . . Std. Passive Alarm Only
Parking Index Rating . . . . Hard
Where Made. . . . . Fremont, CA
Fuel Factor:
  MPG Rating (city/hwy) . . . . Very Good-88/90
  Driving Range (mi.) . . . . –
  Fuel Type . . . . Electricity
  Annual Fuel Cost . . . . Very Low-$473
  Gas Guzzler Tax . . . . No
  Greenhouse Gas Emissions (tons/yr.) . . . . Very Low-4.1
  Barrels of Oil Used per year . . . . Very Low-0.2

How the Competition Rates

Competitors	Rating	Pg.
Chevrolet Volt	–	125
Lexus ES	8	191
Nissan Leaf	4	226

Price Range

Price Range	Retail	Markup
60 kWh	$69,900	0%
85 kWh	$80,000	0%
85D kWh	$85,000	0%
P85D kWh	$105,000	0%

Safety Checklist

Crash Tests:
  Frontal . . . . Good
  Side . . . . Very Good
Airbags:
  Torso . . . . Front Pelvis/Torso from Seat
  Pelvis . . . . Front Pelvis/Torso from Seat
  Roll Sensing. . . . . Yes
  Knee Bolster . . . . Standard Front
Crash Avoidance:
  Collision Avoidance . . . . Standard CIB & DBS
  Blind Spot Detection . . . . Standard
  Lane Keeping Assist . . . . .Optional
  Backup Camera . . . . Standard
  Pedestrian Crash Avoidance . . . . None
General:
  Auto. Crash Notification . . . . None
  Day Running Lamps . . . . Standard
Safety Belt/Restraint:
  Dynamic Head Restraints . . . . None
  Adjustable Belt. . . . . None

^Warning feature does not meet government standards.
*Backup camera does not meet government standards.

Tesla Model S

Specifications

Drive . . . . .RWD
Engine . . . . All Electric
Transmission . . . .–
Tow Rating (lbs.) . . . . –
Head/Leg Room (in.) Average-38.8/42.7
Interior Space (cu. ft.). Cramped-94
Cargo Space (cu. ft.) Roomy-31.6
Wheelbase/Length (in.) 116.5/196

See page 278 for more detail.

Ratings—10 Best, 1 Worst

Combo Crash Tests	1
Safety Features	5
Rollover	1
Preventive Maintenance	9
Repair Costs	4
Warranty	2
Fuel Economy	2
Complaints	10
Insurance Costs	5
OVERALL RATING	**3**

Toyota 4Runner

Toyota 4Runner

At-a-Glance

Status/Year Series Started Unchanged/2006
Twins . . . . Lexus GX
Body Styles . . . . .SUV
Seating 5/7
Anti-Theft Device . . . . .Std. Pass. Immobil.
Parking Index Rating . . . . .Average
Where Made. . . . . .Tahara, Japan

Fuel Factor:
MPG Rating (city/hwy) . . . . Very Poor-17/21
Driving Range (mi.) Long-427.7
Fuel Type . . . . Regular
Annual Fuel Cost . . . . Very High-$1,694
Gas Guzzler Tax . . . . No
Greenhouse Gas Emissions (tons/yr.). . Very High-10.0
Barrels of Oil Used per year . . . . Very High-18.3

How the Competition Rates

Competitors	Rating	Pg.
Chevrolet Tahoe	4	122
Ford Expedition	7	138
Nissan Armada	–	223

Price Range	Retail	Markup
SR5 2WD	$33,510	9%
SR5 Premium 4WD	$38,065	9%
Trail Edition Prem 4WD	$39,095	9%
Limited 4WD	$43,860	9%

Safety Checklist

Crash Tests:
Frontal. . . . . Very Poor
Side. . . . . .Poor

Airbags:
Torso . . . . Front Pelvis/Torso from Seat
Pelvis . . . . Front Pelvis/Torso from Seat
Roll Sensing. . . . . Yes
Knee Bolster . . . . Standard Front

Crash Avoidance:
Collision Avoidance . . . . None
Blind Spot Detection . . . . None
Lane Keeping Assist . . . . None
Backup Camera . . . . Standard
Pedestrian Crash Avoidance . . . . None

General:
Auto. Crash Notification . . . . .Operator Assist.-Fee
Day Running Lamps . . . . Standard

Safety Belt/Restraint:
Dynamic Head Restraints . . . . Standard Front
Adjustable Belt. . . . . Standard Front

^Warning feature does not meet government standards.
*Backup camera does not meet government standards.

Toyota 4Runner

Specifications

Drive. 4WD
Engine 4.0-liter V6
Transmission . . . . 5-sp. Automatic
Tow Rating (lbs.) Low-4700
Head/Leg Room (in.) Cramped-39.3/41.7
Interior Space (cu. ft.). Roomy-128
Cargo Space (cu. ft.) . . . . .Very Cramped-9
Wheelbase/Length (in.) 109.8/190.2

Ratings—10 Best, 1 Worst

Combo Crash Tests	7
Safety Features	9
Rollover	9
Preventive Maintenance	6
Repair Costs	4
Warranty	2
Fuel Economy	5
Complaints	6
Insurance Costs	5
OVERALL RATING	**8**

Toyota Avalon

Toyota Avalon

Safety Checklist

Crash Tests:
Frontal . . . . .Average
Side . . . . Good

Airbags:
Torso . . . . .Fr. & Rr. Pelvis/Torso from Seat
Pelvis . . . . .Fr. & Rr. Pelvis/Torso from Seat
Roll Sensing . . . . Yes
Knee Bolster . . . . Standard Front

Crash Avoidance:
Collision Avoidance . . . . Optional CIB & DBS
Blind Spot Detection . . . . .Optional
Lane Keeping Assist . . . . .Optional
Backup Camera . . . . Standard
Pedestrian Crash Avoidance . . . . .Optional

General:
Auto. Crash Notification . . . . .Operator Assist.-Fee
Day Running Lamps . . . . Standard

Safety Belt/Restraint:
Dynamic Head Restraints . . . . None
Adjustable Belt . . . . Standard Front

^Warning feature does not meet government standards.
*Backup camera does not meet government standards.

At-a-Glance

Status/Year Series Started Unchanged/2013
Twins . . . . .Lexus ES
Body Styles . . . . Sedan
Seating 5
Anti-Theft Device . . . . .Std. Pass. Immobil. & Alarm
Parking Index Rating . . . . Hard
Where Made . . . . Georgetown, KY
Fuel Factor:
MPG Rating (city/hwy) Average-21/31
Driving Range (mi.) Average-417.6
Fuel Type . . . . Regular
Annual Fuel Cost . . . . .Average-$1,282
Gas Guzzler Tax . . . . No
Greenhouse Gas Emissions (tons/yr.) High-7.5
Barrels of Oil Used per year High-13.7

How the Competition Rates

Competitors	Rating	Pg.
Chevrolet Impala	6	116
Ford Taurus	4	147
Hyundai Genesis	7	162

Price Range

Price Range	Retail	Markup
XLE	$32,285	11%
XLE Premium	$34,140	11%
XLE Touring SE	$37,170	11%
Hybrid Limited	$41,700	11%

Toyota Avalon

Specifications

Drive . . . . .FWD
Engine 3.5-liter V6
Transmission . . . . 6-sp. Automatic
Tow Rating (lbs.) .Very Low-1000
Head/Leg Room (in.) . . . . Very Cramped-37.6/42.1
Interior Space (cu. ft.) Average-103.63
Cargo Space (cu. ft.) Cramped-16
Wheelbase/Length (in.) 111/195.3

Ratings—10 Best, 1 Worst

Combo Crash Tests	6
Safety Features	10
Rollover	8
Preventive Maintenance	6
Repair Costs	3
Warranty	2
Fuel Economy	7
Complaints	9
Insurance Costs	3
OVERALL RATING	**7**

Toyota Camry

Toyota Camry

At-a-Glance

Status/Year Series Started. Unchanged/2012
Twins . . . . –
Body Styles . . . . Sedan
Seating 5
Anti-Theft Device Std. Pass. Immobil. & Opt. Pass. Alarm
Parking Index Rating . . . . .Average
Where Made. Georgetown, KY

Fuel Factor:
  MPG Rating (city/hwy) Good-25/35
  Driving Range (mi.) . . . . Very Long-487.7
  Fuel Type . . . . Regular
  Annual Fuel Cost . . . . .Low-$1,098
  Gas Guzzler Tax . . . . No
  Greenhouse Gas Emissions (tons/yr.). Average-6.4
  Barrels of Oil Used per year Average-11.8

How the Competition Rates

Competitors	Rating	Pg.
Ford Fusion	7	144
Honda Accord	10	148
Subaru Legacy	7	242

Price Range	Retail	Markup
LE	$23,070	9%
XSE	$26,310	10%
XLE Hybrid	$30,140	9%
XLE V6	$31,370	10%

Safety Checklist

Crash Tests:
  Frontal. . . . . .Average
  Side. . . . . .Good

Airbags:
  Torso . . . . .Fr. & Rr. Pelvis/Torso from Seat
  Pelvis . . . . .Fr. & Rr. Pelvis/Torso from Seat
  Roll Sensing. . . . . Yes
  Knee Bolster . . . . Standard

Crash Avoidance:
  Collision Avoidance . . . . Optional CIB & DBS
  Blind Spot Detection . . . . .Optional
  Lane Keeping Assist . . . . Warning Only Optional
  Backup Camera . . . . Standard
  Pedestrian Crash Avoidance . . . . None

General:
  Auto. Crash Notification . . . . .Operator Assist.-Fee
  Day Running Lamps . . . . Standard

Safety Belt/Restraint:
  Dynamic Head Restraints . . . . None
  Adjustable Belt. . . . . Standard Front

^Warning feature does not meet government standards.
*Backup camera does not meet government standards.

Toyota Camry

Specifications

Drive. . . . . .FWD
Engine 2.5-liter I4
Transmission . . . . 6-sp. Automatic
Tow Rating (lbs.) .Very Low-0
Head/Leg Room (in.) Cramped-38.8/41.6
Interior Space (cu. ft.). Average-102.7
Cargo Space (cu. ft.) Cramped-15.4
Wheelbase/Length (in.) 109.3/190.9

Ratings—10 Best, 1 Worst

Combo Crash Tests	9
Safety Features	2
Rollover	7
Preventive Maintenance	9
Repair Costs	9
Warranty	2
Fuel Economy	8
Complaints	9
Insurance Costs	3
OVERALL RATING	**9**

Toyota Corolla

Toyota Corolla

At-a-Glance

Status/Year Series Started. Unchanged/2014
Twins . . . . –
Body Styles . . . . Sedan
Seating. 5
Anti-Theft Device . . . . Std. Pass. Immobil.
Parking Index Rating . . . . Easy
Where Made. . . . . Tupelo, MS

Fuel Factor:
MPG Rating (city/hwy). Good-27/36
Driving Range (mi.) Average-401.6
Fuel Type. . . . . Regular
Annual Fuel Cost . . . . .Low-$1,035
Gas Guzzler Tax . . . . No
Greenhouse Gas Emissions (tons/yr.). Low-5.8
Barrels of Oil Used per year Low-10.6

How the Competition Rates

Competitors	Rating	Pg.
Chevrolet Cruze	–	114
Honda Civic	–	149
Nissan Sentra	6	232

Price Range

Price Range	Retail	Markup
L MT	$17,230	6%
LE	$18,665	6%
LE Eco Plus	$19,065	8%
S Premium	$23,055	8%

Safety Checklist

Crash Tests:
Frontal. . . . . Good
Side. . . . . .Very Good

Airbags:
Torso . . . . Front Pelvis/Torso from Seat
Pelvis . . . . Front Pelvis/Torso from Seat
Roll Sensing. . . . . No
Knee Bolster . . . . .Standard Driver

Crash Avoidance:
Collision Avoidance . . . . None
Blind Spot Detection . . . . None
Lane Keeping Assist . . . . None
Backup Camera .Optional*
Pedestrian Crash Avoidance . . . . .Optional

General:
Auto. Crash Notification . . . . None
Day Running Lamps . . . . Standard

Safety Belt/Restraint:
Dynamic Head Restraints . . . . None
Adjustable Belt. . . . . Standard Front

^Warning feature does not meet government standards.
*Backup camera does not meet government standards.

Toyota Corolla

Specifications

Drive. . . . . .FWD
Engine 1.8-liter I4
Transmission . . . . 4-sp. Automatic
Tow Rating (lbs.) . . . . .Very Low-0
Head/Leg Room (in.) Cramped-38.3/42.3
Interior Space (cu. ft.). Average-97.5
Cargo Space (cu. ft.) . . . . .Very Cramped-13
Wheelbase/Length (in.) 106.3/182.6

Ratings—10 Best, 1 Worst

Combo Crash Tests	8
Safety Features	9
Rollover	3
Preventive Maintenance	7
Repair Costs	2
Warranty	2
Fuel Economy	2
Complaints	8
Insurance Costs	5
OVERALL RATING	**7**

Toyota Highlander

Toyota Highlander

At-a-Glance

Status/Year Series Started. Unchanged/2014
Twins . . . . –
Body Styles . . . . .SUV
Seating 7/8
Anti-Theft Device Std. Pass. Immobil. & Opt. Pass. Alarm
Parking Index Rating . . . . Hard
Where Made. . . . . .Princeton, IN

Fuel Factor:
  MPG Rating (city/hwy) . . . . Very Poor-18/24
  Driving Range (mi.) Short-389.4
  Fuel Type. . . . . Regular
  Annual Fuel Cost . . . . .High-$1,553
  Gas Guzzler Tax . . . . No
  Greenhouse Gas Emissions (tons/yr.). . . Very High-9.0
  Barrels of Oil Used per year High-16.5

How the Competition Rates

Competitors	Rating	Pg.
Buick Enclave	5	102
Chevrolet Traverse	4	123
Nissan Pathfinder	1	229

Price Range

Price Range	Retail	Markup
LE I4 FWD	$29,665	10%
LE Plus AWD	$34,650	10%
Limited AWD	$41,550	10%
Hybrid LTD Platinum	$50,240	10%

Safety Checklist

Crash Tests:
  Frontal. . . . . .Average
  Side. . . . . .Very Good

Airbags:
  Torso . . . . Front Pelvis/Torso from Seat
  Pelvis . . . . Front Pelvis/Torso from Seat
  Roll Sensing. . . . . Yes
  Knee Bolster . . . . .Standard Driver

Crash Avoidance:
  Collision Avoidance . . . . Optional CIB & DBS
  Blind Spot Detection . . . . .Optional
  Lane Keeping Assist . . . . Warning Only Optional
  Backup Camera . . . . Standard
  Pedestrian Crash Avoidance . . . . .Optional

General:
  Auto. Crash Notification . . . . .Operator Assist.-Fee
  Day Running Lamps . . . . Standard

Safety Belt/Restraint:
  Dynamic Head Restraints . . . . None
  Adjustable Belt . . . . Standard Front

^Warning feature does not meet government standards.
*Backup camera does not meet government standards.

Toyota Highlander

Specifications

Drive. . . . . .AWD
Engine 3.5-liter V6
Transmission . . . . 6-sp. Automatic
Tow Rating (lbs.) . . . . .Very Low-2000
Head/Leg Room (in.) . . . . Very Roomy-40.7/44.2
Interior Space (cu. ft.). Roomy-144.9
Cargo Space (cu. ft.) Cramped-13.8
Wheelbase/Length (in.) 109.8/191.1

Toyota Prius Compact

Ratings—10 Best, 1 Worst

Combo Crash Tests	—
Safety Features	6
Rollover	—
Preventive Maintenance	9
Repair Costs	5
Warranty	2
Fuel Economy	10
Complaints	—
Insurance Costs	5
OVERALL RATING	—

Toyota Prius

At-a-Glance

```
Status/Year Series Started. . . . . . . . . . . . .All New/2016
Twins . . . . . . . . . . . . . . . . . . . . . . . . . . . . . . . . . . . –
Body Styles . . . . . . . . . . . . . . . . . . . . . . .Hatchback
Seating . . . . . . . . . . . . . . . . . . . . . . . . . . . . . . . . . 5
Anti-Theft Device . . . . . . . . . . . . . . .Std. Pass. Immobil.
Parking Index Rating . . . . . . . . . . . . . . . . . Very Easy
Where Made. . . . . . . . . . . . . . . . . . . . Tsutsumi, Japan
```

Fuel Factor:
```
MPG Rating (city/hwy) . . . . . . . . . . .Very Good-54/50
Driving Range (mi.) . . . . . . . . . . . . . Very Long-589.0
Fuel Type . . . . . . . . . . . . . . . . . . . . . . . . . . . Regular
Annual Fuel Cost . . . . . . . . . . . . . . . . . Very Low-$604
Gas Guzzler Tax . . . . . . . . . . . . . . . . . . . . . . . . . No
Greenhouse Gas Emissions (tons/yr.). . . .Very Low-2.8
Barrels of Oil Used per year . . . . . . . . . .Very Low-6.3
```

How the Competition Rates

Competitors	Rating	Pg.
Chevrolet Volt	—	125
Ford C-MAX	5	135
Lexus CT	—	190

Price Range

Price Range	Retail	Markup
One	$23,215	5%
Three	$25,765	7%
Five	$30,005	7%
Plug-In Hybrid Adv.	$34,905	4%

Toyota Prius

Safety Checklist

Crash Tests:
```
Frontal. . . . . . . . . . . . . . . . . . . . . . . . . . . . . . . . . –
Side. . . . . . . . . . . . . . . . . . . . . . . . . . . . . . . . . . . –
```
Airbags:
```
Torso . . . . . . . . . . . . . . . .Front Torso from Seat
Pelvis . . . . . . . . . . . . . . . . . . . . . . . . . . . . . . None
Roll Sensing. . . . . . . . . . . . . . . . . . . . . . . . . . . . No
Knee Bolster . . . . . . . . . . . . . . . . . . . . . . . . .Driver
```
Crash Avoidance:
```
Collision Avoidance . . . . . . . . . . . Optional CIB & DBS
Blind Spot Detection . . . . . . . . . . . . . . . . . . .Optional
Lane Keeping Assist . . . . . . . . . . . . . . . . . .Optional^
Backup Camera . . . . . . . . . . . . . . . . . . . . Standard*
Pedestrian Crash Avoidance . . . . . . . . . . . .Optional
```
General:
```
Auto. Crash Notification . . . . . . . .Operator Assist.-Fee
Day Running Lamps . . . . . . . . . . . . . . . . . . Standard
```
Safety Belt/Restraint:
```
Dynamic Head Restraints . . . . . . . . . . Standard Front
Adjustable Belt . . . . . . . . . . . . . . . . . . Standard Front
```

^Warning feature does not meet government standards.
*Backup camera does not meet government standards.

Toyota Prius

Specifications

```
Drive. . . . . . . . . . . . . . . . . . . . . . . . . . . . . . . . .FWD
Engine . . . . . . . . . . . . . . . . . . . . . . . . .1.8-liter I4
Transmission . . . . . . . . . . . . . . . . . . . . . . . . . CVT
Tow Rating (lbs.) . . . . . . . . . . . . . . . . . . . . . . . . . –
Head/Leg Room (in.) . . . . . . . . . Very Cramped-34.4/42.3
Interior Space (cu. ft.). . . . . . . . . . . . . . . Cramped-93.1
Cargo Space (cu. ft.) . . . . . . . . . . . . . . . Roomy-24.6
Wheelbase/Length (in.) . . . . . . . . . . . . . 106.3/178.7
```

Toyota Prius c

Ratings—10 Best, 1 Worst

Combo Crash Tests	2
Safety Features	2
Rollover	7
Preventive Maintenance	9
Repair Costs	9
Warranty	2
Fuel Economy	10
Complaints	8
Insurance Costs	—
OVERALL RATING	**6**

Toyota Prius C

Safety Checklist

Crash Tests:
Frontal.................................Poor
Side............................. Very Poor

Airbags:
Torso .... Front Pelvis/Torso from Seat
Pelvis .... Front Pelvis/Torso from Seat
Roll Sensing................................. No
Knee Bolster ....Driver

Crash Avoidance:
Collision Avoidance .... None
Blind Spot Detection .... None
Lane Keeping Assist .... Warning Only Optional^
Backup Camera.........................Optional
Pedestrian Crash Avoidance .... None

General:
Auto. Crash Notification................... None
Day Running Lamps .... Standard

Safety Belt/Restraint:
Dynamic Head Restraints .... None
Adjustable Belt............................ None

^Warning feature does not meet government standards.
*Backup camera does not meet government standards.

Toyota Prius C

At-a-Glance

Status/Year Series Started...........Unchanged/2013
Twins .... –
Body Styles ....Hatchback
Seating 5
Anti-Theft Device .... Optional Pass. Immobil. Only
Parking Index Rating .... Very Easy
Where Made..................... Iwata, Japan

Fuel Factor:
MPG Rating (city/hwy)............Very Good-53/46
Driving Range (mi.) .... Very Long-471.2
Fuel Type........................... Regular
Annual Fuel Cost .... Very Low-$635
Gas Guzzler Tax .... No
Greenhouse Gas Emissions (tons/yr.)....Very Low-3.6
Barrels of Oil Used per year ....Very Low-6.6

How the Competition Rates

Competitors	Rating	Pg.
Chevrolet Sonic	10	119
Ford C-MAX	5	135
Nissan Leaf	4	226

Price Range

Price Range	Retail	Markup
One	$19,540	5%
Two	$20,340	6%
Three	$21,765	7%
Four	$24,475	7%

Toyota Prius C

Specifications

Drive.......................................FWD
Engine 1.5-liter I4
Transmission .... CVT
Tow Rating (lbs.) .... –
Head/Leg Room (in.) Cramped-38.6/41.7
Interior Space (cu. ft.)............. Very Cramped-87.4
Cargo Space (cu. ft.) Average-17.1
Wheelbase/Length (in.) 100.4/157.3

Ratings—10 Best, 1 Worst

Combo Crash Tests	6
Safety Features	6
Rollover	6
Preventive Maintenance	9
Repair Costs	6
Warranty	2
Fuel Economy	10
Complaints	10
Insurance Costs	—
OVERALL RATING	**9**

Toyota Prius V

Toyota Prius V

At-a-Glance

Status/Year Series Started. Unchanged/2013
Twins . . . . —
Body Styles . . . . .Wagon
Seating 5
Anti-Theft Device . . . . .Std. Pass. Immobil.
Parking Index Rating . . . . Easy
Where Made. . . . . Tsutsumi, Japan
Fuel Factor:
  MPG Rating (city/hwy) . . . . .Very Good-44/40
  Driving Range (mi.) . . . . .Very Long-501.1
  Fuel Type. . . . . Regular
  Annual Fuel Cost . . . . Very Low-$748
  Gas Guzzler Tax . . . . No
  Greenhouse Gas Emissions (tons/yr.). . . .Very Low-4.3
  Barrels of Oil Used per year . . . . .Very Low-7.8

How the Competition Rates

Competitors	Rating	Pg.
Chevrolet Volt	–	125
Ford C-MAX	5	135
Lexus CT	–	190

Price Range

	Retail	Markup
Two	$26,675	7%
Three	$28,060	7%
Four	$29,695	7%
Five	$30,935	7%

Safety Checklist

Crash Tests:
  Frontal. . . . . .Poor
  Side. . . . . .Very Good
Airbags:
  Torso . . . . Front Pelvis/Torso from Seat
  Pelvis . . . . Front Pelvis/Torso from Seat
  Roll Sensing. . . . . No
  Knee Bolster . . . . .Standard Driver
Crash Avoidance:
  Collision Avoidance . . . . Optional CIB & DBS
  Blind Spot Detection . . . . None
  Lane Keeping Assist . . . . Warning Only Optional
  Backup Camera . . . . .Optional
  Pedestrian Crash Avoidance . . . . None
General:
  Auto. Crash Notification . . . . .Operator Assist.-Fee
  Day Running Lamps . . . . Standard
Safety Belt/Restraint:
  Dynamic Head Restraints . . . . None
  Adjustable Belt . . . . Standard Front

^Warning feature does not meet government standards.
*Backup camera does not meet government standards.

Toyota Prius V

Specifications

Drive. . . . . .FWD
Engine 1.8-liter I4
Transmission . . . . CVT
Tow Rating (lbs.) . . . . –
Head/Leg Room (in.) Cramped-39.6/41.3
Interior Space (cu. ft.). Average-97.2
Cargo Space (cu. ft.) . . . . Very Roomy-34.3
Wheelbase/Length (in.) 109.4/182.3

Ratings—10 Best, 1 Worst

Combo Crash Tests	6
Safety Features	9
Rollover	4
Preventive Maintenance	4
Repair Costs	4
Warranty	2
Fuel Economy	5
Complaints	9
Insurance Costs	5
OVERALL RATING	**5**

Toyota RAV4

Toyota RAV4

At-a-Glance

Status/Year Series Started	Appearance Change/2013
Twins	Lexus NX
Body Styles	SUV
Seating	5
Anti-Theft Device	Std. Pass. Immobil.
Parking Index Rating	Very Easy
Where Made	Woodstock, Ontario / Tahara, Japan

Fuel Factor:

MPG Rating (city/hwy)	Average-22/29
Driving Range (mi.)	Short-392.4
Fuel Type	Regular
Annual Fuel Cost	Average-$1,276
Gas Guzzler Tax	No
Greenhouse Gas Emissions (tons/yr.)	Average-7.2
Barrels of Oil Used per year	High-13.2

How the Competition Rates

Competitors	Rating	Pg.
Ford Escape	5	137
Honda CR-V	7	154
Hyundai Tucson	7	166

Price Range

	Retail	Markup
LE 2WD	$23,680	7%
LE AWD	$25,080	7%
XLE AWD	$26,640	7%
Limited AWD	$29,850	7%

Safety Checklist

Crash Tests:

Frontal	Poor
Side	Very Good

Airbags:

Torso	Front Pelvis/Torso from Seat
Pelvis	Front Pelvis/Torso from Seat
Roll Sensing	Yes
Knee Bolster	Standard Driver

Crash Avoidance:

Collision Avoidance	Optional CIB & DBS
Blind Spot Detection	Optional
Lane Keeping Assist	Optional
Backup Camera	Standard*
Pedestrian Crash Avoidance	Optional

General:

Auto. Crash Notification	None
Day Running Lamps	Standard

Safety Belt/Restraint:

Dynamic Head Restraints	None
Adjustable Belt	Standard Front

^Warning feature does not meet government standards.
*Backup camera does not meet government standards.

Toyota RAV4

Specifications

Drive	AWD
Engine	2.5-liter I4
Transmission	6-sp. Automatic
Tow Rating (lbs.)	Very Low-1500
Head/Leg Room (in.)	Average-39.8/42.6
Interior Space (cu. ft.)	Average-101.9
Cargo Space (cu. ft.)	Very Roomy-38.4
Wheelbase/Length (in.)	104.7/179.9

Ratings—10 Best, 1 Worst

Combo Crash Tests	—
Safety Features	4
Rollover	—
Preventive Maintenance	6
Repair Costs	3
Warranty	2
Fuel Economy	1
Complaints	9
Insurance Costs	10
OVERALL RATING	—

Toyota Sequoia

At-a-Glance

Status/Year Series Started Unchanged/2008
Twins . . . . —
Body Styles . . . . .SUV
Seating 8
Anti-Theft Device . . . . Std. Pass. Immobil. & Alarm
Parking Index Rating . . . . Very Hard
Where Made . . . . Princeton, IN

Fuel Factor:
MPG Rating (city/hwy) . . . . Very Poor-13/17
Driving Range (mi.) Short-383.8
Fuel Type . . . . Regular
Annual Fuel Cost . . . . Very High-$2,167
Gas Guzzler Tax . . . . No
Greenhouse Gas Emissions (tons/yr.) . . Very High-12.8
Barrels of Oil Used per year . . . . Very High-23.5

How the Competition Rates

Competitors	Rating	Pg.
Chevrolet Suburban	3	121
Ford Expedition	7	138
Nissan Armada	–	223

Price Range	Retail	Markup
SR5 2WD	$44,965	10%
Limited 2WD	$53,755	10%
Limited 4WD	$56,980	10%
Platinum 4WD	$64,720	10%

Toyota Sequoia

Safety Checklist

Crash Tests:
Frontal . . . . –
Side . . . . –
Airbags:
Torso . . . . Front Pelvis/Torso from Seat
Pelvis . . . . Front Pelvis/Torso from Seat
Roll Sensing . . . . Yes
Knee Bolster . . . . Standard
Crash Avoidance:
Collision Avoidance . . . . None
Blind Spot Detection . . . . .Optional
Lane Keeping Assist . . . . None
Backup Camera . . . . Standard
Pedestrian Crash Avoidance . . . . None
General:
Auto. Crash Notification . . . . None
Day Running Lamps . . . . .Optional
Safety Belt/Restraint:
Dynamic Head Restraints . . . . None
Adjustable Belt . . . . Standard Front and Rear

^Warning feature does not meet government standards.
*Backup camera does not meet government standards.

Toyota Sequoia

Specifications

Drive 4WD
Engine 5.7-liter V8
Transmission . . . . 6-sp. Automatic
Tow Rating (lbs.) Average-7100
Head/Leg Room (in.) . . . . Very Cramped-34.8/42.5
Interior Space (cu. ft.) . . . . –
Cargo Space (cu. ft.) Average-18.9
Wheelbase/Length (in.) 122/205.1

Toyota Sienna   Minivan

Ratings—10 Best, 1 Worst

Combo Crash Tests	5
Safety Features	9
Rollover	6
Preventive Maintenance	3
Repair Costs	3
Warranty	2
Fuel Economy	2
Complaints	5
Insurance Costs	5
OVERALL RATING	**3**

Toyota Sienna

Toyota Sienna

At-a-Glance

Status/Year Series Started Unchanged/2004
Twins . . . . –
Body Styles . . . . Minivan
Seating 7/8
Anti-Theft Device Std. Pass. Immobil. & Opt. Pass. Alarm
Parking Index Rating . . . . Hard
Where Made . . . . Princeton, IN

Fuel Factor:
MPG Rating (city/hwy) . . . . Very Poor-18/25
Driving Range (mi.) Average-411.9
Fuel Type . . . . Regular
Annual Fuel Cost . . . . High-$1,530
Gas Guzzler Tax . . . . No
Greenhouse Gas Emissions (tons/yr.) High-8.6
Barrels of Oil Used per year High-15.7

How the Competition Rates

Competitors	Rating	Pg.
Honda Odyssey	8	157
Kia Sedona	7	183
Nissan Quest	–	230

Price Range

Price Range	Retail	Markup
L FWD	$28,600	8%
SE FWD	$34,900	8%
XLE Premium FWD	$38,355	9%
LTD Premium AWD	$46,150	9%

Safety Checklist

Crash Tests:
  Frontal . . . . .Average
  Side . . . . .Average

Airbags:
  Torso . . . . Front Pelvis/Torso from Seat
  Pelvis . . . . Front Pelvis/Torso from Seat
  Roll Sensing . . . . Yes
  Knee Bolster .Standard Driver

Crash Avoidance:
  Collision Avoidance . . . . Optional CIB & DBS
  Blind Spot Detection . . . . .Optional
  Lane Keeping Assist . . . . None
  Backup Camera . . . . Standard
  Pedestrian Crash Avoidance . . . . None

General:
  Auto. Crash Notification . . . . .Operator Assist.-Fee
  Day Running Lamps . . . . .Optional

Safety Belt/Restraint:
  Dynamic Head Restraints . . . . Standard Front
  Adjustable Belt . . . . Standard Front and Rear

^Warning feature does not meet government standards.
*Backup camera does not meet government standards.

Toyota Sienna

Specifications

Drive . . . . .FWD
Engine 3.5-liter V6
Transmission . . . . 6-sp. Automatic
Tow Rating (lbs.) Low-3500
Head/Leg Room (in.) Average-41/40.5
Interior Space (cu. ft.) Roomy-164.4
Cargo Space (cu. ft.) . . . . Very Roomy-39.1
Wheelbase/Length (in.) 119.3/200.2

Ratings—10 Best, 1 Worst

Combo Crash Tests	—
Safety Features	3
Rollover	—
Preventive Maintenance	9
Repair Costs	5
Warranty	2
Fuel Economy	2
Complaints	—
Insurance Costs	5
OVERALL RATING	—

Toyota Tacoma

Toyota Tacoma

At-a-Glance

Status/Year Series Started . . . . .All New/2016
Twins . . . . –
Body Styles . . . . Pickup
Seating 4
Anti-Theft Device . . . . .Opt. Pass. Immbobil. & Alarm
Parking Index Rating . . . . Very Hard
Where Made . . . . .San Antonio, TX / Tijuana, Mexico
Fuel Factor:
  MPG Rating (city/hwy) . . . . Very Poor-19/23
  Driving Range (mi.) Long-434.9
  Fuel Type . . . . Regular
  Annual Fuel Cost .High-$1,528
  Gas Guzzler Tax . . . . No
  Greenhouse Gas Emissions (tons/yr.) High-7.3
  Barrels of Oil Used per year High-16.5

How the Competition Rates

Competitors	Rating	Pg.
Chevrolet Colorado	3	112
GMC Canyon	1	149
Nissan Frontier	—	224

Price Range

Price Range	Retail	Markup
SR Access Cab 2WD MT	$23,300	7%
SR5 Access Cab 2WD AT	$25,385	7%
SR5 Dbl Cab 4WD V6 AT	$31,060	8%
TRD Sport Dbl. Cab 4WD V6 AT	$33,730	8%

Safety Checklist

Crash Tests:
  Frontal . . . . –
  Side . . . . –
Airbags:
  Torso .Front Torso from Seat
  Pelvis . . . . None
  Roll Sensing . . . . Yes
  Knee Bolster . . . . None
Crash Avoidance:
  Collision Avoidance . . . . None
  Blind Spot Detection . . . . .Optional
  Lane Keeping Assist . . . . None
  Backup Camera . . . . Standard
  Pedestrian Crash Avoidance . . . . None
General:
  Auto. Crash Notification . . . . None
  Day Running Lamps . . . . Standard
Safety Belt/Restraint:
  Dynamic Head Restraints . . . . Standard Front
  Adjustable Belt . . . . Standard Front

^Warning feature does not meet government standards.
*Backup camera does not meet government standards.

Toyota Tacoma

Specifications

Drive 4WD
Engine 2.7-liter I4
Transmission . . . . 6-sp. Automatic
Tow Rating (lbs.) Low-3500
Head/Leg Room (in.) Roomy-39.7/42.9
Interior Space (cu. ft.) . . . . Very Cramped-57.5
Cargo Space (cu. ft.) . . . . Very Roomy-33.5
Wheelbase/Length (in.) 127.4/212.3

Ratings—10 Best, 1 Worst

Combo Crash Tests	—
Safety Features	5
Rollover	2
Preventive Maintenance	6
Repair Costs	3
Warranty	2
Fuel Economy	1
Complaints	10
Insurance Costs	5

OVERALL RATING

Toyota Tundra

At-a-Glance

Status/Year Series Started Unchanged/2007
Twins . . . . –
Body Styles . . . . Pickup
Seating 5/6
Anti-Theft Device Std. Pass. Immobil. & Opt. Pass. Alarm
Parking Index Rating . . . . Very Hard
Where Made . . . . San Antonio, TX

Fuel Factor:
MPG Rating (city/hwy) . . . . Very Poor-13/17
Driving Range (mi.) Short-383.8
Fuel Type . . . . Regular
Annual Fuel Cost . . . . Very High-$2,167
Gas Guzzler Tax . . . . No
Greenhouse Gas Emissions (tons/yr.) . . Very High-12.0
Barrels of Oil Used per year . . . . Very High-22.0

How the Competition Rates

Competitors	Rating	Pg.
Chevrolet Silverado	5	118
Ford F-150	9	140
Nissan Titan	–	233

Price Range	Retail	Markup
SR Reg. Cab 2WD 5.7 V8	$29,450	8%
SR5 Dbl. Cab 4WD 5.7 V8	$32,150	8%
Limited Crew Max 4WD 5.7 V8	$43,085	8%
1794 Edition Crew Max 5.7 V8	$49,080	8%

Toyota Tundra

Safety Checklist

Crash Tests:
Frontal . . . . Very Poor
Side . . . . –

Airbags:
Torso . . . . Front Pelvis/Torso from Seat
Pelvis . . . . Front Pelvis/Torso from Seat
Roll Sensing . . . . Yes
Knee Bolster . . . . Standard Front

Crash Avoidance:
Collision Avoidance . . . . None
Blind Spot Detection . . . . .Optional
Lane Keeping Assist . . . . None
Backup Camera . . . . Standard
Pedestrian Crash Avoidance . . . . None

General:
Auto. Crash Notification . . . . None
Day Running Lamps . . . . Standard

Safety Belt/Restraint:
Dynamic Head Restraints . . . . None
Adjustable Belt . . . . Standard Front and Rear

^Warning feature does not meet government standards.
*Backup camera does not meet government standards.

Toyota Tundra

Specifications

Drive 4WD
Engine 5.7-liter V8
Transmission . . . . 6-sp. Automatic
Tow Rating (lbs.) . . . . Very High-10000
Head/Leg Room (in.) Average-39.7/42.5
Interior Space (cu. ft.) . . . .–
Cargo Space (cu. ft.) . . . . Very Roomy-67.1
Wheelbase/Length (in.) 145.7/228.9

Toyota Yaris   Subcompact

Ratings—10 Best, 1 Worst	
Combo Crash Tests	3
Safety Features	2
Rollover	6
Preventive Maintenance	10
Repair Costs	10
Warranty	2
Fuel Economy	9
Complaints	10
Insurance Costs	1
OVERALL RATING	**6**

Toyota Yaris

Safety Checklist

Crash Tests:
Frontal.................................Poor
Side..................................Poor

Airbags:
Torso .... Front Pelvis/Torso from Seat
Pelvis .... Front Pelvis/Torso from Seat
Roll Sensing...............................No
Knee Bolster ....Driver

Crash Avoidance:
Collision Avoidance .... None
Blind Spot Detection .... None
Lane Keeping Assist .... None
Backup Camera...................... Standard
Pedestrian Crash Avoidance .... None

General:
Auto. Crash Notification.................. None
Day Running Lamps ....Optional

Safety Belt/Restraint:
Dynamic Head Restraints .... None
Adjustable Belt.......................... None

^Warning feature does not meet government standards.
*Backup camera does not meet government standards.

Toyota Yaris

Toyota Yaris

At-a-Glance

Status/Year Series Started...........Unchanged/2012
Twins .... –
Body Styles ....Hatchback
Seating 5
Anti-Theft Device .... Std. Pass. Immobil.
Parking Index Rating .... Very Easy
Where Made........................ Iwata, Japan
Fuel Factor:
MPG Rating (city/hwy)...........Very Good-30/36
Driving Range (mi.) ....Very Short-360.0
Fuel Type.............................. Regular
Annual Fuel Cost .... Very Low-$971
Gas Guzzler Tax ....No
Greenhouse Gas Emissions (tons/yr.).......Low-5.6
Barrels of Oil Used per year Low-10.3

How the Competition Rates

Competitors	Rating	Pg.
Chevrolet Sonic	10	119
Kia Rio	6	182
Nissan Versa	3	234

Price Range	Retail	Markup
L 2 Door MT	$14,845	4%
L 4 Door AT	$15,945	4%
LE 4 Door	$16,880	4%
SE 4 Door	$17,620	4%

Toyota Yaris

Specifications

Drive......................................FWD
Engine 1.5-liter I4
Transmission .... 4-sp. Automatic
Tow Rating (lbs.) .... –
Head/Leg Room (in.) Cramped-39.3/40.6
Interior Space (cu. ft.)............. Very Cramped-85.1
Cargo Space (cu. ft.) Cramped-15.6
Wheelbase/Length (in.) 98.8/155.5

Ratings—10 Best, 1 Worst

Combo Crash Tests	4
Safety Features	1
Rollover	9
Preventive Maintenance	5
Repair Costs	4
Warranty	5
Fuel Economy	7
Complaints	5
Insurance Costs	1
OVERALL RATING	**3**

Volkswagen Beetle

Volkswagen Beetle

At-a-Glance

Status/Year Series Started. Unchanged/2012
Twins . . . . –
Body Styles . . . . .Hatchback, Convertible
Seating 4
Anti-Theft Device . . . . .Std. Pass. Immobil. & Alarm
Parking Index Rating . . . . Very Easy
Where Made. . . . . Hai Phong, Vietnam
Fuel Factor:
  MPG Rating (city/hwy) Good-25/33
  Driving Range (mi.) Average-406.9
  Fuel Type . . . . Regular
  Annual Fuel Cost .Low-$1,123
  Gas Guzzler Tax . . . . No
  Greenhouse Gas Emissions (tons/yr.). Average-6.5
  Barrels of Oil Used per year Average-11.8

How the Competition Rates

Competitors	Rating	Pg.
Chevrolet Sonic	10	119
Fiat 500	4	133
Mini Cooper	–	215

Price Range

Price Range	Retail	Markup
S Coupe MT	$19,795	4%
SE Coupe AT	$22,450	4%
SE R-Line Coupe AT	$27,095	4%
SWL R-Line Convertible AT	$36,050	4%

Safety Checklist

Crash Tests:
  Frontal. . . . . .Poor
  Side. . . . . .Average
Airbags:
  Torso . . . . .Front Head/Torso from Seat
  Pelvis . . . . None
  Roll Sensing. . . . . No
  Knee Bolster . . . . None
Crash Avoidance:
  Collision Avoidance . . . . None
  Blind Spot Detection . . . . .Optional
  Lane Keeping Assist . . . . None
  Backup Camera .Optional*
  Pedestrian Crash Avoidance . . . . None
General:
  Auto. Crash Notification . . . . .Operator Assist.-Fee
  Day Running Lamps . . . . Standard
Safety Belt/Restraint:
  Dynamic Head Restraints . . . . None
  Adjustable Belt. . . . . None

^Warning feature does not meet government standards.
*Backup camera does not meet government standards.

Volkswagen Beetle

Specifications

Drive. . . . . .FWD
Engine 1.8-liter I4
Transmission . . . . 6-sp. Automatic
Tow Rating (lbs.) . . . . –
Head/Leg Room (in.) Cramped-39.4/41.3
Interior Space (cu. ft.). . . . . Very Cramped-85.1
Cargo Space (cu. ft.) Cramped-15.4
Wheelbase/Length (in.) 100/168.4

Volkswagen CC

Ratings—10 Best, 1 Worst

Combo Crash Tests	—
Safety Features	4
Rollover	—
Preventive Maintenance	3
Repair Costs	5
Warranty	5
Fuel Economy	5
Complaints	6
Insurance Costs	3
OVERALL RATING	**—**

Volkswagen CC

Volkswagen CC

At-a-Glance

Status/Year Series Started	Unchanged/2009
Twins	—
Body Styles	Coupe
Seating	5
Anti-Theft Device	Std. Pass. Immobil. & Alarm
Parking Index Rating	Average
Where Made	Emden, Germany

Fuel Factor:

MPG Rating (city/hwy)	Average-22/31
Driving Range (mi.)	Very Long-468.2
Fuel Type	Premium
Annual Fuel Cost	High-$1,393
Gas Guzzler Tax	No
Greenhouse Gas Emissions (tons/yr.)	Average-7.2
Barrels of Oil Used per year	High-13.2

How the Competition Rates

Competitors	Rating	Pg.
Acura TLX	10	84
Mercedes-Benz CLA-Class	—	208
Subaru Legacy	7	242

Price Range

Price Range	Retail	Markup
Sport MT	$32,995	4%
R-Line AT	$35,375	4%
Executive	$38,085	4%
VR6 4Motion	$43,575	4%

Safety Checklist

Crash Tests:
Frontal	−
Side	−

Airbags:
Torso	Front Pelvis/Torso from Seat
Pelvis	Front Pelvis/Torso from Seat
Roll Sensing	No
Knee Bolster	None

Crash Avoidance:
Collision Avoidance	Optional CIB^
Blind Spot Detection	None
Lane Keeping Assist	Optional
Backup Camera	Standard*
Pedestrian Crash Avoidance	None

General:
Auto. Crash Notification	Operator Assist.-Fee
Day Running Lamps	Standard

Safety Belt/Restraint:
Dynamic Head Restraints	None
Adjustable Belt	Standard Front

^Warning feature does not meet government standards.
*Backup camera does not meet government standards.

Specifications

Drive	FWD
Engine	2.0-liter I4
Transmission	6-sp. Automatic
Tow Rating (lbs.)	—
Head/Leg Room (in.)	Very Cramped-37.4/41.6
Interior Space (cu. ft.)	Cramped-93.6
Cargo Space (cu. ft.)	Very Cramped-13.2
Wheelbase/Length (in.)	106.7/189.1

Ratings—10 Best, 1 Worst

Combo Crash Tests	4
Safety Features	6
Rollover	8
Preventive Maintenance	3
Repair Costs	8
Warranty	5
Fuel Economy	8
Complaints	1
Insurance Costs	1
OVERALL RATING	**3**

Volkswagen Golf

Volkswagen Golf

At-a-Glance

Status/Year Series Started Unchanged/2015
Twins . . . . Audi A3
Body Styles . . . . .Hatchback
Seating 5
Anti-Theft Device . . . . .Std. Pass. Immobil. & Alarm
Parking Index Rating . . . . Very Easy
Where Made . . . . .Wolfsburg, Germany / Puebla, Mexico

Fuel Factor:
MPG Rating (city/hwy) Good-26/36
Driving Range (mi.) Short-392.2
Fuel Type . . . . Regular
Annual Fuel Cost . . . . .Low-$1,060
Gas Guzzler Tax . . . . No
Greenhouse Gas Emissions (tons/yr.) Average-6.2
Barrels of Oil Used per year Average-11.4

How the Competition Rates

Competitors	Rating	Pg.
Chevrolet Sonic	10	119
Mazda Mazda3	8	204
Subaru Impreza	5	241

Price Range

Price Range	Retail	Markup
Base 2 Door MT	$18,495	4%
S 2 Door AT	$20,675	4%
GTI S 2 Door AT	$26,095	4%
GTI SE 4 Door AT	$29,125	4%

Safety Checklist

Crash Tests:
Frontal . . . . .Poor
Side . . . . .Average

Airbags:
Torso . . . . Front Pelvis/Torso from Seat
Pelvis . . . . Front Pelvis/Torso from Seat
Roll Sensing . . . . No
Knee Bolster . . . . None

Crash Avoidance:
Collision Avoidance . . . . Optional CIB & DBS^
Blind Spot Detection . . . . .Optional
Lane Keeping Assist . . . . .Optional
Backup Camera . . . . Optional*
Pedestrian Crash Avoidance . . . . None

General:
Auto. Crash Notification . . . . .Operator Assist.-Fee
Day Running Lamps . . . . Standard

Safety Belt/Restraint:
Dynamic Head Restraints . . . . None
Adjustable Belt . . . . Standard Front

^Warning feature does not meet government standards.
*Backup camera does not meet government standards.

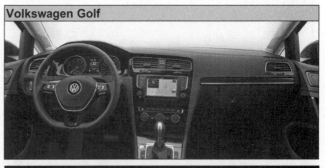

Volkswagen Golf

Specifications

Drive . . . . .FWD
Engine 1.8-liter I4
Transmission . . . . 6-sp. Automatic
Tow Rating (lbs.) . . . . –
Head/Leg Room (in.) . . . . Very Cramped-38.4/41.2
Interior Space (cu. ft.) Cramped-93.5
Cargo Space (cu. ft.) Average-22.8
Wheelbase/Length (in.) 103.8/167.5

Ratings—10 Best, 1 Worst

Combo Crash Tests	7
Safety Features	4
Rollover	8
Preventive Maintenance	5
Repair Costs	5
Warranty	5
Fuel Economy	9
Complaints	6
Insurance Costs	1
OVERALL RATING	**7**

Volkswagen Jetta

Volkswagen Jetta

At-a-Glance

Status/Year Series Started	Unchanged/2011
Twins	–
Body Styles	Sedan
Seating	5
Anti-Theft Device	Std. Pass. Immobil. & Alarm
Parking Index Rating	Easy
Where Made	Puebla, Mexico

Fuel Factor:

MPG Rating (city/hwy)	Very Good-28/39
Driving Range (mi.)	Very Long-465.0
Fuel Type	Regular
Annual Fuel Cost	Very Low-$982
Gas Guzzler Tax	No
Greenhouse Gas Emissions (tons/yr.)	Very Low-4.6
Barrels of Oil Used per year	Low-10.3

How the Competition Rates

Competitors	Rating	Pg.
Ford Focus	6	143
Nissan Sentra	6	232
Toyota Corolla	9	249

Price Range

	Retail	Markup
S	$18,780	4%
SE	$20,095	4%
SEL	$23,605	4%
SEL Premium	$25,380	4%

Safety Checklist

Crash Tests:

Frontal	Average
Side	Very Good

Airbags:

Torso	Front Pelvis/Torso from Seat
Pelvis	Front Pelvis/Torso from Seat
Roll Sensing	Yes
Knee Bolster	None

Crash Avoidance:

Collision Avoidance	Warning Only Optional
Blind Spot Detection	Optional
Lane Keeping Assist	None
Backup Camera	Optional*
Pedestrian Crash Avoidance	None

General:

Auto. Crash Notification	Operator Assist.-Fee
Day Running Lamps	Standard

Safety Belt/Restraint:

Dynamic Head Restraints	None
Adjustable Belt	Standard Front

^Warning feature does not meet government standards.
*Backup camera does not meet government standards.

Volkswagen Jetta

Specifications

Drive	FWD
Engine	1.4-liter I4
Transmission	6-sp. Automatic
Tow Rating (lbs.)	–
Head/Leg Room (in.)	Very Cramped-38.2/41.2
Interior Space (cu. ft.)	Cramped-94.1
Cargo Space (cu. ft.)	Cramped-15.7
Wheelbase/Length (in.)	104.4/183.3

Ratings—10 Best, 1 Worst

Combo Crash Tests	8
Safety Features	5
Rollover	9
Preventive Maintenance	5
Repair Costs	4
Warranty	5
Fuel Economy	8
Complaints	5
Insurance Costs	3
OVERALL RATING	**7**

Volkswagen Passat

Volkswagen Passat

At-a-Glance

Status/Year Series Started... Appearance Change/2012
Twins . . . . –
Body Styles . . . . Sedan
Seating 5
Anti-Theft Device . . . . Std. Pass. Immobil. & Alarm
Parking Index Rating .Average
Where Made. .Chattanooga, TN

Fuel Factor:
MPG Rating (city/hwy) Good-25/38
Driving Range (mi.) . . . . Very Long-546.7
Fuel Type. . . . . Regular
Annual Fuel Cost .Low-$1,066
Gas Guzzler Tax . . . . No
Greenhouse Gas Emissions (tons/yr.). Low-5.0
Barrels of Oil Used per year . . . . .Very Low-0.0

How the Competition Rates

Competitors	Rating	Pg.
Acura TLX	10	84
Ford Fusion	7	144
Volvo S60	10	267

Price Range	Retail	Markup
S 1.8T MT	$21,340	4%
Wolfsburg	$24,375	4%
SE TDI	$27,095	4%
SEL Premium 3.6L	$35,995	4%

Safety Checklist

Crash Tests:
Frontal. . . . . .Very Good
Side. . . . . .Poor

Airbags:
Torso . . . . Front Pelvis/Torso from Seat
Pelvis . . . . Front Pelvis/Torso from Seat
Roll Sensing. . . . . Yes
Knee Bolster . . . . None

Crash Avoidance:
Collision Avoidance . . . . Optional CIB^
Blind Spot Detection . . . . None
Lane Keeping Assist . . . . Warning Only Optional
Backup Camera. Standard*
Pedestrian Crash Avoidance . . . . None

General:
Auto. Crash Notification . . . . .Operator Assist.-Fee
Day Running Lamps . . . . Standard

Safety Belt/Restraint:
Dynamic Head Restraints . . . . None
Adjustable Belt. . . . . Standard Front

^Warning feature does not meet government standards.
*Backup camera does not meet government standards.

Volkswagen Passat

Specifications

Drive. . . . . .FWD
Engine 1.8-liter I4
Transmission . . . . 6-SP. Automatic
Tow Rating (lbs.) . . . . –
Head/Leg Room (in.) . . . . Very Roomy-53.5/42.4
Interior Space (cu. ft.). Average-102
Cargo Space (cu. ft.) Cramped-15.9
Wheelbase/Length (in.) 110.4/191.9

Volkswagen Tiguan

Ratings—10 Best, 1 Worst

Combo Crash Tests	1
Safety Features	3
Rollover	3
Preventive Maintenance	3
Repair Costs	5
Warranty	5
Fuel Economy	4
Complaints	4
Insurance Costs	5
OVERALL RATING	**1**

Volkswagen Tiguan

Volkswagen Tiguan

At-a-Glance

Status/Year Series Started. Unchanged/2009
Twins . . . . .Audi Q3
Body Styles . . . . .SUV
Seating 5
Anti-Theft Device . . . . .Std. Pass. Immobil. & Alarm
Parking Index Rating .Average
Where Made. . . . . Puebla, Mexico

Fuel Factor:
MPG Rating (city/hwy) Poor-21/26
Driving Range (mi.) Short-388.5
Fuel Type. . . . . Premium
Annual Fuel Cost . . . . .High-$1,533
Gas Guzzler Tax . . . . No
Greenhouse Gas Emissions (tons/yr.) High-7.8
Barrels of Oil Used per year High-14.3

How the Competition Rates

Competitors	Rating	Pg.
Ford Escape	5	137
Lexus NX	5	195
Toyota RAV4	5	254

Price Range

Price Range	Retail	Markup
S	$24,890	4%
SE 4Motion	$26,865	4%
R-Line 4Motion	$30,675	4%
SEL	$34,445	4%

Safety Checklist

Crash Tests:
Frontal. . . . . Very Poor
Side. . . . . .Poor
Airbags:
Torso . . . . Front Pelvis/Torso from Seat
Pelvis . . . . Front Pelvis/Torso from Seat
Roll Sensing. . . . . Yes
Knee Bolster . . . . None
Crash Avoidance:
Collision Avoidance . . . . None
Blind Spot Detection . . . . None
Lane Keeping Assist . . . . None
Backup Camera . . . . Standard*
Pedestrian Crash Avoidance . . . . None
General:
Auto. Crash Notification . . . . .Operator Assist.-Fee
Day Running Lamps . . . . Standard
Safety Belt/Restraint:
Dynamic Head Restraints . . . . None
Adjustable Belt. . . . . Standard Front

^Warning feature does not meet government standards.
*Backup camera does not meet government standards.

Volkswagen Tiguan

Specifications

Drive. . . . . .FWD
Engine 2.0-liter I4
Transmission . . . . 6-sp. Automatic
Tow Rating (lbs.) . . . . .Very Low-2200
Head/Leg Room (in.) . . . . Very Cramped-39.1/40.1
Interior Space (cu. ft.). Cramped-95.4
Cargo Space (cu. ft.) Roomy-23.8
Wheelbase/Length (in.) 102.5/174.5

Ratings—10 Best, 1 Worst

Combo Crash Tests	—
Safety Features	5
Rollover	—
Preventive Maintenance	3
Repair Costs	2
Warranty	5
Fuel Economy	2
Complaints	5
Insurance Costs	5
OVERALL RATING	—

Volkswagen Touareg

At-a-Glance

Status/Year Series Started	Unchanged/2011
Twins	–
Body Styles	SUV
Seating	5
Anti-Theft Device	Std. Pass. Immobil. & Alarm
Parking Index Rating	Hard
Where Made	Bratislava, Slovakia

Fuel Factor:

MPG Rating (city/hwy)	Very Poor-17/23
Driving Range (mi.)	Very Long-508.5
Fuel Type	Premium
Annual Fuel Cost	Very High-$1,830
Gas Guzzler Tax	No
Greenhouse Gas Emissions (tons/yr.)	Very High-9.4
Barrels of Oil Used per year	Very High-17.3

How the Competition Rates

Competitors	Rating	Pg.
Acura MDX	6	82
BMW X5	6	101
Volvo XC60	10	269

Price Range	Retail	Markup
Sport VR6	$42,705	5%
Sport TDI	$50,245	5%
Lux TDI	$54,750	5%
Executive TDI	$63,245	5%

Volkswagen Touareg

Safety Checklist

Crash Tests:
Frontal	–
Side	–

Airbags:
Torso	Front Pelvis/Torso from Seat
Pelvis	Front Pelvis/Torso from Seat
Roll Sensing	Yes
Knee Bolster	None

Crash Avoidance:
Collision Avoidance	Optional CIB & DBS
Blind Spot Detection	Optional
Lane Keeping Assist	Warning Only Optional
Backup Camera	Optional*
Pedestrian Crash Avoidance	None

General:
Auto. Crash Notification	None
Day Running Lamps	Standard

Safety Belt/Restraint:
Dynamic Head Restraints	None
Adjustable Belt	Standard Front

^Warning feature does not meet government standards.
*Backup camera does not meet government standards.

Volkswagen Touareg

Specifications

Drive	AWD
Engine	3.6-liter V6
Transmission	8-sp. Automatic
Tow Rating (lbs.)	High-7716
Head/Leg Room (in.)	Cramped-39.6/41.4
Interior Space (cu. ft.)	Average-103.6
Cargo Space (cu. ft.)	Roomy-32.1
Wheelbase/Length (in.)	113.9/188.8

Ratings—10 Best, 1 Worst

Combo Crash Tests	9
Safety Features	10
Rollover	9
Preventive Maintenance	5
Repair Costs	7
Warranty	8
Fuel Economy	7
Complaints	9
Insurance Costs	5
OVERALL RATING	**10**

Volvo S60

Volvo S60

At-a-Glance

Status/Year Series Started Unchanged/2011
Twins . . . . –
Body Styles . . . . Sedan
Seating 5
Anti-Theft Device . . . Std. Pass. Immobil. & Active Alarm
Parking Index Rating . . . . .Average
Where Made. . . . . Ghent, Belgium
Fuel Factor:
MPG Rating (city/hwy) Good-25/37
Driving Range (mi.) . . . . Very Long-521.0
Fuel Type . . . . Regular
Annual Fuel Cost . . . . Low-$1,076
Gas Guzzler Tax . . . . No
Greenhouse Gas Emissions (tons/yr.) Average-6.2
Barrels of Oil Used per year Average-11.4

How the Competition Rates

Competitors	Rating	Pg.
Acura TLX	10	84
Audi A6	8	88
Subaru Legacy	7	242

Price Range

	Retail	Markup
T5 FWD	$33,950	6%
T5 Premier AWD	$38,100	6%
T6 Platinum FWD	$43,100	6%
T6 R Design Platinum AWD	$47,700	6%

Safety Checklist

Crash Tests:
Frontal. . . . . .Very Good
Side. . . . . .Average
Airbags:
Torso . . . . .Front Pelvis/Torso/Shoulder from Seat
Pelvis . . . . Front Pelvis/Torso from Seat
Roll Sensing. . . . . Yes
Knee Bolster . . . . None
Crash Avoidance:
Collision Avoidance . . . . Standard CIB & DBS
Blind Spot Detection . . . . .Optional
Lane Keeping Assist . . . . .Optional
Backup Camera .Optional*
Pedestrian Crash Avoidance . . . . .Optional
General:
Auto. Crash Notification . . . . . . .Operator Assist.- Free
Day Running Lamps . . . . Standard
Safety Belt/Restraint:
Dynamic Head Restraints . . . . None
Adjustable Belt. . . . . Standard Front

^Warning feature does not meet government standards.
*Backup camera does not meet government standards.

Volvo S60

Specifications

Drive . . . . .FWD
Engine 2.0-liter I4
Transmission . . . . 8-sp. Automatic
Tow Rating (lbs.) . . . . –
Head/Leg Room (in.) Cramped-39.3/41.9
Interior Space (cu. ft.). Cramped-92
Cargo Space (cu. ft.) . . . . .Very Cramped-12
Wheelbase/Length (in.) 109.3/182.5

Ratings—10 Best, 1 Worst

Combo Crash Tests	—
Safety Features	10
Rollover	—
Preventive Maintenance	3
Repair Costs	7
Warranty	8
Fuel Economy	7
Complaints	—
Insurance Costs	5
OVERALL RATING	**—**

Volvo V60

Volvo V60

At-a-Glance

Status/Year Series Started. Unchanged/2015
Twins . . . . —
Body Styles . . . . .Wagon
Seating. 5
Anti-Theft Device . . . Std. Pass. Immobil. & Active Alarm
Parking Index Rating .Average
Where Made. . . . . .Torslanda, Sweden
Fuel Factor:
  MPG Rating (city/hwy) Good-25/37
  Driving Range (mi.) . . . . Very Long-521.0
  Fuel Type. . . . . Regular
  Annual Fuel Cost .Low-$1,076
  Gas Guzzler Tax . . . . No
  Greenhouse Gas Emissions (tons/yr.). Average-6.2
  Barrels of Oil Used per year Average-11.4

How the Competition Rates

Competitors	Rating	Pg.
Subaru Outback	7	243
Toyota Prius V	9	253
Volkswagen Jetta	7	263

Price Range

	Retail	Markup
T5 FWD	$35,950	6%
T5 Premier FWD	$37,900	6%
T5 Platinum FWD	$41,550	6%
T6 R-Design Platinum AWD	$49,200	6%

Safety Checklist

Crash Tests:
  Frontal. . . . . −
  Side. . . . . −
Airbags:
  Torso . . . . .Front Pelvis/Torso/Shoulder from Seat
  Pelvis . . . . Front Pelvis/Torso from Seat
  Roll Sensing. . . . . Yes
  Knee Bolster . . . . None
Crash Avoidance:
  Collision Avoidance . . . . Standard CIB & DBS
  Blind Spot Detection . . . . .Optional
  Lane Keeping Assist . . . . .Optional
  Backup Camera . . . . Optional*
  Pedestrian Crash Avoidance . . . . .Optional
General:
  Auto. Crash Notification . . . . . . .Operator Assist.- Free
  Day Running Lamps . . . . Standard
Safety Belt/Restraint:
  Dynamic Head Restraints . . . . None
  Adjustable Belt. . . . . Standard Front

^Warning feature does not meet government standards.
*Backup camera does not meet government standards.

Volvo V60

Specifications

Drive. . . . . .FWD
Engine 2.0-liter I4
Transmission . . . . 8-sp. Automatic
Tow Rating (lbs.) Low-3500
Head/Leg Room (in.) Cramped-38.7/41.9
Interior Space (cu. ft.). Cramped-92
Cargo Space (cu. ft.) Roomy-28
Wheelbase/Length (in.) 109.3/182.5

Volvo XC60   Medium SUV

Ratings—10 Best, 1 Worst

Combo Crash Tests	9
Safety Features	9
Rollover	4
Preventive Maintenance	5
Repair Costs	7
Warranty	8
Fuel Economy	2
Complaints	8
Insurance Costs	10
OVERALL RATING	**10**

Volvo XC60

Volvo XC60

At-a-Glance

Status/Year Series Started. Unchanged/2009
Twins . . . . –
Body Styles . . . . .SUV
Seating 5
Anti-Theft Device . . . Std. Pass. Immobil. & Active Alarm
Parking Index Rating . . . . .Average
Where Made. . . . . Ghent, Belgium
Fuel Factor:
  MPG Rating (city/hwy) . . . . Very Poor-17/24
  Driving Range (mi.) . . . . .Very Short-362.0
  Fuel Type . . . . Regular
  Annual Fuel Cost . . . . Very High-$1,610
  Gas Guzzler Tax . . . . .No
  Greenhouse Gas Emissions (tons/yr.). . . Very High-9.0
  Barrels of Oil Used per year High-16.5

How the Competition Rates

Competitors	Rating	Pg.
Audi Q5	5	90
BMW X3	7	100
Lexus RX	–	197

Price Range

Price Range	Retail	Markup
T5 FWD	$36,400	6%
T5 Platinum AWD	$45,450	6%
T6 R AWD	$46,950	6%
T6 R Platinum AWD	$51,050	6%

Safety Checklist

Crash Tests:
  Frontal. . . . . .Very Good
  Side. . . . . Good
Airbags:
  Torso . . . . .Front Pelvis/Torso/Shoulder from Seat
  Pelvis . . . . Front Pelvis/Torso from Seat
  Roll Sensing. . . . . Yes
  Knee Bolster . . . . None
Crash Avoidance:
  Collision Avoidance . . . . Standard CIB & DBS
  Blind Spot Detection . . . . .Optional
  Lane Keeping Assist . . . . Warning Only Optional
  Backup Camera. . . . . .Optional*
  Pedestrian Crash Avoidance . . . . .Optional
General:
  Auto. Crash Notification . . . . .Operator Assist.-Fee
  Day Running Lamps . . . . Standard
Safety Belt/Restraint:
  Dynamic Head Restraints . . . . None
  Adjustable Belt. . . . . Standard Front

^Warning feature does not meet government standards.
*Backup camera does not meet government standards.

Volvo XC60

Specifications

Drive. . . . . .AWD
Engine 3.0-liter I6
Transmission . . . . 6-sp. Automatic
Tow Rating (lbs.) Low-3500
Head/Leg Room (in.) Cramped-39.1/41.2
Interior Space (cu. ft.). Average-99
Cargo Space (cu. ft.) Roomy-30.8
Wheelbase/Length (in.) 109.2/182.8

Ratings—10 Best, 1 Worst

Combo Crash Tests	—
Safety Features	8
Rollover	—
Preventive Maintenance	7
Repair Costs	7
Warranty	8
Fuel Economy	5
Complaints	—
Insurance Costs	10
OVERALL RATING	—

Volvo XC70

Volvo XC70

At-a-Glance

Status/Year Series Started. Unchanged/2008
Twins . . . . –
Body Styles . . . . .Wagon
Seating. 5
Anti-Theft Device . . . Std. Pass. Immobil. & Active Alarm
Parking Index Rating . . . . .Average
Where Made. . . . . Torslanda, Sweden
Fuel Factor:
  MPG Rating (city/hwy). Average-23/31
  Driving Range (mi.) . . . . Very Long-481.4
  Fuel Type. . . . . Regular
  Annual Fuel Cost . . . . .Average-$1,211
  Gas Guzzler Tax . . . . No
  Greenhouse Gas Emissions (tons/yr.). Low-5.7
  Barrels of Oil Used per year Average-12.7

How the Competition Rates

Competitors	Rating	Pg.
BMW X5	6	101
Lexus RX	–	197
Mercedes-Benz GLC-Class	–	211

Price Range	Retail	Markup
T5 FWD	$37,100	6%
T5 AWD	$38,600	6%
T5 Premier AWD	$42,050	6%
T5 Platinum AWD	$47,175	6%

Safety Checklist

Crash Tests:
  Frontal. . . . . –
  Side. . . . . –
Airbags:
  Torso . . . . .Front Pelvis/Torso/Shoulder from Seat
  Pelvis . . . . Front Pelvis/Torso from Seat
  Roll Sensing. . . . . No
  Knee Bolster . . . . None
Crash Avoidance:
  Collision Avoidance . . . . Standard CIB & DBS
  Blind Spot Detection . . . . .Optional
  Lane Keeping Assist . . . . Warning Only Optional
  Backup Camera. . . . . .Optional*
  Pedestrian Crash Avoidance . . . . .Optional
General:
  Auto. Crash Notification. . . . . . . .Operator Assist.-Fee
  Day Running Lamps . . . . Standard
Safety Belt/Restraint:
  Dynamic Head Restraints . . . . None
  Adjustable Belt. . . . . Standard Front

^Warning feature does not meet government standards.
*Backup camera does not meet government standards.

Volvo XC70

Specifications

Drive. . . . . .FWD
Engine 2.0-liter I4
Transmission . . . . 8-sp. Automatic
Tow Rating (lbs.) . . . . –
Head/Leg Room (in.) Cramped-38.8/41.9
Interior Space (cu. ft.). Roomy-134.9
Cargo Space (cu. ft.) . . . . Very Roomy-33.3
Wheelbase/Length (in.) 110.8/190.5

So you're cosidering an electric vehicle? You're not alone! A recent survey by the Consumer Federation of America found that about one-third of potential car buyers would consider an EV. So it's no surprise that 12 major auto manufacturers have new electric vehicles on the market with choices ranging from subcompacts to the luxury laden Tesla. While they're still more expensive than the corresponding gas powered vehicles, EV prices are on the way down and their benefits may warrant the added expense.

Energy from electricity is something we are all familiar with and, in fact, take for granted. We live in a plug-in world where most electrically powered products are extraordinarily convenient and highly functional. Imagine every night doing the same thing with your car as you do with your cell phone—simply plugging it in for the power it needs the next day. And then getting into a nearly silent, clean running car that glides effortlessly out of your driveway and likely has faster pickup than your gas powered car.

While there are a number of environmental reasons for buying an electric vehicle, the simplicity of operation, quiet ride and responsive performance are also major benefits. When you consider the complexity of a gasoline powered engine (most of us can't even identify the items under the hood!) and associated maintenance costs, the simplicity of electric power is refreshing, understandable, and very reliable. Owners of EVs report very low maintenance costs as there's very little to maintain.

SHOULD I EVEN CONSIDER AN ELECTRIC?

The big question most consumers have about EVs is: will I run out of power at the worst time possible—or anytime! Who hasn't needed a flashlight or tried to make a cell phone call only to find the battery is dead. In addition, many of us find it hard to imagine that the same type of engine that runs our blender, sewing machine or drill could possibly power a car! Finally, will I easily be able to plug this thing in at home? These concerns often dissuade people from looking further into the purchase of an electric vehicle.

The fact is, according to a recent analysis of consumer readiness for electric vehicles by the publishers of *Consumer Reports* and the Union of Concerned Scientists, 42% of car buyers meet the typical driving patterns, charging needs, and model preferences of the electric vehicles already on the market. Of households, 56% have access to charging, 95% transport 4 or fewer passengers, 79% don't require hauling, and 69% drive less than 60 miles on weekdays, well within the range of most battery-electric vehicles. Bottom-line, there's an excellent chance that an EV will meet your driving needs.

WHAT ARE MY CHOICES?

EVs come in various sizes, styles and price ranges. In addition, there are various types of EVs. The industry is trying to settle on acronyms to describe the different types, but here's a simple overview:

All Electric:

BEVs (Battery Powered Electric Vehicles) simply have a battery and an electric motor which powers the car. They are the simplest and most 'pure' form of electric vehicle. Because they depend solely on battery power, the battery systems have to be large which increases the cost of these vehicles. In addition to charging up at home, there are a growing number of publically available charging stations (over 10,000 to date) in shopping centers, employee parking lots, and along the highway. The range of these vehicles is from 62-208 miles per charge.

Electric with Built-In Charging Systems:

EREVs (Extended Range Electric Vehicles) have a gas powered auxiliary power source, that can recharge the battery if you run low on power before getting home or to a charging station. They tend to have smaller batteries and depend on the auxiliary gas powered recharger in place of a larger battery. The battery range on these vehicles is from 40-81 miles. With the auxiliary recharging engines, the range is 150-420 miles. Two cars in this category of vehicle, the

Chevy Volt and Cadillac ELR, have gas engines that initially recharge the battery and then will actually power the vehicle at speeds of over 37 mph when the batteries are down.

Dual Electric and Gasoline Vehicles:

PHEVs (Plug in Hybrid Electric Vehicles) have both an electric and gasoline motor which powers the wheels. They are different from the now common hybrid vehicles, because you can plug them in to recharge. If your daily mileage is low, then these can be used like exclusively electric vehicles. Because the gasoline engine will kick in when the battery depletes, the range of these vehicle is similar to gasoline powered vehicles. The electric range is 11-20 miles per charge and the gasoline engine range is 330-550 miles.

WHAT ABOUT CHARGING?

There are three basic types of charging systems, two of which will work in your home.

Level 1: This is the simplest and least expensive system to set up in your home. All you need is a dedicated circuit (nothing else being used on the circuit) and a common household outlet. Level 1 charging is the slowest method because it uses standard 120 volt household current. Your electric vehicle will come with a Level 1 charging cord that you plug into a regular household outlet. The cord comes with a control box which monitors charging. Typically, it will take about an hour to get 4.5 miles of range. Complete charging times range from 3 to 52 hours.

Level 2: This requires a dedicated 220-240 volt circuit, the same one you would need for an electric dryer or other large appliance. First, your home has to have 220 electrical service (all newer homes will) and second, if there is not a readily available line, it will have to be run to where it is needed from the circuit breaker box. Not only will this require an electrician, but if walls or ceilings are disturbed, carpentry, drywall and painting may also be necessary. In addition, once the circuit is available, you will need a special device to plug into the circuit which monitors the electrical charge to the car. Depending on features, these devices can range from $500-$2500. Before these costs scare you off, it is worth investigating the actual cost (you may be lucky enough to have a circuit box in your garage or very close) and determine if your utility company will offer any financial assistance (many do as they want to sell you more electricity). In addition, you need to consider the fact that this installation will save you hundreds of dollars in gasoline costs as well as being much more convenient than going to a gas station to refuel. Typically an hour's charging will provide 24 miles of driving. Complete charging times range from 1.5 to 10 hours.

Level 3 or DC Fast Charge: This feature enables the car to be connected to a public charging station, many of which have very fast charging systems. This is great if you have an EV and your office provides charging stations or you're on the road and find one on the highway or in a shopping center. You can get up to 40 miles of range with just 10 minutes of charging. Overall charging times can be as low as 20 minutes.

One of the issues the industry is struggling with is a universal plug. There are three types of fast charge plugs, one of which is proprietary to the Tesla. Tesla does offer adaptors that can be used in the various types of outlets. If you are planning to charge your vehicle at work, be sure to check out the DC fast charge plug before you buy.

FOLLOWING IS *THE CAR BOOK'S* SNAPSHOT GUIDE TO THE 2016 EVs:

This is a very basic guide to many of the key features on today's EVs. It's important to take a good, long test drive in order to make a selection that best meets your needs and to get the details behind the features that are really important to you.

You'll find the following items in the EV snapshot:

Range: The first number is how far you can go on a single charge on just battery power. The second number shows the range with auxiliary power. In some cases that auxiliary power just recharges the battery, in other cases it powers the wheels just like a gas engine. In addition to the estimated range, we have provided two comparative ratings. The first rating is the total electric range which includes the range added with an auxiliary recharging engine.

The second includes the range with the auxiliary engine that directly powers the wheels. This range is compared to the range of standard gasoline engines. The ratings for electric and electric + auxiliary vehicles range compares just these vehicles.

Charging Time: This is the total time for a complete charge using Level 1 and Level 2 systems. We did not include the DC fast charging time because there is significant variation in the power of public stations.

MPGe: This is the equivalent of the traditional gasoline miles per gallon converted to electricity (thus the small 'e' at the end). While not actually miles per gallon, it gives you a way to compare the efficiency of EVs with gas powered vehicles. We've presented the 'combined' mileage rating which combines highway and city driving. The ratings (Very Good, Good, etc.) for electric MPGe are based on comparing the vehicle just among the EVs. The ratings for the MPG when auxiliary power is used are compared to all gas powered vehicles.

Introduction: This is the year the vehicle was first introduced. The longer the production time, the more likely the manufacturer is to have worked out any bugs. On the other hand, more recent introductions will contain more sophisticated technology and safety features.

Price: This is the manufacturer's suggested retail price which gives you a general idea of EV pricing. It's important to

check for federal and local rebate programs and to comparison shop. Car pricing is notoriously variable and that's no different for EVs. To get the best price consider using the services of the non-profit CarBargains program (page 68).

Size Class/Seating: This provides a general idea of the size of the car. Most consumers compare vehicles within the same size class.

On Board Charger: The greater the KW (kilowatt) rating, the faster the charger. In addition we indicate which vehicles have DC Fast Charging (Level 3) built-in which enables you to take advantage of speedy (and sometimes free) public charging facilities.

Power: This indicates the type of engine system the vehicle has. While they all have electric motors, some have auxiliary gas powered generators that recharge the batteries and others have more traditional gas engines which both recharge the batteries and power the car. See the descriptions on pages 271-272.

Crash Test Rating: Not all EVs have been crash tested. This tells you which one's were crash tested and how they performed using *The Car Book's* rating system based on government's tests. (See page 19.)

Safety Features: Safety has become critically important to today's car buyer, so we've identified 3 key safety features and indicated if the EV has those

features. AEB stands for *Automatic Emergency Braking* – this system automatically applies the brakes if a collision is imminent. We do not indicate, here, if the vehicle has other forms of automatic braking technologies such as brake assist or forward crash warning. *Rear Cameras* have become one of the best ways to avoid the tragic consequences of hitting a small child as well as serve as a wonderful parking assistant. *Lane Assist* moves you back into your lane if you're drifting. We do not indicate if the car simply provides a warning.

Warranty: Warranties vary so here's how the car's overall warranty stacks up in comparison with all other warranties.

Battery Warranty: Electric vehicle batteries are relatively new products and critical to the car's operation. As such, you want to be sure that your *battery* comes with a good, long warranty.

Interior Space/Cargo Space: This is another indication of the car's size. The ratings are relative compared to all of the vehicles in the *The Car Book*.

Parking Index: This rating takes into consideration the vehicle's key dimensions and determines an estimate for 'ease of parking' compared to other models. This is a general guide and no substitute for a good long test drive.

Sales: This indicates the total sales for the 2014 version of the vehicle indicating the general popularity of the EV.

BMW i3

Introduction:	2014
Range:	81 mi.–Avg./Aux. Pwr.–150 mi.–Vry. Short
Charging Time:	Lvl. 1 (10 hrs.)–Fast/Lvl. 2 (3 hrs.)–Fast
MPGe:	Elec.-124–Vry. High/Aux. Pwr.-39–Vry. High

On Board Charger:	7.4 kW; DC fast charge optional
Power:	All Electric (w/opt. Gas Recharging Generator); EREV
Crash Test Rating:	–
Safety Features	AEB-Yes; Rear Camera-Yes; Lane Asst-No
Warranty:	4 years/50,000 mi.
Battery Warranty:	8 years/100,000 mi.
Size Class/ Seating:	Subcompact/4
Interior/Cargo Space:	83.1 cf–Vry. Cramped/2.8 cf–Vry. Cramped
Parking Index:	Very Easy
Sales:	11,024
Price:	$42,400 (MSRP)/$46,250 w/battery ext.
Notes:	

BMW i8

Introduction:	2014
Range:	15 mi.–Vry. Short/Aux. Pwr.–330 mi.–Vry. Short
Charging Time:	Lvl. 1 (3.5 hrs.)–Vry. Fast/Lvl. 2 (1.5 hrs.)–Vry. Fast
MPGe:	Elec.-76–Vry. Low/Aux. Pwr.-28–High

On Board Charger:	5 kW; DC fast charge standard
Power:	Electric and Gas Power the Wheels; PHEV
Crash Test Rating:	–
Safety Features	AEB-Yes; Rear Camera-Yes; Lane Asst-No
Warranty:	4 years/50,000 mi.
Battery Warranty:	8 years/100,000 mi.
Size Class/ Seating:	Compact/4
Interior/Cargo Space:	80.9 cf.–Vry. Cramped/4.7 cf–Vry. Cramped
Parking Index:	Hard
Sales:	2,265
Price:	$140,700 (MSRP)
Notes:	

Cadillac ELR

Introduction:	2014
Range:	40 mi.–Short/Aux. Pwr.–340 mi.–Vry. Short
Charging Time:	Lvl. 1 (18 hrs.)–Avg./Lvl. 2 (5 hrs.)–Slow
MPGe:	Elec.-82–Low/Aux. Pwr.-32–Vry. High

On Board Charger:	3.3 kW
Power:	Electric and Gas Power the Wheels; EREV
Crash Test Rating:	–
Safety Features	AEB-Yes*; Rear Camera-Yes; Lane Asst-No
Warranty:	4 years/50,000 mi.
Battery Warranty:	8 years/100,000 mi.
Size Class/ Seating:	Compact/4
Interior/Cargo Space:	83.4 cf–Vry. Cramped/10.6 cf–Vry. Cramped
Parking Index:	Average
Sales:	1,024
Price:	$65,000 (MSRP)
Notes:	*Indicates optional feature

Chevrolet Spark EV

Introduction:	2013
Range:	82 mi.–Long
Charging Time:	Lvl. 1 (20 hrs.)–Slow/Lvl. 2 (<7 hrs.)–Vry. Slow
MPGe:	119–Very High

On Board Charger:	3.3 kW; DC fast charge optional
Power:	All Electric
Crash Test Rating:	–
Safety Features	AEB-No; Rear Camera-Yes; Lane Asst-No
Warranty:	3 years/36,000 mi.
Battery Warranty:	8 years/100,000 mi.
Size Class/ Seating:	Subcompact/4
Interior/Cargo Space:	86.3 cf–Vry. Cramped/9.6 cf–Vry. Cramped
Parking Index:	Very Easy
Sales:	2,629
Price:	$25,995 (MSRP)
Notes:	Only available in Maryland, California and Oregon

Chevrolet Volt

Introduction:	2011
Range:	53 mi.–Short/Aux. Pwr.–420 mi.–Avg.
Charging Time:	Lvl. 1 (13 hrs.)–Avg./Lvl. 2 (4.5 hrs.)–Avg.
MPGe:	Elec.–106–Avg./Aux. Pwr.–42–Vry. High

On Board Charger:	3.6 kW
Power:	Electric and Gas Power the Wheels; EREV
Crash Test Rating:	-
Safety Features	AEB-Yes*; Rear Camera-Yes; Lane Asst-Yes*
Warranty:	3 years/36,000 mi.
Battery Warranty:	8 years/100,000 mi.
Size Class/ Seating:	Compact/5
Interior/Cargo Space:	90 cf–Vry. Cramped/10.6 cf–Vry. Cramped
Parking Index:	Easy
Sales:	15,393
Price	$33,170 (MSRP)
Notes:	*Indicates optional feature

Fiat 500e

Introduction:	2013
Range:	87 mi.–Long
Charging Time:	Lvl. 1 (<24 hrs.)–Vry. Slow/Lvl. 2 (<4 hrs.)–Avg.
MPGe:	116–Vry. High

On Board Charger:	6.6 kW
Power:	All Electric
Crash Test Rating:	–
Safety Features	AEB-No; Rear Camera-Yes*; Lane Asst-No
Warranty:	4 years/50,000 mi.
Battery Warranty:	8 years/100,000 mi.
Size Class/ Seating:	Subcompact/2
Interior/Cargo Space:	71.6 cf–Vry. Cramped/7 cf–Vry. Cramped
Parking Index:	Very Easy
Sales:	6,149
Price	$31,800 (MSRP)
Notes:	*Indicates optional feature

Ford C-Max Energi

Introduction:	2013
Range:	20 mi.–Vry. Short/Aux. Pwr.–550 mi.–Vry. Long
Charging Time:	Lvl. 1 (7 hrs.)–Fast/Lvl. 2 (2.5 hrs.)–Fast
MPGe:	Elec.-88–Low/Aux. Pwr.-38–Vry. High

On Board Charger:	3.3 kW
Power:	Electric and Gas Power the Wheels; PHEV
Crash Test Rating:	–
Safety Features	AEB-No; Rear Camera-Yes; Lane Asst-No
Warranty:	3 years/36,000 mi.
Battery Warranty:	8 years/100,000 mi.
Size Class/ Seating:	Midsize/5
Interior/Cargo Space:	99.7 cf–Avg./19.2 cf–Avg.
Parking Index:	Average
Sales:	7,591
Price	$31,770 (MSRP)
Notes:	

Ford Focus Electric

Introduction:	2012
Range:	76 mi.–Avg.
Charging Time:	Lvl. 1 (20 hrs.)–Slow/Lvl. 2 (3.6 hrs.)–Fast
MPGe:	105–Average

On Board Charger:	6.6 kW
Power:	All Electric
Crash Test Rating:	Front-Good;Side-Average;Overall-Average
Safety Features	AEB-No; Rear Camera-Yes; Lane Asst-No
Warranty:	3 years/36,000 mi.
Battery Warranty:	8 years/100,000 mi.
Size Class/ Seating:	Compact/5
Interior/Cargo Space:	90 cf–Vry. Cramped/14.2 cf–Cramped
Parking Index:	Easy
Sales:	1,582
Price	$29,170 (MSRP)
Notes:	Limited Availability

Ford Fusion Energi

Introduction:	2013
Range:	20 mi.–Vry. Short/Aux. Pwr.–550 mi.–Vry. Long
Charging Time:	Lvl. 1 (7 hrs.)–Fast/Lvl. 2 (2.5 hrs.)–Fast
MPGe:	Elec.-88–Low/Aux. Pwr.-38–Vry. High

On Board Charger:	3.3 kW
Power:	Electric and Gas Power the Wheels; PHEV
Crash Test Rating:	Front-Very Good;Side-Poor;Overall-Good
Safety Features	AEB-Yes*; Rear Camera-Yes; Lane Asst-No
Warranty:	3 years/36,000 mi.
Battery Warranty:	8 years/100,000 mi.
Size Class/ Seating:	Midsize/5
Interior/Cargo Space:	102.8 cf–Roomy/8.2 cf–Vry. Cramped
Parking Index:	Average
Sales:	9,750
Price:	$33,900 (MSRP)
Notes:	*Indicates optional feature

Kia Soul EV

Introduction:	2015
Range:	87 mi.–Long
Charging Time:	Lvl. 1 (22 hrs.)–Slow/Lvl. 2 (3.5 hrs.)–Fast
MPGe:	84–Low

On Board Charger:	6.6 kW; DC fast charge optional
Power:	All Electric
Crash Test Rating:	–
Safety Features	AEB-No; Rear Camera-Yes; Lane Asst-Yes
Warranty:	5 years/60,000 mi.
Battery Warranty:	8 years/100,000 mi.
Size Class/ Seating:	Compact/5
Interior/Cargo Space:	97.1 cf–Avg./18.8 cf–Avg.
Parking Index:	Very Easy
Sales:	1,015
Price:	$31,950 (MSRP)
Notes:	Only available in CA, GA, HI, MD, NJ, NY, OR, TX, and WA.

Mercedes-Benz B-Class

Introduction:	2014
Range:	62 mi.–Avg.
Charging Time:	Lvl. 1 (22 hrs.)–Slow/Lvl. 2 (6 hrs.)–Slow
MPGe:	112–High

On Board Charger:	10 kW
Power:	All Electric
Crash Test Rating:	–
Safety Features	AEB-Yes; Rear Camera-Yes; Lane Asst-No
Warranty:	4 years/50,000 mi.
Battery Warranty:	8 years/100,000 mi.
Size Class/ Seating:	Midsize/5
Interior/Cargo Space:	—/21.6 cf–Avg.
Parking Index:	Very Easy
Sales:	1,906
Price:	$41,450 (MSRP)
Notes:	

Mitsubishi i-Miev

Introduction:	2012
Range:	62 mi.–Avg.
Charging Time:	Lvl. 1 (22 hrs.)–Slow/Lvl. 2 (6 hrs.)–Slow
MPGe:	112–High

On Board Charger:	3.3 kW; DC fast charge standard
Power:	All Electric
Crash Test Rating:	–
Safety Features	AEB-No; Rear Camera-Yes; Lane Asst-No
Warranty:	5 years/60,000 mi.
Battery Warranty:	8 years/100,000 mi.
Size Class/ Seating:	Subcompact/4
Interior/Cargo Space:	84.7 cf–Vry. Cramped/13.2 cf–Cramped
Parking Index:	Very Easy
Sales:	115
Price:	$22,995 (MSRP)
Notes:	

Nissan Leaf S

Introduction:	2011
Range:	84 mi.–Long
Charging Time:	Lvl. 1 (21 hrs.)–Slow/Lvl. 2 (8 hrs.)–Vry. Slow
MPGe:	114–High

On Board Charger:	3.6 kW; DC fast charge optional
Power:	All Electric
Crash Test Rating:	Front-Very Poor;Side-Very Poor;Overall-Very Poor
Safety Features	AEB-No; Rear Camera-Yes; Lane Asst-No
Warranty:	36 years/36,000 mi.
Battery Warranty:	8 years/100,000 mi.
Size Class/ Seating:	Compact/5
Interior/Cargo Space:	92.4 cf–Cramped/24 cf–Avg.
Parking Index:	Very Easy
Sales:	17,269
Price	$29,010 (MSRP)
Notes:	

Nissan Leaf SV/SL

Introduction:	2016
Range:	107 mi.–Very Long
Charging Time:	Lvl. 1 (NA)/Lvl. 2 (NA)
MPGe:	114–High

On Board Charger:	6.6 kW; DC fast charge optional
Power:	All Electric
Crash Test Rating:	Front-Very Poor;Side-Very Poor;Overall-Very Poor
Safety Features	AEB-No; Rear Camera-Yes; Lane Asst-No
Warranty:	36 years/36,000 mi.
Battery Warranty:	8 years/100,000 mi.
Size Class/ Seating:	Compact/5
Interior/Cargo Space:	92.4 cf–Cramped/24 cf–Avg.
Parking Index:	Very Easy
Sales:	17,269
Price	$34,200/$36,790 (MSRP)
Notes:	

Porsche Cayenne S E-Hybrid

Introduction:	2015
Range:	14 mi.–Vry. Short/Aux. Pwr.–480 mi.–Vry. Long
Charging Time:	Lvl. 1 (11 hrs.)–Fast/Lvl. 2 (3.6 hrs.)–Fast
MPGe:	Elec.-47–Vry. Low/Aux. Pwr.-22–Poor

On Board Charger:	3.6 kW
Power:	Electric and Gas Power the Wheels; PHEV
Crash Test Rating:	–
Safety Features	AEB-Yes*; Rear Camera-Yes*; Lane Asst-Yes*
Warranty:	4 years/50,000 mi.
Battery Warranty:	8 years/100,000 mi.
Size Class/ Seating:	Midsize SUV/5
Interior/Cargo Space:	—/20.5 cf–Avg.
Parking Index:	Hard
Sales:	1.103
Price	$77,200 (MSRP)
Notes:	*Indicates optional feature

Porsche Panamera S E-Hybrid

Introduction:	2013
Range:	16 mi.–Vry. Short/Aux. Pwr.–540 mi. –Vry. Long
Charging Time:	Lvl. 1 (>11 hrs.)–Fast/Lvl. 2 (2.3 hrs.)–Vry. Fast
MPGe:	Elec.-51–Vry. Low/Aux. Pwr.-25–Avg.

On Board Charger:	3.6 kW
Power:	Electric and Gas Power the Wheels; PHEV
Crash Test Rating:	–
Safety Features	AEB-Yes*; Rear Camera-Yes*; Lane Asst-Yes*
Warranty:	4 years/50,000 mi.
Battery Warranty:	8 years/100,000 mi.
Size Class/ Seating:	Large/5
Interior/Cargo Space:	—/11.8 cf–Vry. Cramped
Parking Index:	Very Hard
Sales:	407
Price	$96,100 (MSRP)
Notes:	*Indicates optional feature

Smart forTwo Electric Drive

Introduction:	2011
Range:	68 mi.–Short
Charging Time:	Lvl. 1 (13 hrs.)–Avg./Lvl. 2 (6 hrs.)–Slow
MPGe:	107–Avg.

On Board Charger:	3.3 kW
Power:	All Electric
Crash Test Rating:	–
Safety Features	AEB-No; Rear Camera-Yes*; Lane Asst-No
Warranty:	4 years/50,000 mi.
Battery Warranty:	8 years/100,000 mi.
Size Class/ Seating:	Subcompact/2
Interior/Cargo Space:	45.4 cf–Vry. Cramped/7.8 cf–Vry. Cramped
Parking Index:	Very Easy
Sales:	1.387
Price:	$25,000 (MSRP)
Notes:	Offers Battery Assurance Plus, a battery rental program; *Opt. feature

Tesla Model S

Introduction:	2012
Range:	208 mi.–Vry. Long
Charging Time:	Lvl. 1 (52 hrs.)–Vry. Slow/Lvl. 2 (10 hrs.)–Vry. Slow
MPGe:	101–Avg.

On Board Charger:	11 kW; DC fast charge optional
Power:	All Electric
Crash Test Rating:	Front-Good;Side-Very Good;Overall-Very Good
Safety Features	AEB-Yes; Rear Camera-Yes; Lane Asst-Yes
Warranty:	4 years/50,000 mi.
Battery Warranty:	8 years/100,000 mi.
Size Class/ Seating:	Large/5
Interior/Cargo Space:	94 cf–Cramped/31.6 cf–Vry. Roomy
Parking Index:	Hard
Sales:	22,635
Price:	$69,900 (MSRP)
Notes:	

Toyota Prius Plug-in (2015 Model)

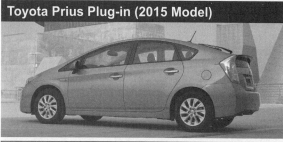

Introduction:	2012
Range:	11 mi.–Vry. Short/Aux. Pwr.–540 mi.–Vry. Long
Charging Time:	Lvl. 1 (3 hrs.)–Vry. Fast/Lvl. 2 (1.5 hrs.)–Vry. Fast
MPGe:	Elec.-95–Low/Aux. Pwr.-50–Vry. High

On Board Charger:	6.6 kW
Power:	Electric and Gas Power the Wheels; PHEV
Crash Test Rating:	Front-Poor;Side-Average;Overall-Poor
Safety Features	AEB-Yes; Rear Camera-Yes; Lane Asst-No
Warranty:	3 years/36,000 mi.
Battery Warranty:	8 years/100,000 mi.
Size Class/ Seating:	Midsize/5
Interior/Cargo Space:	93.7 cf–Cramped/21.6 cf–Avg.
Parking Index:	Very Easy
Sales:	184,794
Price:	$29,990 (MSRP)
Notes:	On hold.

VW e-Golf

Introduction:	2015
Range:	83 mi.–Avg.
Charging Time:	Lvl. 1 (20 hrs.)–Slow/Lvl. 2 (4 hrs.)–Avg.
MPGe:	116–Vry. High

On Board Charger:	7.2 kW; DC fast charge standard
Power:	All Electric
Crash Test Rating:	–
Safety Features	AEB-Yes*; Rear Camera-Yes; Lane Asst-No
Warranty:	3 years/36,000 mi.
Battery Warranty:	8 years/100,000 mi.
Size Class/ Seating:	Compact/5
Interior/Cargo Space:	93.5 cf–Cramped/22.8 cf–Avg.
Parking Index:	Easy
Sales:	4.232
Price:	$28,995 (MSRP)
Notes:	*Indicates optional feature